SEC ADMINISTRATIVE POLICY RE: BALANCE-SHEET TREATMENT OF DEFERRED INCOME-TAX CREDITS

(Part 1 of Two Parts)

CASES IN
PUBLIC ACCOUNTING PRACTICE

Volume 5

ARTHUR ANDERSEN & CO.

1961

Copyright, 1961, by
ARTHUR ANDERSEN & CO.
Chicago, Illinois
Publisher

COPIES OF THIS BOOK MAY BE
OBTAINED FROM THE PUBLISHER.

Library of Congress

Catalog Card Number: 61-18184

PREFACE

This is the fourth in a series of Cases in Public Accounting Practice. The purpose of this series is to provide a source to which practitioners, professors and students can turn for the record of cases that have established important precedents in the practice of public accounting. We are undertaking to compile these volumes in a form suitable for reference, research and educational purposes.

This case relates to the administrative policy of the Securities and Exchange Commission in regard to the balance-sheet treatment of deferred income-tax credits. The two volumes covering this case consist of (1) a brief factual resumé with no editorial comment, (2) the pertinent Commission releases, (3) the written views and comments filed with the Commission by accountants, financial analysts and institutions, governmental regulatory authorities, public utility associations and companies, attorneys and others, and (4) the record of the public hearing including exhibits filed.

This case is of considerable interest in that it gives the widely divergent views which were presented for consideration of the Commission in reaching a final decision on this matter.

A copy of each volume is furnished without charge to the libraries of colleges and universities that offer any courses in accounting. Additional copies may be obtained from the publisher, at cost.

ARTHUR ANDERSEN & CO.

TABLE OF CONTENTS

PART 1 OF TWO PARTS (VOLUME 5)

SEC ADMINISTRATIVE POLICY

RE: BALANCE-SHEET TREATMENT OF

DEFERRED INCOME-TAX CREDITS

RESUME

On December 30, 1958, the Securities and Exchange Commission (SEC) gave notice of its intention to announce an interpretation of administrative policy regarding the balance-sheet treatment of credits equivalent to reductions in income taxes. The notice, given in SEC Release No. 4010[1] under the Securities Act of 1933 (and bearing other release numbers under other Acts administered by the Commission) read in part as follows:

"Notice is hereby given that any financial statement which designates as earned surplus or its equivalent or includes as a part of equity capital (even though accompanied by words of limitation such as 'restricted' or 'appropriated') the accumulated credit arising from accounting for reductions in income taxes for various items including those under sections 167 and 168 of the Internal Revenue Code of 1954, filed with this Commission dated as of December 31, 1958, or thereafter, will pursuant to the administrative policy on financial statements announced in Accounting Series Release No. 4, be presumed by this Commission 'to be misleading or inaccurate despite disclosure contained in the certificate of the accountant or in footnotes to the statements provided the matters involved are material'."

The Commission invited interested parties to file their written views and comments, and subsequently held public hearings (in April, 1959) on the proposed policy statement.

On February 29, 1960, the Commission issued its Statement of Administrative Policy Regarding Balance Sheet Treatment of Credit Equivalent

---

1. Release No. 4010, together with releases No. 4023 and 4038, which extended the time for submitting views and for the public hearing, are included on pages 19-23.

to Reduction in Income Taxes as Accounting Series Release No. 85[2], effective April 30, 1960, providing that:

" . . . any financial statement filed with this Commission which designates as earned surplus (or its equivalent) or in any manner as a part of equity capital (even though accompanied by words of limitation such as 'restricted' or 'appropriated') the accumulated credit arising from accounting for reductions in income taxes resulting from deducting costs for income tax purposes at a more rapid rate than for financial statement purposes will be presumed by the Commission to be misleading or inaccurate despite disclosure contained in the certificate of the accountant or in footnotes to the statements, provided the amounts involved are material."

Both in the Commission's Notice of Intention to Announce Interpretation of Administrative Policy (Release No. 4010, December 30, 1958) and in the resulting written views filed with, and oral testimony before, the Commission, it was apparent that attention was focused primarily on the balance-sheet treatment of the deferred income-tax credits arising from the more rapid deduction of depreciation for tax purposes under Section 167 (liberalized depreciation) and Section 168 (accelerated amortization) of the Internal Revenue Code of 1954, than for book purposes. With respect to depreciation, the Commission stated in ASR No. 85:

"With specific reference to depreciation, since the total deduction allowed over the life of an asset is limited to its cost and hence is not affected by the method by which it is deducted from income, acceleration of tax deductions in earlier years results in deferring to later years the payment of taxes on an amount equivalent to the cost differential. Because of the interrelationship between income taxes and depreciation, the Commission is of the view that in the earlier years the charge equivalent to the tax reduction should be treated either (1) as a provision for future taxes in the income statement with a corresponding credit in the balance sheet to a non-equity caption such as a deferred tax credit, or (2) as additional depreciation in the income statement with a corresponding addition to the accumulated provision for depreciation in the balance sheet. In the Commission's view it is improper to charge income with an item required for

---

2. ASR No. 85 is included on pages 24-30.

the proper determination of net income and concurrently to credit earned surplus.

"A number of comments indicated that, should the Commission take the foregoing position, it should be limited to matters connected with depreciation and amortization or, if not so limited, any additional items embraced within this principle should be clearly specified. It is the Commission's view, however, that comparable recognition of tax deferment should be made in all cases in which there is a tax reduction resulting from deducting costs for tax purposes at faster rates than for financial statement purposes." (Footnotes omitted.)

"The Committee on Accounting Procedure of the American Institute of Certified Public Accountants agrees with the position expressed above."

With respect to the intent of the paragraphs quoted above, the Chief Accountant of the Commission subsequently commented as follows in a letter made public as ASR No. 86[3]:

"It was not the Commission's intention by the publication of this release (No. 85), stating an administrative policy regarding balance sheet treatment of the credit equivalent to the reduction in income taxes when deferred tax accounting is employed, to make mandatory the use of deferred tax accounting beyond the requirements of generally accepted accounting principles."

The effect of the policy set forth in ASR No. 85, as supplemented by the above comments of the Chief Accountant in ASR No. 86, on financial statements filed with the Commission after April 30, 1960, may be summarized as follows:

(1) Deferred-tax accounting must be followed to the extent required by generally accepted accounting principles.

(2) When deferred-tax accounting is followed, the resulting credit must be excluded from the equity-capital section of the financial statements.

3. ASR No. 86 is included on pages 33-34.

Behind these SEC releases lay a controversy that had extended over several years among accountants, regulatory authorities, business enterprises (principally public utility companies) and financial analysts regarding the proper accounting for the income-tax effect of using accelerated amortization or liberalized depreciation for income-tax purposes only. ASR No. 85 was directed toward eliminating one of the differences in practice resulting from this controversy. It addresses itself specifically to the balance-sheet treatment of the deferred-tax credits arising from the resulting income-tax reductions.

Depreciation for Tax Purposes

Accelerated amortization originated with the addition of Section 124 to the Internal Revenue Code as of January 1, 1940. It was extended as Section 124 A in the Code in 1950 and is now Section 168 in the 1954 Code. Accelerated amortization does not change the total depreciation allowed, but it permits the cost of property to the extent covered by certificates of necessity to be amortized over a five-year period for income-tax purposes, irrespective of the fact that useful life may be longer.

Liberalized depreciation in its present form (sometimes referred to herein as declining-balance depreciation) first appeared as Section 167 of the 1954 Code, and applies only to new property additions after 1953. Like accelerated amortization, it does not change the total depreciation allowable over the life of the property; it merely permits an acceleration of depreciation deductions for income-tax purposes. In the early years, its use results in depreciation charges which are higher than those under the commonly used straight-line method, with corresponding reductions in the later years.

Accelerated amortization and liberalized depreciation are therefore similar in effect, since both allow faster-than-straight-line write-off for income-tax purposes of the cost of property -- accelerated amortization, over a five-year period; liberalized depreciation, over the useful life but at higher rates in the early years.

Depreciation for Book Purposes

As Accounting Research Bulletin (ARB) No. 44 (Revised)[4] on declining-balance depreciation issued by the Committee on Accounting Procedure, American Institute of Certified Public Accountants, points out, "In those cases where the expected productivity or revenue-earning power of the asset is relatively greater during the earlier years of its life, or where maintenance charges tend to increase during the later years, the declining-balance method may well provide the most satisfactory allocation of cost." Many companies, however, particularly public utilities, have continued to use straight-line or other appropriate methods of depreciation for financial-accounting purposes even though using liberalized depreciation or accelerated amortization for income-tax purposes.

Recognition of Deferred Income Taxes

Where one of these faster methods of depreciation or amortization is used for income-tax purposes but not for book purposes, ARB No. 43[5], Chapter 9 (accelerated amortization), and ARB No. 44 (Revised) (declining-balance depreciation), state that recognition generally should be given to the deferred income taxes if the amounts thereof are material. In other words, it is recognized that an election to deduct property costs for income-tax purposes at a rate faster than they are depreciated for book purposes creates deferred income taxes, not income. An exception, however, is made in ARB No. 44 for certain "rare cases" such as are mentioned in paragraph 8, which reads as follows:

"Many regulatory authorities permit recognition of deferred income taxes for accounting and/or rate-making purposes, whereas some do not. The committee believes that they should permit the recognition of deferred income taxes for both purposes. However, where charges for deferred income taxes are not allowed for rate-making purposes, accounting recognition need not be given to the deferment of taxes if it may reasonably

---

4. Infra, pp. 912-7.

5. Committee on Accounting Procedure, American Institute of Accountants: Accounting Research Bulletin No. 43, Restatement and Revision of Accounting Research Bulletins, American Institute of Accountants, 1953.

be expected that increased future income taxes, resulting from the earlier deduction of declining-balance depreciation for income-tax purposes only, will be allowed in future rate determinations."

ARB No. 43, Chapter 9, paragraphs 12 and 13, expresses the opinion that it is " . . . desirable to treat the charge (for deferred income taxes resulting from accelerated amortization) as being for additional income taxes. The related credit in such cases would properly be made to an account for deferred income taxes." This Bulletin recognized, however, that giving effect to the amount of deferred income taxes may acceptably but less desirably be ". . . accomplished by making a charge in the income account for additional amortization or depreciation." Under this procedure, the related credit would be carried to " . . . an accumulated amortization or depreciation account as a practical means of recognizing the loss of future deductibility . . . for income tax purposes."

With respect to liberalized depreciation, ARB No. 44 (Revised), paragraph 5, states that, "Where it may reasonably be presumed that the accumulative difference between taxable income and financial income will continue for a long or indefinite period, it is alternatively appropriate, instead of crediting a deferred tax account, to recognize the related tax effect as additional amortization or depreciation applicable to such assets in recognition of the loss of future deductibility for income-tax purposes."

Classification of Deferred-Tax Credit

Neither of these accounting research bulletins specifies where the "account for deferred income taxes" or the "deferred tax account," as the credits are variously described, should be classified in the balance sheet.

So far as commercial and industrial enterprises are concerned, this problem of classifying the deferred-tax credit has presented little, if any, problem. Those companies which have not recorded on their books the same accelerated amortization or liberalized depreciation claimed for tax purposes generally have included the credit resulting from the charge for deferred taxes in a reserve for deferred taxes, classified as a reserve on the liability side of the balance sheet, or in a reserve for depreciation or amortization.

Public utility companies generally have continued to use straight-line depreciation rather than accelerated amortization or liberalized depreciation on their books. Many of these companies, however, have claimed accelerated amortization and/or liberalized depreciation for income-tax purposes. At least in part because of treatment prescribed by regulatory authorities, there has been a great diversity among utility companies in the accounting treatment accorded the income-tax effect of the resulting difference between the amounts of accelerated amortization and liberalized depreciation claimed for income-tax purposes, and the amounts of depreciation recorded for financial-accounting (book) purposes. The two methods used can be summarized as follows:

Deferred-tax method (sometimes referred to as normalization). Under this method a charge is made in the income statement for the amount of the income taxes deferred, either as a provision for deferred taxes or as an additional provision for depreciation and/or amortization, with a contra credit to one of the following four accounts:

Reserve for deferred income taxes, shown as a reserve on the liability side of the balance sheet.

Earned surplus restricted or appropriated for deferred income taxes, generally included in stockholders' equity but in a few cases shown outside of the stockholders' equity section.

Accumulated deferred taxes on income, shown on the liability side of the balance sheet but classified neither as a part of earned surplus nor as a reserve.

Reserve for depreciation and/or amortization.

Flow-through method. Under this method only those taxes actually payable for each year are charged in the income statement. This is the method referred to in paragraph 8 of ARB No. 44 (Revised) (see page 5) which the American Institute Committee on Accounting Procedure did not favor but considered acceptable in "rare cases."

Notice of Proposed SEC Action

Confronted with this wide diversity of accounting treatment among companies, particularly public utilities, claiming accelerated amortization and/or liberalized depreciation for income-tax purposes only, the Securities and Exchange Commission, on December 30, 1958, issued its Release No. 4010 referred to earlier, giving notice of its intention to announce an interpretation of administrative policy regarding the balance-sheet treatment of the resulting deferred income-tax credits.

Views Submitted by Interested Persons

Pursuant to Release No. 4010, a number of persons and organizations presented written statements of their views and comments.[6] These fall into the following categories:

Accountants -- firms, individuals and associations

Financial analysts and institutions

Governmental regulatory authorities

Public utility associations and companies

Attorneys

Others.

Public hearings commenced on April 8, 1959, and after a one-day recess were concluded on April 10, 1959. Appearances were made by 23 persons.[7]

The principal arguments supporting and opposing the proposed SEC policy announcement, as set forth in the written statements and presented at the public hearing, may be summarized as follows:

---

6. All statements filed with the Commission are included on pages 62-776.

7. The testimony and related exhibits are included on pages 777-992.

Supporting

(1) As set forth in ARB No. 44 (Revised), generally accepted accounting principles require the recognition of deferred taxes, if material, in all except "rare cases" (see page 5) in order to accomplish an equitable matching of costs and revenues.[8]

(2) A deferred-tax credit does not represent a tax saving but merely a postponement of the tax. Even though the balance in the deferred-tax account may remain large, and perhaps even increase over the years in a growing utility, the fact remains that the tax relating to any specific item involved is ultimately paid.

Tax deferment credits are, therefore, reserves for taxes that will be payable in later years and are in no sense a part of stockholders' equity. Even those commissions prescribing restricted-surplus treatment generally retain jurisdiction and require that the credit be used only in the same manner as a reserve.[9]

(3) Provision for deferred taxes amounts to recognition that a cost has been incurred by using up the right of deducting depreciation for tax purposes; an item cannot be a cost or an income charge and a credit to stockholders' equity at the same time.[10]

(4) The name "deferred tax account" used in ARB No. 44 (Revised) in itself implies that the credit should not be considered a part of capital, and the Committee on Accounting Procedure subsequently issued an interpretive letter in 1959, a draft of which was introduced into the testimony at page 780, stating that it used "the phrase in its ordinary

8. Infra, pp. 86-7, 209-11, 347-8, 350 et seq., 515-6, 524, 566, 628, 645 et seq., 724-5 and 773.

9. Infra, pp. 64, 66, 80 et seq., 157, 161-2, 205-6, 348, 462, 465, 529, 724-5, 783 and 792-5.

10. Infra, pp. 72, 88, 347-8, 422, 525, 629, 773 and 783.

connotation of an account to be shown in the balance sheet as a liability or a deferred credit."[11]

(5) The fact that different accounting treatments (such as flow-through or the restricted-surplus classification of the deferred-tax credit) are authorized or required for public utilities by different Federal and state regulatory bodies does not justify refraining from establishing a uniform accounting standard; authorization of a particular accounting presentation by a regulatory body does not in itself prevent such presentation from being misleading.[12]

(6) It is misleading to investors and the general public to permit materially diverse treatment of a comparable item among various companies.[13]

(7) Improper income determination or misclassification of items in the financial statements cannot be cured by disclosure in the form of footnotes or captions.[14]

Opposing

(1) Income should be charged with only those taxes currently payable for which there is an actual liability (flow-through), at least in cases where growth will result in a continued and increasing tax deferment. Paragraph 8 of ARB No. 44 (Revised), which permits use of flow-through accounting only in certain "rare cases" such as those involving regulated companies where there is reasonable expectation that the in-

---

11. Infra, pp. 86, 103 and 780-1. Three subsidiaries of American Electric Power Company sought an injunction in the Federal courts against the issuance by the Committee of its interpretative letter. The injunction was denied and the U. S. Supreme Court refused certiorari on November 9, 1959. See Cases in Public Accounting Practice, Vol. 1, The AICPA Injunction Case Re: ARB No. 44 (Revised), published by Arthur Andersen & Co. in 1960.

12. Infra, pp. 73, 147, 149, 152, 157-8, 207 et seq., 353, 518-9 and 796.

13. Infra, pp. 146, 152, 156-7, 162, 348-9, 395, 518-9, 524, 782, 798 and 826.

14. Infra, p. 157.

creased taxes payable in the future will be allowed in future rate determinations, is ambiguous and is too limited in its application. Deferred-
tax accounting is inconsistent with Commission policy as previously enunciated in ASR No. 53 which states in conclusion that " . . . amounts shown
should be in accordance with the historical facts and should not be altered
to reflect amounts that the draftsman considers to be more normal or likely
to recur in future years."[15]

(2) Where deferred-tax accounting is followed, the charge to income is not the recognition of a cost and the credit is not a liability -- at
least not one which must be paid in the foreseeable future. In a growing
utility the deferment is permanent and the tax will never have to be paid.
The charge is a matter of income normalization and the credit must, therefore, be a part of stockholders' equity.[16]

(3) Classification of the deferred-tax credit as restricted earned
surplus has substantial authoritative support. This classification in reports filed with state and Federal regulatory authorities, including the
Securities and Exchange Commission, and in reports to stockholders, has
been considered to be in accordance with generally accepted accounting
principles, and ARB No. 44 (Revised) contains no language proscribing
such treatment.[17]

(4) As long as there is adequate disclosure as to the nature of
the deferred-tax credit by the use of captions or footnotes, absolute uniformity of classification in the financial statements is unnecessary; in
fact under certain circumstances it is even undesirable and may be un-
attainable.[18]

---

15. Infra, pp. 105, 140-1, 355, 396 et seq., 400-1, 404, 473 and 475 et seq.,
    563-4, 610, 663 et seq., 739, 742 et seq., 752 et seq., 758-9, 771,
    786, 801 et seq., 816, 819 and 853.

16. Infra, pp. 104-5, 119, 124, 332 et seq., 425, 443-5, 568, 626, 658,
    675-6, 686, 736, 801 and 876 et seq.

17. Infra, pp. 68, 112, 114, 130-2, 253, 305-7, 329, 333, 413-4, 433 et seq.,
    475 et seq., 510-3, 536, 554, 560-1, 563-5, 569-70, 571-3, 585, 606-9,
    625-6, 657-8, 708, 715-6, 721-2, 802 et seq., 839, 843, 858, 860 et seq.,
    867, 872, 880, 882 and 884 et seq.

18. Infra, pp. 67, 114-5, 143, 155, 159-60, 218-9, 253, 269-70, 278, 344, 388-9,
    409-10, 415, 434, 446, 477-8, 496-7, 512-3, 553, 561, 563, 569-70,
    573, 581, 585, 618-9, 638, 686, 708, 718-9, 814, 821, 850, 853 and
    855 et seq.

(5) It is inconsistent to permit a company using flow-through accounting in accordance with the "rare cases" provision of paragraph 8 of ARB No. 44 (Revised) to credit all tax reductions to earnings but to deprive those companies which normalize taxes in the income statement of the same increment to stockholders' equity.[19]

(6) Since a utility company's rates and accounting are closely interrelated, financial statements are most meaningful if prepared on a basis consistent with the accounting and rate treatment authorized by the applicable regulatory bodies.[20]

(7) The proposed treatment would result in inevitable conflicts with orders of certain regulatory authorities, many of which have primary jurisdiction over accounting and rates.[21]

(8) Some companies' rates, trust indentures, loan agreements, financing plans, etc., have been premised on accounting treatments which would be prohibited by the proposed interpretation, thereby subjecting them to serious problems.[22]

(9) Inclusion of the deferred-tax credit in stockholders' equity benefits consumers and investors, since the improved capitalization ratios reduce capital costs.[23]

---

19. _Infra_, pp. 69, 109, 336, 446, 493 and 877.

20. _Infra_, pp. 131, 195-6, 199, 326 et seq., 389-90, 450, 477, 495-6, 527-8, 626-7, 665-6, 674, 689, 719, 816, 857 and 874 et seq.

21. _Infra_, pp. 109, 113, 131, 155, 164, 195, 252, 271 et seq., 306-7, 326 et seq., 385 et seq., 391, 392, 410, 414, 425, 450, 466, 493, 494-5, 551 et seq., 560-1, 563, 572, 585 et seq., 606 et seq., 613-4, 618-9, 625, 634, 637, 668, 674 et seq., 682, 687, 707, 822 et seq., 839 and 853.

22. _Infra_, pp. 63, 68, 114-5, 116-7, 200, 285-6, 493, 581-2, 618, 658 et seq., 682, 709, 823, 839, 841 et seq. and 856.

23. _Infra_, pp. 159-60, 200, 233, 285, 328, 338 et seq., 390-1, 434, 493, 535, 573, 675, 682, 688-9, 719, 810, 844-5, 852 et seq., 856 and 891 et seq.

(10) The proposed interpretation would exceed the Commission's statutory authority.[24]

(11) Aside from the merits of the proposed treatment, there is a question whether an "interpretation" is the proper vehicle for attaining the desired result, since it might cast a cloud over previously filed financial statements, branding them as inaccurate or misleading.[25]

(12) The proper time for the proposed action, assuming it were sound, would have been several years ago when the accelerated-amortization and liberalized-depreciation provisions were first included in the Internal Revenue Code; in any event, amounts previously reported as equity capital should not now be required to be reclassified.[26]

Both those supporting and those opposing the proposed announcement raised questions with respect to interpretation of certain provisions of the proposed SEC policy statement, and there were suggestions for amending or expanding certain parts. The more significant of these were covered by the Commission in ASR No. 85, which has been reproduced at page 24.

Significant Points in the SEC Releases

In ASR No. 85 and No. 86, the Commission reviewed the reasons for its position and commented briefly on certain of the questions raised in written statements by interested parties and in the public hearing. These may be summarized as follows:

In accordance with the Commission's authority and responsibility to require adequate and fair disclosure in financial statements, the statement of policy is designed to advise interested parties of " . . . the Commission's views as to the presentation in financial statements filed with the

---

24. _Infra_, pp. 271 _et seq._, 307, 330 _et seq._, 434, 447 _et seq._, 485 _et seq._, 496 _et seq._, 512-3, 682, 707-8, 717 _et seq._, 813-4, 845-6, 868 _et seq._, 873-4 and 880.

25. _Infra_, pp. 63, 68, 108, 111, 115, 116-7, 196, 342-3, 452, 585, 607, 689-90, 709-10 and 720 _et seq._

26. _Infra_, pp. 115, 287, 690.

Commission of the credit arising when deferred tax accounting is employed. It pertains to the propriety of designating as earned surplus (or its equivalent) or in any manner as a part of equity capital, in financial statements filed with this Commission, the accumulated credit arising from accounting for reductions in income taxes for various items, including those under Section 167 (liberalized depreciation) and Section 168 (accelerated amortization of emergency facilities) of the Internal Revenue Code of 1954." It is not intended to prescribe any system of accounts or to affect the requirements of any other governmental agency with respect to the manner in which books shall be kept. (see page 25).

Deferred tax accounting is necessary to achieve a proper matching of costs and revenues and is in accordance with generally accepted accounting principles. The Commission, however, " . . . raises no question as to the propriety of the exception" with respect to regulated companies under certain circumstances as set forth in paragraph 8 of ARB No. 44 (Revised). This is the "rare cases" exception which appears on page 5.

In providing for deferred taxes, the charge equivalent to the tax reduction in the earlier years " . . . should be treated either (1) as a provision for future taxes in the income statement with a corresponding credit in the balance sheet to a non-equity caption such as a deferred tax credit, or (2) as additional depreciation in the income statement with a corresponding addition to the accumulated provision for depreciation in the balance sheet. In the Commission's view, it is improper to charge income with an item required for the proper determination of net income and concurrently to credit earned surplus." (Underscoring supplied) (see page 27).

Notwithstanding comments suggesting that the policy be limited to matters connected with depreciation and amortization, it is the Commission's view " . . . that comparable recognition of tax deferment should be made in all cases in which there is a tax reduction resulting from deducting costs for tax purposes at faster rates than for financial statement purposes." In its subsequent ASR No. 86, which was issued in response to a comment regarding this view, it is stated that it was not the Commission's intention " . . . to make mandatory the use of deferred tax accounting beyond the requirements of generally accepted accounting principles" (see page 34).

Since the Commission's ASR No. 4 states that the question of authoritative support is pertinent only where the position of the Commission has not previously been published in official releases, " . . . the fact that there may be some authoritative support for different methods of classifying this deferred tax account does not preclude the Commission from determining for the future the manner in which the item should be classified in financial statements filed with it" (see page 28).

While it is entirely " . . . appropriate that regulatory agencies treat the accumulated credit arising from deferred tax accounting in whatever manner they deem most relevant to their purposes," the arguments advanced that from analytical and rate-making viewpoints the treatment prescribed might have undesirable results upon investors and consumers were rejected. In rejecting these arguments, it was pointed out that " . . . alleged adverse results as to investors and consumers are no different from those complained of whenever any requirement designed to assure financial stability is imposed" (see page 29).

Although some comments questioned the authority of the Commission to deal with this matter, the Commission is of the opinion that it is authorized to issue a statement of administrative policy which " . . . is merely an announcement of the manner in which the Commission intends to enforce the statutes which it administers" (see page 29).

In concluding its statement, the Commission summarized its position as follows (see page 30):

" . . . on and after the effective date of this statement of administrative policy, any financial statement filed with this Commission which designates as earned surplus (or its equivalent) or in any manner as a part of equity capital (even though accompanied by words of limitation such as 'restricted' or 'appropriated') the accumulated credit arising from accounting for reductions in income taxes resulting from deducting costs for income tax purposes at a more rapid rate than for financial statement purposes will be presumed by the Commission to be misleading or inaccurate despite disclosure contained in the certificate of the accountant or in footnotes to the statements, provided the amounts involved are material.

"This statement of administrative policy shall become effective on April 30, 1960."

Kentucky Power Company Matter

On September 6, 1960, the Commission gave notice of a hearing on an application of Kentucky Power Company (Kentucky), a public utility subsidiary of American Electric Power Company, Inc. (American Electric), regarding a proposal to sell to banks not to exceed $40,000,000 of unsecured notes.

In its notice of hearing the Commission noted that the consolidated balance sheet of American Electric and its subsidiaries as of March 31, 1960, filed as a part of an amendment to the application, contained an amount of $86,976,332 identified as "Earned Surplus Restricted for Future Federal Income Taxes," and that the corporate balance sheet of Kentucky as of the same date filed as a part of this amendment contained an amount of $731,441 identified in the same manner. The Commission further stated that in respect to these items the financial statements did not appear to conform with its Statement of Administrative Policy Regarding Balance Sheet Treatment of Credit Equivalent to Reduction of Income Taxes (Holding Company Act, Release No. 14173, February 29, 1960).

Arthur Andersen & Co., believing that the Commission's Statement of Administrative Policy Regarding Balance Sheet Treatment of Credit Equivalent to Reduction of Income Taxes was within the power of the Commission, was in the public interest, and was necessary for the protection of investors and consumers, and believing that it (Andersen) had an economic interest in the maintenance of this Policy, requested leave to participate as a party to the proceedings.

As stated in Note 1 on page 2 of SEC Holding Company Act Release No. 14353, the request was denied by the hearing examiner. The record indicates that the request was denied on the basis that there was no issue concerning the modification or revocation of the Commission's Statement of Administrative Policy, with the understanding that if the issue of such modification or revocation should come up, the examiner would reconsider Andersen's request at that time. Since this issue did not come up, the question of Andersen's participation did not again arise.

As stated in the Commission's January 13, 1961, summary of Holding Company Act Release No. 35-14353:

"After several weeks of hearings during which testimony was offered by Kentucky and American Electric in support of their balance sheet treatment of the accumulated reduction, counsel for the two companies and counsel for the SEC Division of Corporate Regulation entered into discussions looking to the possible settlement of the accounting issue which had been raised. An agreement was reached, which was submitted to and approved by the Commission.

"Under the settlement proposal, as approved, supplemental financial statements have been filed by both companies which the Commission has found not in contravention of its statement of policy. In the new financial statements, the accumulated reductions are carried under a designation reading: 'Accumulated Amount Invested in the Business Equivalent to Reduction in Federal Income Taxes Resulting from Accelerated Amortization and Liberalized Depreciation, Which is Recorded as Earned Surplus Restricted for Future Federal Income Taxes in Accounts Maintained Pursuant to State Regulatory Requirements.'

"As part of the settlement, the Commission also approved certain ratio tests concerning the capital structure of the various companies in the American Electric holding-company system. In future financings by companies in the system, the Commission will give due weight to the existence of the accumulated tax reduction and its size in determining appropriate capitalization ratios; and, so long as the consolidated balance sheet of American Electric and its subsidiaries or the corporate balance sheet of any subsidiary includes a substantial amount of accumulated tax reduction, the Commission will not take any adverse action in respect of capitalization ratios where, upon completion of the financing: (a) common stock equity is not less than 30% of total capitalization, including surplus; (b) mortgage debt is not in excess of 60% of total capitalization, including surplus; and (c) total long-term debt is not in excess of 65% of total capitalization, including surplus. For purposes of these tests, any accumulated tax reduction resulting from charges against income as an operating revenue reduction in respect of accelerated amortization or liberalized depreciation for Federal income tax purposes will not be included as a part of common stock equity or as part of capitalization, including surplus.

"The Commission observed in its decision that by its statement of policy on accumulated tax reductions it had not intended to and, of course, could not foreclose rating agencies, financial analysts, investors, and others from regarding the amount of accumulated tax reductions in any manner they deem appropriate for their purposes."

The findings, opinion and order of the Commission were issued as of January 13, 1961, as Holding Company Act, Release No. 14353, which has been reproduced in full, starting at page 35.

END OF RESUMÉ

For IMMEDIATE Release, Tuesday, December 30, 1958

SECURITIES AND EXCHANGE COMMISSION
Washington 25, D. C.

SECURITIES ACT OF 1933
Release No. 4010
SECURITIES EXCHANGE ACT OF 1934
Release No. 5844
PUBLIC UTILITY HOLDING COMPANY ACT OF 1935
Release No. 13894
INVESTMENT COMPANY ACT OF 1940
Release No. 2814

NOTICE OF INTENTION TO ANNOUNCE
INTERPRETATION OF ADMINISTRATIVE POLICY

Notice is hereby given that the Securities and Exchange Commission has under consideration the announcement of an interpretation of administrative policy on financial statements regarding balance sheet treatment of credits equivalent to the reductions in income taxes. In view of the importance of the amounts involved, any interested person may on or before January 31, 1959, file in triplicate with the Secretary of the Commission written views and comments to be considered in this matter. Except where it is requested that such views and comments not be disclosed, they will be considered available for public inspection.

The proposed announcement follows:

Interpretation of administrative policy on financial statements regarding balance sheet treatment of credit equivalent to reduction of income taxes.

Notice is hereby given that any financial statement which designates as earned surplus or its equivalent or includes as a part of equity capital (even though accompanied by words of limitation such as "restricted" or "appropriated") the accumulated credit arising from accounting for reductions in income taxes for various items including those under sections 167 and 168 of the Internal Revenue Code of 1954, filed with this Commission dated as of December 31, 1958, or thereafter, will pursuant to the administrative policy on financial statements announced in Accounting Series

Release No. 4, be presumed by this Commission "to be misleading or inaccurate despite disclosure contained in the certificate of the accountant or in footnotes to the statements provided the matters involved are material."

The Commission considers that the action thus taken is necessary or appropriate in the public interest or for the protection of investors and is consistent with the intent of Congress, as expressed in section 167 (liberalized depreciation) and section 168 (accelerated amortization) of the Internal Revenue Code of 1954. The effect of these sections is to permit the tax-free recovery from operations of capital invested in plant at a faster rate than would be possible by depreciation methods previously permitted for income tax purposes.[1] The cash working capital is thus temporarily increased by an amount equal to the current tax reduction resulting from the excess depreciation deductions taken for tax purposes in earlier years. This procedure will result in reduced depreciation deductions in future years for tax purposes on the related plant with a resulting increase in income taxes over the amount of taxes which otherwise would be payable.

In order that the net income from operations of a corporation which deducts liberalized depreciation or accelerated amortization for tax purposes but only normal depreciation in its books of account be not overstated in the earlier years and understated in the later years, it is necessary, except in rare cases, to charge current income with an amount equal to the tax reduction.[2] The exception to this procedure is found in those cases described in paragraph 8 of Accounting Research Bulletin

---

1. That this was the intent of these sections of the Code is disclosed by the Report of the House Committee on Ways and Means and the Report of the Senate Committee on Finance. See H. Rep. No. 1337 (83rd Cong., 2nd Sess.), p. 24, and Sen. Rep. No. 1622 (83rd Cong., 2nd Sess.), p. 26.

2. This charge to income is not necessary where the corporation treats the related tax effect in its books of account as additional amortization or depreciation applicable to the asset in question in recognition of the loss of future deductibility for income tax purposes, or charges liberalized depreciation or accelerated amortization in its books of account.

No. 44 (Revised), <u>Declining-Balance Depreciation</u>, issued in July 1958 by the Committee on Accounting Procedure of the American Institute of Certified Public Accountants.[3] The contra credit should be accumulated in an appropriately captioned balance sheet account[4] and returned to income proportionately in later years when the depreciation then allowed for tax purposes is less than the normal depreciation charged to income in the books of account.

It is not contemplated that the portion returned to income will offset exactly the actual tax to be paid in future years, as it is made only for the purpose of allocating to future periods the effect on income of the tax reduction taken. These tax reductions therefore enter into the determination of income and to the increase of equity capital only through the passage of time.

By the Commission.

Orval L. DuBois
Secretary

---

3. "Many regulatory authorities permit recognition of deferred income taxes for accounting and/or rate-making purposes, whereas some do not. The Committee believes that they should permit the recognition of deferred income taxes for both purposes. However, where charges for deferred income taxes are not allowed for rate-making purposes, accounting recognition need not be given to the deferment of taxes if it may reasonably be expected that increased future income taxes, resulting from the earlier deduction of declining-balance depreciation for income tax purposes only, will be allowed in future rate determinations."

4. Companies required to comply with a uniform system of accounts of the Federal Power Commission shall use the balance sheet captions and classification of deferred taxes prescribed by that Commission in its Orders No. 203 and 204, Dockets No. R-158 and R-159 respectively, issued May 29, 1958. Other companies may use the same or other appropriate captions and classification provided they avoid any implication that the credit balance in question is a part of earned surplus or of equity capital.

For IMMEDIATE Release Wednesday, January 28, 1959

SECURITIES AND EXCHANGE COMMISSION
Washington 25, D. C.

SECURITIES ACT OF 1933
Release No. 4023

EXTENSION OF TIME FOR SUBMITTING COMMENTS
ON NOTICE OF INTENTION TO ANNOUNCE
INTERPRETATION OF ADMINISTRATIVE POLICY

On December 30, 1958, the Securities and Exchange Commission, in Securities Act Release No. 4010 and related releases under the Acts administered by the Commission, invited all interested persons to file written views and comments on a proposed interpretation of administrative policy on financial statements regarding balance sheet treatment of the accumulated credit arising from the recognition in such statements of the deferral to future periods of current reductions in income taxes.

It was requested that such written views and comments be submitted in triplicate on or before January 31, 1959. Pursuant to requests the Commission has extended the time for submitting such views and comments to February 28, 1959, and announces that a public hearing will be held on the release in Room 193 of its offices at 425 Second Street, N. W., Washington, D. C., on March 25, 1959, at 10:00 a.m.

Any person interested in presenting his views on the proposed interpretation of administrative policy at the public hearing should, not later than February 28, 1959, submit to the Commission in writing a statement of his intention to appear at the hearing, together with a written statement of his views, in triplicate, and should limit his request for time to make oral presentation so as to provide an opportunity for all interested persons to be heard. Except where it is requested that views and comments not be disclosed, they will be considered available for public inspection.

By the Commission.

Orval L. DuBois

For IMMEDIATE Release, Wednesday, February 25, 1959

SECURITIES AND EXCHANGE COMMISSION
Washington, D. C.

SECURITIES ACT OF 1933
Release No. 4038

POSTPONEMENT OF PUBLIC HEARING AND FURTHER EXTENSION OF
TIME FOR SUBMITTING COMMENTS ON NOTICE OF INTENTION TO
ANNOUNCE INTERPRETATION OF ADMINISTRATIVE POLICY

On December 30, 1958, the Securities and Exchange Commission, in Securities Act Release No. 4010 and related releases under the Acts administered by the Commission, invited all interested persons to file written views and comments on a proposed interpretation of administrative policy on financial statements regarding balance sheet treatment of the accumulated credit arising from the recognition in such statements of the deferral to future periods of current reductions in income taxes. On January 28, 1959, in Securities Act Release No. 4023, pursuant to requests the Commission extended the time for submitting such views and comments to February 28, 1959, and announced that a public hearing would be held on March 25, 1959.

At the request of interested persons, the Commission is further extending until March 25, 1959, the date upon which any person may submit, in triplicate, a written statement of his views and comments on the proposed interpretation of administrative policy. The date for public hearing is also postponed until April 8, 1959, at 10:00 A.M. in Room 193 at the offices of the Commission at 425 Second Street, N. W., Washington, D.C. Except where it is requested that views and comments not be disclosed, they will be considered available for public inspection.

By the Commission.

Orval L. DuBois
Secretary

For IMMEDIATE Release Monday, February 29, 1960

SECURITIES AND EXCHANGE COMMISSION
Washington 25, D. C.

SECURITIES ACT OF 1933
Release No. 4191
SECURITIES EXCHANGE ACT OF 1934
Release No. 6189
HOLDING COMPANY ACT
Release No. 14173
INVESTMENT COMPANY ACT OF 1940
Release No. 2977
ACCOUNTING SERIES
Release No. 85

STATEMENT OF ADMINISTRATIVE POLICY REGARDING
BALANCE SHEET TREATMENT OF CREDIT EQUIVALENT
TO REDUCTION IN INCOME TAXES

On December 30, 1958, in Securities Act Release No. 4010[1] the Commission gave notice of its intention to announce a statement of administrative policy regarding the balance sheet treatment, in financial statements filed with the Commission, of the credit equivalent to the reduction of income taxes arising from the deduction of costs for income tax purposes at a more rapid rate than for financial statement purposes. Comments and views thereon were submitted and oral presentation before the Commission was made by interested persons on April 8 and 10, 1959.

Under various statutes administered by it, the Commission has the authority and the corresponding responsibility to require that the financial statements filed with it be prepared in a manner which provides adequate and fair disclosure. This statement of policy is designed to advise all interested persons of the Commission's views as to the presentation in financial statements filed with the Commission of the credit arising when deferred tax accounting is employed. It pertains to the propriety of designating as earned surplus (or its equivalent) or in any manner as a part of equity capital, in financial statements filed with this Commission, the accumulated credit arising from accounting for reductions in income taxes for various items, including those under Section 167 (liberalized depreciation) and Section 168 (accelerated

---

[1] This was also issued as Securities Exchange Act Release No. 5844; Holding Company Act Release No. 13894; and Investment Company Act Release No. 2814. It was also published in 24 Federal Register 271 and bears Federal Register Document No. 59-243.

amortization of emergency facilities) of the Internal Revenue Code of 1954. It is not intended to direct or establish any system of accounts or to specify the manner in which a particular item shall be recorded on the books of the reporting companies, nor is it intended in any way to affect the requirements of any other governmental agency, federal or state, with respect to the manner in which such books of account shall be kept.[2]

The problem arises from the deduction of costs for income tax purposes at a faster rate than for financial statement purposes where the difference is material. The amount of income tax payable for any period is affected by the amount of costs deducted in determining taxable income. In a year in which costs are deducted for tax purposes in amounts greater than those used for financial statement purposes, then, unless corrected, there is a failure properly to match costs and revenues in the financial statements by the amount of the tax effect of the cost differential. To correct the resultant distortion in periodic net income after taxes, it is therefore necessary to charge income in earlier years with an amount equal to the tax reduction and to return this amount to income in subsequent years when the amount charged for financial state-

---

[2]Representatives of companies subject to the jurisdiction of the Commission under the Public Utility Holding Company Act of 1935 as registered holding companies or subsidiary companies thereof have contended that this Commission has no power to prescribe the manner in which the accumulated credit arising from deferred tax accounting should be classified in the accounts of the company. In support of this contention, reference was made to Section 20(b) of that Act. That section provides that "in the case of the accounts of any company whose methods of accounting are prescribed under the provisions of any law of the United States or of any State, the rules and regulations or orders of the Commission in respect of accounts shall not be inconsistent with the requirements imposed by such law or any rule or regulation thereunder;..."(emphasis supplied) For reasons stated above, this contention misconceives the nature of the action herein taken.

In this connection the Commission today modified Rule 28 promulgated under the Public Utility Holding Company Act of 1935 (17 CFR 250.28) so as to conform the language of that rule with the policy here announced. Rule 28 provided, so far as is here pertinent, that no registered holding company or subsidiary thereof could publish financial statements inconsistent with its book accounts. The rule as modified provides, in effect, that a registered holding company or subsidiary thereof need not conform its published financial statements with its book accounts where such deviation is authorized or required by this Commission by rule, regulation, order, statement of administrative policy, or otherwise. (Holding Company Act Release No. 14172)

ment purposes exceeds the amount deducted for tax purposes.[3] It is our understanding that such deferred tax accounting is in accordance with generally accepted accounting principles.[4]

With specific reference to depreciation, since the total deduction allowed over the life of an asset is limited to its cost and hence is not affected by the method by which it is deducted from income, acceleration of tax deductions in earlier years results in deferring to later years the payment of taxes on an amount equivalent to the cost differential.[5] Because of the interrelationship between income taxes and depreciation,

---

[3] Since the deferral is made for the purpose of allocating to future periods the effect on income of the current tax reduction, it is not contemplated that the portion returned to income will exactly offset the increased tax to be paid in future years. The amount of additional taxes payable in future years may vary from the reduction obtained earlier because of changes in the tax rates or because of failure to earn taxable income corresponding to the tax reduction previously taken.

[4] Accounting Research Bulletins issued by the Committee on Accounting Procedure of the American Institute of Certified Public Accountants: No. 42, November 1952; No. 43, June 1953, Chs. 9c and 10b; No. 44, October 1954; No. 44 (Revised), July 1958.

An exception to this practice is stated in paragraph 8 of Accounting Research Bulletin No. 44 (Revised), which provides that:

"Many regulatory authorities permit recognition of deferred income taxes for accounting and/or rate-making purposes, whereas some do not. The committee believes that they should permit the recognition of deferred income taxes for both purposes. However, where charges for deferred income taxes are not allowed for rate-making purposes, accounting recognition need not be given to the deferment of taxes if it may reasonably be expected that increased future income taxes, resulting from the earlier deduction of declining-balance depreciation for income-tax purposes only, will be allowed in future rate determinations."

It is the understanding of this Commission that the exception recognizes the position of those regulatory agencies which permit public utilities to deduct only the actual taxes payable in a given year, and the Commission raises no question as to the propriety of the exception.

[5] Where there is no difference between the amount of cost deducted for income taxes and the amount deducted for financial statement purposes, such as where declining-balance depreciation is taken both for tax and financial statement purposes, there is, of course, no occasion for deferred tax accounting.

the Commission is of the view that in the earlier years the charge equivalent to the tax reduction should be treated either (1) as a provision for future taxes in the income statement with a corresponding credit in the balance sheet to a non-equity caption such as a deferred tax credit, [6] or (2) as additional depreciation in the income statement with a corresponding addition to the accumulated provision for depreciation in the balance sheet.[7] In the Commission's view it is improper to charge income with an item required for the proper determination of net income and concurrently to credit earned surplus.

A number of comments indicated that, should the Commission take the foregoing position, it should be limited to matters connected with depreciation and amortization or, if not so limited, any additional items embraced within this principle should be clearly specified. It is the Commission's view, however, that comparable recognition of tax deferment should be made in all cases in which there is a tax reduction resulting from deducting costs for tax purposes at faster rates than for financial statement purposes.[8]

The Committee on Accounting Procedure of the American Institute of Certified Public Accountants agrees with the position expressed above. Accounting Research Bulletin No. 44 (Revised) states, in connection with the deduction of depreciation for income tax purposes at a

---

[6] This would not prohibit companies from utilizing in financial statements filed with this Commission the balance sheet captions and classification of deferred taxes prescribed by the Federal Power Commission in its Orders Nos. 203 and 204, Dockets Nos. R-158 and R-159, respectively, issued May 29, 1958. Nor has there been called to the Commission's attention the provisions of any law of the United States or any rule or regulation thereunder prescribing methods of accounting which would prohibit any companies from following, in reports filed with us pursuant to the Securities Exchange Act of 1934, the balance sheet treatment set forth herein. See Section 13(b) of that Act.

[7] In either case there should be an appropriate explanation with disclosure of the amounts involved.

[8] This is, of course, subject to the general qualification under our rules that the amounts in question are material. The term "material," when used to qualify a requirement for the furnishing of information as to any subject, unless the context of a provision in a form otherwise requires, limits the information required to those matters as to which an average prudent investor ought reasonably to be informed before buying or selling the security registered. (See the rules and regulations under certain of the pertinent Acts: 17 CFR 230.405; 17 CFR 240.12b-2; 17 CFR 270.8b-2.)

more rapid rate than for financial accounting purposes, that the accounting company should employ deferred tax accounting and that it is "alternatively appropriate, instead of crediting a deferred tax account, to recognize the related tax effect as additional amortization or depreciation applicable to such assets in recognition of the loss of future deductibility for income-tax purposes." A difference of opinion arose among certifying accountants whether the language of this bulletin permitted the deferred tax account to be classified as earned surplus restricted for future income taxes. To resolve the controversy, the Committee on Accounting Procedure sent a letter dated April 15, 1959, to all members of the Institute in which it clarified the bulletin on the point. The pertinent portion of the letter reads:

"Question has been raised with respect to the intent of the committee on accounting procedure in using the phrase 'a deferred tax account' in Accounting Research Bulletin No. 44 (Revised), Declining-balance Depreciation, to indicate the account to be credited for the amount of the deferred income tax (see paragraphs 4 and 5).

"The committee used the phrase in its ordinary connotation of an account to be shown in the balance sheet as a liability or a deferred credit. A provision in recognition of the deferral of income taxes, being required for the proper determination of net income, should not at the same time result in a credit to earned surplus or to any other account included in the stockholders' equity section of the balance sheet."[9]

While some accounting firms that appeared before the Commission urged that it was appropriate to designate as a part of earned surplus the credit arising from deferred tax accounting despite the opinion of the Committee on Accounting Procedure, the Commission disagrees. Moreover, the fact that there may be some authoritative support for different methods of classifying this deferred tax account does not preclude the Commission from determining for the future the manner in which the item should be classified in financial statements filed with it. In fact, as enunciated by the Commission in Accounting Series Release No. 4, dated April 25, 1938, the question of authoritative support is

---

[9] It may be noted that 18 of the 21 members of the Committee approved the letter. The three who did not merely dissented to the issuance at that time of any letter interpreting the bulletin.

pertinent only where the position of the Commission has not previously been published in official releases.[10]

Arguments have been advanced, particularly on behalf of public utility companies, to the effect that from analytical and rate-making viewpoints the treatment prescribed herein might have undesirable results upon investors and consumers. However, it is entirely appropriate that regulatory agencies treat the accumulated credit arising from deferred tax accounting in whatever manner they deem most relevant to their purposes.[11]

Some of the comments on Release No. 4010 questioned the authority of the Commission to deal with the subject of this release. But these comments apparently fail to recognize that a statement of administrative policy is merely an announcement of the manner in which the Commission intends to enforce the statutes which it administers. Publication of a statement of administrative policy such as this is in accord with long-established Commission practice expressed in Accounting Series Release No. 4, quoted above. Although the Commission is of the view that there is ample authority for it to adopt specific rules as to the form and content of financial statements filed with it with respect to the sub-

---

[10] That release provided in pertinent part:

> "In cases where there is a difference of opinion between the Commission and the registrant as to the proper principles of accounting to be followed, disclosure will be accepted in lieu of correction of the financial statements themselves only if the points involved are such that there is substantial authoritative support for the practices followed by the registrant and the position of the Commission has not previously been expressed in rules, regulations, or other official releases of the Commission, including the published opinions of its chief accountant."

[11] So far as this Commission is concerned, since it believes that classifying the item as a component part of common stock equity is misleading for financial statement purposes, it does not intend to consider the item as a part of common stock equity for analytical purposes, although it may give consideration to the item as one of a number of relevant factors in appraising the overall financial condition of a company. The Commission, of course, does not have jurisdiction over rate-making, although under the Public Utility Holding Company Act of 1935 it is concerned with the interests of consumers. Alleged adverse results as to investors and consumers are no different from those complained of whenever any requirement designed to assure financial stability is imposed.

ject of this release,[12] it is, instead, hereby announcing that, since any requirement in the statutes it administers calling for the filing of financial statements contemplates that they not be misleading or inaccurate, the filing with it of such statements which do not conform to the policy expressed herein would require appropriate action to be taken by the Commission.[13]

For the foregoing reasons, on and after the effective date of this statement of administrative policy, any financial statement filed with this Commission which designates as earned surplus (or its equivalent) or in any manner as a part of equity capital (even though accompanied by words of limitation such as "restricted" or "appropriated") the accumulated credit arising from accounting for reductions in income taxes resulting from deducting costs for income tax purposes at a more rapid rate than for financial statement purposes will be presumed by the Commission to be misleading or inaccurate despite disclosure contained in the certificate of the accountant or in footnotes to the statements, provided the amounts involved are material.

This statement of administrative policy shall become effective on April 30, 1960.

By the Commission.

Orval L. DuBois
Secretary

February 29, 1960

---

[12] See, e.g., Section 19(a) and paragraphs 25 and 26 of Schedule A of the Securities Act of 1933; Sections 12, 13, and 23 of the Securities Exchange Act of 1934; Sections 5(b)(2), 7(a), 10(a), 14, and 20(a) of the Public Utility Holding Company Act of 1935; and Sections 30 and 38 of the Investment Company Act of 1940.

[13] For example, in connection with application filed under Section 6(b) or declarations filed under Section 7 of the Public Utility Holding Company Act of 1935, where the financial statements do not conform to the policy expressed herein, the Commission would presumably condition any order granting the application or permitting the declaration to become effective so as to require that such financial statements do so conform.

For IMMEDIATE Release Monday, February 29, 1960

SECURITIES AND EXCHANGE COMMISSION
Washington, D.C.

HOLDING COMPANY ACT
Release No. 14172

AMENDMENT OF RULE 28

The Securities and Exchange Commission today announced an amendment of Rule 28 of the General Rules and Regulations under the Public Utility Holding Company Act of 1935. Rule 28 provides that no registered holding company or subsidiary company thereof shall distribute to its security holders, or publish, financial statements which are inconsistent with the book accounts of such company or financial statements filed with this Commission by, or on behalf of, such company. The amendment will continue such requirement except as otherwise authorized or required by the Commission by rule, regulation, order, statement of administrative policy, or otherwise.

The Commission is of the opinion that under certain circumstances the public interest or the interest of investors does not require the financial statements of a company subject to the Act and published or distributed to its security holders to be consistent in all respects with the book accounts of such company.

The text of the Commission's action follows:

The Securities and Exchange Commission, acting pursuant to authority conferred upon it by the Public Utility Holding Company Act of 1935, particularly Sections 5(b)(2), 7(a), 10(a), 14, and 20(a) thereof, and deeming such action appropriate in the public interest and for the protection of investors, hereby amends Rule 28 of the General Rules and Regulations under the Public Utility Holding Company Act of 1935 by inserting the words "Except as otherwise authorized or required by the Commission by rule, regulation, order, statement of administrative policy, or otherwise," before the words "No registered holding company or subsidiary company thereof" and changing the word "No" appearing as the first word in the rule to read "no". This amendment of Rule 28 being in the nature of a modification of the substantive provisions of the rule and having the effect of relieving a restriction, the Commission finds that the preliminary notice and public procedures provided for in Section 4(a) and Section 4(b) of the Administrative Procedure Act are unnecessary and declares the amendment of Rule 28 effective immediately pursuant to Section 4(c) of that Act.

The text of the Rule as amended follows:

Rule 28. Inconsistent Financial Statements

Except as otherwise authorized or required by the Commission by rule, regulation, order, statement of administrative policy, or otherwise, no registered holding company or subsidiary company thereof shall distribute to its security holders, or publish, financial statements which are inconsistent with the book accounts of such company or financial statements filed with this Commission by, or on behalf of, such company. This rule shall not be deemed to prevent the distribution or publication of reasonable condensations or of unaudited financial statements or of financial statements (on a cash or other basis) pursuant to the requirements of an indenture or mortgage given to secure bonds or similar instruments, or of appropriate financial statements of a receiver or trustee appointed by a court of the United States.

By the Commission.

Orval L. DuBois
Secretary

February 29, 1960

For IMMEDIATE Release Tuesday, April 12, 1960

SECURITIES AND EXCHANGE COMMISSION
Washington 25, D.C.

ACCOUNTING SERIES
Release No. 86
SECURITIES ACT OF 1933
Release No. 4206
SECURITIES EXCHANGE ACT OF 1934
Release No. 6233
HOLDING COMPANY ACT
Release No. 14209
INVESTMENT COMPANY ACT OF 1940
Release No. 3010

RESPONSE TO COMMENT ON STATEMENT OF
ADMINISTRATIVE POLICY REGARDING BALANCE SHEET
TREATMENT OF CREDIT EQUIVALENT TO REDUCTION
IN INCOME TAXES

The Securities and Exchange Commission today made public a letter sent by its Chief Accountant, Andrew Barr, to Mr. Carman G. Blough, Director of Research, American Institute of Certified Public Accountants, in response to his comment on this Commission's Statement of Administrative Policy Regarding Balance Sheet Treatment of Credit Equivalent to Reduction in Income Taxes published February 29, 1960. The text of the letter follows:

"The Commission has authorized me to respond to your letter in which you express concern over the wording of the last sentence in the first full paragraph on page 4 and the first sentence of the paragraph immediately following it in Securities Act of 1933 Release No. 4191 (also identified as Securities Exchange Act of 1934 Release No. 6189, Holding Company Act Release No. 14173, Investment Company Act of 1940 Release No. 2977, and Accounting Series Release No. 85). The full paragraph to which you refer and the following sentence read as follows:

'A number of comments indicated that, should the Commission take the foregoing position, it should be limited to matters connected with depreciation and amortization or, if not so limited, any additional items embraced within this principle should be clearly specified. It is the Commission's view, however, that comparable recognition of tax deferment should be made in all cases in which there is a tax reduction resulting from deducting costs for tax purposes at faster rates than for financial statement purposes. (Footnote omitted.)

'The Committee on Accounting Procedure of the American Institute of Certified Public Accountants agrees with the position expressed above.'

"It was not the Commission's intention by the publication of this release, stating an administrative policy regarding balance sheet treatment of the credit equivalent to the reduction in income taxes when deferred tax accounting is employed, to make mandatory the use of deferred tax accounting beyond the requirements of generally accepted accounting principles."

(Holding Company Act Release No. 14353)

SECURITIES AND EXCHANGE COMMISSION
Washington, D.C.
January 13, 1961

In the Matters of	
KENTUCKY POWER COMPANY File No. 70-3890	
AMERICAN ELECTRIC POWER COMPANY, INC. KENTUCKY POWER COMPANY File No. 60-22	FINDINGS AND OPINION OF THE COMMISSION
(Public Utility Holding Company Act of 1935)	

ISSUANCE OF SECURITIES

Exemption

Application for exemption by public utility subsidiary company of registered holding company, pursuant to Section 6(b) of the Public Utility Holding Company Act of 1935, with respect to the issue and sale of promissory notes to banks, granted, where the issue and sale of such notes are solely for the purpose of financing the business of such subsidiary company and have been expressly authorized by the State commission of the State in which such subsidiary company is organized and doing business.

ACCOUNTING

Proceeding instituted by the Commission, pursuant to Sections 6(b) and 20(a) of the Public Utility Holding Company Act of 1935, to determine, in light of the Commission's Statement of Administrative Policy Regarding Balance Sheet Treatment of Credit Equivalent to Reduction in Income Taxes, what action, if any, should be required with respect to the item included in the balance sheets filed in the proceeding and identified as "Earned Surplus Restricted for Future Federal Income taxes," dismissed, in view of the filing of supplementary financial statements in which the questioned item is identified in a manner which the Commission finds as not being in contravention of the Commission's Statement of Administrative Policy.

APPEARANCES:

Chester C. Davis, Richard M. Dicke, and Richard Hawkins, of Simpson Thacher & Bartlett, and Herbert B. Cohn, for Kentucky Power Company and American Electric Power Company, Inc.

Clarence H. Ross and Lowell E. Sachnoff, of Ross, McGowan & O'Keefe, for Arthur Andersen & Co., petitioner for intervention.

Solomon Freedman, for the Division of Corporate Regulation of the Commission.

- - - - -

This is a consolidated proceeding with respect to (a) an application, filed pursuant to Section 6(b) of the Public Utility Holding Company Act of 1935 ("Act"), by Kentucky Power Company ("Kentucky"), an electric utility subsidiary company of American Electric Power Company, Inc. ("American"), a registered holding company, regarding the issue and sale to four commercial banks, from time to time prior to December 31, 1962, of not to exceed an aggregate face amount of $40,000,000 of unsecured notes each to be due December 31, 1965; and (b) a proceeding instituted by the Commission pursuant to Sections 6(b) and 20(a) of the Act to determine what action, if any, should be taken with respect to the item, included in the corporate financial statements of Kentucky and the consolidated financial statements of American and its subsidiary companies filed with this Commission in this proceeding, identified as "Earned Surplus Restricted for Future Federal Income Taxes," in the light of the Commission's Statement of Administrative Policy Regarding Balance Sheet Treatment of Credit Equivalent to Reduction in Income Taxes (Holding Company Act Release No. 14173) issued Feburary 29, 1960, and effective with respect to financial statements filed on and after April 30, 1960.

After appropriate notice, a public hearing was held.[1] After Kentucky had introduced a portion of its direct case, discussions were held between Kentucky and American and our Division of Corporate Regulation ("Division") with a view to arriving at a mutually acceptable proposal for the disposition of the issues raised in the consolidated proceeding. As a result of the discussions, the Division has, with Kentucky and American, worked out a proposed settlement of such issues which the Division recommends that we accept and adopt. The matter is before us, upon the record thus presented, to determine if we should grant the application of Kentucky and dispose of the various issues raised in the manner proposed by the Division, Kentucky, and American. The filing of proposed findings, briefs in support thereof, and of a recommended decision by the hearing officer were waived, and Kentucky and American agreed that the Division might assist us in the preparation of our Findings and Opinion. On the basis of the record, we make the following findings.

---

[1] A request for leave to participate, filed by Arthur Andersen & Co., a public accounting firm, was denied by the hearing examiner.

DESCRIPTION OF THE COMPANIES INVOLVED

American is a registered holding company. The American holding-company system operates an interconnected electric utility system covering portions of the seven states of Kentucky, Virginia, West Virginia, Indiana, Ohio, Michigan, and Tennessee.[2] At September 30, 1960, the system's consolidated electric utility plant (stated at original cost), less reserves for depreciation, depletion, and amortization totaled some $1,333,000,000. For the twelve months ended September 30, 1960, the system's consolidated electric operating revenues totaled approximately $335,460,000, its consolidated gross income was some $78,851,000, and its consolidated net income for common stock was about $53,963,000.

Kentucky is incorporated under the laws of the Commonwealth of Kentucky and all of its common stock is owned by American. Kentucky is engaged in the purchase, transmission, and distribution of electric power in the eastern section of Kentucky. Its utility assets constitute an integral part of the integrated electric utility system of American. The population in the service area of Kentucky totals approximately 370,000 and it serves some 93,000 customers. At September 30, 1960, Kentucky's electric utility plant (stated at original cost), less reserve for depreciation, totaled some $33,546,000. For the twelve months ended September 30, 1960, Kentucky's electric operating revenues totaled some $15,454,000, its gross income was $2,037,000, and its net income was $1,471,000.

At the present time Kentucky has no generating facilities of its own. It purchases all of its power requirements from Appalachian Power Company, an associate company in the American holding-company system. Kentucky estimates that the peak demands on its own system in the period 1960-1963 will increase to such an extent that the installation by it of its own generating equipment will be warranted. It therefore pro-

---

[2] In 1945, we found that, except for certain properties which have since been divested, the electric properties of the American holding-company system comprised an integrated electric utility system as defined in Section 2(a)(29)(A) and are retainable under common control under the standards of Section 11(b)(1) of the Act. American Gas and Electric Company, 21 S.E.C. 575. Subsequent to that determination, American acquired 37.8% of the common stock of Ohio Valley Electric Corporation, which in turn holds all of the common stock of Indiana-Kentucky Electric Corporation. Both of those companies operate electric generating facilities used principally to supply the energy requirements of an installation of the Atomic Energy Commission. As to the status of American's holdings of the common stock of Ohio Valley Electric Corporation, see Ohio Valley Electric Corporation et al., 34 S.E.C. 323 (1952) and Holding Company Act Releases No. 13313 (November 16, 1956) and No. 13350 (December 27, 1956).

poses to construct, in the State of Kentucky on the Big Sandy River, a tributary of the Ohio River, a new steam-electric generating station having an estimated capability of 265,000 kilowatts. This generating station, it is contemplated, will be completed and available for commercial service in the latter part of 1962. This Big Sandy plant will be interconnected with the transmission facilities of other companies in the American holding-company system and will become an integral part of that system's integrated operations. Kentucky estimates that the construction of this plant and miscellaneous routine construction will require it to secure capital funds approximating $41,000,000 in addition to such funds as are anticipated will be available from internal sources.

PROPOSED TRANSACTIONS

Kentucky proposes that, under a bank loan agreement dated as of April 1, 1960 between Kentucky and four commercial banks, Kentucky will, from time to time prior to December 31, 1962, issue promissory notes to such banks up to their several commitments, not to exceed an aggregate of $40,000,000. [3]

Each promissory note will be dated when issued, and will mature December 31, 1965, and, during the periods in which the borrowings are made, the interest rate on the notes will be 1/4 of 1% plus the prime rate for commercial loans (now 4-1/2% per annum) from time to time charged by Irving Trust Company, which interest rate shall change whenever such prime rate shall change, thirty days after the effective date of such change.

After the earlier of December 31, 1962, or the date when an aggregate of $40,000,000 has been borrowed, the interest rate on the promissory notes will be 1/2 of 1% plus the prime rate for commercial loans from time to time charged by Irving Trust Company, which interest rate shall change whenever such prime rate shall change, thirty days after the effective date of such change, and, until December 31, 1962, substitute interest will be paid on the daily average unused amount of the commitment at the rate of 1/4 of 1% per annum.

---

[3] The amount of the notes to be issued will be subject to certain limitations in respect of capitalization ratios described infra.

The names of the commercial banks and the maximum amounts of their respective commitments are as follows:

Irving Trust Company	New York, N.Y.	$10,000,000
Continental Illinois National Bank and Trust Company of Chicago	Chicago, Ill.	10,000,000
The Hanover Bank	New York, N.Y.	10,000,000
Manufacturers Trust Company	New York, N.Y.	10,000,000
		$40,000,000

Two of these banks now hold all of Kentucky's outstanding promissory notes which, at December 31, 1960, totaled $7,000,000 face amount.

The promissory notes will be prepayable at any time, in whole or in part, in the amount of $100,000 or multiples thereof, without premium, unless prepayment is made from the proceeds of, or in anticipation of, bank borrowings at an interest rate equal to or less than the then applicable interest rate on the notes, in which event there will be payable a premium computed at the rate of 1/4 of 1% per annum on the amount of the prepayment for the unexpired term thereof.

The proceeds of the notes will be used to pay outstanding promissory notes ($7,000,000 face amount being outstanding at December 31, 1960), and the remainder will be applied to the payment of the cost of constructing the Big Sandy plant and related facilities.

The application states that Kentucky has been advised that American will supply it with capital funds in 1962, either by a capital contribution or the purchase of additional shares of Kentucky's common stock, to the extent, not exceeding $7,000,000 in the aggregate, required to enable Kentucky to complete the proposed bank financing.

The notes are to be paid from the proceeds of a public financing to be effectuated prior to December 31, 1965, the maturity date of the notes.

The Public Service Commission of Kentucky ("Kentucky Commission"), the State Commission of the State in which Kentucky is organized and doing business, (1) has expressly authorized the issue and sale of the promissory notes, pursuant to the terms of the bank loan agreement, to the extent that, at each issuance, the total principal amount of all indebtedness of Kentucky for borrowed money (other than short-term debt as defined in the bank loan agreement) does not, after giving effect to the issuance of such notes and the application of the proceeds thereof, exceed 65% of the capitalization, as defined in the bank loan agreement, of Kentucky, and (2) subject to certain exceptions, has prohibited Kentucky from distributing to its customers or its security holders, or publishing, financial statements which are inconsistent with the accounts which Kentucky maintains pursuant to rules, regulations and orders of the Kentucky Commission or the financial statements contained in Kentucky's financial and statistical report to the Kentucky Commission.

CONSOLIDATION OF PROCEEDINGS

The Division, after a preliminary examination of the application of Kentucky, as amended, under Section 6(b) of the Act, advised us that the balance sheet of Kentucky, as of March 31, 1960, contained an amount of $731,441 identified as "Earned Surplus Restricted for Future Federal Income Taxes"; and that such amount represented the aggregate of the accumulations, as of that date, of balance sheet credits ("accumulated tax reduction") arising from the inclusion in the income statement, as an operating revenue deduction, of items identified as "Provision for Future Federal Income Taxes". The Division, after a preliminary examination of the consolidated balance sheet, as of March 31, 1960, of American and its consolidated subsidiaries, advised us that said consolidated balance sheet contained an accumulated tax reduction, on a consolidated basis, as of that date of $86,976,332 identified as "Earned Surplus Restricted for Future Federal Income Taxes".

This consolidated accumulated tax reduction resulted from the accounting for and reporting, pursuant to requirements of State regulatory authorities having jurisdiction over the principal operating electric utility subsidiaries of American, of reductions in Federal income taxes resulting from liberalized depreciation and accelerated amortization deductions permitted by Sections 167 and 168, respectively, of the Internal Revenue Code of 1954, as amended. The accounting orders of these respective State regulatory authorities in general require that (1) amounts recorded as depreciation in accounts maintained pursuant to such requirements shall be continued on a straight-line basis; (2) during the early years of the life of any property with respect to which accelerated amortization or liberalized depreciation is taken for Federal income tax purposes, there shall be charged against income in such accounts as "Provision For Future Federal Income Taxes" the amount by which such taxes have been currently reduced as a result of accelerated amortization or liberalized depreciation deductions for tax purposes, with a contra-credit to a restricted earned surplus balance sheet account maintained pursuant to such requirements; and (3) in the latter years, when accelerated amortization or liberalized depreciation deductions for tax purposes are less than would have been available if depreciation had been taken on a straight-line basis for tax purposes and Federal income taxes are accordingly increased, there be a "feed-back" from the restricted earned surplus account by charging the amount recorded as restricted earned surplus in such accounts and crediting to income an amount equivalent to such increased taxes.[4]

On May 29, 1958, the Federal Power Commission issued its Order No. 204 (Docket No. R-159) and, on October 22, 1959, its Order No. 216

---

[4] Exceptions to this are (i) in Ohio where, in respect of liberalized depreciation, the State Commission's order requires that the contra-credit be denoted a reserve (said reserve amounting to $5,670,541 at March 31, 1960), (ii) in West Virginia where, in respect of liberalized depreciation, the State Commission's order now provides that no charge is to be made as an operating revenue deduction against income and, instead, only actual taxes are charged at all times, and (iii) in Tennessee where, with the approval of the State Commission, no provision is made in the income statement for any future increased taxes either in respect of accelerated amortization or liberalized depreciation but actual taxes are charged at all times.

(Docket No. R-180), providing that where, in accounts maintained pursuant to FPC requirements tax reductions resulting from the taking of accelerated amortization and liberalized depreciation are charged against income, the contra-credits shall be recorded in a balance sheet account as "Accumulated Deferred Taxes on Income" which is not classified by the FPC as either a reserve or a restricted surplus account. American's operating subsidiaries interpret the provisions of Order No. 204 to permit such subsidiaries to elect to charge, and they have so charged, only actual taxes against income in accounts maintained for FPC purposes and in reports to the FPC. On October 28, 1959, the FPC initiated a proceeding directed to Appalachian Power Company, one of American's subsidiaries, to determine whether it has been complying with the FPC's requirements. A hearing was commenced and the matter is pending.

The Division indicated, on the basis of its preliminary examination of the financial statements filed with Kentucky's application, that such financial statements of Kentucky and American did not appear to conform with our Statement of Admininstrative Policy Regarding Balance Sheet Treatment of Credit Equivalent to Reduction in Income Taxes, dated February 29, 1960.[5] In that Statement, we discussed the proper treatment of the accumulated credit arising from accounting for reductions in income taxes resulting from deducting costs for income tax purposes at a more rapid rate than for financial statement purposes. We stated that on and after its effective date any financial statement filed with us would be presumed to be misleading or inaccurate, provided that amounts involved were material,[6] if it designated such accumulated credit as earned surplus (or its equivalent) or in any manner as a part of equity capital, even though such designation was accompanied by words of limitation, such as "restricted" or "appropriated", and even though disclosure was contained in the certificate of the accountant or in footnotes to the statement.

We thereupon ordered that a proceeding be instituted, pursuant to Sections 6(b) and 20(a) of the Act, with respect to the application of our Statement of Administrative Policy to the financial statements filed with Kentucky's application under Section 6(b) of the Act, in order to

---

[5] See Holding Company Act Release No. 14173.

[6] With respect to the question of materiality, it may be noted that in a footnote to Kentucky's financial statements, it was represented that the accumulated tax reduction would significantly increase to a point where it would represent a material part of the capitalization, as defined in the bank loan agreement, of Kentucky. Insofar as the accumulated tax reduction in the consolidated balance sheet is concerned, the amount of $86,976,332 as of March 31, 1960, is clearly material in amount.

determine whether such financial statements should be held to be inconsistent with our Statement of Administrative Policy. We further ordered that the proceeding in respect of Kentucky's application under Section 6(b) of the Act be consolidated with the proceeding which we instituted under Sections 6(b) and 20(a) of the Act.

Another issue involved the terms and conditions, if any, which should be imposed in the public interest or for the protection of investors or consumers regarding the capitalization ratios of Kentucky and of American and its consolidated subsidiary companies, as such ratios might be affected by the promissory notes proposed to be issued by Kentucky.

During the course of the public hearing, Kentucky introduced evidence, as a portion of its direct case, for the purpose of establishing that the financial statements of Kentucky and of American and its subsidiaries consolidated were not in contravention of the Statement of Administrative Policy.[7]

PROPOSALS REGARDING RESOLUTION OF ISSUES

Discussions were held between Kentucky and American and the Division with a view to arriving at a mutually acceptable proposal for the disposition of the issues raised in the consolidated proceeding. In such discussions the Division asserted that it could not at this time recommend any disposition which did not involve the filing of supplementary financial statements in a form which, in the view of the Division, would eliminate any question which might be raised as to conformity with our Statement of Administrative Policy.

The managements of Kentucky and American were concerned with whether any such supplementary financial statements might affect the terms and conditions which might be imposed with respect to the proposed issuance by Kentucky of its promissory notes and which might adversely affect future financings by American and/or its subsidiaries submitted for our consideration under Sections 6(b) and 7 of the Act. In this connection, officials of American noted that, on the basis of inclusion in the consolidated common stock equity and in total capitalization, including surplus, as of March 31, 1960, of the consolidated accumulated tax reduction of $92,646,873,[8] the system had capitalization

---

[7]In adopting our Statement of Administrative Policy we did not, of course, intend to impugn in any way financial statements which, prior to April 30, 1960, were filed with us on behalf of various utility companies, including Kentucky and American. Rather, it was our intention to establish on a prospective basis requirements applicable to financial statements which were to be filed with us after that date.

[8]This is the sum of $86,976,332 of accumulated tax reduction recorded as Earned Surplus Restricted for Future Federal Income Taxes and $5,670,541 recorded as Reserve for Future Federal Income Taxes.

ratios consisting of debt of 53.7%, preferred stock of 7.6%, and common stock equity of 38.7%; and that on the basis of exclusion of this item from common stock equity and from total capitalization, including surplus, the respective ratios were 57.7%, 8.1%, and 34.2%. The exclusion of this item, therefore, increased the system's debt ratio by 4.0 percentage points and the preferred stock ratio by 0.5 percentage point, and reduced the common equity ratio by 4.5 percentage points.

American's officials also stated that the 38.7% consolidated common equity ratio as of March 31, 1960, which it computed on the basis of inclusion therein of the accumulated tax reduction, was substantially higher than the consolidated common equity ratio, computed on such basis, which the system had in the past generally strived to maintain. It appears that this excess has been occasioned primarily by the fact that American issued and sold, in October 1959, $55,512,000 of additional common stock. American's officials stated it was intended that such consolidated common equity ratio would be substantially reduced from 38.7% as a result of normal system debt financing in connection with system construction expenditures effected within the next few years.

For the same reason, they stated, the consolidated common equity ratio, computed without the benefit of the accumulated tax reduction, of 34.2% as of March 31, 1960, would necessarily also be substantially reduced after giving effect to the debt financing projected by the system for the next few years.

The officials of American were particularly concerned that, in passing upon future debt or equity financings of its system companies under the Act, we would exclude the accumulated tax reduction from the calculation of common equity ratios and would impose terms and conditions under Section 6(b) or make adverse findings under Section 7(d)(1)[9] which would have the effect of requiring that the common equity ratios of individual system companies or of the system on a consolidated basis exceed, and that the debt ratios be reduced from, the respective ratios which the system has attempted to maintain during the past few years, computed on a basis which included the accumulated tax reduction as a part of common equity and of capitalization, including surplus.

In this connection, American's officials stated that the accumulated tax reduction in the system is expected to grow substantially over the

---

[9] Section 7(d)(1) provides in pertinent part that the Commission shall permit a declaration regarding the issue or sale of a security to become effective unless the Commission finds that--

"(1) the security is not reasonably adapted to the security structure of the declarant and other companies in the same holding-company system."

next several years.[10]   They testified that if the Commission, by the exclusion of the accumulated tax reduction were in effect to require an increase in common equity and a concomitant decrease in debt, such requirement would result in a substantial increase in the cost of capital and taxes of the American System; that any such increase in cost of capital and taxes would necessarily have an adverse effect on rates charged for its services and would thus impose an unnecessary and unwarranted burden on consumers; and that such a result would be inconsistent with the proper protection of consumers which is one of the primary objectives of the Act.

The Division indicated that it did not believe that any such consequence was intended by, or would result from, the proper application of the provisions of the Statement of Administrative Policy. The Division pointed out that, in our Statement of Administrative Policy, it was indicated in Note 11 thereof that, although we did not intend to consider a company's accumulated tax reduction as a part of common stock equity for analytical purposes, we would nevertheless give consideration to the item as one of a number of relevant factors in appraising the overall financial condition ot such company.[11]   The Division also

---

[10] The following tabulation sets forth estimates submitted by American's officials of the system's consolidated amounts of accumulated tax reduction as at the ends of 1961, 1965, and 1970, and the ratios of such amounts to estimated total capitalization, including surplus. For purposes of computing such ratios, the management included the accumulated tax reduction (both that recorded as Restricted Earned Surplus and that recorded as a Reserve) in the base amount of capitalization, including surplus.

| At Year-end | American's Estimates of Total Capitalization, Including Surplus (000's) | Accumulated Tax Reduction (000's) | | | | | |
| | | Accelerated Amortization | | Liberalized Depreciation | | Total | |
		Amount	%	Amount	%	Amount	%
1961	$1,440,207	$108,241	7.5	$ 20,301	1.4	$128,542	8.9
1965	1,799,546	137,251	7.6	48,923	2.7	186,174	10.3
1970	2,409,204	104,420	4.3	104,612	4.3	209,032	8.6

[11] It should also be borne in mind that, by the very nature of the accumulated tax reduction, whether it be in respect of accelerated amortization or liberalized depreciation, the amounts which have heretofore been, and which will hereafter be, credited to this account through charges to the income account, will be returned to income during the remaining life of the related physical assets, generally in proportion to the increased amount of income taxes to which a company will become subject in later years as the depreciation de-

correctly pointed out that by our Statement of Administrative Policy we did not intend to and of course could not foreclose rating agencies, financial analysts, investors, and others from regarding the amount of accumulated tax reduction in any manner they deem appropriate for their purposes.

In view of the foregoing, a settlement proposal was developed between the Division and Kentucky and American which the Division is now recommending to us for approval and adoption. The proposal is that (1) supplementary financial statements be filed in the consolidated proceeding which designate the accumulated tax reduction in the manner described below; (2) in any proceeding involving American or any of its system's subsidiary companies under Section 6(b) or Section 7 of the Act, the Commission will give due weight to the existence of the accumulated tax reduction and its size in determining appropriate capitalization ratios; and (3) so long as the consolidated balance sheet of American and its subsidiary companies or the corporate balance sheet of any public utility subsidiary company of American includes an account, involving a substantial amount, representing an accumulated reduction in Federal income taxes arising from the deduction of accelerated amortization or liberalized depreciation for Federal income tax purposes, the Commission will not impose any terms and conditions under Section 6(b), or make adverse findings under Section 7 of the Act, in respect of capitalization ratios with respect to any proposed financing of the American system where upon completion of the financing:

(a) Common stock equity is not less than 30% of total capitalization, including surplus.

(b) Mortgage debt is not in excess of 60% of total capitalization, including surplus.

---

ductions for income tax purposes applicable to such assets become less than the straight-line depreciation deductions taken as depreciation in the accounts. In that sense, therefore, the accumulated tax reduction may properly be regarded as a deferred credit to income in that it represents a source of enhancement of future income by way of mitigation, for financial accounting purposes, of a future expense--namely, income tax expense. It will thus furnish the basis for future accretions to unrestricted earned surplus. While this may be more readily apparent where the accumulated tax reduction relates to accelerated amortization where necessity certificates are no longer being issued by the Federal Government than where it relates to liberalized depreciation where, in a growing company, the balance in the accumulated tax reduction account may be expected to grow, nevertheless the existing balance as of any given time in the accumulated tax reduction account, regardless of the nature of the credits, will ultimately be returned to income and thence to unrestricted earned surplus.

(c) Long-term debt is not in excess of 65% of total capitalization, including surplus.

For purposes of these tests:

(i) The computation of common stock equity, mortgage debt and long-term debt ratios is to be on a system consolidated basis or on a subsidiary corporate basis as is appropriate;

(ii) The terms "common stock equity" and "total capitalization, including surplus" are not to include any accumulated tax reduction resulting from charges against income as an operating revenue deduction in respect of accelerated amortization or liberalized depreciation for Federal income tax purposes;

(iii) The term "long-term debt" is to include all indebtedness for borrowed money having, at the date of issuance, renewal or the guaranty thereof, a maturity of more than 12 months; and

(iv) The term "total capitalization, including surplus" is to include long term debt, the aggregate of the par value of, or stated capital represented by, the outstanding shares of all classes of stock, any premium on stock, and surplus.

The settlement proposal presented to us includes a filing of supplementary financial statements, as at September 30, 1960, in which the accumulated tax reduction is captioned in the corporate balance sheet of Kentucky as "Accumulated Amount Invested in the Business Equivalent to Reduction in Federal Income Taxes Resulting From Accelerated Amortization and Liberalized Depreciation, Which is Recorded as Earned Surplus Restricted for Future Federal Income Taxes in Accounts Maintained Pursuant to State Regulatory Requirements", and in the consolidated balance sheet of American and its consolidated subsidiaries as "Accumulated Amount Invested in the Business Equivalent to Reduction in Federal Income Taxes Resulting From Accelerated Amortization and Liberalized Depreciation, Which is Recorded as Earned Surplus Restricted ($94,698,293), or as a Reserve ($6,600,874), for Future Federal Income Taxes in Accounts Maintained Pursuant to State Regulatory Requirements."

We have reviewed the settlement proposal submitted to us and have considered it under the standards of the Act and in light of our Statement of Administrative Policy. We find that the supplementary financial statements do not contravene our Statement of Administrative Policy. It is unnecessary, in view of this finding, for us to consider further the financial statements originally filed with the application of Kentucky under Section 6(b) of the Act [12]

In appraising the settlement proposal regarding capitalization ratios, with particular reference to the system's consolidated capital structure, we have considered the maximum amount of long-term debt and the minimum amount of common stock equity which American contended the system could issue pursuant to a commitment made by American in a declaration filed with us in 1952 in connection with a financing, as against the respective amounts of securities it could issue under the settlement proposal. Under that commitment long-term debt is limited to a maximum of 60% of total capitalization, including surplus, and common stock equity to a minimum of 30% thereof. [13]

---

[12] In accordance with Orders of the Public Service Commission of West Virginia, subsidiaries of American are no longer charging income with a provision for future taxes in connection with the taking of liberalized depreciation on property in West Virginia but are, instead, charging only actual taxes paid against income. (Where state regulatory agencies authorize such accounting, we regard such procedure as falling within the exception in paragraph 8 of Accounting Research Bulletin No. 44 (Revised) which is referred to in our Statement of Administrative Policy (see page 3 of Holding Company Act Release No. 14173).) In such cases, to the extent that only actual taxes paid are charged against income and the income statement contains no provision for future Federal income taxes, there will, of course, no longer be any contra-credits to the accumulated tax reduction in the balance sheet.

[13] In that declaration (File No. 70-2878), which involved the issue and sale of its 3-3/8% Sinking Fund Debentures due 1977, American agreed that so long as any of such Debentures remain outstanding, if, at the end of any calendar year, the consolidated common equity ratio of American and its subsidiaries should be less than 30% of total consolidated capitalization, including surplus, or, if at the end of any calendar year, the consolidated funded debt ratio should be in excess of 60% of such total capitalization, including surplus, American would initiate appropriate proceedings designed to bring such common equity ratio above 30% and such debt ratio below 60%, as the case may be.

For purposes of computing permissible security issuances under the 1952 commitment, American treats as a part of common stock equity and total capitalization, including surplus, the accumulated tax reduction recorded on the books of its subsidiary companies as Restricted Earned Surplus.

American estimates, on the basis of its projections as to consolidated capitalization, including surplus, that under the settlement proposal the maximum amount of system debt at the end of 1961 would be $6,000,000 less than that issuable under its 1952 commitment; that at the end of 1965 it would be $24,000,000 less than under the 1952 commitment; and that at the end of 1970 the two amounts would be substantially the same.

Accordingly, giving due consideration to the source and the substantial amount of the accumulated tax reductions in American's system companies and having due regard for all of the other circumstances pertaining to the financial condition of the American system, we find that the capitalization ratio tests included in the settlement proposal recommended by the Division are appropriate for that system. Moreover, so long as future financings of American's system companies fall within such limits and the amount of the accumulated tax reduction continues to be substantial, we believe it would be unnecessary for us to impose any terms or conditions under Section 6(b) or to make adverse findings under Section 7 in respect of capitalization ratios. We turn then to the question whether under Section 6(b) of the Act the proposed issue and sale of the promissory notes by Kentucky require the imposition of terms and conditions in any other respect.

EFFECTS OF PROPOSED NOTE ISSUANCES ON KENTUCKY AND AMERICAN

Attached hereto as Appendix A is a condensed balance sheet of Kentucky as at September 30, 1960, filed as described above, and pro forma giving effect to the proposed issue and sale of the 5-year promissory notes. Appendix B contains a condensed statement of income of Kentucky for the twelve months ended September 30, 1960, actual and pro forma giving effect to the proposed note transaction. Appendix C contains a condensed consolidated balance sheet of American and its subsidiary companies as at September 30, 1960, also filed as described above, and pro forma giving effect to the proposed note transaction. Appendix D contains a condensed consolidated statement of income of American and its subsidiary companies for the twelve months ended September 30, 1960, actual and pro forma giving effect to the proposed note transaction.

There is set forth below a table of capitalization, including surplus, of Kentucky on the basis of actual figures as at September 30, 1960, and as estimated by the company as at year-ends for the period 1960-1965. We have excluded from the table the accumulated tax reduction which at September 30, 1960, amounted to $831,825 and which the company estimates will increase to $3,938,000 by December 31, 1965.

Table I

Amounts (000's)	Actual- Sept. 30 1960	As Estimated by Company					
		Dec. 31 1960	Dec. 31 1961	Dec. 31 1962	Dec. 31 1963	Dec. 31 1964	Dec. 31 1965
Debt:							
First mortgage bonds - 3%, due 1979	$10,000	$10,000	$10,000	$10,000	$10,000	$10,000	$10,000
Notes payable to banks - due Dec. 31, 1965	-	-	18,000	40,000	40,000	40,000	40,000
Notes payable to banks - due within one year	5,100	7,000	-	-	-	-	-
Total	$15,100	$17,000	$28,000	$50,000	$50,000	$50,000	$50,000
Common stock and surplus:							
Common stock - $25 par value per share	$12,647	$12,647	$12,647	$12,647	$12,647	$12,647	$12,647
Capital surplus	2,800	2,800	2,800	9,800	9,800	9,800	9,800
Earned surplus	2,438	2,594	3,711	4,538	4,703	4,877	5,063
Total	$17,885	$18,041	$19,158	$26,985	$27,150	$27,324	$27,510
Total capitalization, including surplus	$32,985	$35,041	$47,158	$76,985	$77,150	$77,324	$77,510
Percents							
Debt	45.8%	48.5%	59.4%	64.9%	64.8%	64.7%	64.5%
Common stock and surplus	54.2	51.5	40.6	35.1	35.2	35.3	35.5
Total	100.0%	100.0%	100.0%	100.0%	100.0%	100.0%	100.0%

The effect of the bank loan agreement and the Kentucky Commission order is to require Kentucky to maintain a ratio of debt to total capitalization, including surplus, of not more than 65% (as those terms are defined). Kentucky states that, to enable it to comply with these capitalization ratio limitations, its parent company, American, will increase its investment in the common stock equity of Kentucky in 1962, either in the form of a cash capital contribution or through the purchase by American of additional shares of Kentucky's common stock, up to a maximum of $7,000,000.

For purposes of computing capitalization ratios under the bank loan agreement, debt is defined as not including short-term debt not exceeding 10% of capitalization, including surplus, exclusive of short-term debt, and the ratio computations are to be made on the basis of the accounts maintained by the company pursuant to the requirements of accounting orders issued by the Kentucky Commission. Since the Kentucky Commission has directed Kentucky to classify the accumulated tax reduction referred to above as common equity in its books of account and in published financial statements, the ratio computations for purposes of the bank loan agreement are to be based on inclusion of this item in common stock equity.[14]

At September 30, 1960, Kentucky had net utility plant of $33,546,055 and outstanding mortgage bonds in the principal amount of $10,000,000, or 29.8% thereof. If an amount equal to the sum of (a) the projected increase in total capitalization, including surplus, between September 30, 1960, and December 31, 1965, of $44,525,000, and (b) the projected increase in the accumulated tax reduction of $3,106,000 between the same two dates, were assumed to be invested in net utility plant, the resultant net utility plant by the end of 1965 would amount to $81,177,055. If it were further assumed, as Kentucky has for purposes of analysis, that the $40,000,000 face amount of promissory notes were refinanced

---

[14]The amounts of the accumulated tax reduction per books as at September 30, 1960, and as estimated by Kentucky as at year-ends for the period 1960-1965, together with the resultant capitalization ratios as computed by the company, are shown below.

	Accumulated Tax Reduction (000's)	Capitalization Ratios as Computed by Kentucky	
		Debt(%)	Common Stock Equity (%)
September 30, 1960--actual	$ 832	44.7	55.3
December 31, 1960--estimated	888	47.3	52.7
December 31, 1961-- "	1,122	58.0	42.0
December 31, 1962-- "	1,527	63.7	36.3
December 31, 1963-- "	2,462	62.8	37.2
December 31, 1964-- "	3,257	62.1	37.9
December 31, 1965-- "	3,938	61.4	38.6

at maturity with $33,000,000 principal amount of additional first mortgage bonds and $7,000,000 principal amount of other securities, the resultant principal amount of mortgage debt to be outstanding at that date would aggregate $43,000,000. This would amount to 53.0% of the estimated amount of net utility plant as of that date.

Kentucky also submitted income statements reflecting actual figures for the year 1959 and estimated figures for each of the years during the period 1960-1965 giving pro forma effect to the issuance of the 5-year notes. The company also presented computations showing actual and estimated coverages, before Federal income taxes, of interest charges on debt securities. Pertinent data from the Kentucky exhibit, together with computations of interest coverages after Federal income taxes, are shown below.

<u>Table II</u>

Year	Gross Revenues (000's)	Gross Income a/ (000's)	Interest Charges b/ (000's)	Times Interest Charges Earned Before Taxes	After Taxes
1959 - actual	$14,874	$2,007	$ 500	6.64	4.01
1960 - estimated	16,567	2,243	667	5.73 c/	3.36 c/
1961 - estimated	17,703	2,532	957	4.29	2.65
1962 - estimated	18,803	3,101	1,824	2.40	1.70
1963 - estimated	19,930	5,628	2,401	3.68	2.34
1964 - estimated	21,185	5,867	2,401	3.88	2.44
1965 - estimated	22,456	6,146	2,401	4.11	2.56

a/ After deducting Federal income taxes and provisions for future Federal income taxes (net) as follows: 1959--$1,312,000; 1960--$1,577,000; 1961--$1,576,000; 1962--$1,277,000; 1963--$3,202,000; 1964--$3,441,000; 1965--$3,720,000.

b/ Kentucky has assumed, for purposes of financial analysis, that the 5-year notes will bear interest at the rate of 5-1/4% per annum.

c/ Actual coverages for the twelve months ended September 30, 1960, were 6.20 and 3.71 times, respectively.

There is set forth below a condensed consolidated table of capitalization, including surplus, of American and its subsidiary companies as at September 30, 1960, on the basis of actual figures and also on a pro forma basis giving effect to the proposed issue and sale by Kentucky of the 5-year promissory notes. As in the case of the capitalization figures for Kentucky (see Table I), we have excluded from the following table the accumulated tax reduction which, on a consolidated basis at September 30, 1960, amounted to $101,299,167.

Table III

Amounts (000's)	As at September 30, 1960	
	Actual	Pro Forma
Long-term debt:		
Subsidiaries:		
First mortgage bonds, due 1965 to 1989	$ 668,535	$ 668,535
Serial notes and notes payable to banks, due 1961 to 1967	25,492	65,492
American Electric Power Company, Inc.:		
Serial notes due serially to 1965	9,785	9,785
Sinking fund debentures due 1977	16,081	16,081
Total	$ 719,893	$ 759,893
Preferred stocks of subsidiary companies and premiums	101,766	101,766
Total	$ 821,659	$ 861,659
Common stock of American Electric Power Company, Inc. and surplus:		
Common stock - par value $10 per share	$ 213,699	$ 213,699
Premium on common stock	54,217	54,217
Capital surplus	36	36
Earned surplus	164,980	164,980
Total	$ 432,932	$ 432,932
Total capitalization, including surplus	$1,254,591	$1,294,591

Percents	As at September 30, 1960	
	Actual	Pro Forma
Long-term debt:		
Mortgage debt	53.3%	51.6%
Unsecured debt	4.1	7.1
Total debt	57.4%	58.7%
Preferred stock	8.1	7.9
Total	65.5%	66.6%
Common stock, including surplus	34.5	33.4
Total	100.0%	100.0%

For the twelve months ended September 30, 1960, the system's interest charges were earned 4.64 times before Federal income taxes and 2.94 times after taxes. On a pro forma basis for the same period, giving estimated effect to the proposed issuance of the 5-year notes by Kentucky, these coverages would become 4.33 and 2.78 times, respectively.

For the same twelve-month period, consolidated interest charges plus subsidiaries' preferred dividend requirements were earned 2.53 times after Federal income taxes. On a pro forma basis for the same period, giving estimated effect to the proposed notes, the coverage would become 2.41 times.

In view of the above, we observe no basis for imposing any terms or conditions arising from the nature of the capital structure or earnings coverages.

OTHER MATTERS

Maturity Date and Interest Rate of the Notes

The issue and sale of the proposed notes are excepted from the competitive bidding requirements of Rule 50 promulgated under the Act by reason of paragraph (a)(2) thereof, which provides an exception for, among other things, notes issued to a commercial bank having a maturity of ten years or less.

The management of Kentucky is of the opinion that the maturity date of December 31, 1965, and the interest rate are appropriate under the circumstances. Kentucky's officials estimated that approximately 2-1/2 years would be required to construct the Big Sandy plant and place it in commercial operation. As a consequence, the size of Kentucky will more than double in a relatively short period of time.

Kentucky's officials testified that, on the basis of actual earnings for the year 1959, if Kentucky were required to finance the construction by the issuance of long-term debt at this time, at an estimated 5-1/2% annual interest cost, the interest charges on all debt to be outstanding would have been earned only 1.3 times before Federal income taxes. It was their view, therefore, that the most economical means of raising the necessary construction funds would be by the issuance of promissory notes to banks, with the funds being obtained as needed. The notes would be refinanced at a later date on a permanent or long-term basis.

It was also pointed out by the management that there would be a reduction in interest coverages through the year 1962 during the period of construction and that an improvement in coverages would be effected only after the plant has been placed in commercial operation. They were, therefore, of the opinion that to require the notes to mature before Kentucky had developed an earnings history based upon the operation of the plant, would compel Kentucky to refinance the notes on an extremely unfavorable and uneconomical basis. Accordingly, they believed that the proposed maturity date under the bank loan agreement, of December 31, 1965, would enable Kentucky to obtain the required construction funds on the most economical basis available and would permit the company to refinance the notes after a reasonable period of demonstrated earning power.[15]

---

[15] In projecting Kentucky's capital structure to December 31, 1965, on the basis of the proposed 5-year notes, one of Kentucky's officials

Negotiations with respect to terms of the notes were conducted, initially, with one bank. That bank was willing to commit itself for $10,000,000 of the $40,000,000 required by Kentucky, at an interest rate of 1/2 of 1% plus the then prime rate for commercial loans of 5% per annum, plus also a stand-by charge of 1/4 of 1% per annum on the average unused amount of the commitment. The bank also desired that the loan be repaid at the end of five years from the date of the bank loan agreement. Since the bank loan agreement was executed as of April 1, 1960, the maturity date would have been April 1, 1965.

The management of Kentucky, however, insisted on a maturity date of December 31, 1965, or some 5-3/4 years from the time of the negotiations, and an interest rate which, during the period of the borrowings, would equal 1/4 of 1% plus the prime rate, and which would be increased to 1/2 of 1% plus the prime rate after the earlier of December 31, 1962, or the date when the entire $40,000,000 has been borrowed. In addition, the management of Kentucky asserted that the interest rate should be related to changes in the prime rate rather than to the prime rate in existence at the time of entering into the bank loan agreement. Further, the management expressed its unwillingness to pay a stand-by charge until after all required approvals of regulatory agencies had been obtained.

After consideration of Kentucky's views, the bank agreed thereto. The management of Kentucky then negotiated an additional $10,000,000 credit with a second bank without advising it of the negotiations with the first bank. Although the second bank initially offered substantially the same terms as originally offered by the first bank, the management of Kentucky was able to obtain a $10,000,000 commitment on the same terms as it obtained from the first bank. On the basis of commitments totaling $20,000,000 on terms which it regarded as being favorable to it, Kentucky then contacted a third bank, which upon being advised by the company as to the terms which the first two banks had agreed on, offered an identical commitment for $10,000,000 of credit. A fourth bank made the same commitment, thereby providing Kentucky with an aggregate of $40,000,000 of credit on the terms contained in the bank loan agreement.

---

also projected figures indicating the feasibility of refinancing at that date the $40,000,000 face amount of notes through the issuance of $33,000,000 principal amount of additional first mortgage bonds and $7,000,000 principal amount of other debt securities. He recognized, of course, and so stated, that our granting of the instant application regarding the 5-year notes should in no manner be construed as indicating our approval at this time of the kind of refinancing to be undertaken upon the maturity of the notes.

In the light of the foregoing, we are satisfied that the maturity date and the interest rate of the notes are appropriate and that there has been a maintenance of competitive conditions with respect to the issue and sale of the notes.

Fees and Expenses

The record is not complete as to fees and expenses incurred or to be incurred by Kentucky in respect of the proposed issue and sale of the promissory notes. We shall therefore reserve jurisdiction over the payment of all such fees and expenses.

CONCLUSIONS

We conclude that the recommendation of the Division with respect to the resolution of the issues relating to the financial statements filed herein and maintenance of capitalization ratios within the limits described is an appropriate basis for disposing of such issues and we therefore adopt and approve the settlement proposal.[16] Further, we observe no basis for the imposition of any terms or conditions in any other respect in connection with the issue and sale by Kentucky of the promissory notes, subject to the reservation of jurisdiction with respect to fees and expenses applicable thereto. In addition, we shall terminate the proceeding instituted under Sections 6(b) and 20(a) of the Act directed to American and Kentucky with respect to the financial statements filed herein. An appropriate order will issue.

By the Commission (Chairman Gadsby and Commissioners Hastings, Woodside, and McCauley).

/s/ ORVAL L. DUBOIS

Orval L. DuBois
Secretary

---

[16] In effect, we have before us an offer of settlement similar to those contemplated by Section 5(b) of the Administrative Procedure Act: 60 Stat. 239 (1946), 5 U.S.C. 1004 (b) (1952). The Commission's Rules of Practice also provide for such offers of settlement: 17 C.F.R. 201.8.

KENTUCKY POWER COMPANY

Condensed Balance Sheet as at September 30, 1960 — Actual and Pro Forma
Giving Effect to Proposed Issue and Sale of $40,000,000 Face Amount
of Promissory Notes

Assets and Other Debits	Actual	Pro Forma Adjustments (Net)	Pro Forma
Electric Utility Plant	$45,987,197	$ --	$45,987,197
Less Reserve for Depreciation	12,441,142	--	12,441,142
Net Electric Utility Plant	$33,546,055	$ --	$33,546,055
Investment and Fund Accounts — Net of Reserve	$ 262,606	$ --	$ 262,606
Current Assets:			
Cash	$ 1,484,168	$49,038,095) (5,100,000))	$45,422,263
Other	2,173,866	--	2,173,866
Total Current Assets	$ 3,658,034	$43,938,095	$47,596,129
Deferred Debits	$ 57,234	$ --	$ 57,234
Total Assets and Other Debits	$37,523,929	$43,938,095	$81,462,024

Liabilities and Other Credits	Actual	Pro Forma Adjustments (Net)	Pro Forma
Long-Term Debt	$10,000,000	$40,000,000	$50,000,000
Common Stock, Par Value $25 per Share	12,646,525	--	12,646,525
Capital Surplus	2,800,000	--	2,800,000
Earned Surplus as Recorded in Unrestricted Accounts Maintained Pursuant to State Regulatory Requirements	2,438,457	--	2,438,457
Aggregate of Proposed Increases in One or More of the Accounts for Common Stock, Capital Surplus and Earned Surplus as Recorded in Unrestricted Accounts Maintained Pursuant to State Regulatory Requirements	-	9,038,095 a/	9,038,095 a/
Accumulated Amount Invested in the Business Equivalent to Reduction in Federal Income Taxes Resulting from Accelerated Amortization and Liberalized Depreciation, Which is Recorded as Earned Surplus Restricted for Future Federal Income Taxes in Accounts Maintained Pursuant to State Regulatory Requirements	831,825	-	831,825
Current Liabilities	8,292,761	(5,100,000)	3,192,761
Deferred Credits and Miscellaneous Reserves	155,419	-	155,419
Contributions in Aid of Construction	358,942	-	358,942
Total Liabilities and Other Credits	$37,523,929	$43,938,095	$81,462,024

( ) Denotes red figure.

a/ Represents increase in common stock equity necessitated by issuance of $40,000,000
face amount of promissory notes. Related issuances of additional common stock to,
or capital contributions from, American Electric Power Company, Inc. will be the
subject of appropriate applications or declarations under the Public Utility
Holding Company Act of 1935.

KENTUCKY POWER COMPANY
Condensed Statement of Income for the Twelve Months Ended September 30, 1960 —
Actual and Pro Forma Giving Effect to Proposed Issue and Sale of $40,000,000 Face
Amount of Promissory Notes

	Actual	Pro Forma Adjustments	Pro Forma
Operating Revenues — Electric	$15,454,713	$ —	$15,454,713
Operating Revenue Deductions:			
Operation (including purchased power)	$ 9,312,613	$ —	$ 9,312,613
Maintenance	792,723	—	792,723
Depreciation	1,395,665	—	1,395,665
Taxes, other than Federal income taxes	556,779	—	556,779
Federal income taxes	1,166,771	(1,014,348)	152,423
Provision for future Federal income taxes	204,505	—	204,505
Portion of current Federal income taxes provided for in prior years (credit)	(4,750)	—	(4,750)
Total	$13,424,306	$(1,014,348)	$12,409,958
Operating Income	$ 2,030,407	$1,014,348	$ 3,044,755
Other Income	6,418	—	6,418
Gross Income	$ 2,036,825	$1,014,348	$ 3,051,173
Income Deductions:			
Interest on long-term debt	$ 300,000	$2,200,000	$ 2,500,000
Interest on short-term debt (notes payable to banks)	249,331	(249,331)	—
Interest charged to construction (credit)	(9,280)	(1,919,500)	(1,928,780)
Other interest and miscellaneous deductions	25,629	—	25,629
Total	$ 565,680	$ 31,169	$ 596,849
Net Income	$ 1,471,145	$ 983,179	$ 2,454,324

( ) Denotes red figure.

AMERICAN ELECTRIC POWER COMPANY, INC. AND SUBSIDIARY COMPANIES
Condensed Consolidated Balance Sheet as at September 30, 1960--Actual and Pro Forma
Giving Effect to Proposed Issue and Sale by a Subsidiary Company of $40,000,000 Face
Amount of Promissory Notes

Assets and Other Debits	Actual	Pro Forma Adjustments	Pro Forma
Utility Plant:			
Electric Plant (at original cost)	$1,717,987,472	$ -	$1,717,987,472
Less Reserves for Depreciation, Depletion, and Amortization	384,545,238	-	384,545,238
Electric Plant, less Reserves	$1,333,442,234	-	$1,333,442,234
Heating Plant (less Reserve, $1,133,970)	211,248	-	211,248
Total Utility Plant, less Reserves	$1,333,653,482	-	$1,333,653,482
Excess of Cost of Investments in Subsidiaries Consolidated over Book Value at Dates of Acquisition	$ 31,661,602	-	$ 31,661,602
Investment and Fund Accounts	$ 16,441,324	$ -	$ 16,441,324
Current Assets:			
Cash	$ 39,479,674	$40,000,000) (5,100,000))	$ 74,379,674
Other	73,916,721		73,916,721
Total Current Assets	$ 113,396,395	$34,900,000	$ 148,296,395
Deferred Debits	$ 5,241,295	-	$ 5,241,295
Total Assets and Other Debits	$1,500,394,098	$34,900,000	$1,535,294,098
Liabilities and Other Credits			
Long-Term Debt (less current maturities)	$ 719,893,000	$40,000,000	$ 759,893,000
Preferred Stocks of Subsidiaries (including premiums $3,047,481)	101,732,881	-	101,732,881
Common Stock of American Electric Power Company, Inc., outstanding 21,369,889 shares, par value $10 per share	213,698,890	-	213,698,890
Premium on Common Stock	54,216,942	-	54,216,942
Capital Surplus	36,082	-	36,082
Earned Surplus as Recorded in Unrestricted Accounts Maintained, in the Case of the Principal Electric Utility Subsidiaries, Pursuant to State Regulatory Requirements	164,980,168	-	164,980,168
Accumulated Amount Invested in the Business Equivalent to Reduction in Federal Income Taxes Resulting from Accelerated Amortization and Liberalized Depreciation, Which is Recorded as Earned Surplus Restricted ($94,698,293), or as a Reserve ($6,600,874), for Future Federal Income Taxes in Accounts Maintained Pursuant to State Regulatory Requirements	101,299,167	-	101,299,167
Current Liabilities	132,669,751	(5,100,000)	127,569,751
Contractual Liability	673,000	-	673,000
Deferred Credits and Miscellaneous Reserves	8,334,211	-	8,334,211
Contributions in Aid of Construction	2,860,006	-	2,860,006
Total Liabilities and Other Credits	$1,500,394,098	$34,900,000	$1,535,294,098

( ) Denotes red figure.

AMERICAN ELECTRIC POWER COMPANY, INC, AND SUBSIDIARY COMPANIES
Condensed Consolidated Statement of Income for the Twelve Months
Ended September 30, 1960 -- Actual and Pro Forma Giving Effect
to Proposed Issue and Sale by a Subsidiary Company of $40,000,000
Face Amount of Promissory Notes

	Actual	Pro Forma Adjustments	Pro Forma
Operating Revenues -- Electric	$335,459,899	$ -	$335,459,899
Operating Revenue Deductions:			
Operation	$113,511,269	$ -	$113,511,269
Maintenance	24,531,575		24,531,575
Depreciation	43,849,559		43,849,559
Taxes, other than Federal income taxes	29,800,757		29,800,757
Federal income taxes	28,316,985	(1,014,348)	27,302,637
Provision for future Federal income taxes	19,636,435	-	19,636,435
Portion of current Federal income taxes provided for in prior years (credit)	(2,357,018)	-	(2,357,018)
Total	$257,289,562	$(1,014,348)	$256,275,214
Operating Income	$ 78,170,337	$ 1,014,348	$ 79,184,685
Other Income, net	681,320	-	681,320
Gross Income	$ 78,851,657	$ 1,014,348	$ 79,866,005
Income Deductions:			
Interest on long-term debt	$ 25,564,556	$ 2,200,000	$ 27,764,556
Amortization of debt premium, discount, and expense -- net (credit)	(133,681)	-	(133,681)
Interest on short-term debt	1,242,605	(249,331)	993,274
Other interest and miscellaneous deductions	400,107	-	400,107
Interest charged to construction (credit)	(6,522,234)	(1,919,500)	(8,441,734)
Total	$ 20,551,353	$ 31,169	$ 20,582,522
Consolidated Net Income, before Preferred Stock Dividend Requirements of Subsidiaries	$ 58,300,304	$ 983,179	$ 59,283,483
Deduct Preferred Stock Dividend Requirements of Subsidiaries	4,336,800	-	4,336,800
Consolidated Net Income Applicable to Common Stock of American Electric Power Company, Inc.	$ 53,963,504	$ 983,179	$ 54,946,683

( ) Denotes red figure.

UNITED STATES OF AMERICA
before the
SECURITIES AND EXCHANGE COMMISSION

January 13, 1961

In the Matters of

KENTUCKY POWER COMPANY
File No. 70-3890

AMERICAN ELECTRIC POWER COMPANY, INC.
KENTUCKY POWER COMPANY
File No. 60-22

(Public Utility Holding Company Act of 1935)

ORDER GRANTING SECTION 6(b)
APPLICATION AND TERMINATING
PROCEEDINGS

Kentucky Power Company ("Kentucky"), a public utility subsidiary company of American Electric Power Company, Inc. ("American"), a registered holding company, having filed with this Commission an application, as amended, pursuant to Section 6(b) of the Public Utility Holding Company Act of 1935 ("Act"), regarding the issue and sale to banks of not to exceed an aggregate face amount of $40,000,000 of unsecured notes; and

The Commission, pursuant to Sections 6(b) and 20(a) of the Act, having instituted a proceeding with respect to Kentucky and American for the purpose of determining what action, if any, should be taken in respect of the item identified on the corporate balance sheet of Kentucky, and the consolidated balance sheet of American and its subsidiary companies, filed in this proceeding as "Earned Surplus Restricted for Future Federal Income Taxes"; and

The Commission having consolidated the proceedings for the purpose of hearing and consideration; and

A hearing having been held after appropriate notice, in the course of which Kentucky and American, on the one hand, and the Division of Corporate Regulation of the Commission, on the other hand, having entered into a settlement proposal with respect to the various issues involved in the consolidated proceedings, and the Commission having considered the matter and having this day issued its Findings and Opinion, on the basis of such Findings and Opinion:

IT IS ORDERED that the application, as amended, of Kentucky, filed pursuant to Section 6(b) of the Act, be and hereby is granted, effective forthwith, subject to (a) the terms and conditions contained in Rule 24 promulgated under the Act, and (b) the reservation of jurisdiction with respect to the fees and expenses incurred in connection with such application, as amended.

IT IS FURTHER ORDERED that the proceeding instituted by the Commission pursuant to Sections 6(b) and 20(a) of the Act and directed to Kentucky and American be, and hereby is, dismissed.

IT IS FURTHER ORDERED that these consolidated proceedings be, and hereby are, terminated, except to the extent of the reservation of jurisdiction with respect to the fees and expenses noted above.

By the Commission.

/s/ ORVAL L. DUBOIS

Orval L. DuBois
Secretary

AMERICAN INSTITUTE OF CERTIFIED PUBLIC ACCOUNTANTS

270 Madison Avenue
New York 16, N. Y.

January 28, 1959

Mr. Andrew Barr, Chief Accountant
Securities and Exchange Commission
Washington 25, D. C.

Dear Andy:

Enclosed is a memorandum which contains a summary of and excerpts from the comments received from thirteen members of the committee on accounting procedure on Securities Act Release No. 4010 giving notice of the Commission's intention to announce an interpretation of administrative policy on financial statements regarding balance-sheet treatment of the credit equivalent to the reduction of income taxes, or, in other words, the treatment of the credit for deferred income taxes.

If additional comments are received before your deadline, I shall send you a supplementary memorandum so as to include them in the record of the committee's reaction.

Sincerely yours,

/s/   PERRY

Perry Mason
Research Associate

PM:eh
Enclosure

RELEASE No. 4010, SECURITIES ACT OF 1933, December 30, 1958
The credit arising from accounting for reductions of income taxes excluded
from stockholders' equity section of the balance sheet.

Summary of and excerpts from comments of members of committee on accounting procedure, American Institute of Certified Public Accountants

Summary of Comments

Thirteen members (out of twenty-one) of the committee have submitted comments on the proposed interpretation. Ten members definitely
approved or have no objections to the release. Three oppose or have
serious doubts as to the desirability of its issuance.

Principal Points in Opposition

1. May seriously affect the rate used by some state regulatory agencies.

2. May seriously affect the legal position of a utility under existing
   indentures.

3. May have adverse effect upon future financing arrangements.

4. May create a problem of civil liability of those concerned with previous
   filings.

5. No definite position was taken by the committee on accounting procedure as to the nature of the credit.

6. The proper course for the Commission to follow in cases of this kind
   is to amend Regulation S-X, rather than to issue an administrative
   ruling which is likely to cast a cloud over previous SEC filings.

Suggested Changes

1. Release should be clarified to indicate that it does not apply to corporations that have not accounted for tax reductions prior to 1958, in
   other words, indicate that it does not have a retroactive application to
   such corporations.

2. Should be made clear that the term "equity capital" refers to stockholders' equity capital.

3. Caption should indicate that the position taken covers both the determination of income and the balance sheet treatment.

4. Clarify footnote 2. Rather than saying that the charge to income is not necessary, indicate that it already has been made.

Excerpts from Comments

. . . I think your position is sound.

I think you will get many objections to it from state commissions and perhaps some of their accountants (but I hope on non-accounting grounds), as I am sure you are well aware. I also assume there is no question as to the Commission's power under the Securities Acts to require a treatment different than that called for by some of the state utility commissions.

— — — — —

The proposed SEC release is in agreement with the suggestion which I made in my letter of April 18, 1958, regarding ARB No. 44 (Revised), as follows:

"I believe that we should clearly indicate that the 'reserve' should in no case be considered as restricted surplus or any other form of equity capital."

While I still feel that way, I can see the difficulty that some utility companies face, since they are probably not going to get the benefit of the reserve as a part of their rate base unless it is included in equity capital. In effect, they say that they are being deprived of the benefit intended by Congress unless they can include the reserve in their rate base. In other words, unless they can include the admitted cash savings (or the plant built with such savings) to increase their ultimate earnings, as non-regulated companies are free to do, what advantage to their stockholders will result from adopting the liberalized depreciation methods permitted by the 1954 Internal Revenue Code? If they conclude that there is no advantage, and therefore do not adopt such methods, then to that extent the purpose of Congress in encouraging plant expansion is defeated.

My belief is that this is a problem which they will have to resolve with the regulatory commissions, but that it hardly justifies treatment of the reserve as equity capital for financial statement purposes.

— — — — —

While I am not sure that the proposed release will accomplish much greater uniformity in deferred tax treatment among utilities (see footnote 3), I do not see that our committee can offer any valid objections to it.

I don't understand why the caption of the proposed release refers only to balance sheet treatment, when the third paragraph includes reference to determination of income. Possibly the latter consideration is presumed to be covered by ARB 44 (revised) but if the Commission is going to state a position, I think it should cover both income and balance sheet treatment, and the caption should so indicate. This may be a piece of unsolicited advice but I think it is worth offering.

— — — — —

I see no objections to the proposed release. . . In some ways I am sorry that the Committee on Accounting Procedure could not have made such a release unnecessary.

— — — — —

The proposed SEC release seems to me to be a step in the right direction. . .

I do not see how anyone can read into our bulletin, permission to carry the reserve as a part of surplus. . .

— — — — —

Generally, I am in agreement with the basic idea of the proposed SEC release that whatever the balance sheet item growing out of deferred tax accounting is, it certainly is not earned surplus. If it were, it doesn't seem to me there should have been any tax allocation accounting.

The wording of footnote 2 on page 2 bothers me a little bit, possibly because I fail to understand what it is driving at. It seems to me that rather than saying that the charge to income is not necessary under the circumstances mentioned, the real situation is that the charge has already been made.

I do not know enough about the practical and procedural questions raised by [two other members], but certainly think they should be carefully considered by the SEC before a release of this type should be issued.

I like the last paragraph of the release very much, particularly the first sentence thereof, and I rather wish that our committee had said it. It seems to me that accounting is on sound ground when it allocates to appropriate periods the effect on income of material income tax reductions or increases occurring in a different period from the recognition of the related income or losses for accounting purposes, and that we should not have to establish a definite liability which will be paid in order to have a credit balance account for the purpose of properly stating income.

. . .I am bothered by the inconsistency between the situation of companies who have and those who have not employed deferred tax accounting in the past, but it seems to me there are many such cases if bulletins are not applied retroactively.

— — — — —

I assume that the term "equity capital," as used in the first paragraph and in footnote 4 of the proposed announcement, refers to stockholders' equity capital. If so, the language might be clarified. . . Otherwise, the proposed announcement seems to me a sound statement of accounting principle and a logical extension of the views expressed in footnote 35 of Accounting Series Release No. 53 (footnote 96 in the bound edition). . .

— — — — —

The proposed SEC release is in accord with my views on the treatment of the credit arising in deferred income tax accounting. Although my letter of about a year ago indicates my support for the view that the credit might reasonably be treated "as unrecognized income by reflecting an appropriate amount in the depreciation charge," I have been consistently of the view that the item has many characteristics of a liability. Despite the impact of the Income Tax Rules which allows a corporation to be taxed as a partnership and other special situations which weaken the view that the item is a liability, I yet believe in most situations it is normally a liability. . . In any event, I agree with the SEC proposal that it not be included as part of equity capital.

– – – – –

I have reviewed the SEC release, and express my approval of its issuance. However, since ARB 44 (revised) is not retroactive, the SEC's release should be clarified with respect to what is to be done in those instances where corporations do not choose to make retroactive adjustment for any previously unaccounted for reductions in taxes. It should, in my judgment, state specifically that they are not required to do so.

– – – – –

I have never considered the inclusion of a provision for deferred taxes in the equity section of the balance sheet as particularly misleading when such provision was adequately described and where the tax deferral could reasonably be expected to be indefinite or long term. Although, in my opinion, accountants are approaching agreement on recognizing a deferred tax debit or its equivalent in the income statement in order to present earnings fairly, I feel there is still considerable difference of opinion on the balance sheet presentation of the resulting credit and its significance. However, I have no strong views on the balance sheet presentation and therefore no objection to the proposed policy announcement.

I do feel, however, that the phrase "the accumulated credit arising from accounting for reductions in income taxes" could be clarified so as to make it clear that it is the classification of amounts which have been specifically set aside for deferred taxes, not the amount of cumulative tax reductions as a literal reading of the release would indicate, which is at issue. Thus, where a company did not provide for deferred taxes prior to ARB No. 44 (revised) but "accounted" for such tax reductions by taking them into income, it is not intended that it be required to make a transfer out of earned surplus retroactively.

– – – – –

From the standpoint of existing accounting theory, the position of the Commission as to the balance-sheet classification of deferred income taxes probably is sound. On practical grounds, however, it may be subject to question. Several large public utility companies have classified deferred income taxes as restricted earned surplus for a number of years now, and a reclassification of this item is likely to be a serious matter for some of them, as affecting especially their regulatory position vis-a-vis state authority, their legal position under existing indentures, and their future financing arrangements. Whether the theoretical advantages of a change outweigh the practical disadvantages may be doubtful.

The form of the proposed action also is questionable. The release indicates that the Commission simply proposes to make an announcement saying that all statements dated December 31, 1958 and subsequently are false and misleading if they classify deferred income taxes as restricted earned surplus. This is likely to cast a cloud over previous filings notwithstanding the language of the proposed announcement, and to create problems as to civil liability in connection with previous filings on the part of everyone, including accountants, who had anything to do with them. The proper course for the Commission to follow in cases of this kind is to amend Regulation S-X. I understand this course was not followed in this case because the adoption or amendment of a rule is a lengthy process and the staff wanted fast action. I think the form of the proposed action of the Commission in this matter should be protested vigorously.

– – – – –

I think the SEC should go easy on this, and I think we should so suggest.

ARB 44 Revised should have a chance to stand on its own feet for a season before "interpretations" of it are issued. There is nothing in the Bulletin implying that the credit is a part of surplus, but if someone chooses to infer that it may be, properly earmarked and described, I am hard put to find the irrefutable counter-argument.

There was enough uncertainty about the real nature of the credit in our Committee — was it a liability, a deferred credit to income, a depreciation reserve, or what, and how was it to be disposed of in the final analysis? — to make me hesitate to rule out segregated surplus. At the same time, I am quite satisfied that the charge to income is a proper one and that it has nothing to do with income-leveling or income-equalization.

Besides that, there are regulated companies that may find themselves in a box under this interpretation. . .

Some of my concern comes about because of the conflict between the accumulated credit resting in earned surplus of those corporations that have not previously accounted for reductions in taxes and the accumulated credit resting in a reserve or liability account of those that have. As 44 Revised is not retroactive, there may be many cases where substantial amounts that should have been, but were not, charged to income will remain in earned surplus, although there is a tax "lien" on the corporation in equal amount. When the SEC says "accumulated credit arising from accounting," I take it to mean just that, but I think the release should be clarified to be sure that corporations that have not accounted for reductions prior to 1958 will not be required to apply 44 Revised retroactively to remove a previously-unaccounted-for credit from surplus.

This conflict between the content of the surplus accounts of corporations that have previously accounted for the reductions and those that have not (assuming that the have-nots will not make retroactive adjustment) makes me think that the SEC ought to strengthen and clarify its position on accounting for the charge to income before it begins to deal with the credit arising from the charge.

— — — — —

I subscribe to the views expressed both in regard to clarifying the
.mplication of retroactivity and the prohibition against including the
deferred credit in earned surplus, particularly in the case of certain regulated companies. . .

I admit that I did not at first read into the release the implication of
the retroactivity above referred to, but several of our clients who have
commenced providing for the deferred income tax in 1958 and have no
intention of making retroactive provisions have questioned us about the
meaning of the SEC release; therefore, it appears that clarification is
required.

— — — — —

GARRETT T. BURNS
CHATEAU ROCHAMBEAU
SCARSDALE, N. Y.

February 16, 1959

Mr. Andrew Barr, Chief Accountant
Securities and Exchange Commission
Washington 25, D. C.

Re: Tax Allocation -- S.E.C. Release
(With reference also to A.R.B.
No. 44 (Revised))

Dear Andy:

On reviewing the summarization prepared by
the office of the American Institute of Certified
Public Accountants, I was unable to identify any
of the comments that I submitted. I have just
talked with Perry Mason, and apparently his copy
of my letter went astray -- at least he could not
find it.

Inasmuch as I desire my views to be on record,
I am sending you a copy of my letter of January
13th to Perry Mason, and I have informed him that
I am taking this action.

Sincerely yours,

/s/ GARRETT

Enclosure

GARRETT T. BURNS

January 13, 1959

Mr. Perry Mason, Research Director
American Institute of
  Certified Public Accountants
270 Madison Avenue
New York 16, N. Y.

Re: Tax Allocation -- S.E.C. Release
    (With reference also to A.R.B.
    No. 44 (Revised))

Dear Perry:

Dick Lytle, in his letter of January 6, 1959, suggested that comments be submitted to you on the above S.E.C. Release.

I strongly urge that this release be endorsed and supported by the committee. The only defect in it is that it does not go far enough and deal with the more important objective of fairly presenting net income.

The proponents of the earned surplus credit treatment (the have-your-cake-and-eat-it-too-school) argue, so I understand, that the debit is not a cost of doing business, but an "equalizer," made necessary because of an income-tax election (although the election is not necessary or mandatory, and some hold the view that the benefits may be taken away).

How the aforementioned "school" can justify ignoring Par. 2 of Chapter 8 of A.R.B. No. 43, with regard to the avoidance of income equalization, is beyond me. But it is even more difficult for me to comprehend how an item can be a cost or an income charge and a part of earned surplus at the same time.

I still regret the inclusion of "except in those rare cases" in Par. 4, and also Par. 8 and Par. 9 in A.R.B. No. 44 (Revised). The majority who approved the foregoing must have done so in the spirit of compromise. The so-called "rare cases" rest on the premise that "it may reasonably be expected" that the resultant higher income taxes will be allowed in future rate determinations. However, no present regulatory commission would attempt, or have the power, to bind a future commission, and the uncertain future economic and political environments also remove entirely any basis for a <u>reasonable</u> expectation.

The case for so-called "matching" rests on such an expectation, but, meantime, the flow-through method permits current net income to be increased, utilities in some states to report net income differently from those in other states, and even utilities in the same state to do so where accelerated depreciation is not claimed for income-tax purposes by one company.

Lastly, the permanent benefit position is clearly a cash-basis accounting approach and could be applied to level amounts of accounts payable and liability accruals.

I should like to see the exception in Par. 4 of A.R.B. No. 44 (Revised) and Par. 8 and Par. 9 eliminated by our committee before the S.E.C. moves ahead to income statements in a subsequent release.

Sincerely,

/s/ GARRETT

Copies to:

  Members of the Committee on Accounting Procedure
  Mr. John L. Carey, Executive Director
  Mr. Carman G. Blough, Research Director
  Mr. Richard C. Lytle, Director of Technical
    Services

AMERICAN INSTITUTE OF CERTIFIED PUBLIC ACCOUNTANTS

270 Madison Avenue
New York 16, N. Y.

March 30, 1959

The Securities and Exchange Commission
Washington 25, D. C.

Gentlemen:

This is in support of my telegram to Mr. Andrew Barr, Chief Accountant for the Commission, requesting an opportunity to testify at the hearing to be held on April 8, 1959 as a representative of the American Institute of Certified Public Accountants with respect to Securities Act of 1933, Release No. 4010, "Notice of Intention to Announce Interpretation of Administrative Policy."

This request grows out of the fact that question has been raised with respect to the intent of the American Institute of Certified Public Accountants' committee on accounting procedure in using the phrase "a deferred tax account" in Accounting Research Bulletin No. 44 (Revised), dated July, 1958, to indicate the account to be credited for the amount of the deferred income tax referred to in that Bulletin. It is our intention to testify as to the meaning of this term as it was used by the committee.

If I am permitted to testify, it is my intention to state that the committee used the phrase in its ordinary connotation of an account to be shown in the balance sheet as a liability or a deferred credit, and that a provision in recognition of the deferral of income taxes, being required for the proper determination of net income, should not at the same time result in a credit to earned surplus or to any other account included in the stockholders equity section of the balance sheet.

Very truly yours,

/s/ CARMAN G. BLOUGH

Director of Research

CGB:dum

SECURITIES AND EXCHANGE COMMISSION
Washington 25, D. C.

March 31, 1959

Mr. Carman G. Blough
Director of Research
American Institute of Certified
  Public Accountants
270 Madison Avenue
New York 16, N. Y.

Dear Carman:

As I told you over the telephone earlier to-day, your letter of March 30, 1959, was received this morning, and your telephone call of yesterday was in time to include the Institute's name on the schedule of appearances which we have prepared to send all those who have requested time at the hearing on our Release No. 4010. I am enclosing a copy of the form letter which I have been sending along with the schedule.

I am glad that the Institute has decided it should be represented, as there has been considerable confusion expressed in some of the comments we have received as to the meaning of Research Bulletin 44 (Revised). Your appearance should set the record straight.

Sincerely yours,

Andrew Barr
Chief Accountant

Enclosures - 2

AMERICAN INSTITUTE OF CERTIFIED PUBLIC ACCOUNTANTS

270 Madison Avenue
New York 16, N.Y.

March 8, 1960

Mr. Andrew Barr, Chief Accountant
Securities and Exchange Commission
Washington 25, D. C.

Dear Andy:

Thank you for your letter of February 29 with which you enclosed copies of your releases dealing with the deferred tax problem. I appreciate your sending them to me and I also appreciate your kind comments with respect to my appearance before the Commission stating the position of the accounting procedure committee in clarifying Accounting Research Bulletin No. 44 (Revised).

It was very gratifying to me to see the extent to which your release relied upon the public statements by the committee on accounting procedure and I want to express my congratulations upon the well considered statement with respect to the treatment of the credit for deferred taxes. I can see no way in which it could have been improved, from my viewpoint.

I do have a little concern, however, over the wording of the last sentence in the first full paragraph on page 4 and the first sentence in the paragraph immediately following it in Securities Act of 1933, Release No. 4191 which read as follows:

"It is the Commission's view, however, that comparable recognition of tax deferment should be made in all cases in which there is a tax reduction resulting from deducting costs for tax purposes at faster rates than for financial statement purposes.

"The Committee on Accounting Procedure of the American Institute of Certified Public Accountants agrees with the position expressed above."

There are some situations, notably intangible drilling costs, on which quite a few members of the committee did not think it had yet spoken. The last sentence in paragraph 1 of Chapter 10 (B) of ARB 43 reads:

> "The section does not apply where there is a presumption that particular differences between the tax return and the income statement will recur regularly over a comparatively long period of time."

This sentence has been a particular area of uncertainty.

On the other hand, there are those who interpret paragraph 4 of Accounting Research Bulletin No. 23 (now paragraph 11 of Chapter 10 (B) of ARB 43) as being all-inclusive. However, it is a fact that the members of the committee, in recent years, were not in agreement as to whether the application of the bulletin to a variety of problems, including intangible drilling costs, was sufficiently clear to afford a reasonable guide.

One of the recommendations made to the accounting principles board by the committee on accounting procedure when it went out of existence was that the board should give early consideration to the clarification of all phases of the tax allocation problem. As a result, the board has asked the new Accounting Research Division to make a study of this subject, and Professor Homer Black of Florida State University has undertaken to do it.

You can see why I might wish that the Commission had not covered the matter quite as broadly as it did. I have always felt that the Commission's policy of letting the profession lead in matters of accounting principles was to the advantage of all concerned.

With kindest regards and best wishes, I remain

Sincerely,

/s/ CARMAN G. BLOUGH

Director of Research

CGB:dum
cc: George Wagner, Chairman, Committee on Relations with SEC
    Weldon Powell, Chairman, Accounting Principles Board
    Perry Mason, Acting Director, Accounting Research Division

SECURITIES AND EXCHANGE COMMISSION
Washington 25 D. C.

April 8, 1960

Mr. Carman G. Blough
Director of Research
American Institute of Certified
  Public Accountants
270 Madison Avenue
New York 16, N. Y.

Dear Mr. Blough:

The Commission has authorized me to respond to your letter in which you express concern over the wording of the last sentence in the first full paragraph on page 4 and first sentence of the paragraph immediately following it in Securites Act of 1933 Release No. 4191 (also identified as Securities Exchange Act of 1934 Release No. 6189, Holding Company Act Release No. 14173, Investment Company Act of 1940 Release No. 2977, and Accounting Series Release No. 85). The full paragraph to which you refer and the following sentence read as follows:

> "A number of comments indicated that, should the Commission take the foregoing position, it should be limited to matters connected with depreciation and amortization or, if not so limited, any additional items embraced within this principle should be clearly specified. It is the Commission's view, however, that comparable recognition of tax deferment should be made in all cases in which there is a tax reduction resulting from deducting costs for tax purposes at faster rates than for financial statement purposes. (Footnote omitted.)

      "The Committee on Accounting Procedure
of the American Institute of Certified Public
Accountants agrees with the position expressed
above."

      It was not the Commission's intention by the publication of this release, stating an administrative policy regarding balance sheet treatment of the credit equivalent to the reduction in income taxes when deferred tax accounting is employed, to make mandatory the use of deferred tax accounting beyond the requirements of generally accepted accounting principles.

                  Yours very truly,

                    Andrew Barr
                    Chief Accountant

ARTHUR ANDERSEN & CO..

120 South LaSalle Street
Chicago 3

January 28, 1959

Mr. Orval L. DuBois, Secretary
Securities and Exchange Commission
425 Second Street, N. W.
Washington 25, D.C.

Re: Proposed announcement of policy regarding
balance-sheet treatment of credits
equivalent to income-tax reductions.

Gentlemen:

We are a firm of independent public accountants. In our practice, we are responsible for examining and expressing our opinion on the financial statements of a large number of commercial and public utility companies. Many of these companies file their financial statements with the Securities and Exchange Commission under the Securities Act of 1933, the Securities Exchange Act of 1934, the Public Utility Holding Company Act of 1935, or the Investment Company Act of 1940. Therefore, we are vitally interested in the proposed policy announcement.

We understand it is the intention of the proposed announcement to exclude from the equity-capital section of the balance sheet, the accumulated credits arising from accounting for reductions in income taxes for various items, including liberalized depreciation under Section 167 and accelerated amortization under Section 168 of the Internal Revenue Code of 1954, a problem which arises when costs are deductible for income-tax purposes in an earlier period, or at a faster rate, than they are recognized in the accounts.

This letter and the accompanying memorandum relate only to that particular phase of deferred-tax accounting.

The credits arising from accounting for the tax reductions that result from the use of liberalized-depreciation and/or accelerated-amortization deductions for income-tax purposes only, clearly, in our opinion, represent tax deferment, not tax savings. Such credits are, in effect, reserves for the future taxes that will become payable when the amounts of the costs (such as depreciation or amortization) deductible for tax purposes fall below those deducted in the accounts. When this takes place, these credits will be returned to income proportionately to offset the effect of the higher current income taxes payable because of having taken liberalized depreciation or accelerated amortization in prior years. Accordingly, we believe that where these accumulated credits are relatively material in amount, their inclusion in the equity-capital section of the balance sheet overstates the stockholders' equity.

In our opinion, generally accepted accounting principles require that where the credits arising from accounting for income-tax reductions represent tax deferment (as in the case of liberalized depreciation or accelerated amortization), the resulting accumulated credits should not be included in the equity-capital section of the balance sheet. Accordingly, we concur in the proposed announcement of interpretation of administrative policy on financial statements regarding the balance-sheet treatment of credits equivalent to reductions of income taxes.

The accompanying memorandum states our views in greater detail. We shall be pleased to discuss these matters with you further, if you would like us to do so.

Very truly yours,

/s/ ARTHUR ANDERSEN & CO.

ARTHUR ANDERSEN & CO.

120 South LaSalle Street
Chicago 3

DEFERRED-TAX ACCOUNTING

MEMORANDUM RE SECURITIES AND EXCHANGE COMMISSION'S
PROPOSED ANNOUNCEMENT OF POLICY REGARDING BALANCE-SHEET
TREATMENT OF CREDITS EQUIVALENT TO INCOME-TAX REDUCTIONS

The proposed announcement of the Securities and Exchange Commission, of which notice was released on December 30, 1958, would exclude from the equity-capital section of the balance sheet, the accumulated credits arising from accounting for reductions in income taxes for various items, including liberalized depreciation under Section 167 and accelerated amortization under Section 168 of the Internal Revenue Code of 1954.

Equity-capital treatment problem arises
 mainly with public utilities—

The problem of tax deferment arises where costs are deductible for income-tax purposes in an earlier period, or at a faster rate, than in the accounts.

It is principally with respect to accelerated amortization and liberalized depreciation that the problem of statement presentation of the accumulated credit arising from accounting for the tax deferment is encountered.

Commercial companies generally treat the accumulated credit as a reserve for deferred income taxes, or in some cases as an addition to the depreciation reserve in recognition of the loss of future deductibility for income-tax purposes. We know of no commercial companies that treat the accumulated credit as a part of equity capital.

Most public utilities are subject to state regulatory commissions. Some of these commissions do not permit accounting recognition of the deferred tax arising from use of accelerated amortization or liberalized depreciation, but allow the tax benefit to flow through income into earned surplus. A majority of the state commissions, however, recognize deferred-tax accounting. Some of them require treatment of the accumulated credit as a deferred-tax reserve while others regard it as restricted or appropriated surplus which some companies classify as part of equity capital. A few companies, even though they have restricted-surplus orders, classify the credit outside of the equity-capital section in their published balance sheets.

Since the problem relates almost entirely to public utilities, our discussion herein is directed to the treatment of the accumulated credit arising from accounting for the tax deferment due to the use of accelerated amortization and liberalized depreciation by regulated public utilities.

Accelerated amortization and
 liberalized depreciation—

Accelerated amortization originated with the addition of Section 124 to the Internal Revenue Code in 1940. It was extended as Section 124A in the Code in 1950, and is now Section 168 in the 1954 Code. Accelerated amortization does not change the total depreciation allowed, but it permits the cost of the property, to the extent covered by Certificates of Necessity, to be amortized over a five-year period for tax purposes. In many cases the property has a useful life of more than five years, and is depreciated in the accounts over the longer useful life.

Liberalized depreciation in its present form first appeared as Section 167 of the Internal Revenue Code of 1954, and applies only to new property additions after 1953. It does not change the total depreciation allowable over the life of the property. But it permits higher depreciation charges in the early years, thus reducing taxes in those years and deferring payment of this tax until later years when depreciation deductions for tax purposes applicable to such property will be lower than the depreciation reflected in the accounts.

Accelerated amortization and liberalized depreciation are similar in effect. Both permit deferment of income tax by allowing faster-than-normal write-off of the <u>cost</u> of the related property--accelerated amortization, over a five-year period; liberalized depreciation, over the useful life but at higher rates in the early years. For convenience herein, they will be referred to together as "accelerated depreciation."

Accelerated depreciation results
 in tax deferment—

Neither Sections 167 nor 168 of the 1954 Internal Revenue Code allows depreciation in excess of the cost of the related property. They do not change the aggregate allowance for depreciation over the life of the property; they change only the timing of the depreciation deduction for tax purposes.

By allowing larger depreciation deductions in the early years, these sections have the effect of reducing the income-tax payments in those years. But the depreciation deduction for tax purposes decreases in later years, or ceases entirely after five years in case of accelerated amortization; hence, the income tax becomes correspondingly larger in the later years. The effect is to allow a forward shift in the depreciation deductions and a consequent deferment of income tax.

That the effect of the liberalized depreciation is merely to shift the depreciation deductions between years and to defer the tax, is clearly pointed out in the comments in the report of the Ways and Means Committee of the House of Representatives (House Report No. 1337 83d Congress, 2d Session, page 25). In discussing the section allowing the liberalized depreciation (which later became Section 167 of the 1954 Code), the report stated: "The changes made by your committee's bill merely affect the timing and not the ultimate amount of depreciation deductions with respect to a property." Also, on page 3 of that committee report there is a table summarizing the "Effect on receipts, fiscal year 1955, of measures contained in your committee's bill." This summary classifies the tax effect of liberalized depreciation deductions under the subheading "Items Which Merely Shift Deductions or Income Between Taxable Years."

Accumulated credit is a reserve for
  deferred taxes--not a portion of
  the equity capital—

The aggregate of the depreciation deductions, being limited to the cost of the property, is the same, no matter which method is used for income-tax purposes. Accordingly, the total taxes to be paid over the life of the property are the same, assuming that the company has taxable profits in all years and that there is no change in the income-tax rate. It is only the periods in which the taxes must be paid that are changed. Since the aggregate amount of taxes to be paid is the same under either method, there is no income-tax saving; there is only a deferral of the tax payment.

Thus, it is evident that the accumulated credit arising from accounting recognition of the current income-tax deferment through the use of accelerated depreciation for tax purposes and normal depreciation in the accounts, is a reserve for the deferred income taxes that will be payable in later years. It is in no sense an equity balance.

The principal argument advanced for classifying the credit as part of equity capital is that in order to "normalize" the income, it is necessary to normalize the income-tax provision; and, since no present tax cost or liability is incurred (there being only a future tax cost) the credit arising from such normalization should be included in the equity capital rather than in a reserve account that implies provision for a current cost. Further it is argued, where no charge is made against income to recognize the tax deferral, the result is to allow the effect of the deferral to flow through income into earned surplus which is part of equity capital; and if this is acceptable treatment, there ought to be no objection where the tax is "normalized," to including the credit under equity capital as a separate restricted-surplus account.

We believe that a current cost is incurred where depreciation or amortization deductions for income-tax purposes are higher than those recorded on the books, and that accordingly, the credit arising from recognition of the tax deferral should go to a reserve, rather than into equity capital as restricted surplus. Those who would "normalize" the income, but argue that there is no current cost involved, destroy their support for normalization.

Generally accepted accounting principles
require recognition of deferred tax,
if material—

Since the income-tax reduction from use of accelerated depreciation is only a temporary deferment, not a permanent saving, the taxes must eventually be paid. Hence, generally accepted accounting principles require recognition of and accounting for the tax reductions, if material, by charge against current income and credit to a reserve for deferred taxes, not to restricted surplus or some other equity-capital account. We know of no accounting principle which permits classifying as stockholders' equity a credit arising from provision for a cost that eventually will have to be recognized, no matter how long deferred.

Accounting recognition of the deferred taxes is necessary to accomplish an equitable matching of costs and revenues and to avoid overstating net income in the early years when the tax reduction is greatest and understating net income in the later years when the tax payable exceeds the tax on current book income.

The requirement for accounting recognition of the tax deferment has been stated in the accounting research bulletins issued by the Accounting Procedure Committee of the American Institute of Certified Public Accountants. (ARB No. 43, Chapt. 9C, Par. 11 and 12, re accelerated amortization; ARB No. 44 (Revised) Par. 4, re declining-balance (liberalized) depreciation.)

While ARB No. 44 (Revised) dealing with accelerated (liberalized) depreciation does not specifically state that the credit arising from the tax deferment shall be treated as a reserve rather than in equity capital, we believe this was clearly the intention. For instance, in paragraph 5, it speaks of "crediting a deferred tax account." The bulletin requires recognition of the deferred tax (with the exception referred to in Note 3 on page 2 of the Commission's proposed announcement), in order to accomplish an equitable matching of costs and revenues and to avoid income distortion, even when the payment of the tax is deferred for relatively long periods. We see no possibility of reading into this bulletin any indication that the credit arising from the tax deferment can be treated as equity capital.

Furthermore, where a public utility company, pursuant to paragraph 8 of ARB No. 44, gives no accounting recognition to the tax deferment, in our opinion, its financial statements should clearly disclose the basis for the reasonable expectation that increased future income taxes, resulting from the earlier deduction of higher depreciation for income-tax purposes only, will be allowed in future rate determinations.

Argument that deferred tax will never
 have to be paid and therefore need
 not be treated as a reserve for
 future tax, is fallacious—

One of the principal arguments for not recognizing the deferred-tax credit as a reserve for future tax is that in the case of a utility property there is a constantly growing volume of property additions, with the result, it is argued, that the deferred tax will never have to be paid in the foreseeable future.

We disagree with this thinking. Those who advance this view will agree that with respect to a given unit of property, or even a year's property additions treated as a whole, it is clear that there is a deferral of income tax that will have to be paid in later years of the life of such property. They contend, however, that with respect to the property as a whole, the higher depreciation deductions on subsequent additions will offset the smaller depreciation deductions in later years of the life of the present property. In other words, they argue that the whole is different from the sum of its parts.

It is true that in the case of growing utility properties, the aggregate of the tax deferrals will be extended as long as such methods of depreciation are permitted for income-tax purposes. However, this does not mean that the taxes deferred this year will never have to be paid; they will have to be paid at some time in the future if the company continues to have taxable income. What happens is that the taxes deferred this year become payable, say, twelve years hence, assuming twenty-five year life and the sum of the years-digits depreciation method. At that time, accelerated depreciation on additions of that year may give rise to a new tax deferment, but this does not mean that this borrowing from the future should not be recognized and recorded.

If the reserve for deferred taxes continues to grow on an aggregate basis, this is merely a reflection of the amount of future tax benefit that has been used up to date as a result of claiming higher depreciation deductions for tax purposes than in the accounts. The fact that this reserve may continue to grow does not change its character or the purpose for which it is provided. It remains a reserve for deferred taxes payable in future years. Surely no one would argue that just because the depreciation reserves continue to grow they should be included in surplus account; and no one would argue that because a growing company has an increasingly large total balance of accounts payable or of long-term debt the present balance will never have to be paid and thus should be treated as a part of earned surplus and need not be treated as a liability in the accounts.

That accelerated depreciation results in tax deferment rather than a tax saving was well stated by the Federal Power Commission in its opinion June 30, 1956, in the case of Amere Gas Utilities Company, et al., Docket No. G-6358:

> "It is clear that the charging of greater depreciation during the early life of property and the charging of less during the later life operates to create a deferral of income taxes. The fact that there may be continuing additions to plant, year by year, with the results that there will be a balance in the reserve account at all times in the foreseeable future, does not prove that there is no tax deferral. On the contrary, it proves that there is a continuing tax deferral so long as additional facilities are being installed. This is precisely what Congress intended."

Furthermore, it should be recognized that there is always the possibility that the Congress may repeal the accelerated amortization or liberalized depreciation provisions of the Internal Revenue Code. If this were done, the balance in the tax-deferral account would cease to increase and would steadily decrease as it was used to meet the subsequent increases in future taxes resulting from the use of accelerated depreciation for tax purposes only in prior years. In this event, the permanent-tax-deferral argument falls apart.

Some state commissions prescribe classification
  of the credit as restricted surplus, but permit
  it to be used only in the same way as a reserve—

Notwithstanding the fact that the accumulated credit is clearly a reserve for future taxes, a number of the state regulatory commissions have prescribed restricted (or appropriated) surplus treatment.

In prescribing restricted-surplus treatment the commissions generally retained jurisdiction and permitted the account to be used only in the same manner as if it were a reserve for deferred taxes--i.e., to be returned to income to offset the effect of higher current income taxes payable because of having taken accelerated depreciation in prior years. Thus, in effect, the restricted surplus is treated as a deferred-tax reserve, and hence it should not be treated as part of common stock equity.

Some companies have expressed a preference for the restricted-surplus treatment, believing that it gave the appearance of larger equity capital, thereby improving their financial position and bonding power, and enabling them to borrow funds at lower interest cost. It would seem that this could follow only if the lenders were misled as to the nature of the so-called restricted surplus.

USCA held credit to be a reserve
  (Panhandle case)—

That the credit arising from the tax deferral was in the nature of a reserve rather than stockholders' equity was the position taken by the United States District Court of Appeals for the District of Columbia in the Case of City of Detroit vs. Federal Power Commission, 230F. (2d) 810, 821-22 (1956, Certiorari denied 352 U.S. 829--Rehearing denied 352 U.S. 919).

In this case the Federal Power Commission's treatment of accelerated amortization under Section 124A (now Section 168) of the Internal Revenue Code in the Panhandle Eastern Pipe Line Company case (FPC Opinion No. 269) was under consideration. The Court stated:

> "Since, however, Congress intended by Section 124A only to defer tax liability, and not to provide a fund which could be diverted by Panhandle to the payment of dividends,

the Commission further states, 'The accruals for taxes in excess of those actually paid should logically be treated by Panhandle, not as free and unrestricted income, but earmarked to provide for future meeting of such liability.' After the facilities have been fully depreciated under the accelerated amortization plan, income taxes will normally be greater, since no further deductions for depreciation will be possible. By setting up a special reserve for the tax saving of the first five years, the Commission insures that this amount will go to meet the increased taxes after that period, rather than being paid out in dividends."

That the accumulated credits resulting from the use of liberalized depreciation under Section 167 of the Internal Revenue Code are no different from those arising under Section 168 (formerly Section 124A), was well stated by the Federal Power Commission in the first paragraph of its opinion dated June 30, 1956, in the Amere Gas Utilities Company case (Docket No. G-6358):

"We are in agreement with the decision of the presiding examiner. We can find no legal difference between the problem now before us and that which was presented to us by Section 124A (now Section 168) of the Internal Revenue Code, pertaining to five year amortization of defense facilities pursuant to a certificate issued by a defense agency of the United States. Therefore, what was said in our Opinion No. 264 in Docket No. R-126, and in our Opinion No. 269 in Panhandle Eastern Pipe Line Company, Docket No. G-1116, et al., and what was said by the United States Circuit Court of Appeals for the District of Columbia Circuit in City of Detroit vs. Federal Power Commission, on December 15, 1955, in which the Commission's treatment of accelerated depreciation in the Panhandle case was fully approved, is completely controlling in this matter."

Federal Power Commission excludes
credit from equity capital—

In its Orders Nos. 203 and 204, dated May 29, 1958, amending its uniform system of accounts for natural gas companies and electric companies to provide for the accounting and reporting of deferred taxes on income, the Federal Power Commission declined to permit the accumulated credit from deferred-tax accounting to be treated as restricted surplus.

Instead, the Commission provided a new balance-sheet classification for accumulated deferred taxes on income (that neither identified the accumulated amounts as a reserve or restricted surplus), and made provision for two new accounts thereunder--one for accelerated amortization and one for liberalized depreciation. The deferred-tax provisions charged to income are to be credited to these accounts. These accounts are then to be charged and income credited for the amounts by which the taxes currently payable are greater because of the use of accelerated amortization or liberalized depreciation in prior years.

In its order for this amendment of the system of accounts, Federal Power Commission stated with respect to the argument for restricted-surplus treatment:

> "In favor of the restricted-surplus treatment, it is argued that the temporary classification of deferred tax amounts as equity capital sufficiently provides for such accumulations as may be needed for future taxes while improving the rating of the company's securities and reducing its cost of financing. On the other hand, it is evident that classification of tax deferrals as surplus, even though restricted, tends to disregard their essential character as provisions from income committed to the single purpose of providing for future taxes."

Congressional subcommittee recommends reserve treatment for railroads—

While in general the railroads are not subject to the Securities and Exchange Commission, it may be pertinent here to review briefly the matter of accounting for deferred taxes as it affects them.

The railroads, following the accounting prescribed by the Interstate Commerce Commission, have allowed the benefit of the current tax reduction from accelerated amortization to flow through their income accounts instead of crediting it to a reserve for deferred taxes. As a result, in many instances the railroad income was materially overstated during the five-year amortization period, and will be correspondingly understated in later years when the taxes are higher because the amortization had been used up for tax purposes.

This deficiency in railroad accounting practice, among others, was considered by the Subcommittee on Legal and Monetary Affairs, of the Committee on Government Operations, House of Representatives, 85th Congress, 1st session. In its report, dated August 14, 1957, the Subcommittee referred to the six variations in railroad accounting requiring correction to conform with generally accepted accounting principles, that were stated in a report to the Interstate Commerce Commission by the American Institute of Accountant's committee on relations with that commission. One of these variations related to deferred-tax accounting, as follows:

> "3. Income taxes are dealt with on the basis of charging railway operating expenses for essentially all accruals and adjustments of income tax, whereas other industries allocate a portion of such taxes to other accounts and/or to other years when there are divergencies between the handling of major items of income or expense for tax purposes and for financial accounting purposes. Also no reserves are maintained for deferred taxes resulting from tax amortization or accelerated depreciation."

That the Subcommittee on Legal and Monetary Affairs believed reserves for deferred taxes should be established is clear from the following comments contained in its report dated August 14, 1957. There is no indication in these comments that such reserves were in any way considered to be in the nature of restricted or appropriated surplus or equity capital.

B. Reserves for Deferred Taxes

> "1. The record of the Interstate Commerce Commission in this field leaves much to be desired.

"While belatedly recognizing the error of its 1951 decision, the Interstate Commerce Commission in its 1956 decision again rejected the reserve concept, principally because of the 'shock' to the rate structure that reserves would presumably cause. While the subcommittee is in no position to assess the effect on railroads' financial structure, of establishing reserves for deferred taxes due to tax amortization,[13] it seriously questions the statement in the Commission's 1956 decision that 'shippers of the future' may have to assume 'a portion of the burden * * * in the form of higher freight rates' as a result of the failure of the Interstate Commerce Commission to require reserves for deferred taxes.

"It is difficult to conceive why a 'paper' reserve for a future tax liability would inhibit the railroads in any area of activity except dividend distribution or why there would be such a shock to 'going rates' or why the public must be penalized for the Commission's admitted deficiencies. It would appear that the ICC is sanctioning some kind of mathematical aberration through a fiction of higher earnings currently as a result of its failure to prescribe adherence to generally accepted accounting principles in a procedure which is also at variance with that prescribed by other Federal regulatory agencies and most State regulatory agencies.

"The possibility of overstatement of earnings and misleading the investor has been accorded recognition by the Commission effective January 1, 1957, on annual statements, through footnoted explanations referred to on page 23 supra. There is no reason why such footnoted explanations should not be contained in the body of financial reports submitted to stockholders. While it may be true, as Commissioner Arpaia pointed out, that the railroads live in a 'glass house' as far as financial reports are concerned, the stated policy of the

---

13 The 1956 decision notes that the Federal Power Commission amended its uniform system of accounts in April 1954 to require such reserve for natural-gas companies (209 I.C.C. 463,466).

Securities and Exchange Commission (in its Accounting Service release of August 5, 1947) with respect to footnotes is most persuasive:

> In cases where financial statements filed with this Commission, pursuant to its rules and regulations under the Securities Act of 1933, or the Securities Exchange Act of 1934, are prepared in accordance with accounting principles for which there is no substantial authoritative support, such financial statements will be presumed to be misleading, or inaccurate, despite disclosures contained in the certificate of the accountant or in the footnotes to the statements provided the matters involved are material.'

"The AIA in its report with respect to footnoted explanations in railroad financial reports said:

> 'while such disclosures may be helpful, they do not in our opinion cure the basic variation from generally accepted accounting practices.'

"The AIA committee chairman stated that the failure to provide for reserves for deferred taxes would prevent accountants from certifying that financial reports of railroads have been prepared in accordance with generally accepted principles of accounting.

"The subcommittee endorses the testimony of the AIA committee chairman that—

> 'holders of railroad securities should be entitled to the same protection as the holders of any other securities of comparable corporate structures.'

"The subcommittee therefore recommends that the Commission consider institution of rulemaking procedures with a view to conforming financial statements submitted to stockholders and investors to generally accepted accounting principles in the foregoing connection.

"2. Closely allied with the above question is consideration of establishing reserves for deferred taxes as a result of the use of methods of accelerated depreciation routinely available to taxpayers under the provisions of the recently enacted Internal Revenue Code of 1954.

"No objection was interposed to this recommendation of the AIA committee by any witness before the subcommittee. The AAR stated that this matter 'should be thoroughly considered.'

"It is therefore recommended that the Commission consider institution of rulemaking procedures with respect to establishing such reserves."

Possible conflict of proposed SEC policy
  with state regulatory commission orders—

In amending its uniform system of accounts for natural gas companies and electric companies previously referred to herein, the Federal Power Commission was faced with the problem that some of the utilities over which it has jurisdiction were also subject to state regulatory commissions that had prescribed the restricted-surplus treatment. This raised the question of conflicting treatment if these utilities complied with the requirements of both the Federal and state commissions. On this point the Federal Power Commission stated:

"In view of the fact that some state regulatory commissions also having accounting jurisdiction have specified the restricted surplus treatment and others the reserve treatment, some parties urge that we adopt accounting provisions which would permit either such treatment. In our opinion, this dual or alternative treatment would cause intolerable confusion and conflict in the Commission's prescribed accounting and would be contrary to the public interest. We regret the inconsistency which has arisen among the several state commissions. Under the circumstances, however, we see no reasonable solution to the problem for those utilities which are required by a state commission to report deferred taxes as a reserve or restricted surplus but to classify the deferred taxes in accordance with state requirements for state purposes, and to use the treatment specified by this order for the purposes of this Commission.''

As in the case of the Federal Power Commission, the proposed policy of the Securities and Exchange Commission to exclude the accumulated tax-deferment credits from equity capital would conflict with the presentation followed by those companies which include the restricted surplus prescribed by some state regulatory commissions as a part of the common stockholders' equity. In view of the state commission's restrictions on the use of restricted surplus, as previously mentioned herein, we question whether such state orders require or approve the inclusion of such deferred-tax credits in common stockholders' equity. However, it would seem that the same position would prevail--that notwithstanding the inconsistency, utility reports to the Securities and Exchange Commission should exclude the accumulated deferred tax credit from the equity-capital section, even though included therein for state reporting purposes.

Conclusion—

Since the accumulated credit arising from accounting recognition of the current income-tax deferment through the use of accelerated depreciation for tax purposes and normal depreciation in the accounts, is clearly a reserve for the deferred income taxes that will be payable in later years, in our opinion, it would be contrary to generally accepted accounting principles to include it as a part of equity capital, even though accompanied by words of limitation such as ''restricted surplus'' or ''appropriated surplus.''

Accordingly, we concur in the proposed announcement of interpretation of administrative policy on financial statements regarding balance-sheet treatment of credits equivalent to reductions of income taxes.

ARTHUR ANDERSEN & CO.

/s/ ARTHUR ANDERSEN & CO.

Chicago, Illinois,

January 28, 1959.

ARTHUR ANDERSEN & CO

120 South LaSalle Street
Chicago 3

February 20, 1959

Mr. Orval L. DuBois, Secretary
Securities and Exchange Commission
425 Second Street, N. W.
Washington 25, D. C.

Re: Securities Act of 1933
Release No. 4023

Dear Mr. DuBois:

This is to inform you that Mr. Leonard Spacek, Managing Partner of our Firm, intends to appear at the public hearing March 25, 1959, with respect to the Commission's proposed interpretation of administrative policy on financial statements regarding balance sheet treatment of the accumulated credits arising from recognition in such statements of the deferral to future periods of current reductions in income taxes.

The views of our Firm on this matter were previously submitted to the Commission in triplicate; hence, no written statement of views accompanies this letter.

We do not expect that the presentation of our views at the hearing will require more than 15 minutes.

Very truly yours,

/s/ ARTHUR ANDERSEN & CO.

SECURITIES AND EXCHANGE COMMISSION
Washington 25, D. C.

February 25, 1959

Mr. Leonard Spacek
Arthur Andersen & Co.
120 South La Salle Street
Chicago 3, Illinois

Dear Leonard:

This is to inform you that your request for
15 minutes of time at the public hearing on Securities Act Release 4010 has been noted. The Commission will no doubt make an equitable distribution
of time among the parties, but I am sure that they
would be interested in hearing your full discussion.

You will note from the enclosed release that
the hearing has been postponed to April 8, 1959.

Very truly yours,

Andrew Barr
Chief Accountant

Enclosure
  Release 4038

ARTHUR ANDERSEN & CO.
120 South LaSalle Street
Chicago 3

March 13, 1959

Mr. Andrew Barr, Chief Accountant
Securities and Exchange Commission
Washington, D. C.

Dear Andy:

You have confirmed receipt of my request for time to appear at the public hearing on Securities Act Release 4010 on April 8, 1959. My original request was for 15 minutes. Your reply mentioned that you thought the Commission probably would want to hear my full discussion.

As I have been thinking more about this matter, I believe that 15 minutes would be a little short. If it could be arranged, I would appreciate having a longer time, say 30 minutes.

Cordially yours,

/s/ LEONARD SPACEK

SECURITIES AND EXCHANGE COMMISSION
Washington 25, D. C.

March 17, 1959

Mr. Leonard Spacek
Arthur Andersen & Co.
120 South La Salle Street
Chicago 3, Illinois

Dear Leonard:

I have your letter of March 13, 1959, and
note that in the assignment of time for the public
hearing on our Release No. 4010 you would like to
have 30 minutes instead of 15. When all of the requests have been received, the Commission will
make an appropriate allocation of time among those
who appear at the hearing.

Sincerely yours,

Andrew Barr
Chief Accountant

AMERICAN INSTITUTE OF CERTIFIED PUBLIC ACCOUNTANTS

270 Madison Avenue
New York 16, N.Y.
January 8, 1959

Mr. Andrew Barr, Chief Accountant
Securities and Exchange Commission
Washington 25, D. C.

Dear Andy:

Under date of December 31, you sent me 30 copies of your Securities Act Release No. 4010 giving notice of the Commission's intention to announce an interpretation of administrative policy on financial statements regarding balance-sheet treatment of credit equivalent to reduction of income taxes. As I said in my letter of January 2, these have been sent to the members of our committee on accounting procedure with a request for any comments they may feel appropriate. Without waiting for the committee members' comments, I am taking this opportunity to express my own views with respect to the proposal and give you a little background that may be of interest to you.

In my opinion, the position which the Commission proposes to take, as indicated in this Release, is sound. It has always been my opinion that the inclusion, as a part of equity capital, of the accumulated credit arising from accounting for reduction in income taxes due to differences in accounting for depreciation in the tax return as compared with the books of account has no justification in accounting principles.

When Accounting Research Bulletin No. 42 "Emergency Facilities-- Depreciation, Amortization, and Income Taxes" was under consideration by the committee on accounting procedure, representatives of the Edision Electric Institute and of the American Gas Association met with a subcommittee of the committee on accounting procedure for the purpose of discussing the application of the proposed bulletin to public utilities. One of the points which appeared to cause the greatest concern at this discussion was the classification of the credit as set forth in the second sentence of paragraph 12 of what ultimately became Bulletin 42. After the representatives of the public utilities were convinced that there was

no chance of the committee on accounting procedure so wording the bulletin as to exclude public utilities from its coverage, they asked what the attitude of accountants would be in case the regulatory body had issued an order requiring classification of the tax credit as restricted surplus. Our subcommittee expressed the view that the philosophy of the bulletin was such that the credit could not logically be treated as a part of surplus.

However, one of the members of the subcommittee then voiced the opinion that in the case of most of the utilities with which he was familiar, the significance of classifying the credit as a restricted surplus item in the stockholders' equity section, rather than outside of that section, would not be so material that he, personally, would feel he had to take an exception in his opinion in the case of a Commission order, provided adequate disclosure were made. Others of the subcommittee indicated that they held the same view. Later it seemed to develop that no good line could be drawn between a case in which a Commission had issued an order and one in which it had not. It seemed apparent, from the remarks of the members of the subcommittee on this point, that they were expressing only their own personal judgments and that their views did not necessarily coincide with the views of the other members of their respective firms or of the committee as a whole.

Shortly after this meeting, in a conference at the Securities and Exchange Commission, representatives of a public utility company asserted that our subcommittee had said it would be acceptable, under the bulletin, to carry to surplus the credit mentioned in the second sentence of paragraph 12. Earle King challenged this statement, and I was called upon, by telephone, to verify it. I reported substantially as I have outlined above. After several talks with Earle and the independent auditor for the company in question who insisted that either the subcommittee or I should be willing to put in writing what had been said orally, that subcommittee authorized me to write a letter, the last paragraph of which read as follows:

"One of the points which appeared to cause concern was the conflict between the provisions of the bulletin as to the accounting for the credit for deferred taxes and the fact that, in line with numerous recent orders of regulatory commissions, many public utility companies classify such credits as restricted surplus. While, as it was pointed out, the philosophy of the bulletin does not support the latter treatment, nevertheless certain members of the subcommittee voiced the opinion that they personally, would not consider such classification of this item in the balance sheet of a public utility to be so significant as to require them to take an exception in their opinion, provided adequate disclosure were made. Those present could not, of course, speak on this latter point for the other members of the committee."

When Bulletin 44 was issued, as I remember, no serious consideration was given to the inclusion of any statement with respect to the treatment of the credit item. It was generally assumed that accountants would know what to do with it. When Bulletin 44 was revised, the two alternatives in accounting for the credit are set forth in paragraph 5. While this paragraph does not say anything about whether "a deferred tax account" is to be included among the liabilities or in the proprietorship section, it seems to me that its very name implies that it should be treated either as a liability or as a deferred credit to an expense. In neither case would it be included, in my opinion, under the capital section.

I think it should be said, in justification of the position taken by the members of our subcommittee who considered this question before the issuance of Bulletin 42, that their great concern was with the avoidance of distortion in the income statement. I think many of them had the feeling that if the income statement were properly reflected, their big job would be accomplished and that the residual effect in the balance sheet of most public utilities would not be very significant. Whether they would still feel the same, in the light of what has taken place both under the accounting for emergency facilities and in the use of the declining-balance method for tax purposes and straight-line method for accounting purposes, I do not know.

In closing, I want to reiterate that this letter expresses only my own personal opinion, except where it clearly indicates views expressed in 1952. I have not consulted with any member of the present committee in writing this letter.

Very truly yours,

/s/ CARMAN G. BLOUGH

Director of Research

CGB:dum

cc: Mr. William W. Werntz, chairman of the
committee on accounting procedure

56 PINE STREET
New York 5

January 14, 1959

Securities and Exchange Commission
Washington 25, D. C.

Gentlemen:

Re: SECURITIES ACT OF 1933
RELEASE NO. 4010

Accounting in its basic principles is pure
and clear. In its mechanics of application it is
at times complex and contradictory. Please reconsider Release No. 4010 in the light of basic principles:

I. The Misplaced Credit

1. A = L+C is a principle we all learned years
ago that told us that the assets of a
business represented the interests of outsiders to whom the business was indebted
or the capital interest of the owners.

2. Accounting Research Bulletin No. 44 grants
that there are situations where the tax
"deferment" "would be built up during the
earlier years which would tend to remain
relatively constant thereafter." It also
grants that there are situations where the
amount of "deferred" taxes will continue
to increase.

3. In such situations where the "deferred"
amounts are never to be settled by payments
to outsiders how can they be considered
liabilities? (Liabilities - per S-X "Items

due and payable"; per Webster "A debt; an amount which is owed")

4. If such "deferred" amounts do not represent the interests of outsiders in the assets, must they not represent the interest of the owners? Where is the interest of the owners shown but under the heading of capital!

II. The Fraudulent Debit

1. As stated above there are situations where the "deferred" amounts are permanently deferred and never extinguished by payment.

2. I submit that to classify as an expense an item, that is never expected to be paid, violates basic accounting principles to an extent so as to constitute fraud.

Recommendation

Your release be modified to provide in those situations where the "deferment" is foreseen to be permanent that:

A. At least, the credit be shown with the other capital accounts.

B. Preferably, the charging of income with taxes not expected to be paid be prohibited.

Yours very truly,

/s/ K. G. CADEMATORI

Kenneth G. Cadematori

CONTROLLERS INSTITUTE OF AMERICA
Two Park Avenue
New York 16, N. Y.
MUrray Hill 5-0470

January 27, 1959

Securities and Exchange Commission
Washington 25, D. C.

Attention: Secretary

Gentlemen:

Copies of your "Notice of Intention to Announce Interpretation of Administrative Policy"
dated December 30, 1958, have been distributed for
comment to members of the National Committee on Securities and Exchange Regulation of the Controllers
Institute of America. This "Notice of Intention"
was issued as Release No. 4010 under the Securities
Act of 1933 and Release No. 5844 under the Securities Exchange Act of 1934.

Replies received from Committee members indicated that there is a wide divergence of views in
respect to this Release and no unanimity of opinion
is evident. Therefore, under these circumstances,
the Committee will refrain from submitting any
views or comments for Commission consideration.
However, the distribution of this proposal to the
members of the Committee probably will result in
the submission of individual views which we hope
will be helpful to you.

We appreciate being extended the opportunity
of commenting on this "Notice of Intention".

Yours very truly,

/s/ Wm. H. ZIMMER

Wm. H. Zimmer, Chairman
National Committee on
Securities and Exchange
Regulation

COLUMBIA UNIVERSITY
In the City of New York
OFFICE OF BUSINESS AFFAIRS
New York 27, N.Y.

January 6, 1959

Secretary,
Securities and Exchange Commission,
Washington 25, D. C.

Sir:

Securities Act of 1933, Release No. 4010, etc.

The proposed release (relating to a corporation which deducts liberalized depreciation in its tax return but not on its books) is a step in the right direction, but it does not go far enough. It eliminates segregated retained earnings but allows the "contra credit" to be made to a "deferred tax liability" account. There is, of course, no deferred tax liability and the use of that kind of accounting has done nothing but produce confusion. The simple fact is that the company has used part of its "tax deductibility" and the asset should be reduced accordingly. The rule should be to charge current income in an amount equal to the tax reduction and credit that amount to accrued depreciation. Under such a rule accounts would be more accurate and more understandable for all purposes.

In passing, I do not understand footnote #2. If the related tax effect is treated as additional amortization or depreciation, I assume it will be charged in the income account as well as credited to accrued depreciation. The footnote should read "This separate charge to income is not necessary where the charge for depreciation on the books is increased by the amount of the tax reduction."

Yours truly,

/s/ JAMES L. DOHR

James L. Dohr
Professor of Accounting

JLD:dbc

ERNST & ERNST
Union Commerce Building
Cleveland 14, Ohio

ACCOUNTANTS-AUDITORS
MANAGEMENT SERVICES

January 27, 1959

Secretary
Securities and Exchange Commission
Washington 25, D. C.

Re: Notice of Intention to Announce Interpretation of
Administrative Policy — Securities Act of 1933
Release No. 4010

Dear Sir:

In response to your invitation for written views and comments on the subject matter of the above-mentioned notice, we present the following views for the Commission's consideration:

1. The import of the Release is of such breadth and gravity that an "Interpretation of Administrative Policy" is not a suitable procedure for making it effective. It more probably requires formal amendment of the Commission's accounting regulations, to be accomplished only after affected corporations and industries have an opportunity to be heard.

2. The timing of the proposed announcement is unfortunate, since it relates to filings dated as of December 31, 1958, but cannot possibly be issued before February 1959. During this period many corporations will release their financial statements for the year 1958, without a definitive interpretation of the Commission to guide them. If the interpretation is announced, we believe its effective date should be subsequent to the date of announcement to permit appropriate preparatory action on the part of subject corporations.

3. There is much uncertainty, and wide difference of opinion, within the accounting profession about the true nature of the credit arising from the accounting for deferred taxes and how the ultimate disposal of the credit will be accomplished. There is a strong and sound presumption that the credit is not a part of stockholders' equity, but we do not believe that the presumption is so strong and sound that every statement in which the credit might be displayed, properly described and segregated, as a

component of the equity accounts is necessarily misleading, much less inaccurate. If the presentation is misleading on and after December 31, 1958, it would seem that it must have been equally so prior to that date, a situation with possibly serious implications to some corporations and some accountants.

4. A requirement for segregation of the accumulated credit will place many regulated companies in the position of being unable to comply with the accounting requirements of their respective regulatory commissions, which stipulate that the accumulated credit shall be presented as a segregated surplus.

5. The important phase of the problem is the one of obtaining an appropriate charge to income for the effect of the deferred taxes. We believe the Commission should give further thought to strengthening and clarifying its position with respect to the charge to income before dealing with the credit arising from the charge.

6. The proposed announcement does not seem to recognize the conflict between the content of the earned-surplus accounts of those corporations which have not accounted for deferred taxes and the content of the surplus accounts of those which have. In the case of the corporation which has not accounted for the deferred tax, the credit has flowed through the income account and come to rest, undisclosed, in earned surplus. In the other case, the credit has been accounted for by charges to income and has come to rest in a liability or reserve account. Consideration should be given to the disparity in balance-sheet presentation resulting from these two methods of accounting, and the corporation that has accounted for the credit should not summarily be denied the right to display it as a component of stockholders' equity, inasmuch as the many corporations which have not accounted for the credit have passively achieved that presentation.

7. If the Interpretation is issued, it should be clarified with respect to possible retroactive application. A corporation which has not accounted for deferred taxes prior to 1958 should not now be required to make a retroactive adjustment to remove from its earned surplus the credits which have accumulated therein, unless it chooses so to do. We do not believe the Interpretation intends that it should, but the language is not clear in that regard.

Respectfully submitted,

/s/   ERNST & ERNST

HASKINS & SELLS
CERTIFIED PUBLIC ACCOUNTANTS

Executive Office
67 Broad Street
New York 4

February 27, 1959

Mr. Orval L. DuBois, Secretary,
Securities and Exchange Commission,
Washington 25, D. C.

Dear Sir:

We are enclosing three copies of our letter dated February 26, 1959 containing our comments concerning "Notice of Intention to Announce Interpretation of Administrative Policy (Securities Act Release 4010, Securities Exchange Act Release 5844, Public Utility Holding Company Act Release 13894, and Investment Company Act Release 2814)."

Yours very truly,

/s/ HASKINS & SELLS

Enclosures

HASKINS & SELLS
CERTIFIED PUBLIC ACCOUNTANTS

EXECUTIVE OFFICE
67 Broad Street
New York 4

February 26, 1959

Securities and Exchange Commission,
  Washington 25, D. C.

Attention of Mr. Orval L. DuBois, Secretary.

Dear Sirs:

Notice of Intention to Announce
Interpretation of Administrative Policy
(Securities Act Release 4010,
Securities Exchange Act Release 5844,
Public Utility Holding Company Act Release 13894,
and Investment Company Act Release 2814)

As independent certified public accountants who express opinions on the financial statements of numerous companies, we are deeply concerned as to certain implications of the above release, and we wish to present our views and comments for the consideration of the Commission in this matter.

We assume that the Commission recognizes the vital importance of this matter to issuers and others, but we wish at the outset to emphasize it. There is at issue here something more than a choice of words or the position of an item in a financial statement. Action by the Commission in the manner proposed in the release as we understand it, would have far-reaching effect.

Although the Acts administered by the Commission appear to give it considerable authority in accounting matters, in general we believe that the Commission should not undertake to prescribe what are generally accepted accounting principles but that on the contrary it should expect this to be done within the business community. But if the Commission does determine to do this, we think that it should be accomplished through the adoption of pertinent rules or regulations as an amendment to Regulation S-X in the regular way; and that new rules or regulations should provide clearly that they are to be applied prospectively only, not retroactively.

As to the action now proposed, it is our understanding that the Commission would seek to accomplish its objective by an "interpretation of administrative policy." Under it, the Commission would deem to be "misleading or inaccurate" those financial statements which display a particular item, namely, the accumulated credit arising from accounting for certain reductions in income taxes, in the balance sheet in a particular way, namely, in earned surplus, or equity capital. This would be so because, following Accounting Series Release 4 of April 25, 1938, the Commission now would be of the opinion that there was no "substantial authoritative support" for displaying the item in question in the manner specified, irrespective of the completeness of the designation of this item or of the applicable footnotes, and irrespective of the obvious meaning of the item and the applicable footnotes to the average prudent investor. But the Commission would have this opinion solely as to financial statements dated as of December 31, 1958 or thereafter, and then only if the amounts were material.

We are not aware of any recent development in the field of generally accepted accounting principles which would require action on the part of the Commission in the manner proposed (although the Commission may consider that its proposed action is called for by the issuance by the Federal Power Commission on May 29, 1958 of Orders 203 and 204 amending its Uniform Systems of Accounts for Public Utilities and Licensees and Natural Gas Companies to provide for the accounting and reporting of deferred taxes on income). The latest pronouncement of the accounting profession concerning deferred income taxes is contained in Accounting Research Bulletin 44 (Revised), which was issued during 1958 by the Committee on Accounting Procedure of the American Institute of Certified Public Accountants; it, however, concerned itself largely with the treatment of deferred income taxes in the income statement, not in the balance sheet.

If, as we believe to be the case, there has been in the past "substantial authoritative support" for the reporting to which the Commission now proposes to take exception, there must be such support now. In this connection, it should be noted that for several years numerous public utility companies have reported the accumulated credits arising from certain reductions in income taxes, in their balance sheets in earned surplus or equity capital, upon the order or with the approval of state or local regulatory authorities having jurisdiction, and with the concurrence of their independent certified public accountants, among whom are national or international firms, including ourselves; and the Commission has accepted their reports. If the Commission were to take the action proposed in the release, it might create problems for itself and for some companies subject to the jurisdiction of the Public Utility Holding Company Act of 1935. For example, how would the explicit restrictions on the Commission under Section 20(b) of that Act be reconciled with such state orders or approvals, and how would a regulated company comply with Rule U-28 under the Act and keep its books and make its reports in accordance with such orders and approvals and with the requirements proposed by the release?

If there is not now "substantial authoritative support" for this reporting, there must not have been such support when the reports as of dates and for periods prior to December 31, 1958 were issued. Some of those reports were prepared in connection with substantial issues of securities made during the past several years. The proposed "interpretation of administrative policy" would tend to cast a cloud over those issues, and to impose the risk of civil liability upon the issuers and their directors and principal officers, the accountants, and the underwriters.

The proposed action of the Commission would place these persons in jeopardy not only with respect to filings with the Commission during the past several years, but also with respect to certain of those now pending or about to be made.

For example, let us assume that a registration statement under the 1933 Act is filed in early 1959 with financial statements as of December 31, 1958 and for the three years then ended, which, consistent with the registrant's practice in the past, show the accumulated credit arising from accounting for certain reductions in income taxes in the balance sheet as restricted earned surplus; and that before the effective date of the registration statement the Commission, by the adoption of its proposed announcement, characterizes financial statements which so treat such item as "misleading or inaccurate." This would place all persons having anything to do with such financial statements in an untenable position even though the Commission (or its staff) were to determine administratively that no action would be taken against them in the matter.

Again, let us assume that the proposed announcement is made after the effective date of the registration statement but before the independent accountants are to deliver a letter to the underwriters of an issue to the effect that the audited financial statements in the registration statement have been prepared in accordance with generally accepted accounting principles and comply with the applicable accounting requirements of the Commission. In these circumstances the accountants would have difficulty in issuing such a letter without noting some exception, and if they were to note an exception the underwriters would have difficulty in taking delivery of the securities.

Manifestly, we did not consider the financial statements in the reports of our public-utility-company clients referred to above "misleading or inaccurate" in any respect when we issued our opinions on them and we do not consider them "misleading or inaccurate" in any respect now. On the contrary, it was, and is, our opinion that they were prepared in conformity with generally accepted accounting principles. In each case the practice followed was made clear.

Furthermore, we thought then, and we think now, that there were, and are, in some cases, important practical considerations in favor of the classification of the accumulated credit arising from accounting for certain reductions in income taxes, in the balance sheets of some public utility companies as a part of earned surplus or in equity capital.

Since some state commissions apparently consider that the credits arising from accounting for certain reductions in income taxes have sufficient characteristics of earned surplus or equity capital to treat them as such for regulatory purposes, and since these commissions have a responsibility for the financial stability of the companies subject to their jurisdiction, we suggest that appropriate weight should be given to their views. These commissions have considered such credits as equity capital for the purpose of determining the type of securities they would permit utilities to issue; this, of course, affects the cost of financing and, in turn, the rates the utilities charge their customers.

Enforced reclassification of the tax credits now, it seems to us, might affect the legal position of some public utility companies under indentures or other agreements, especially in connection with dividend payments, future financing arrangements, and similar matters. These indentures and other agreements were drafted by the issuers and their counsel and were executed by the issuers in the light of generally accepted accounting principles which were carefully considered and well understood by the parties at the time. Retroactive action by the Commission could jeopardize, rather than protect, the interests of investors.

The time for the Commission to take a firm position (assuming such a position were sound) against the inclusion of the accumulated credit arising from the accounting for certain reductions in income taxes, in the balance sheet in earned surplus or equity capital, was some years ago when provision for the liberalization of depreciation and amortization allowances was made in the Internal Revenue Code. If such a position is to be taken now, the Commission should make clear that it is not intended to be retroactive. We think that any pronouncement of the Commission on the subject should provide specifically that it will not require the revision of financial statements as of prior dates or for prior periods or the reclassification in future financial statements of amounts previously reported as earned surplus or equity capital. Also, Rule U-28 under the Public Utility Holding Company Act of 1935 should be appropriately amended.

In conclusion, we should like to reiterate that the proper method of accounting for deferred income taxes is one upon which there is not unanimity of view in accounting circles, and to say that until such future time, if any, as some degree of unanimity is more nearly reached, financial statements which include in earned surplus or equity capital the credits arising from accounting for certain reductions in income taxes, with adequate disclosure, are not (and by fiat of the Commission cannot properly be made or deemed) "misleading or inaccurate."

Yours very truly,

/s/ HASKINS & SELLS

LYBRAND, ROSS BROS. & MONTGOMERY

90 Broad Street
New York 4

February 19, 1959.

Securities and Exchange Commission,
425 Second Street, N. W.,
Washington 25, D. C.

Dear Sirs:

I am writing in response to the invitation contained in Release No. 4010 under the Securities Act of 1933 regarding the proposed announcement by the Commission of an interpretation of administrative policy on financial statements with respect to the balance sheet treatment of credits equivalent to the reductions in income taxes.

I am particularly concerned about the procedure the Commission proposes to follow in adopting a new and important policy on an accounting question. Many utility companies have included the deferred taxes in the equity section of their balance sheets with the knowledge, approval, or pursuant to order of the public service commission having jurisdiction over the accounting of such companies. I am certain you are familiar with the arguments for including the item in question in the equity section, and shall not repeat them.

These utility companies have prepared their financial statements on a basis approved or ordered by their regulatory commissions and have filed them with the SEC without objection (until recently) by the Commission. You now propose to adopt a policy which, because of the manner of its adoption, would, in effect, stigmatize as misleading all previous filings that do not conform to the proposed policy. Many issuers, their directors, officers, and underwriters have a continuing statutory liability with respect to filings that included the deferred tax item in the equity section of the balance sheet. Some of them have entered into indentures, bank loans, and other agreements which were based on a similar treatment of the item. For the SEC now to adopt a policy which, in effect, characterizes as misleading what these companies have done openly and with no intent to mislead might have serious consequences and might even subject them to suit.

If, despite the views of the companies affected, and the orders of the regulatory commissions, the SEC concludes that it disapproves of including the tax item in the equity section, I believe that the way to accomplish it is by amending Regulation S-X. This would properly avoid associating the misleading label with prior filings.

There is ample precedent for the procedure I am suggesting. For years the Commission accepted filings by public utilities in which the depreciation reserve was shown on the credit side of the balance sheet as permitted by the uniform systems of accounts of the state regulatory commissions. By amendment to Regulation S-X, the SEC made it clear that after a certain date it would require the reserve to be deducted from the plant account, and has insisted on compliance with the revised regulation despite contrary provisions in the uniform systems.

From the Commission's own point of view it seems to me that the preferable route to follow would be to amend Regulation S-X. The SEC does not knowingly permit a registration statement to become effective which is misleading on its face. Many registrations were filed on a basis which your proposal would now imply were misleading. The conclusion is obvious.

Very truly yours,

/s/ LOUIS H. RAPPAPORT

LHR

SECURITIES AND EXCHANGE COMMISSION
Washington 25, D. C.

February 26, 1959

Mr. Louis H. Rappaport
Lybrand, Ross Bros. & Montgomery
90 Broad Street
New York 4, N. Y.

Dear Mr. Rappaport:

I have not had the time, as you may suspect, to acknowledge except by postcard all of the letters of comment on our proposed accounting for deferred taxes presented in Release No. 4010.

However, in your case I think I should point out that the rule-making procedure being followed is identical with that which would be required for an amendment of Regulation S-X and, as you know, that regulation now incorporates the Accounting Series Releases. I realize that it may not be clear from the release as published that upon completion of the process, assuming that the proposal in some form is adopted by the Commission, it would appear as an Accounting Series Release. The matter of retroactivity will also be clarified. I believe this will take care of the principal points made in your letter.

Very truly yours,

Andrew Barr
Chief Accountant

NILES & NILES
CERTIFIED PUBLIC ACCOUNTANTS

165 Broadway
New York 6, N. Y.

March 23, 1959.

Securities and Exchange Commission,
Washington 25, D. C.

Gentlemen:

Referring to your Notice of December 30, 1958, "Of Intention to Announce Interpretation of Administrative Policy * * * regarding Balance Sheet Treatment of Credit Equivalent to Reduction of Income Taxes," we offer the following brief comment.

It appears to us that the policy as described in the announcement will lead away from the preferred direction of producing informative financial statements. As we understand it, the proposal would result in a substantial amount in the balance sheet which would be classified neither as a liability nor as an element of capital equity. The reader of the statement would have to make the classification which should have been made for him. It is doubtful that the reader would be satisfied with the idea that the equity in a large portion of the corporate assets could not be determined. He would at least have the right to request an explanation, and if told that there was no identifiable creditor involved he would probably wonder why the absence of a creditor did not cause the amount to fall into the capital equity classification.

In "A Dictionary for Accountants" by Eric L. Kohler, second edition, 1957, a balance sheet is defined as "A statement of financial position * * * disclosing as of a given moment its assets, * * * its liabilities, and the equity of owners * * * ." In the same book, Equity is defined as "any right or claim to assets * * * . An equity holder may be a creditor or a proprietor." It seems to us that the proposed policy would not produce a balance sheet that would fit these generally accepted definitions.

Orders Nos. 203 and 204 of the Federal Power Commission, which under the proposal companies subject to those orders would have to follow, require the use of a balance sheet which would show participations in a company's assets about as follows:

1. Stockholders' Equity, $

2. Creditors' Equity,

3. Equity of neither stockholders nor creditors, to be described as "Accumulated Deferred Taxes on Income",

Total equal to Assets, $

Referring to the foregoing list of three kinds of equity, the first two are well known but the third is a newcomer which was devised by the Federal Power Commission to meet its question " * * * whether accumulated deferred taxes should be included in a reserve account * * * or in some other account such as a restricted surplus account." It concluded that " * * * the Congressional purposes * * can reasonably be achieved by employing the procedures contemplated * * * but providing a balance sheet treatment that neither identifies the accumulated amounts as a reserve or as restricted surplus." *

The Federal Power Commission has not shown how it concluded that its required indecisive balance sheet treatment would aid in the achievement of Congressional purposes, but elsewhere in its order it found it necessary to say that " * * * the deferred tax accounting provided for * * * is not mandatory for any utility which, in accordance with a consistent policy, elects not to follow deferred tax accounting * * * ."

---

* The quoted words were taken from page 4 of Order No. 204 as issued by the Federal Power Commission on May 29, 1958, in which the reference to Congressional purposes was supported by a quotation from both House and Senate Committee reports as to the purposes of more liberal depreciation allowances, but with no directions or suggestions on accounting procedures.

Also, at another point in its discussion of the balance sheet treatment, it said that " * * * while making provision for future tax liability, it will not foreclose financial analysts, investors, and others from considering these amounts as part of equity capital if they think proper, with such consequential benefits to the rating of the company's securities and costs of financing as may result therefrom."

These quotations from the Federal Power Commission's order indicate that, while an incomplete classification was decided upon for the accumulated credits, there was no criticism of those companies which, by electing not to follow deferred tax accounting, had previously classified these amounts as part of the stockholders' equity and were proposing to continue to do so in the accounts required to be maintained in accordance with the Commission's orders. In fact, there was a definite acknowledgement of the propriety of the stockholders' equity classification, not only in the acceptance of the procedure of those who did not follow deferred tax accounting, but also in the recognition of the right of financial analysts, investors, and others to classify these amounts as part of the stockholders' equity where deferred tax accounting was being followed.

Although we disagree with the conclusion of the Federal Power Commission in its devising an unclassified equity account for the accumulation of these credits for balance sheet purposes, we can not avoid the contrast between that Commission's recognition of there being two sides to this question with the proposal in the Notice of December 30, 1958, to declare that those companies which espouse one side shall be declared to be presenting misleading and inaccurate financial statements and acting in a manner not consistent with the intent of Congress and contrary to the public interest. Moreover, we can not reconcile the last sentence of the Notice with the expressed intention of the Proposal. That sentence reads as follows: "These tax reductions therefore enter into the determination of income and to the increase of equity only through the passage of time." The reference is to the accumulated credit item in the balance sheet, which represents an amount of assets on the other side of the balance sheet equal to the amount of the reductions in taxes. These assets, which the reductions in taxes did not encumber, are being used in the business and have been so used ever since the tax reductions occurred. They are not to be used in payment of subsequent taxes, because those taxes are to be provided for out of income earned on which the taxes accrue. The passage of time to which the notice refers has no effect on these assets as far as the Company's ownership of them and right to their use are concerned. Careful consideration of whether or not anything happens to these assets during this passage of time to remove them, according to the notice, from what might be called a state of limbo and to place them in their rightful class of assets owned by the proprietor, should show that those who prefer the stockholders' equity classification throughout the period have a realistic basis for their preference.

It is our opinion that, contrary to the proposed announcement, any financial statement that did not clearly present the equities might be said to be incomplete and possibly misleading, and, if so, not in accordance with accepted principles of accounting. It follows, therefore, in our opinion, that any financial statement that does clearly present the equities, and in doing so includes in the stockholders' equity the accumulated credit amounts resulting from reductions in income taxes, has been prepared in accordance with accepted principles of accounting and generally recognized practice and is in no way misleading.

Yours truly,

/s/ NILES & NILES

PEAT, MARWICK, MITCHELL & CO.
ACCOUNTANTS AND AUDITORS

Seventy Pine Street
New York 5, N. Y.

January 15, 1959

Mr. Andrew Barr, Chief Accountant
Securities and Exchange Commission
Washington 25, D. C.

Dear Mr. Barr:

Securities Act, Release No. 4010 —
Proposed Announcement of Interpretation
of Administrative Policy

I believe the wording of the draft statement incorporated in Release No. 4010, taken literally, goes considerably beyond what I understand is the intention.

The difficulty is centered in the portion of the first sentence which reads: "which designates as earned surplus . . . the accumulated credit arising from accounting for reductions in income taxes . . . " If the accumulated reduction in income taxes is taken up as income and thus automatically flows into earned surplus, is it designated as earned surplus because it is included in earned surplus?

I understand that the present purpose is merely to be sure that if an amount equal to the tax reductions has been set up in a separate account (as distinguished from being taken into income) the accumulated amount thereof thus set up and included in a separate account shall not be added in with the earned surplus or equity capital however it is described.

I think this major difficulty, and possible ambiguity, could be overcome by changing the words "the accumulated credit arising from accounting for reductions in income taxes . . . " to read: "the accumulated credit which has been set up in the accounts to reflect the accounting for reductions in income taxes . . . "

The statement will be substantially limited to utility companies which have endeavored to make the best showing possible for the computation of their debt ratios, a matter of some importance to them and one which will become of increasing importance as the amount of the accumulated credit grows.

This brings us to some consideration as to the nature of the credit. This was discussed to some extent in the Federal Power Commission's Order No. 203 to which the release makes reference.

Personally, I think that there is a great deal of merit in many cases to deducting the credit from the fixed assets as a reflection of a diminution in value of the fixed assets to the owner which arises solely by reason of the fact that he has already used up a part of his inherent right to deduct their cost (less salvage) for tax purposes over the useful life of the asset. However, I would not expect utilities to follow this alternative because it would almost be an open invitation to exclude the amount involved from their rate base.

When we come to regard the item as one to be reflected on the liabilities side of the balance sheet, my own preference is to regard it, not as a liability, but rather as an allocation of the tax benefit which has already arisen to the future period in which the depreciation allowance on the specific assets will be correspondingly reduced. It is hard to refute the arguments of those who oppose setting up the credit that no liability is involved and that even if there was it is one which would never have to be paid if we assume that the accounting is that of a going concern. In such circumstances we have what is, in effect, interest-free financing assistance under the tax law in plant replacement or expansion; this is what Congress intended. In most cases the amount is one which will increase until it substantially levels off and one which, thereafter, will be added to by new credits as the older credits decline or expire — a kind of revolving fund.

In these circumstances I doubt whether we can regard the "accumulated credit" as anything in the nature of a liability or debt. If, as has increasingly been suggested in recent years, all items on the liabilities side of the balance sheet should be reflected either as debt or as equity capital, there is some question in my mind whether the credit does not partake more of the nature of capital than of debt, particularly for the purpose of computing the long-term debt ratio.

It seems to me that whether one presentation or the other is "misleading" depends more upon the specific words used to describe the credit than upon its precise location.

Very truly yours, .

/s/ S. J. BROAD

S. J. Broad

SJB:IN

PRICE WATERHOUSE & CO.

56 Pine Street
New York 5

January 19, 1959

Mr. Orval L. Dubois,
Secretary
Securities and Exchange Commission
425 Second Street, N. W.
Washington 25, D. C.

Dear Sir:

We enclose three copies of our letter of this
date commenting on the Commission's proposed interpretation of administrative policy as described
in the Securities Act of 1933 Release No. 4010.
The enclosed letter is in response to the invitation for comment contained in the Release.

Yours very truly,

/s/ PRICE WATERHOUSE & CO.

Enclosure - 3
    Letter

PRICE WATERHOUSE & CO.

56 Pine Street
New York 5
January 19, 1959

Securities and Exchange Commission
Washington 25, D. C.

Dear Sirs:

Securities Act of 1933 Release No. 4010
Notice of Intention to Announce
Interpretation of Administrative Policy

Under date of December 30, 1958 the Securities and Exchange Commission gave notice that it had under consideration the announcement of an interpretation of administrative policy regarding treatment in the balance sheet of credits equivalent to the reductions in income taxes. This letter is in reply to an invitation contained in the Notice for views and comments on this matter.

On the basis of initial reactions conveyed to us by a number of our clients and after consideration of the text of the proposed release by members of our organization, we have concluded that the wording in the first paragraph of the proposed announcement may be susceptible to misinterpretation. We suggest that the wording of this paragraph be revised along the lines indicated below in order to make clear that the policy outlined in such paragraph is intended to apply solely to those situations where accounting recognition already has been given to deferred taxes and the accumulated credit arising from such accounting recognition has been classified as a part of equity capital:

Proposed revision to first paragraph of announcement
(Brackets indicate deletion; underscoring indicates new material)

Notice is hereby given that any financial statement filed with this Commission dated as of December 31, 1958, or thereafter, which designates as earned surplus or its equivalent or includes as a part of equity capital (even though accompanied by words of limitation such as "restricted" or "appropriated") the accumulated credit arising from accounting for   the recognition in such statement of the deferral to future periods of current reductions in income taxes for various items including those under sections 167 and 168 of the Internal Revenue Code of 1954   filed with this Commission dated as of December 31, 1958, or thereafter will pursuant to the administrative policy on financial statements announced in Accounting Series Release No. 4, be presumed by this Commission "to be misleading or inaccurate despite disclosure contained in the certificate of the accountant or in footnotes to the statements provided the matters involved are material."

First paragraph of announcement as revised

Notice is hereby given that any financial statement filed with this Commission dated as of December 31, 1958, or thereafter, which designates as earned surplus or its equivalent or includes as a part of equity capital (even though accompanied by words of limitation such as "restricted" or "appropriated") the accumulated credit arising from the recognition in such statement of the deferral to future periods of current reductions in income taxes for various items including those under sections 167 and 168 of the Internal Revenue Code of 1954, will pursuant to the administrative policy on financial statements announced in Accounting Series Release No. 4, be presumed by this Commission "to be misleading or inaccurate despite disclosure contained in the certificate of the accountant or in footnotes to the statements provided the matters involved are material."

It is our belief that a revision along the lines indicated above would permit a clearer understanding of the Commission's interpretation of administrative policy. Further, such a revision would tend to minimize the possibility of any misunderstanding on the part of the public that it is the Commission's intent to require retroactive application of the procedures prescribed by Accounting Research Bulletin No. 44 (revised) to accounting periods prior to the date of official release of the Bulletin by the Committee on Accounting Procedures of the American Institute of Certified Public Accountants.

Yours very truly,

/s/ PRICE WATERHOUSE CO.

PRICE WATERHOUSE & CO.

56 Pine Street
NEW YORK 5

March 18, 1959

Mr. Orval L. DuBois, Secretary
Securities and Exchange Commission
Washington 25, D.C.

Dear Mr. DuBois:

Pursuant to the invitation contained in
Securities Act of 1933, Release No. 4010, we are
sending you three copies of a letter dated March
17, 1959 setting forth our views and recommendations
regarding the proposed interpretation of administrative policy.

Yours very truly,

/s/ PRICE WATERHOUSE & CO.

Enclosures - 3
    Letter

PRICE WATERHOUSE & CO.

56 Pine Street
New York 5

March 17, 1959

Securities and Exchange Commission
Washington 25, D. C.

Dear Sirs:

Notice of Intention to Announce
Interpretation of Administrative Policy
(Securities Act Release No. 4010,
Securities Exchange Act Release No. 5844,
Public Utility Holding Company Act Release No. 13894
and Investment Company Act Release No. 2814)

We have previously submitted, in a letter dated January 19, 1959, certain suggestions for clarification of language of the Commission's proposed interpretation of administrative policy. The purpose of this letter is to deal with the substantive aspects of the proposed action by the Commission.

The first paragraph of the interpretation reads as follows:

"Notice is hereby given that any financial statement which designates as earned surplus or its equivalent or includes as a part of equity capital (even though accompanied by words of limitation such as 'restricted' or 'appropriated') the accumulated credit arising from accounting for reductions in income taxes for various items including those under sections 167 and 168 of the Internal Revenue Code of 1954, filed with this Commission dated as of December 31, 1958, or thereafter, will pursuant to the administrative policy on financial statements announced in Accounting Series Release No. 4, be presumed by this Commission 'to be misleading or inaccurate despite disclosure contained in the certificate of the accountant or in footnotes to the statements provided the matters involved are material'."

The financial statements of numerous public utilities, showing such credits as restricted surplus, have been reported upon, without qualification, by many independent certified public accountants, including our firm. Such financial statements have been included in registration statements and reports filed with the S.E.C. under both the Securities Act and the Securities Exchange Act. Many millions of dollars of securities have been sold in the past on the basis of such statements, and registration statements for new issues are being cleared currently by the S.E.C. We do not believe these financial statements "to be misleading or inaccurate" and, therefore, we are unable to see that there is appropriate foundation for the Commission's proposed presumption to that effect. It seems to us, the Commission would be treading on dangerous ground if it went so far in indicting a wide segment of financial statements of public utilities, which are based upon an accounting treatment prescribed or authorized by numerous State Public Service Commissions and accepted by Certified Public Accountants and by the S.E.C. itself.

The entire first sentence of Accounting Series Release No. 4 reads as follows:

"In cases where financial statements filed with this Commission pursuant to its rules and regulations under the Securities Act of 1933 or the Securities Exchange Act of 1934 are prepared in accordance with accounting principles for which there is no substantial authoritative support, such financial statements will be presumed to be misleading or inaccurate despite disclosures contained in the certificate of the accountant or in footnotes to the statements provided the matters involved are material."

The State Commissions in Alabama, Colorado, Florida, Kentucky, Michigan, New Jersey, New Mexico, North Carolina, Ohio, Oklahoma, South Carolina, Utah, Virginia, West Virginia, Washington and Wyoming have prescribed or authorized the use of surplus for the credits arising from accounting for income tax reductions due to accelerated amortization and depreciation. We believe this alone constitutes substantial authoritative support so that the first sentence of Accounting Series Release No. 4 does not apply.

It is clear to us that the second sentence of Release No. 4 is properly applicable to the problem. This sentence is quoted below:

"In cases where there is a difference of opinion between the Commission and the registrant as to the proper principles of accounting to be followed, disclosure will be accepted in lieu of correction of the financial statements themselves only if the points involved are such that there is substantial authoritative support for the practices followed by the registrant and the position of the Commission has not previously been expressed in rules, regulations, or other official releases of the Commission, including the published opinions of its chief accountant."

The treatment of income tax reductions arising from accelerated depreciation in regulated public utilities and railroads is one of the most complicated problems which State and Federal regulatory agencies and the accounting profession have faced in many years. We are sure the Commission is fully informed as to the extensive hearings by other Commissions preceding their orders and of studies given the matter by the N.A.R.U.C. In the light of the wide diversity of viewpoints, it is to be expected that the S.E.C. would have its own views and preferences. But doesn't this illustrate conclusively why the matter falls within the second sentence of Release No. 4?

As accountants we are fully aware of the apparent incongruity in charging expenses with amounts equivalent to income tax reductions arising from accelerated depreciation and then returning the credits to surplus. The justification, we believe, arises from the fact that the State Commissions have both rate making and accounting authority. Where a State Commission has authorized these credits as equity capital for accounting purposes there is at least some implication that such a viewpoint will be entitled to some weight when the Commission exercises rate making authority. In such circumstances, insistence on a different accounting treatment in statements filed with the S.E.C., in our view, would be erroneous. Such action might hinder the judgment of the State Commissions upon how much of the benefits of accelerated depreciation should go to the utility and how much to the customers, which is an important substantive matter.

We recommend that the proposed interpretation of administrative policy be withdrawn on the grounds, first, that it would be contrary to the past policies of the Commission as expressed in Accounting Series Release No. 4 and in Rule U-27 and, second, that the financial statements of utilities, wherein the credits arising from tax reductions attributable to accelerated depreciation are shown in restricted surplus, are based on substantial authoritative support and, assuming full disclosure, they are not "misleading or inaccurate." The issue involved in the presentation of these credits in balance sheets is not sufficiently important to justify such a major step as interfering with the accounting of utilities which is already subject to state and/or federal regulations. If, contrary to the foregoing recommendation, the Commission decides to require the classification of these credits outside the equity section, we respectfully request that the requirement be made effective as to the future by such wording as will not indict past statements.

Yours very truly,

/s/ PRICE WATERHOUSE & CO.

SCOVELL, WELLINGTON & COMPANY

ACCOUNTANTS AND AUDITORS
MANAGEMENT CONSULTANTS

110 State Street
Boston 9, Mass.

January 23, 1959

Orval L. DuBois, Secretary
Securities and Exchange Commission
Washington 25, D. C.

Gentlemen:

The Commission's "Notice of Intention to Announce Interpretation of Administrative Policy" release under date of December 30, 1958, regarding balance sheet treatment of credit equivalent to reduction of income taxes, requested comments concerning this proposed change in administrative policy of the Commission. Although we are in agreement with the general application of the proposed policy, we know of at least one situation in which we believe inflexible application of the proposed policy would be unreasonable and would not result in improved accounting for net income or in any better annual presentation of financial position and results of operations over a period of years.

The situation which we believe should be excepted from the proposed policy exists in many companies conducting non-ferrous mining operations. In this industry it has been generally accepted accounting practice, followed by the companies for many years, not to recognize or charge depletion in the accounts or in the financial statements. On the other hand, federal income tax laws permit deduction from taxable income of a provision for depletion; and such allowable deduction, limited by the amount of net income, is usually taken on the tax return but not on the books. Because such a deduction is a continuing one and does not represent a deferring of tax liability to future years, the tax provision made against book income before income taxes has normally been taken at the reduced rate, reflecting deduction of depletion; and, therefore, the amount of tax shown on the income statement does not bear the relationship to net income before taxes that normally is expected in the case of non-mining enterprises.

Where a mining company has taken and deducted accelerated depreciation or amortization, there is an interaction between the allowance for depletion for tax purposes and the additional depreciation or amortization resulting from the limitations of percentage depletion based on amounts of net income. Therefore, in years where greater depreciation or amortization is taken on the tax return than is taken on the books, the amount of depletion allowable as deduction for purposes of computing income tax will be reduced. Since the selling prices of minerals mined are characteristically subject to material fluctuations, it cannot be estimated with any degree of accuracy whether or to what extent this loss of depletion will be recovered in future years when taxable income no longer is being charged with accelerated amortization or depreciation.

Because of this interaction of the allowance for depletion for income tax purposes and the deductions only for tax purposes of accelerated depreciation and/or amortization, it does not appear to be possible to establish any reasonable and consistent method or basis for allocating to future years any overall reduction of the actual income tax charge for initial and early years. An attempt to make such a proration to future years would be more nearly an effort to equalize income than an effort to account properly for discrepancies between book and tax income.

In recognition of this situation that exists in many mining companies, and the general acceptance of the practices mentioned above, and in view of the difficulty of determining a reasonable proration of taxes, we believe that companies faced with the problems outlined should be allowed to continue to account for discrepancies between book and taxable income without providing on the balance sheet a liability for income taxes deferred to future years. We believe that the proposed administrative policy should not be applied in such situations, but that a full and clear disclosure of the facts in the footnotes to the financial statement should suffice.

Very truly yours,

/s/ SCOVELL, WELLINGTON & COMPANY

RW/clm

TOUCHE, NIVEN, BAILEY & SMART
ACCOUNTANTS AND AUDITORS

233 Broadway
New York 7, N. Y.

January 5, 1959

Mr. Andrew Barr, Chief Accountant
Securities and Exchange Commission
Washington 25, D. C.

Dear Andy:

I have your letter of December 31st enclosing a copy of Securities Release No. 4010. I think your position is sound.

I think you will get many objections to it from state commissions and perhaps some of their accountants (but I hope on non-accounting grounds), as I am sure you are well aware. I also assume there is no question as to the Commission's power under the Securities Acts to require a treatment different than that called for by some of the state utility commissions.

Sincerely,

/s/ BILL WERNTZ

WWW:ala

TOUCHE, NIVEN, BAILEY & SMART
ACCOUNTANTS AND AUDITORS

233 Broadway
New York 7, New York

January 21, 1959

Mr. Andrew Barr, Chief Accountant
Securities and Exchange Commission
Washington 25, D. C.

Dear Andy:

Since writing you an earlier letter with
respect to your release 4010, two things have come
to my attention which I felt I should pass on to
you.

Several of my clients, after reading the proposed release, have stated that they felt it was
unclear from the language used as to whether the
intent of the release was to require retroactive
establishment of equalization reserves. As you
know, Bulletin 44 encourages making the adjustment
retroactively but emphasizes that the operation of
the bulletin is not retroactive. In view of the
fact that many companies had already released
earnings for a part of the current year, it was
also my feeling and that of the Committee that no
great harm would be done in a particular case if
the bulletin's requirements commenced to be met
beginning with the next fiscal year, usually
January 1, 1959. While a number of my clients
have made the adjustment retroactively (none was
material), others are planning to start the accumulation with the first of the new year so as not
to change in the middle of the year. In my own
case, I think most of these were also not really
material situations.

I did not read the proposed language in such
a way as to have it imply that the adjustment must

be made retroactively to 1954, and I would not
think it would be wise for the Commission to use
language that was susceptible to this interpretation. If, on consideration, the Commission feels
that the operation of the bulletin should be
retroactive, I am inclined to feel that there
would be substantial objection from all or nearly
all of the Committee members, as well as many
companies. I also think it might cast unwarranted
doubt on registration statements where the old
method had been used, which would seem to me to
be undesirable.

The other question which has been raised
involves clients in the natural resources areas
who, under the tax codes, are permitted to take
percentage depletion. The language of the proposed
release refers to "various items including those
under Sections 167 and 168". Two or three of
these clients have felt that the use of the words
"various items" is so broad as to include differences in depletion allowances between the tax
and book bases. I feel fairly certain that this
was not intended, but I thought it best to call it
to your attention so that you could consider the
desirability of some alternate form of language.

Sincerely,

/s/ BILL WERNTZ

WWW:ala

SECURITIES AND EXCHANGE COMMISSION
Washington 25, D. C.

January 29, 1959

Mr. William W. Werntz
Touche, Niven, Bailey & Smart
233 Broadway
New York 7, N. Y.

Dear Bill:

You realize from your committee experience
and past experience here that no matter how hard
you try nor how careful you think you have been in
getting language that is clear in proposals such
as our Release 4010, others quickly find ambiguities or think they do. That, of course, is one
reason for exposure for comment.

It was our intention to deal principally with
the classification of the credit which arises when
deferred tax accounting is adopted. This, of
course, is prevalent only in the utilities. It
was our feeling that your Bulletin 44 (Revised)
dealt with the question in other areas. Our release might well have caused some industrial companies and their accountants to review their
policies. I have not made a detailed survey, but
I know of cases where retroactive application of
the bulletin has been made, and others (at least
one) where the bulletin was made effective the
month after its adoption, which was a few months
after the close of the fiscal year. I think this
is a matter for accountants to review as to whether
they can certify in a given case without qualification. Any suggestions you may have for clarification of language or insertion of additional
material would be very helpful.

The words "various items" I think you
recognize as necessary to cover matters other
than those growing out of Sections 167 and 168 of
the Internal Revenue Code. It has been my understanding that most accountants would not include
percentage depletion differences as one of these
items requiring tax adjustment. The Federal Power
Commission Orders 203 and 204 include accounts to
take care of "other items", and the Civil Aeronautics Board's recent rule-making designated as
Regulation ER-230, adopted March 12, 1958, provides
for such items as pre-operating, new aircraft integration, or extension and development expenses.
I think it would be impracticable for us to enumerate all of the items which some registrants and
their accountants might feel material enough to
warrant deferred tax accounting. These matters,
except for the utilities, should be covered by the
Institute's bulletins on tax allocation. Any suggestions you have for dealing with this matter
would be appreciated.

Sincerely yours,

Andrew Barr
Chief Accountant

Enclosure
ABarr:mmg

March 23, 1959

Mr. Orval L. DuBois, Secretary
Securities and Exchange Commission
425 Second Street, N. W.
Washington 25, D. C.

Dear Sir:

> Comments on Proposed Accounting Policy
> On Deferred Tax Credits
> Securities Act Release No. 4010
> Exchange Act Release No. 5844

All of the logical basic objections were admirably stated in the Commission's Accounting Series Release No. 53 under date of November 15, 1945. We quote, with underlining added.

" . . . . With such information at hand the reader of the statement is informed of what the past operations were, and of the conditions or transaction, which in the draftman's judgment, are apt to be unusual and not apt to recur. In our opinion, this is the boundary line of financial accounting. It is the place at which the financial accountant in his capacity as such should stop. He is, we feel, essentially a historian, not a prophet.

"This desire to prepare statements in a form more readily usable in estimating the future has led some to attempt to present what can be called a 'normal' income statement, the inference being that the statement shows about what can be expected to happen year after year. The broad justification alleged for the practice is that if the actual results of the year's operations are unusual a reader may be misled into thinking the abnormalities will recur and that the best, if not the only way, to avoid such misconceptions is to 'normalize' the statement--that is, to exclude therefrom the effects of some or all of the conditions which in the opinion of the draftsman are deemed to be unusual.

"The dangers inherent in such a practice are numerous. In the first place, the draftsman's judgment as to what is abnormal can scarcely be considered infallible. In the second place, there is certainly as much danger that the reader will fail to understand what has been done by the draftsman as that he will fail to recognize that the unadjusted statements are abnormal. Finally, the method is extremely susceptible of misuse through conscious or unconscious bias in making decisions as to what is unusual or abnormal about the current year. To a degree, of course, the care with which disclosure is made of the extent of normalization may serve to minimize the possibility of misleading the reader. But in general we are satisfied that a statement purporting to reflect the actual results of operations is far less likely to be misleading if abnormalities are explained than if they are eliminated by adjustment in the statement even with an explanation of the elimination set forth in a note. If, of course, a clear and full explanation of the adjustments made is not given, the practice is highly deceptive and may be fraudulent. It may be noted in passing that accountants have long condemned such undisclosed 'adjustments' terming them at times a device akin to 'equalizing earnings'.

"We conclude, then that the proper function of an income statement presenting the results of operations is to present an accurate historical record. On this basis, it is evident that the items included therein should clearly and accurately reflect only actual operations. It is accordingly our view that the amounts shown should be in accordance with the historical facts and should not be altered to reflect amounts that the draftsman considers to be more 'normal' or likely to recur in future years."

Would it not be in order for the Commission to give an explanation as what has happened which causes the Commission to completely reverse its views expressed in 1945? It would seem that corporate managements, among others, would be interested in finding out whether it is the intention of the Commission to delegate to the American Institute of Certified Public Accountants the sole right to formulate and state "generally accepted accounting principles" to be followed by all corporations required to report to the Securities and Exchange Commission. Is the investing public now being asked to believe that the judgment of certified public accountants is to be considered infallible?

The Institute's 1958 revision of Accounting Research Bulletin No. 44 emphasizes that the use of one depreciation method for tax accounting, coupled with a different depreciation method for financial accounting statements, is a factor (together with other factors) resulting in the situation that income statements of different companies, as well as income statements of the same company for different years, are not truly comparable. Undue emphasis appears to be given to a highly theoretic idea as to a resulting "overstatement of income."

The reporting corporation can either pass on, by means of increased selling prices, the entire increase in depreciation arising from the change from straight-line depreciation to one of the accelerated methods, or it cannot pass on this increase. If it can pass on the increase, it would seem that the reporting corporation should be required to record the increased depreciation for financial reporting purposes. In this situation, permitting the reporting corporation to use the suggested "reserve" method appears to be a somewhat doubtful compromise.

In the opposite situation where the reporting corporation cannot pass on the increased depreciation through increased selling prices, it is not too clear where the suggested "reserve" method comes out. If, under the going-concern theory, additions to depreciable assets are relatively uniform as to dollar amount from year to year, it is arithmetically demonstrable that the change in method will increase the annual depreciation charge for a few years, followed by a decreasing trend until the annual depreciation charge comes back to where it was before the change. Ultimately, of course, when the corporation starts to fall apart and no longer adds to its depreciable assets, then the annual depreciation charge decreases at a more rapid rate under one of the accelerated depreciation methods than it would if the straight-line method had been continued. Just what is the suggested "reserve" method supposed to accomplish in such a situation?

Many have long realized that it is completely impossible for an investment analyst to determine solely by a review of income statements that the market price of one company's common stock will go up while that of another will go down. There is nothing new in the knowledge that income statements lack exact comparability. One company uses one "cost" theory of valuing inventory, while another uses an entirely different "cost" theory. To date, the magic formula as to how to achieve exact comparability of financial statements, in terms of the purchasing power of the dollar among other factors, has not been found by either the American Institute of Certified Public Accountants or by others. What can possibly be gained by setting apart the one factor of depreciation for special treatment while ignoring other equally important factors?

The Commission has fulfilled its purpose well in requiring corporations to reveal important facts that affect financial statements. Can it ever hope to achieve its pot-of-gold-at-the-end-of-the-rainbow search for absolute uniformity?

Very truly yours,

/s/ RALPH WANSER

Ralph Wanser
C.P.A. (New York, Massachusetts, California)
Not in public practice currently

3729 Warrensville Center Road
Shaker Heights 22, Ohio

ARTHUR YOUNG & COMPANY
Certified Public Accountants
165 Broadway
New York 6

February 26, 1959

Securities and Exchange Commission
Washington 25, D. C.

Release No. 4010
Securities Act of 1933

Gentlemen:

Regarding the Notice of Intention To Announce Interpretation of Administrative Policy issued on December 30, 1958 (Release No. 4010 under the Securities Act of 1933), we agree in principle with the suggested treatment of the accumulated credit arising from accounting for deferred income taxes.

We assume that, when the proposed treatment becomes effective, the date of the financial statements affected (December 31, 1958 in the present release) will be appropriately revised to a date following the effective date of the policy.

Yours very truly,

/s/ ARTHUR YOUNG & COMPANY

THE FINANCIAL ANALYSTS SOCIETY OF DETROIT

PRESIDENT
DAVID D. WILLIAMS
NATIONAL BANK OF DETROIT
DETROIT 32, MICHIGAN

January 29, 1959

Mr. Orval L. DuBois, Secretary
Securities & Exchange Commission
Washington 25, D.C.

Dear Sir:

It has come to my attention that the S.E.C. has under consideration issuance of a statement interpreting administrative policy concerning balance sheet treatment of credits resulting from reduction of income taxes arising from application of liberalized depreciation and accelerated amortization rules.

A number of us in the business of security analysis here have discussed this problem on several occasions among ourselves, as a result of which I should like to inform you, in my capacity as president of The Financial Analysts Society of Detroit, that we are firmly in favor of the administrative policy which is proposed by your Commission.

Sincerely,

/s/ DAVID D. WILLIAMS

David D. Williams,
    President
The Financial Analysts
    Society of Detroit

DDW:bl
encl. 2

FINANCIAL ANALYSTS OF PHILADELPHIA
1632 Chestnut Street
Philadelphia 3, Pa.

February 16, 1959

Mr. Orval L. DuBois, Secretary
Securities and Exchange Commission
Washington 25, D.C.

To the Commission:

As President of the Financial Analysts of
Philadelphia, a group of 370 representatives of
leading financial institutions and investment
firms in this area, I am writing with regard to
your proposals concerning <u>more uniform financial
requirements with respect to tax credits arising
from the use of formulas for liberalized depreciation or accelerated amortization.</u> It would seem
that investors should have clear disclosures concerning tax credit information and that it should
be so reported that earnings and net worth are not
improperly distorted.

The Directors of our Society would like to
encourage the Commission in its efforts (1) to require more uniform practice on this subject in
public statements by corporations under its jurisdiction, and (2) to require that additional earnings, arising from such tax credits, shall be
disclosed as deferred income in published income
statements and shall be separately set up as reserves in published balance sheet statements.

Although I have not brought this subject to a
vote of our individual members, I believe this
letter to be consistent with the normal thinking
throughout our group, since the more accurate presentation of financial reports to investors has
been a principal aim of the Financial Analyst
organizations.

Sincerely,

/s/ S. FRANCIS NICHOLSON

S. F. Nicholson,
President.

SFN:MAP

HARRIS TRUST AND SAVINGS BANK
115 West Monroe Street
Chicago 90, Illinois

January 29, 1959

Mr. Orval L. Du Bois, Secretary
Securities and Exchange Commission
Washington 25, D. C.

Dear Mr. Du Bois:

Accounting for Accelerated Depreciation
and Deferred Income Taxes

In response to your release dated December
30, 1958, we are writing to say that we favor your
proposed rule regarding balance sheet treatment of
deferred tax provisions. We would not be in favor
of any exceptions, however, since our interest lies
in uniformity of financial statements for ready
analysis and comparison, regardless of varying re-
gulatory-policies for the regulated companies.

It is our understanding from your release that
companies would also, in effect, be required to
make a provision for deferred taxes on the income
statement.

As you pointed out in your release, the rule
is not required for those concerns which charge
additional depreciation in the amount of the tax
saving. We concur with this view, and also add
that it is not required in cases where the depreciation charge is equivalent to tax depreciation.

Yours very truly,

/s/ WILLIAM C. NORBY

Vice President

William C. Norby
JMR

The Investment Analysts Society
of Chicago
Clarence E. Torrey, Jr., President
c/o A. G. Becker & Co., Incorporated
120 South LaSalle Street
Chicago 3, Illinois

January 28, 1959

Mr. Orval L. DuBois
Secretary
Securities and Exchange Commission
Washington 25, D. C.

> Re: SECURITIES ACT OF 1933
> Release No. 4010
> SECURITIES EXCHANGE ACT OF 1934
> Release No. 5844
> PUBLIC UTILITY HOLDING COMPANY ACT OF 1935
> Release No. 13894
> INVESTMENT COMPANY ACT OF 1940
> Release No. 2814

NOTICE OF INTENTION TO ANNOUNCE
INTERPRETATION OF ADMINISTRATIVE POLICY

To the Commission:

The following comments are with respect to the Commission's proposed announcement of an interpretation of administrative policy on financial statements regarding balance sheet treatment of credits equivalent to the reduction in income taxes. The views expressed herein have the approval of the Board of Governors of the Investment Analysts Society of Chicago, which has a membership of approximately 300 resident and 100 non-resident security and financial analysts.

In general, we are heartily in accord with the proposed announcement. However, we would urge that consideration be given to broadening its scope along the following lines:

(1) The emphasis in the proposed announcement is on the impropriety of including the accumulated credit arising from reduction of income taxes through accelerated amortiza-

tion or liberalized depreciation as a part of equity capital. We are in full agreement with this, but would suggest further that it be required that the amount of credits or debits to the deferred item for the period be set forth in the accompanying income statements.

(2) The language of the proposed announcement does not specifically require that all companies subject to Securities and Exchange Commission jurisdiction charge income and credit a deferred income account for the amount of estimated tax savings where they are material, and we feel that it should. We believe that the first sentence of the second to the last paragraph of the release dated December 30, 1958, should employ stronger language than the phrase "it is necessary" regarding the matter of charging current income with an amount equal to the estimated tax reduction.

(3) Furthermore, we object to the exception to this normalizing procedure described in Paragraph 8 of Accounting Research Bulletin No. 44 (Revised) of the Committee on Accounting Procedure of the American Institute of Certified Public Accountants. In this matter, we are in agreement with certain of the members of that committee who assented to the bulletin with qualification. In our opinion, the circumstance that a corporation is subject to the jurisdiction of a rate-making body which happens to have adopted rules and regulations which are in conflict with generally accepted accounting principles does not justify a departure from the general rule.

(4) It is our view that an understatement of earnings through a deviation from accounting principles in general use can be just as misleading as an overstatement. We refer here to companies which charge the whole of accelerated amortization or liberalized depreciation in their reported earnings, rather than normalizing earnings with a provision for the estimated tax savings. Companies which are reporting earnings and financial statements on this ultra-conservative basis should at least be required to footnote their income and financial statements to indicate the effect of their departure from

the generally accepted procedure. This situation is further complicated by the fact that certain major steel companies which report to stockholders on this basis with respect to amortization and depreciation of their own facilities are at the same time charging net income with their share of the reduction in present Federal income taxes arising from necessity certificate amortization, financing costs, and development expenditures of affiliates in which they have minority interests (pursuant to closing agreements with the Treasury Department).

While we are of the opinion that the proposed announcement should be broadened as described above in order not to mislead investors, we believe that the amount of estimated tax savings should be left to the discretion of the company managements and their independent auditors, so that they may take into consideration such experience factors as property retirements and salvage. Further, companies should not be required to make such provisions where the amounts involved are not material.

Respectfully submitted,
The Investment Analysts Society
 of Chicago

/s/ CLARENCE E. TORREY, JR.

CLARENCE E. TORREY, JR.
President

CET/ml

THE NATIONAL FEDERATION OF
FINANCIAL ANALYSTS SOCIETIES

February 2, 1959

Mr. Orval L. DuBois
Secretary
Securities and Exchange Commission
Washington 25, D. C.

> Re: SECURITIES ACT OF 1933
>   Release No. 1010
>   SECURITIES EXCHANGE ACT OF 1934
>   Release No. 5844
>   PUBLIC UTILITY HOLDING COMPANY ACT OF
>   1935 Release No. 13894
>   INVESTMENT COMPANY ACT OF 1940
>   Release No. 2814

NOTICE OF INTENTION TO ANNOUNCE
INTERPRETATION OF ADMINISTRATIVE POLICY

To the Commission:

The National Federation of Financial Analysts
Societies consists of autonomous societies of financial analysts in twenty cities in the United
States and two in Canada with a membership of over
six thousand. The nature of our work in appraising
the relative investment value of securities is such
that we believe our membership more nearly represents the interests of the investor than other
groups in the accounting and securities industry
whose interests are often more closely identified
with corporate management than with that of the
individual investor.

While the following comments cannot be said
to represent the views of all analysts, they do
represent the opinion of our Standing Committee
empowered to deal with such matters and of the

Executive Committee of the Federation. As such,
the views presented herein can be said to be representative of the general thinking of the financial
analysts, and hence of the individual investor.

In general, we are in hearty accord with the
proposed announcement of an interpretation of administrative policy on financial statements regarding
balance sheet treatment of credits equivalent to
the reduction in income taxes. We believe, however:

1. That the amount of credits or debits to the de-
    ferred balance sheet item for the period should
    be set forth in the income statements.

2. That all companies subject to the Security and
    Exchange Commission's jurisdiction should be
    required to charge income and credit to a de-
    ferred income account the amount of estimated
    tax savings without regard to the exceptions
    noted in Paragraph 8 of Accounting Research
    Bulletin No. 44.

3. That the amount of deferred taxes for the year
    and changes in the reserve be required to be
    shown in the financial statements.

We believe that a lack of uniformity in income and balance sheet accounting is misleading to
the investor. The National Federation of Financial
Analysts, therefore, as a matter of general principle, is in favor of measures such as that now being
proposed by the Commission leading in the direction
of uniform accounting practice.

Respectfully submitted,

/s/ M. DUTTON MOREHOUSE

M. Dutton Morehouse,
Chairman, Government Relations
Committee NATIONAL FEDERATION
OF FINANCIAL ANALYSTS SOCIETIES

MDM EH

THE NEW YORK SOCIETY OF SECURITY ANALYSTS, Incorporated

40 Exchange Place
New York 5, N. Y.

March 23, 1959

Mr. Orval L. DuBois, Secretary
Securities and Exchange Commission
Washington 25, D. C.

Re: SECURITIES ACT OF 1933
Release No. 4010
SECURITIES EXCHANGE ACT OF 1934
Release No. 5844
PUBLIC UTILITY HOLDING COMPANY
ACT OF 1935
Release No. 13894
INVESTMENT COMPANY ACT OF 1940
Release No. 2814

NOTICE OF INTENTION TO ANNOUNCE
INTERPRETATION OF ADMINISTRATIVE POLICY

To the Commission:

The undersigned Special Committee has been appointed by the Board of Directors of the New York Society of Security Analysts, Inc. to express its views and comments concerning the Notice of Intention of the Securities and Exchange Commission as set forth in the Releases enumerated above. The New York Society has a membership of some 2,500 financial analysts and is substantially the largest member society of the National Federation of Financial Analysts Societies.

The Special Committee deems it particularly important that this expression of views be submitted to the Securities and Exchange Commission in view of the statement addressed to the Commission by the National Federation of Financial Analysts Societies. The Special Committee does not concur in that statement and seriously doubts that the views presented therein are representative of the general thinking of financial analysts.

The following comments represent the unanimous views of the Special Committee, with the exception of one member whose views are set forth in a separate letter attached hereto, and of a majority of the Board of Directors of the New York Society.

(1) The Special Committee believes that the Notice of Intention referred to above is insufficiently clear as to the scope of its intended coverage to permit any affirmative endorsement of such intention at this time.

(2) In making this statement the Special Committee has reference to the words "for various items" included in the sentence referring to "the accumulated credit arising from accounting for reductions in income taxes for various items including those under sections 167 and 168 of the Internal Revenue Code of 1954, . . . ".

(3) The general impression obtained by a reading of the Notice of Intention is that it refers specifically to the accounting treatment of income tax reductions resulting from section 167 and 168 of the Internal Revenue Code of 1954. This general impression may be completely inaccurate.

(4) The Special Committee fully recognizes that many items in corporate financial accounting may be accorded one treatment in reporting for income tax purposes and a very different treatment in corporate accounts as reported to stockholders.

(5) The Special Committee seriously questions the wisdom of any attempt on the part of the Securities and Exchange Commission to establish a rule or regulation which seeks to reconcile what is but one facet of the difference between financial reporting for income tax and ordinary corporate purposes.

(6) Any attempt to reconcile all of the differences between the two accounting presentations referred to above would involve many considerations of the gravest import. No such attempt should be undertaken without the most comprehensive study.

(7) In respect to public utility companies, the Special Committee recognizes that the various state regulatory commissions having jurisdiction thereover have prescribed differing accounting treatments for the reduction in income taxes under sections 167 and 168 of the Internal Revenue Code of 1954 and have similarly adopted differing treatment thereof for rate making purposes. While uniformity of treatment might be desirable, it seems questionable, at the least, whether such uniformity would be obtained by the Commission's proposed intention, with particular reference being hereby made to Section 20(b) of the Public Utility Holding Act of 1935.

(8) The Special Committee believes that at the present time the public interest and protection of investors would be adequately served by a requirement of full disclosure in the financial accounts or footnotes thereto of any differences in the provisions for income taxes resulting from the adoption of accelerated amortization and/or liberalized depreciation and the taxes that would be payable under the depreciation method used for ordinary corporate purposes.

(9) Therefore and for the above reasons the Special Committee cannot express its agreement with the proposed interpretation of administrative policy as set forth in the above Releases and believes that any such course of action by the Securities and Exchange Commission would at this time be premature.

In accordance with your request this expression of views is being sent to you in triplicate.

Respectfully submitted,

/s/ CHARLES TATHAM

Charles Tatham, Chairman,
Special Committee

C. J. VANDERHYDE

59 Wall Street
New York 5, New York

March 18, 1959

Mr. Orval L. DuBois, Secretary
Securities and Exchange Commission
Washington 25, D. C.

> Re: SECURITIES ACT OF 1933
> Release No. 4010
> SECURITIES EXCHANGE ACT OF 1934
> Release No. 5844
> PUBLIC UTILITY HOLDING COMPANY
> ACT OF 1935
> Release No. 13894
> INVESTMENT COMPANY ACT OF 1940
> Release No. 2814

NOTICE OF INTENTION TO ANNOUNCE
INTERPRETATION OF ADMINISTRATIVE POLICY

To the Commission:

As a member of the Special Committee appointed by the Board of Directors of The New York Society of Security Analysts, Inc. to express views and comments on this matter, I wish to take this opportunity to express my personal ideas on this subject since they differ in some particulars from those of other members of the Special Committee.

(1) In general, I support efforts to bring about greater uniformity in accounting practices and in the presentation of financial information, regardless of whether the effort is being made by Government or private agencies. The SEC, the NARUC, the AICPA, the NYSSA and other analysts societies have done a great deal of work along these lines in the past. Their efforts have furthered the comparability of financial reports and I believe that this is in the interest of investors.

(2) I agree with the Special Committee that the scope of the intended coverage of the Commission's policy is not clear. As stated, it is possible to interpret the scope very broadly-- probably more broadly than is intended.

(3) My interpretation is that the proposed rule is limited to eliminating deferred tax credits from earned surplus accounts even where they are earmarked and to require that they be segregated in a separate Reserve for Deferred Taxes outside of the capitalization. If this is the intended purpose, I agree that it is a desirable objective from the standpoint of investors.

(4) I do not agree that a footnote in an annual report or occasional prospectus adequately protects investors in this matter. It is plain that the footnote is disregarded by managements of some companies that advocate its use. They base their financial policies on the contention that the "restricted surplus" is a substitute for common equity money and to the extent that there is "restricted surplus" they refrain from marketing an equivalent amount of common stock. These managements deny the validity of the more rational view that deferred taxes are more nearly equivalent to long-term debt-- an interest-free loan of tax money by the Government repayable in installments over a long period of years. Since it does, in reality, make a difference whether management puts the deferred taxes into a separate reserve or includes them in earmarked surplus, the argument that a footnote will take care of the problem does not hold water.

(5) This problem has aspects like Gresham's Law which holds that bad currencies tend to drive out the good. If steps are not taken to eliminate an undesirable accounting practice, competition will drive others into adopting it.

(6) A much more serious problem is the use by public utility companies of "flow-through" accounting in connection

with accelerated depreciation. This problem also calls for the adoption or imposition of some standards for the protection of investors, but as I read the notice this practice is not to be scrutinized by the Commission at this time.

In accordance with your request, this letter is being sent to you in triplicate.

Respectfully submitted,

/s/ C. J. VANDERHYDE

C. J. Vanderhyde

CJV:pbe

TRI-CONTINENTAL CORPORATION
65 Broadway
New York 6, N. Y.

January 26, 1959

Mr. Orval L. DuBois, Secretary
Securities and Exchange Commission
Washington 25, D. C.

Dear Mr. DuBois:

Securities Act of 1933 - Release No. 4010
Securities Exchange Act of 1934 - Release No. 5844
Public Utility Holding Co. Act of 1935 -
    Release No. 13,894
Investment Company Act of 1940 - Release No. 2814

Your release dated December 30, 1958 states
that the Commission has under consideration the
announcement of an interpretation of administrative
policy on financial statements regarding balance
sheet treatment of credits equivalent to the reductions in income taxes. Interested parties were
asked to submit views and comments by January 31,
1959.

As substantial investors in public utility
securities, we are opposed to the proposed interpretation. We do not believe that the term "restricted" surplus is misleading, and we believe that
such an account offers the investor just as much
protection as would a reserve account. While many
companies may regard "restricted" surplus as part
of their equity capital, the investor is not hurt
by the company's doing so. Under current standards
of accounting, equity ratios are amply strong and,
moreover, in many instances are understated. With
an account labelled "restricted" surplus, the investor is able to decide for himself whether or
not he wishes to regard this as part of equity capital. If the tax savings were required to be

placed in a reserve account, in no way could they
be considered a part of the equity. As such, many
companies would be forced to sell a disproportion-
ate amount of common stock which would become costly and would hurt both investors and consumers over
the long run.

Very truly yours,

/s/ FREDERICK W. PAGE

Frederick W. Page
Vice President

C. J. VANDERHYDE

59 Wall Street
New York 5, New York
March 13, 1959

Securities and Exchange Commission
Washington 25, D. C.

Dear Sirs:

This is in response to the invitation extended to interested persons to submit views and comments on the matter set forth in your Notice of Intention to Announce an Interpretation of Administrative Policy on Financial Statements regarding balance sheet treatment of credits equivalent to the reductions in income taxes (Securities Act of 1933, Release No. 4010).

As a practicing public utility investment analyst I wish to express personal agreement with this proposal and regret that it does not go further. Unless I misunderstand, it does not touch those companies that do not "normalize" earnings for the tax reduction but allow it to flow through and be reflected in earnings and dividends and in earned surplus without segregation or earmarking.

As I see it, companies that use the flow-through procedure give away shareholders' capital to the Federal Government in return for a deferral (not forgiveness) of income taxes and then turn around and give the tax deferral to customers without charge. They do so in the hope that at some time in the distant future they will be permitted to adjust rates and recover the amount given away (AICPA Bulletin). Whether matters will work out this way or whether future recoveries of the tax credits from customers will be lost in a welter of conflicting issues, remains to be seen.

It is clear to me that, in making available the accelerated depreciation option, Congress intended to confer a benefit on stockholders by allowing companies to retain for a time (without interest) some cash that otherwise would be paid to the Federal Government in taxes. The purpose was to encourage modernization of facilities and the construction of ample capacity for production in the interest of national defense.

Companies that permit the deferred income taxes to flow through to net income pervert this purpose. Their practice produces no additional cash that might be devoted by the company to the purpose Congress had in mind. It simply results in lower rates for present consumers and higher rates for future consumers while building up a contingent tax liability for investors. However worthy lower rates may be, Congress did not intend that they be achieved in this way.

"Normalization" of earnings with the credit to a separate Reserve for Deferred Taxes is the only procedure that accomplishes the purpose of Congress while protecting investors and dealing fairly with consumers. The only alternative procedure that would accomplish the purpose of Congress while protecting investors would be for a company to use accelerated depreciation on its books as well as its tax returns. This, of course, would mean higher rates for present consumers and lower rates for future consumers.

The current situation is reminiscent of the 1920's and 1930's when utilities used retirement reserve accounting on their books and much higher straight-line depreciation on their tax returns. Your study of utility depreciation practices brought out the differences that prevailed. The results were very costly to investors, especially when the Excess Profits Tax of World War II came along and also when Commissions forced huge transfers from "earned" surplus to bolster depreciation reserves per books. Who can foretell the twists and turns of future events and give positive assurance that the "flow through" policy will not some day prove equally detrimental to long-term investors in the common stocks of these companies?

An observer cannot help noting that the flow-through method has found greatest favor with (or met the least resistance from) companies that have been having difficulty in showing significant increases in earnings. The "flow-through" method is attractive to such companies for two reasons: (1) it increases current earnings and (2) produces an automatic year to year increase in reported earnings per share. The resultant "earnings" and "earnings growth" are being reflected in the dividends paid and in market prices of the stocks of these companies.

Investors and analysts are being confused and misled by present conflicting practices in this field. Your efforts to protect investors are welcomed.

Very truly yours,

/s/ C. J. VANDERHYDE

C. J. Vanderhyde

CJV:pbe

FEDERAL POWER COMMISSION

Washington 25

February 12, 1959

Honorable Edward N. Gadsby
Chairman, Securities & Exchange Commission
Washington 25, D. C.

Dear Chairman Gadsby:

This Commission has noted your press release of December 30, 1958, wherein you gave notice of intention to issue an interpretation of administrative policy on financial statements with respect to balance sheet treatment of credits equivalent to reductions in federal income taxes resulting from the taking of depreciation or amortization under Sections 167 and 168 of the Internal Revenue Code of 1954. As this Commission has a vital interest in the integrity of financial statements of electric and natural gas utilities subject to its jurisdiction, we appreciate your invitation to submit comments. We note your Release No. 4023 of January 28, 1959, extends the time for filing comments to February 28, 1959.

We have held that where electric utilities and natural gas companies subject to our accounting jurisdiction are regularly recording deferrals of income taxes through periodic charges to income, the concurrent credits shall be classified in Account 266, Accumulated Deferred Taxes on Income; further, that Account 266 is to be reported in the company's balance sheet under a new and distinctly separate balance sheet classification, which is neither a part of earned surplus nor reserves (See orders No. 203 and No. 204 in Docket Nos. R-158 and R-159). In view of the provisions of these orders, we believe that for financial reporting purposes it would be improper and contrary to our requirements for a company under our accounting jurisdiction to report as a part of equity capital (even though accompanied by words of limitation such as "restricted" or "appropriated"), the amounts of accumulated credits resulting from deferrals of income taxes. We are, accordingly, in agreement with the proposal expressed in Note 4 on page 2 of your press release of December 30, 1958, that companies under our jurisdiction be required in their balance sheet statements to use the balance sheet captions and classifications for the accumulated deferrals on income taxes which we have prescribed. We believe that the force of this Commission's accounting jurisdiction requires that prescribed classifications be observed in financial statements distributed to the public, including prospective investors.

In both of our accounting orders, No. 203 and No. 204, we held that the deferred tax accounting is not mandatory for a company under our accounting jurisdiction which in accordance with a consistent policy elects not to follow deferred tax accounting even though accelerated amortization or liberalized depreciation is used in computing taxes on income. We consider such non-mandatory feature is desirable, among other reasons, to avoid conflict, to the extent possible, with requirements which may be prescribed by state regulatory authorities having major rate responsibilities, some of which may authorize and others deny deferred tax accounting. We, accordingly, respectfully suggest that your proposed statement of policy to the extent it may set up an accounting requirement for companies subject to our jurisdiction which do not elect to follow deferred tax accounting, may offer considerable difficulty and result in confusion in this important aspect.

It is not entirely clear from the language appearing in the first paragraph of page 2 of your press release of December 30, 1958, or from your reference to Accounting Research Bulletin No. 44 (Note 3) what exceptions, if any, would be permitted from the proposed general rule "to charge current income with an amount equal to the tax reduction." It is urged that you recognize the non-mandatory features of our accounting rules in order to avoid almost inevitable conflicts between regulatory agency requirements.

Subject to the above observations, this Commission favors your proposed interpretation of administrative policy.

Sincerely yours,

/s/ JEROME K. KUYKENDALL

Chairman

SECURITIES AND EXCHANGE COMMISSION
Washington 25, D. C.

March 4, 1959

Honorable Jerome K. Kuykendall
Chairman, Federal Power Commission
Washington 25, D. C.

Dear Chairman Kuykendall:

I want to thank you personally for the consideration that you and your staff have given to our
notice of intention to announce interpretation of
administrative policy on financial statements with
respect to balance sheet treatment of credits equivalent to reduction in federal income taxes resulting from the taking of depreciation or amortization
under Sections 167 and 168 of the Internal Revenue
Code of 1954. We realize that our interests in
the matter are closely related, and your comments
will receive careful consideration.

You may be interested to know, if it has not
yet come to your attention, that in response to
numerous requests we have again extended the time
for filing comments to March 25, 1959, and have
reset the date for hearing to April 8, 1959. From
the number of requests for time at the public hearing, it would appear that there will be a lively
discussion of the question.

Sincerely yours,

Edward N. Gadsby
Chairman

ABarr:mmg
3/4/59

PUBLIC UTILITIES COMMISSION
State of California

California State Building
San Francisco 2, Calif.

January 21, 1959

File No. C-6148

AIR MAIL

Secretary of the Commission
Securities and Exchange Commission
Washington 25, D. C.

Dear Sir:

This is with reference to the Securities and
Exchange Commission's release of December 30, 1958
regarding "Interpretation of Administrative Policy
on Financial Statements Regarding Balance Sheet
Treatment of Credit Equivalent to Reduction of Income Taxes."

It seems clear from the release that your Commission proposes to consider misleading or inaccurate any financial statement which designates as
earned surplus or its equivalent or includes as
part of equity capital the accumulated credit a-
rising from accounting for reductions in income
taxes for various items including those under Sections 167 and 168 of the Internal Revenue Code of
1954. The release, however, does not appear to be
clear as to your Commission's intent with respect
to those situations where charges for deferred income taxes are not allowed for rate making purposes
or where companies are permitted by a regulatory
agency to utilize the "flow through" basis for accelerated depreciation. We would appreciate clarification of the intent of your interpretation of
administrative policy on financial statements in
this connection.

Also your release mentions "the accumulated credit arising from accounting for reductions in income taxes for various items including those under Sections 167 and 168." We would appreciate being advised as to the various items which you intend to cover other than those included under Sections 167 and 168 of the Internal Revenue Code.

We would appreciate your providing us with more complete information as to your Notice of Intention to Announce Interpretation of Administrative Policy as promptly as possible in order that we may have such information before us in considering whether or not we will file written views or comments on or before January 31, 1959.

Very truly yours,

PUBLIC UTILITIES COMMISSION,
STATE OF CALIFORNIA

By /s/ R. J. PAJALICH

R. J. Pajalich, Secretary

SECURITIES AND EXCHANGE COMMISSION
Washington 25, D. C.

January 29, 1959

Public Utilities Commission
State of California
California State Building   File C-6148
San Francisco 2, California

Attention: Mr. R. J. Pajalich, Secretary

Gentlemen:

This will acknowledge receipt of your letter
of January 21, 1959, requesting additional information on our proposal regarding the balance sheet
treatment of the credit equivalent to the reduction
of income taxes.

Your first question, with respect to the "flow
through" basis where deferred taxes are not allowed
for rate making purposes, is intended to be covered
by our footnate 3 which quotes from the American
Institute of Certified Public Accountants Research
Bulletin No. 44 (Revised). The inclusion of "various items" in our release is consistent with the
Federal Power Commission's recent rule-making announced in their Orders 203 and 204, to which reference is made in footnote 4 in our release.
These orders provide accounts to take care of any
other sources of deferred tax accounting adopted
by utilities.

I am enclosing a copy of the release announcing an extension of time for comment and setting a
date for public hearing on our proposal. We would be
pleased to have any comments you care to make.

Very truly yours,

Andrew Barr
Enclosure   Chief Accountant

PUBLIC UTILITIES COMMISSION
of the Territory of Hawaii
1311 Kapiolani Boulevard
Telephones 67737 67738
Honolulu 14, T. H.

March 31, 1959

Honorable Orval L. Dubois, Secretary
Securities and Exchange Commission
Washington, D. C.

Sir:

Reference is made to the Securities and Exchange Commission Securities Act, Release No. 4038,
dated Wednesday, February 25, 1959.

For information purposes only, we are submitting the accounting methods prescribed by this Commission for handling the reserve accrued as a
result of a public utility's election to use accelerated depreciation for income tax purposes.

Attached hereto are:

1. Commission Decision and Order No. 916 pres-
    cribing accounting treatment of accumulated
    credit from deferred income taxes for ac-
    counting purposes.

2. Commission Decision and Order No. 970 pres-
    cribing the treatment of the accumulated
    credit from deferred income taxes for the
    purpose of rate making (page 9).

It so happens that the application of the
Honolulu Rapid Transit Company, Limited was the
first case before this Commission, involving a utility, which had elected to subscribe to accelerated
depreciation method, requesting authority to increase rates and charges.

Although the reasonableness of rates for
transportation utilities are usually judged by
operating ratio in most jurisdictions, this Commission considers three factors : (1) Operating
Ratio, (2) Rate of Return, and (3) Financial
Requirements. It was felt that the problem of
handling deferred taxes should be met at this
time (Docket No. 1375, Decision and Order No. 970).

Yours very truly,

/s/ JACK E. CONLEY

Jack E. CONLEY
Director

JEC:au
Enclosures

BEFORE THE PUBLIC UTILITIES COMMISSION

OF THE TERRITORY OF HAWAII

In the Matter of the Application of

HONOLULU RAPID TRANSIT CO., LTD.

for Approval of Declining-Balance
Method of Depreciation (Accelerated
Depreciation).

DOCKET NO. 1322

DECISION AND ORDER NO. 916

Filed __FEBRUARY 7__ , 1958

At __10:56__ o'clock __A.M.__

__/s/ MARY G. ARIOLI__
Secretary of the Commission

BEFORE THE PUBLIC UTILITIES COMMISSION

OF THE TERRITORY OF HAWAII

In the Matter of the Application of HONOLULU RAPID TRANSIT CO., LTD. for Approval of Declining-Balance Method of Depreciation (Accelerated Depreciation).	DOCKET NO. 1322 DECISION AND ORDER NO. 916

Before: Roger S. Ames — Chairman
James M. O'Dowda — Commissioner
Fred G. Manary — Commissioner
Leo G. Lycurgus — Commissioner
Masaru Shinseki — Commissioner

APPEARANCES:

For the Commission
Harold W. Nickelsen, Esq.   Counsel
Assistant Attorney General

For Honolulu Rapid Transit Co., Ltd.
Edward M. deHarne   Pres. and Gen. Manager
John W. McClaren   Vice-Pres. and Treasurer

D E C I S I O N

This matter first came before the Commission through application filed on December 2, 1957, wherein the HONOLULU RAPID TRANSIT COMPANY, LIMITED, requested authority to adopt the declining-balance method of accelerated depreciation, for income tax purposes, to cover the Company's fleet of 75 new General Motor buses, including spare parts equipment.

The method of depreciation is prescribed under Section 167 of the 1954 Internal Revenue Code. These assets qualify under this section through proviso: "(1) New (not used) tangible property acquired after

1953." The three methods authorized under this section are (1) straight line, (2) declining balance or (3) sum-of-the-digits. At the public hearing held on the 23rd of January 1958, John W. McClaren, Vice-President and Treasurer, stated that the Company proposes to use the declining-balance method of depreciation if the application is granted.

The 75 General Motor buses were purchased in June 1957, at which time the Commission authorized a twelve-year life and an 8.33 per cent annual rate of depreciation.

Mr. William H. Wright, Chief Auditor for the Commission, testified that, under the declining-balance method, accelerated depreciation will be accrued at the annual rate of 16.66 per cent. However, the straight-line basis will continue to be used for rate-making purposes so that this authorization will have no affect on rates. The Commission has previously granted authorization for the use of accelerated depreciation for tax purposes only to several other Territorial public utilities.

The procedure for accounting for deferred income taxes is as follows:

During the period when the allowance for depreciation under the declining-balance method exceeds the accrual under the straight-line method, the amounts representing deferral in income taxes would be carried in a Reserve for Deferred Income Tax account. When the straight-line accrual exceeds the allowance under the declining-balance method, the increased income taxes would be charged against the Reserve account, and such practice would continue until the total amount accumulated therein shall have been exhausted.

Setting up of the accounts mentioned above has been studied and agreed upon by both the Applicant and the staff.

The Commission, having considered the entire record herein and being fully advised in the premises, is of the opinion and finds (1) that the adoption of the accelerated method of depreciation for income tax purposes is not against the public interest and is beneficial to the Applicant in that it provides interest-free working capital; and (2) that, therefore, the application should be approved.

ORDER

IT IS, THEREFORE, HEREBY ORDERED:

(1) That HONOLULU RAPID TRANSIT COMPANY, LIMITED, be and it is authorized to adopt the declining-balance method of accounting for accelerated depreciation for income tax purposes effective retroactively to July 1, 1957.

(2) That during the period when the allowance for depreciation under declining-balance method exceeds the accrual under the straight-line method, the deferral in income taxes be carried in a Reserve for Deferred Income Tax account.

(3) That during the period when the accrual for depreciation under the straight-line method exceeds the allowance under the declining-balance method, the increased income taxes be charged against the Reserve for Deferred Income Tax account until the total amount accumulated in the Reserve has been exhausted.

DONE at Honolulu, City and County of Honolulu, Territory of Hawaii, this 7th day of February 1958.

PUBLIC UTILITIES COMMISSION
TERRITORY OF HAWAII

By___/s/ ROGER S. AMES_____
      Roger S. Ames
      Chairman

By___/s/ JAMES M. O'DOWDA___
      James M. O'Dowda
      Commissioner

By___/s/ FRED G. MANARY_____
      Fred G. Manary
      Commissioner

By___/s/ LEO G. LYCURGUS____
      Leo G. Lycurgus
      Commissioner

By___/s/ MASARU SHINSEKI____
      Masaru Shinseki
      Commissioner

BEFORE THE PUBLIC UTILITIES COMMISSION

OF THE TERRITORY OF HAWAII

In the Matter of the Application of HONOLULU RAPID TRANSIT COMPANY, LIMITED for an Increase in Its Rates of Fare	Docket No. 1375

DECISION AND ORDER NO. 970*

DISSENTING OPINIONS

Filed _____ March 19 _____ , 1959

At ___ 11:50 ___ o'clock ___ A.M. ___

/s/ MARY G. ARIOLI
Secretary of the Commission

Order approved 2/27/59.
Decision approved 3/19/59.

BEFORE THE PUBLIC UTILITIES COMMISSION

OF THE TERRITORY OF HAWAII

In the Matter of the Application of	Docket No. 1375
HONOLULU RAPID TRANSIT COMPANY, LIMITED	
for an Increase in its Rates of Fare	Decision and Order No. 970

Before: J. M. O'Dowda   Chairman
           V. J. Moranz   Commissioner
           F. G. Manary   Commissioner
           L. G. Lycurgus   Commissioner
           M. Shinseki   Commissioner

Appearances:

    For the Commission
      Henry H. Shigekane, Esq.   Counsel
      Deputy Attorney General

    For Honolulu Rapid Transit Co., Ltd.
      Robertson, Castle & Anthony
      By J. Garner Anthony, Esq.   Counsel
         Frank D. Padgett, Esq.   Counsel

DECISION

This matter came before the Commission through application filed December 17, 1958, by the HONOLULU RAPID TRANSIT COMPANY, LIMITED, for authority to increase the adult ticket rate of fare and the fare for the Around-the-Island Tour.

Through Commission approval, the application was received and referred to the staff at the quorum meeting held December 17, 1958, and the date for the Public Hearing was set at 7:30 P.M. Wednesday, January 14, 1959, at the Commission's offices, 1311 Kapiolani Boulevard, Honolulu, Hawaii.

Notices of the Public Hearing were published in accordance with the Provisions of Chapter 104, Section 104-15, Revised Law of Hawaii, 1955, as amended.

The Public Hearing was called to order at 7:35 P.M. on January 14, 1959. No one representing the public appeared. No applications for intervention or letters from the public protesting the granting of the application had been received. Statements were made by Chairman O'Dowda and a brief resumé of the application was presented by J. Garner Anthony, Esquire, Counsel for the Company.

The part of the hearing open for statements by the general public was then closed at 7:43 P.M. The hearing reconvened at 7:49 P.M., at which time the Company was asked to present their case.

Counsel for Applicant requested and was granted permission to amend the original application (for detail of corrections see official transcript). Other than for correcting estimated cost figures and related effect on income and operating ratio, the amendment changed Paragraph III to state the collective bargaining agreement had been ratified and changed Paragraph IV regarding the commission to be paid agents for selling Around-the-Island Tours to provide for a commission of $1.00 or such other rates as prevail within the industry.

The application requests authority to increase the adult ticket fare from two for 30 cents — (15 cents) — to three for 50 cents — (16-2/3 cents) — and the Around-the-Island fare of $4.00 (including Federal Transportation Tax) to $5.50 (including Federal Transportation Tax), all other fares and privileges in effect at this time to remain in effect. Applicant also requested authority to pay a $1.00 commission to agents selling Around-the-Island Tours instead of the 50 cents now being paid.

The application contains, in general, the following allegations in its support: Petitioner can not absorb the additional labor costs and expenses arising out of or caused by the recently negotiated collective bargaining agreement, and that, due to the increase in labor costs and expenses, Petitioner is convinced that it is not possible to render adequate service to the public on a proper operating ratio, and to realize its financial requirements at the existing rates of fare, and that applicant must have the increase asked for in order to obtain the proper operating ratio, and approach its financial requirements.

The collective bargaining agreement, agreed on and retroactive to December 1, 1958, in substance provides for:

> (1) The Company would increase contributions, from $13.00 to $17.00 per employee per month, to the Health and Welfare Fund;

> (2) A wage increase of 15 cents per hour to maintenance employees and 10 cents per hour to operators, construction and certain other employees, and a second wage increase of 10 cents per hour for maintenance employees and 5 cents an hour for operators, construction and certain other employees effective December 1, 1959; and

> (3) Payment of other fringe benefits.

The foregoing increased labor costs, together with increased cost and wages to other employees not covered by aforesaid collective bargaining agreement, according to the Company, will amount to a total of approximately $194,000.00 in operating costs in a Test Year commencing February 1, 1959 and a total increase of $263,000.00 in operating costs in a subsequent year.

Petitioner anticipated a net profit for the Test Year under present rates of approximately $143,000.00, or an operating ratio of 96.8 per cent, and a net profit for a subsequent year of $108,000.00, or an operating ratio of 97.6 per cent. The Company's annual report for 1958 shows an operating ratio of 93.14 per cent and the rate of return at 9.52 per cent. These figures include December 1958, during which time the increased operating cost of approximately $16,200.00 was in effect.

The Company's estimate of its financial requirements per annum after all operating charges, depreciation, and taxes is as follows:

Dividends on Outstanding 5% Preferred Stock.....	$ 21,400.00
Dividends on Outstanding Common at $1.00 Per Share	180,000.00
Interest on Bank Loans	300.00
Surplus Requirements Based on 50% Over and Above Common Stock Dividend	90,000,00
	$291,700.00

Just prior to completing the Company's case on January 15, Counsel for Applicant made a verbal request for the granting of "interim rates" to be effective February 1, 1959.

The reason for this request was the fact that the Union Contract had been retroactive to December 1, 1958 and the additional expense resulting therefrom, together with other expense as outlined in the application (including salary raises to executives assumed as of the same date), amount to some $16,200.00 per month, and the Company could not afford this increased cost--for the months December 1958 and January 1959, and the period which would elapse prior to the time the Commission can render its decision, without some relief.

The Company concluded the formal presentation of their case at 11:59 A.M., January 15, 1959.

The request for interim rates was unanimously denied. Applicant was last before this Commission for a general rate increase in 1953 and since then for an additional increase in its school fares in 1957. Applicant was granted a Certificate of Public Convenience and Necessity for Around-the-Island Tours in 1954.

Evidence was presented by the Applicant and Commission staff[1] in the form of testimony and exhibits as to the past and future (estimated) earnings and operating ratio for Test Year February 1, 1959 to January 31, 1960.

A summary of Staff and Company Estimates (Results of Operations) for the Test Year under both the Present and Proposed Rates is appended hereto and by reference is made a part of this Decision. (Appendix I).

---

[1]Witnesses for Applicant:

Mr. E. M. deHarne	President & Gen. Mgr.
Mr. J. W. McClaren	Vice-President & Treasurer
Mr. G. G. Stancil	Superintendent
Mr. A. P. Moniz	Assistant Treasurer
Mr. Paul Dittmar	Illinois

Witnesses for the Commission:

Mr. J. E. Conley	Director
Mr. W. H. Wright	Chief Auditor
Mr. A. E. Pierce	Chief Engineer
Mr. E. M. deHarne (HRT CO.)	Adverse Witness

The major differences that arose between the staff and Company were:

(1) `$102,319.00 in estimated adult passenger revenues under proposed rates, principally due to a difference in the estimates of adult passengers at present rates and the diminution and ticket utilization factors.

(2) $15,000.00 in the prediction of revenues from charter service, primarily due to the views on the improvement in economic conditions.

(3) In estimated revenues at proposed rates from the Around-the-Island Tour for the Test Year, the staff estimate being higher because they felt, with the Company now paying the same commission as other tour operators and a bigger tourist season anticipated, that these revenues were certain to increase.

(4) In operating expenses due to the disallowance by the staff of $6,750.00 in executives' compensation.

(5) In the treatment of accrued deferred Federal Income Tax.

In the process of developing the earnings of the Applicant, the Commission requested the Company to furnish the recorded financial results of operations and other pertinent facts relative to Honolulu, Limited, a wholly-owned subsidiary, and the staff submitted to the Commission a supplemental report covering this data. This information was received in evidence over the objection of Counsel for Applicant.

Honolulu, Limited was incorporated on November 30, 1954 in accordance with the Resolution of Honolulu Rapid Transit Company, Limited of September 24, 1954, and received in consideration for the exchange of 12,500 common shares of its capital stock at $10.00 per share, or $125,000, the following two parcels of real properties transferred from Honolulu Rapid Transit Company, Limited, viz:

1. Lot at Alapai and Beretania Streets, Tax Key 2-1-42-12, containing an area of 13,059 square feet.

2. Land at Queen, Keawe, South and Halekauwila Streets, sub-divided into six lots, viz:

a. Lot 1, Tax Key 2-1-31-1 , area 16,946 square feet
b. Lot 2, Tax Key 2-1-31-31, area 18,392 square feet
c. Lot 3, Tax Key 2-1-31-32, area 20,039 square feet
d. Lot 4, Tax Key 2-1-31-33, area 19,399 square feet
e. Lot 5, Tax Key 2-1-31-29, area 17,555 square feet
f. Lot 6, Tax Key 2-1-31-30, area 77,301 square feet

Total Area   169,632 square feet

In accordance with a second Resolution of the Honolulu Rapid Transit Company, Limited of December 17, 1954, Honolulu, Limited acquired on December 31, 1954, in exchange for 10,000 shares of Company's common capital stock at $10.00 per share or $100,000.00 and $3,237.17 in cash, real property described, as follows:

Land bounded by King, Alapai and Young Streets, being Lot 4A Tax Key 2-1-42-13, containing an area of 55,118 square feet and Lot 5A, Tax Key 2-1-42-5, containing an area of 8,092 square feet, or a total of 63,210 square feet.

The Applicant adduced no evidence to indicate the value of the properties on the respective dates of transfer.

Honolulu, Limited earnings are as follows:

| | | EARNINGS PER SHARE | |
| | | HON. LTD. | H.R.T. CO. |
YEAR	NET INCOME	STOCK	STOCK
1954	$ 1,149.24	$ .05	$ .006
1955	12,345.09	.55	.07
1956	22,333.23	.99	.12
1957	22,546.63	1.00	.13
1958	265,503.89	11.80	1.47

The staff's estimates of revenues reflected a greater number of adult passengers under present rates than the Applicant's. We are convinced by the staff's analysis, which was complete and well-founded, that an estimate of 24,350,000 adult revenue passengers for the Test Year is fair and reasonable.

We are also persuaded to adopt the staff's estimate of a 25 per cent diminution factor and a 90 per cent ticket utilization factor as applicable to the proposed adult fare structure. The extensive study made by the staff, in the matter of Applicant's recorded fare structure results, appears to us to be conclusively in support of the staff's treatment of estimated revenues for the Test Year under proposed rates (20 cents cash and three tickets for 50 cents). In considering alternate rate structures we are of the opinion that the basis used by the staff relative to ticket utilization under proposed fares will serve equally well for us to conclude that ticket utilization under an adult fare structure of 20 cents cash and five tickets for 75 cents would approximate 88 per cent, and under an adult fare structure of 20 cents cash and five tickets for 80 cents would be 86 per cent.

The Commission felt that:

(1) The Company's estimated revenues for the Test Year were low in view of all economic forecasts for 1959;

(2) Every effort should be made to minimize the cost to the regular everyday rider; and

(3) The present rates are such that they tend to reduce to the minimum the use of the cash fare of 20 cents and that the Company has lost considerable potential revenue by having the ticket fare of 2 for 30 cents as against 2 cash rides for 40 cents.

A couple boarding a bus will buy two tickets — and an individual planning on returning may buy two tickets — two total strangers boarding might also combine for two tickets. In all three cases, the Company has lost 10 cents in revenue because these occasional riders did not pay the cash fare.

By increasing the number of tickets which must be purchased at one time, only the regular rider who actually deserves a discount for his continued patronage would receive
the advantage of the ticket.

The Commission, in arriving at its decision accepted the results
as presented in the staff report (Exhibit B). Consideration was also
given to the possibility of increasing the adult ticket rate to 5 for 80
cents, but it was rejected. The Commission voted to change the ticket
rate to five for 75 cents.

In so doing we do not penalize the everyday rider. The amount of
money he has budgeted for transportation is the same — at the same time
we think that a majority of visitors, occasional Honolulu riders and service personnel will pay the cash fare rather than be burdened with extra
tickets. Further we think that the diminution will be reduced due to the
fact that the adopted fare structure will change the cost of a ride mainly
to the occasional rider.

In approving the 5 tickets for 75 cents adult ticket rate, two Commissioners (Commissioner Moranz and Commissioner Lycurgus) dissented
in favor of no change at all, and their dissenting opinions are attached
hereto.

The approach to the matter of Charter and Around-the-Island Tour
revenues for the Test Year resulted in revenues which are in our opinion,
fair and reasonable.

The Commission voted unanimously to approve the increase in the
Around-the-Island Tour fare (from $4.00 including Federal Transportation
Tax to $5.50 including the Federal Transportation Tax), and at the same
time denied the request of the Company to pay a commission of $1.00 per
ticket "or such other rates as prevail within the industry." It did, however, authorize the payment of a $1.00 commission on the Around-the-
Island Tour fare of $5.50.

We will also disallow the increase in executive salaries reflected in
Applicant's expense estimates. This we do for the reason that such increases were directly related to wage increases arrived at through collec-

tive bargaining between representatives of the Union and Management. The Management representatives included individuals in the executive category, the subsequent recipients of the disallowed salary increases.

The question of disallowance by the staff of the $6,750.00 in executives' compensation does in no way refer to the actual payment of such additional renumeration — nor does it question the right of the directors to award such an increase. It does, however, question the advisability of passing such an expense directly on to the fare payer — in the same manner and at the same time as wage increases to employees in the bargaining units — in awarding a rate increase.

This docket presented to the Commission the first request for a rate increase which involved a public utility which has elected to take advantage of accelerated depreciation under Section 167-168 of the Internal Revenue Code of 1954.

This Section 167-168 explicitly permits the tax payer to apply the "sum of the year digits" or "declining balance" methods of depreciating the cost of facilities constructed, reconstructed or acquired and initially used after December 30, 1953, in the determination of Federal Income Tax Liability.

This Commission, in allowing utilities under its jurisdiction to employ accelerated depreciation, has in effect prescribed the accounting method for each but not the treatment in connection with rate-making.

After studying this matter, the Commission is of the opinion that normalization of taxes, with the reserve for deferred taxes deducted from the rate base, is the most equitable method for rate-making purposes.

The procedure to be followed is that the normal taxes would be set up as a charge against operations for rate-making purposes and that the deferred taxes would flow to a reserve for future payout. The deferred tax reserve would be deducted from the rate base, in addition to the regular depreciation reserve deductions, because the ratepayer has contributed the amounts in the deferred tax reserve prior to the due date for payment to the Government and should not be required to pay a return on it in the meantime.

By handling the reserve in the manner outlined above, the utility itself has the advantage of the interest-free capital to assist it in modernization and expansion of plant, and the ratepayer is protected from paying rates predicated on a rate base which has been increased by the amount of this reserve to which he has contributed.

By letter filed November 30, 1954, Honolulu Rapid Transit Company, Limited advised the Commission regarding the incorporation of the new subsidiary company to handle its non-utility holdings, and also outlined the purposes of the corporation, viz:

1. To take the present non-utility activity out of the parent company, Honolulu Rapid Transit Company, Limited, which should eliminate any criticism of its participation in non-utility activities; and

2. To engage in other activities with the purpose of increasing the over-all earnings of the two companies.

However, Applicant has received no dividend or return whatsoever on its total investment of $225,000 as per books, in Honolulu, Limited.

Applicant alleges to financial requirements to be as follows:

CAPITAL	ESTIMATED FINANCIAL REQUIREMENTS WITH COMMON STOCK DIVIDENDS		
	PRINCIPAL	AT 8%	AT 10%
5% Preferred Stock			
50,000 Shares $10 Par	$ 500,000		
Less:			
7,201 Shares Held in Treasury	72,010		
Total Preferred Stock	$ 427,990	$ 21,400	$ 21,400
Common Equity			
Common Stock			
180,000 Shares			
$10 Par	$1,800,000	$144,000	$180,000
Surplus & Other Credits	1,402,252	72,300*	90,300*
Total Common Equity	$3,202,252	$216,300	$270,300
Total Capital	$3,630,242	$237,700	$291,700

* Surplus based on 50% over common dividend.

In view of the Company's investment in its subsidiary corporation, Honolulu, Limited, it would seem logical that a return be anticipated from this investment as a source which might contribute towards the Company's financial requirements, and thus alleviate a portion of this burden which, otherwise, must be borne by the riding patrons.

It is noted that a loan in excess of $300,000 was made in 1955 by Honolulu Rapid Transit Company, Limited, the Applicant, to its wholly-owned subsidiary, Honolulu, Limited, and it appears that the source of the sum was the depreciation reserve maintained by the Applicant.

This Commission has long felt that depreciation reserve funds should be kept so invested as to be as nearly liquid as possible and should not be loaned or advanced to a subsidiary corporation or invested in any corporation in which the Company is interested.

Applicant requested an increase in rates which would produce additional gross revenues in the amount of $268,937 in the Test Year. It was pointed out that such a rate increase would provide for increased wage and salary costs as well as approach financial requirements based on common dividends of $1.00 per share.

Through the proposed rates the Applicant desires to pass on to the rider all increased costs assumed by management as of December 1, 1958 and in addition, expects at the same time to increase its dividend through the increased revenue produced by these rates.

The ratepayer can not be expected to assume all increase in financial requirements--some responsibility must be assumed by the owners and certainly some assumed by management through development of advertising, charter, ride-shop revenues and returns on their investments.

The concern of Applicant toward the dividend to their stockholders is quite apparent. In contrast, however, is their lack of concern regarding the return on their non-operating investment.

It is our opinion that an increase in the fare for Around-the-Island Tours from $4.00 (including Federal Transportation Tax) to $5.50 (Including Federal Transportation Tax) plus a change in the adult ticket rate from two tickets for 30 cents to five tickets for 75 cents would provide adequate revenues to enable Applicant to meet its reasonable financial requirements, earn $217,591 from operations, and result in a rate of return of 6.82 per cent and an operating ratio of 95.33 per cent, as shown in Appendix II attached hereto and by reference made a part hereof, and that these rates are fair and reasonable.

CONCLUSION

1. The Commission, having considered the entire record herein and being fully advised in the premises, is of the opinion that the granting of the application is against the public interest and therefore the application should be denied.

2. However, the Commission feels that the increase in the Around-the-Island rate of fare is justified and that this increase should be put in effect. Also, that the increase of from 50 cents to $1.00 in commission to agents selling this trip should be authorized.

3. Further, the majority of the Commission feel that adult ticket rate should be revised to stimulate payment of cash fares and the Commission orders the number of tickets to be purchased be changed from two tickets for 30 cents to five tickets for 75 cents.

ORDER

IT IS, THEREFORE, HEREBY

ORDERED: (1) That the proposed increases in rates of fare requested by the HONOLULU RAPID TRANSIT COMPANY, LIMITED be denied:

(2) That Applicant be and it is hereby authorized and directed to place in effect on, or as soon as possible after March 1, 1959, the following adopted rates of fare:

(a) Adult ticket fare of 5 tickets for 75 cents with full transfer privileges.

(b) Around the Island fare of $5.00 plus applicable Federal Transportation Taxes (10%–$5.50), with authority to pay travel agents a commission on the sale of such tickets of $1.00 per ticket.

(3) That all other rates of fare, in effect as of this date, shall remain in effect.

(4) That the Applicant advise the Commission of the exact date these new authorized rates will go in effect and at the same time supply the Commission with copies of notices, advertisements or circulars used to advise the public of the change.

(5) That the rates of fare for Honolulu Rapid Transit Company, Limited, effective on and after March 1, 1959, shall be as follows:

FRANCHISE OPERATIONS

(a) Full-Fare Passengers — 20¢ cash, or 5 tickets for 75¢, with an additional fare of 5¢ cash, or 5 tickets for 20¢, for passengers crossing the boundaries between Zones 1 and 2, or between Zones 1 and 3, with full transfer privileges on all connecting service lines within any zone for which the fare has been paid, subject to the Company's rules relating to such transfers.

(b) School Fares — 15¢ cash, or 5 tickets for 50¢, with full transfer privileges on all connecting service lines, subject to the Company's rules relating to such transfer. No zone fares.

(c) Express Service to and from Pearl Harbor — 30¢ cash, with no transfer privileges.

(d) Other Fares — Such other fares for special services as the Commission may from time to time approve.

CERTIFICATED OPERATION

Scheduled Bus Tour Service Around the Island $5.00 plus transportation tax (or $5.50) per person, together with authority to pay travel agents participating in the sale of tickets for such tours a commission of $1.00 per ticket.

This Decision and Order supersedes Decisions and Orders No. 895 dated July 18, 1957, and No. 913 dated January 23, 1958.

Done at Honolulu, City and County of Honolulu, Territory of Hawaii, this 27th day of February, 1959.

PUBLIC UTILITIES COMMISSION
OF THE TERRITORY OF HAWAII

By /s/ J. M. O'DOWDA
J. M. O'Dowda, Chairman

By _____ *
V. J. Moranz, Commissioner

By /s/ F. G. MANARY
F. G. Manary, Commissioner

By _____ *
L. G. Lycurgus, Commissioner

By /s/ MASARU SHINSEKI
Masaru Shinseki, Commissioner

*Dissented

HONOLULU RAPID TRANSIT COMPANY, LIMITED

COMPARATIVE RESULTS OF OPERATIONS

FOR TEST YEAR ENDING JANUARY 31, 1960

	AT PRESENT RATES			AT PROPOSED RATES		
	Company	Staff	Staff/Co.	Company	Staff	Staff/Co.
REVENUES						
Passenger Revenues	$4,419,499.00	$4,488,990.00	$69,491.00	$4,688,436.00	$4,820,520.00	$132,084.00
Revenue from Other Operations	82,300.00	83,640.00	1,340.00	82,300.00	83,640.00	1,340.00
Total Revenues	$4,501,799.00	$4,572,630.00	$70,831.00	$4,770,736.00	$4,904,160.00	$133,424.00
EXPENSES						
Maintenance of Way & Structure	$ 24,321.74	$ 24,330.00	$ 8.26*	$ 24,321.74	$ 24,330.00	$ 8.26*
Maintenance of Equipment	484,078.71	484,410.00	331.29	481,371.40	483,720.00	2,348.60*
Operating Garage	532,650.51	534,970.00	2,319.49	530,151.25	533,620.00	3,468.75*
Transportation	1,596,217.06	1,596,480.00	262.94	1,587,841.63	1,591,290.00	3,448.37*
Traffic Promotion	79,830.90	77,610.00	2,220.90	81,945.40	81,460.00	485.40
Administration & General	690,487.08	677,330.00	13,157.08	692,000.75	678,900.00	13,100.75
Sub-Total	$3,407,586.00	$3,395,130.00	$12,456.00	$3,397,632.17	$3,393,320.00	$ 4,312.17
Additional Labor Cost	194,374.00	187,760.00	6,614.00	193,503.00	187,210.00	6,293.00
Total Operating Expenses	$3,601,960.00	$3,582,890.00	$19,070.00	$3,591,135.17	$3,580,530.00	$10,605.17
Depreciation	273,851.00	273,820.00	31.00	273,851.00	273,820.00	31.00
Taxes Other Than Income	323,364.00	327,160.00	3,796.00*	337,464.00	344,540.00	7,076.00*
Total Expenses	$4,199,175.00	$4,183,870.00	$15,305.00	$4,202,450.17	$4,198,890.00	$ 3,560.17
NET BEFORE INCOME TAXES	$ 302,624.00	$ 388,760.00	$86,136.00	$ 568,285.83	$ 705,270.00	$136,984.17
INCOME TAXES	$ 159,380.00	$ 210,140.00	$50,760.00	$ 304,172.00	$ 382,650.00	$ 78,478.00
NET FOR RETURN	$ 143,244.00	$ 178,620.00	$35,376.00	$ 264,113.83	$ 322,620.00	$ 58,506.17
OPERATING RATIO	96.82%	96.09%	.73%	94.46%	93.42%	1.04%

*Denotes red figure.

HONOLULU RAPID TRANSITY COMPANY, LIMITED

Results of Operations for Test Year
Under Adopted Rates

Revenues	$4,660,200.00
Expenses:	
Total Expenses	$4,183,870.00
Costs Affected by mileage	2,690.00
Public Utility Tax	4,379.00
P.U.C. Fee	220.00
Total Expenses	$4,185,779.00
Net Before Income Taxes	474,421.00
Income Taxes	256,830.00
NET FOR RETURN	$ 217,591.00
Rate Base	$3,190,412.00
Rate of Return	6.82%
Operating Ratio	95.33%

D I S S E N T I N G   O P I N I O N

After considering the testimony and reviewing the exhibits in Docket No. 1375, the Application of Honolulu Rapid Transit Company, Limited for authority to increase their rates of fare and charges, I find myself in agreement with the majority of the Commission that the Company should be granted an increase in fare for the around-the-island tour together with authority to pay a $1.00 commission to the agents selling this tour.

I also agree with the majority that the staff report be accepted "in toto" and that the information with regard to Honolulu, Limited be accepted in evidence over the protest of the Applicant's counsel.

However, I do not agree with majority in setting the adult ticket rate of 5 tickets for 75¢. I am of the opinion that the adult ticket rate should be left at 2 for 30¢ and that the Company continue their operations with only the increase in the around-the-island tour rate.

I feel that increasing the ticket rate to 5 for 75¢ might possibly reduce the ticket utilization and might also cause a drop in riders. Although I heartily agree with the majority, that the ticket rate of 15¢ for the everyday rider should not be raised, the increase in the number of tickets required in order to realize the ticket rate might result in loss of riders.

The 1958 Annual Report of the Company, which includes the month of December 1958 at increased operating expenses shows it to be in a very good financial position. The operating ratio was 93.14% and a rate of return of 9.52% I consider both of these to be excessive.

I find that the Company, through this Application, is passing on to the rider the expenses incurred through the recently negotiated contract with their unions, the wages that they granted to the non-union employees and in addition, the increase of salaries granted their executives. Furthermore, they state that they desire to raise the dividend to the stockholder from 80¢ to $1.00 and this is also included in the amount of revenue that they estimate to be produced by the increase in rates applied for. This infers that they expect through this application, that the rider will pay all the increased cost assumed by management as of December 1, 1958. I certainly disagree with this thinking. I believe that some expenses of the Company should be assumed by the stockholders.

In 1954 when the Company came before the Commission to have certain lands taken out of the rate base and informed the Commission of their plan to form a subsidiary company, one of the reasons given for this action was that, through diversification, they would be able to increase the revenues to Honolulu Rapid Transit Company. This, they have not done. Listed in the assets of the Company is some 22,500 shares of stock issued as a result of this diversification idea upon which they received no income during the last four years. Now whether this investment is with an outside company or a wholly-owned subsidiary it seems to me that some revenue should have been derived.

I feel very definitely that the rates should remain the same as they were before the Application with the exception, of course, of the Around-the-Island Tour and that the additional expenses needed in the operation of the Company should be supplied by management through an increase in their advertising revenues, development of their charter service, development of further ride-shop plans, and any other ideas which would attract more riders.

Therefore, I agree with all phases of the Decision and Order except that of increasing the adult ticket rate to 5 for 75¢. I feel it should have been left at 2 for 30¢.

/s/ LEO G. LYCURGUS

Leo G. Lycurgus
Commissioner

SECURITIES AND EXCHANGE COMMISSION
Washington 25, D. C.

April 3, 1959

Public Utilities Commission
Territory of Hawaii
1311 Kapiolani Boulevard
Honolulu 14, T. H.

Attention: Mr. Jack E. Conley
Director

Gentlemen:

Thank you very much for your letter of March 31, 1959, with which you sent copies of recent decisions and orders of your Commission relating to the subject of our current proceedings on accounting for deferred income taxes. These orders form an interesting addition to our files on the subject.

Very truly yours,

Andrew Barr
Chief Accountant

IDAHO
Public Utilities Commission
Statehouse
Boise

February 24, 1959

Securities & Exchange Commission
425 2nd Street Northwest
Washington 25, D. C.

RE: Securities Act of 1933 -
       Release Nos. 4010 & 4023

Gentlemen:

Pursuant to Notice of Intention to Announce
Interpretation of Administrative Policy, Securities
Act of 1933 release No. 4010 and extension of time
for submitting comments on Notice of Intention to
Announce Interpretation of Administrative Policy
Securities Act of 1933 release No. 4023, the Idaho
Public Utilities Commission submits herewith views
and comments with respect to Release No. 4010.

Under the Statutes of the State of Idaho, the
Idaho Public Utilities Commission is charged with
the regulatory responsibility for the prescription
of accounting procedures for all privately owned
public utilities subject to its jurisdiction.

The adoption of the proposed policy puts companies which are under regulation as to accounting
in an untenable position. These companies are regulated as to their accounting procedures by both
State and Federal Commissions. The accounting as
prescribed by regulatory Commissions is of primary
importance to the rate payer and the investors
since the earnings and the amount which public utilities will be allowed to earn are directly and
clearly stated in the accounting practices of these
Commissions.

There is, of course, at present, some possibility of confusion where a company is regulated by both a State Commission and a Federal Commission. It is our understanding that the purpose of the Securities Act of 1933 is to require a full disclosure to the public. In the case of regulated utilities this purpose is best served by statements to the public in the form prescribed by regulatory Commissions provided that all possible effects on prospective purchasers of securities are fully disclosed, whether by footnote or otherwise.

Accounting regulations should not result in changing the effect of a post transaction which was properly accounted for at the time the transaction took place if it was made in accordance with all rules in effect. This retroactively affects the regulation and the stability of business enterprises which have previously managed their affairs according to existing practice. The alternative would create confusion not only for the companies and the investing public but for the regulatory Commissions in their primary responsibilities of rate regulation.

We therefore respectfully request that this Commission be allowed a period of time, not exceeding 15 minutes, to present a statement setting forth their position in this matter at the hearing on March 25, 1959, before your Commission.

Yours truly,

/s/ A. O. SHELDON

A. O. Sheldon
President

AOS:ji

IDAHO
Public Utilities Commission
Statehouse
Boise

March 20, 1959

Securities & Exchange Commission
Washington 25, D. C.

Gentlemen:

Pursuant to Release No. 4038, I am transmitting herewith three (3) copies of the Views and Comments of the Idaho Public Utilities Commission Relating to Notice of Intention to Announce Interpretation of Administrative Policy.

Yours truly,

/s/ IRENE A. ROSS

Irene A. Ross
Secretary

IAR:ji

UNITED STATES OF AMERICA

SECURITIES AND EXCHANGE COMMISSION

SECURITIES ACT OF 1933
Release Nos. 4010, 4023, and 4038

VIEWS AND COMMENTS OF THE IDAHO PUBLIC UTILITIES COMMISSION RELATING TO NOTICE OF INTENTION TO ANNOUNCE INTERPRETATION OF ADMINISTRATIVE POLICY

Pursuant to Notice of Intention to Announce Interpretation of Administrative Policy, Securities Act of 1933, Release No. 4010 and extension of time for submitting comments on Notice of Intention to Announce Interpretation of Administrative Policy, Securities Act 1933 Releases No. 4023, and 4038, the Idaho Public Utilities Commission submits herewith its view and comments with respect to Release No. 4010.

The Idaho Public Utilities Commission is a Commission of the government of the State of Idaho vested by statute with authority to regulate public utility companies in the State of Idaho. There is included in the statutes granting to the Commission its authority to regulate public utilities the specific provision for the Commission to establish a system of accounts to be kept by the public utilities subject to the Commission's jurisdiction or to classify these public utilities and to establish a system of accounts for each class and to prescribe the manner in which such accounts are to be kept. The statute required that where the Commission has prescribed a system of accounts for a utility it is thereafter unlawful for a public utility to keep any accounts, records or memoranda other than those prescribed by this Commission.

The Idaho Commission has been in existence since 1913 and has prescribed accounting systems for utilities under its jurisdiction for most of that time. On June 15, 1925, this Commission adopted the Uniform Classification of Accounts that had been developed by the National Association of Railway and Utilities Commissioners for the guidance of its members and for the purpose of assisting the members in formulation a classification of accounts for the use of utilities under their jurisdiction.

The primary function of a state regulatory Commission in its control of the activities of a public utility are generally limited to those matters which bear upon the rates to be charged, the service rendered, the securities to be issued and accounting. It is the function of a regulatory Commission to see that adequate and nondiscriminatory service, as well as reasonable and nondiscriminatory rates are rendered by a public utility or utilities under the Commission's jurisdiction.

Most State Commissions administer their primary function by prescribing reasonable and nondiscriminatory rates through uniform accounting procedures. One of the principal advantages which occurs from uniform accounting procedures is that of uniformity in reports, thus facilitating comparison as between utilities. A proper basis for comparison is necessary if full consideration and fair decisions are to be given these matters by the Commissions. Proper comparisons cannot be made between companies with regard to costs and efficiency or operating ratios unless the companies keep their accounts in the same manner. If the accounts differ greatly one company might charge a certain expenditure to one account while another company might charge the same expenditure to a different account, thus invalidating any comparisons. If correct information is available it is valuable not only from the Commissions viewpoint but also from the standpoint of management. Commissions, through the uniform classification of accounts, should know when a report is submitted, the contents of each item contained in the report and the nature of the expenditure of each item. The facts are immediately available for the regulatory body should cases arise involving rates, service, securities issues or similar matters.

It is for these reasons that State Commissions have prescribed or adopted uniform accounting procedures and in our opinion the adoption of the proposed policy by the Securities and Exchange Commission puts companies that are under regulation as to accounting in an untenable position. These companies are regulated as to their accounting procedures by both State and Federal Commissions. The accounting as prescribed by regulatory commissions is of primary importance to the rate payer and the investor. Since the earnings and the amount which public utilities will be allowed to earn are directly and clearly stated in the accounting practices of these Commissions.

Accounting regulations should not result in changing the effect of a past transaction which was properly accounted for at the time the transaction took place, if it was made in accordance with all rules then in effect. This retroactively affects the regulation and the stability of business enterprises which have previously managed their affairs according to existing practice. The alternative would create confusion not only for the companies and the investing public but for the State Commissions in their primary responsibilities of rate regulation.

In this respect there is one utility coming under the jurisdiction of the Idaho and the State of Washington Commissions that would be required to issue an additional $15,000,000 in Common Stock if the provisions contained in Release 4010 become effective. If this utility is to be required to issue additional Common Stock in such amounts, then it would have to request authority from the Idaho and Washington Commissions for increases in its rates in the approximate amount of $2,000,000 per year.

The Securities and Exchange Commission could, by the proposed action, force rate increase proceedings in every State similarly situated.

We submit that Accounting Release No. 4 should continue to govern the accounting for deferred taxes without imposition of a fixed or inflexible rule, or that regulated utilities be exempt from the provisions of Release 4010.

State of Illinois
William G. Stratton, Governor
ILLINOIS COMMERCE COMMISSION
160 North LaSalle Street
Chicago 1, Illinois

January 29, 1959

Mr. Orville L. DuBois
Secretary
Securities & Exchange Commission
Washington 25, D. C.

Dear Mr. DuBois:

In response to release #4010 under the Securities Act of 1933, we submit herewith as an indication of the position of this Commission, three (3) certified copies of a supplemental order entered on January 28, 1959, denying a request of the Union Electric Company for the cancellation of the original order requiring said company to account for future liability for deferred income taxes resulting from the use for tax purposes of the provisions of Section 167 of the Internal Revenue Code of 1954.

The possible exceptions (to the rule which you propose) as set forth in the first paragraph of page 2 and in footnote 3 of your release, are specifically referred to on page 12 of our order. You will also note that this Commission does not recognize any essential differences between the appropriate treatment of Sections 167 and 168 of the Internal Revenue Code. It may also be of interest to you that this Commission in several rate cases has allowed normalization of income taxes.

Sincerely yours,

/s/ GEORGE R. PERRINE

George R. Perrine
Chairman

GRP:KET:BT
Encl:

STATE OF ILLINOIS

ILLINOIS COMMERCE COMMISSION

In the matter of the Petition of
UNION ELECTRIC COMPANY for an order
authorizing appropriate accounting
entries with respect to deferred
federal income taxes resulting from
accelerated depreciation

No. 43748

SUPPLEMENTAL ORDER

By the Commission:

On September 3, 1958, Union Electric Company (hereinafter some-times called the "Company") filed its verified supplemental petition in the above entitled case (hereinafter sometimes called the "supplemental petition") with the Illinois Commerce Commission under the provisions of "An Act concerning Public Utilities", as amended, now in force in Illinois, which Act, as amended, is hereinafter called the "Illinois Public Utilities Act". By the supplemental petition the Company prays that a supplemental order be issued herein,

(1) canceling the provisions of Paragraphs A, B and C of the Order of the Commission dated December 19, 1956 in this Docket 43758 (hereinafter sometimes called the "original order"). Such paragraphs provide for accounting procedures with respect to facilities for which the Company shall have adopted for federal income tax purposes a method of accelerated depreciation authorized by Section 167 of the Internal Revenue Code of 1954, or any amendments thereto, or statuatory provisions in substitution therefor, thereafter enacted;

(2) authorizing the Company, with respect to all property additions for which it has exercised, or may exercise, its option to claim accelerated depreciation under Section 167 of the Internal Revenue Code of 1954, to record in its income account only its liability for current federal income taxes after giving effect to the exercise of such option; and

(3) authorizing the Company to transfer the balance in
its "Reserve for Federal Income Taxes — Accelerated Depreciation" as of December 31, 1957 to its earned surplus account, and to reverse all entries recorded in the year 1958
which shall have accounted for deferred federal income taxes
resulting from accelerated depreciation in accordance with the
methods authorized by the original order.

A hearing was held at the office of the Commission at Springfield,
Illinois, before a duly authorized Examiner of the Commission, at which
the Company presented its evidence in support of the supplemental petition, and the matter is now submitted to the Commission for disposition.

The Company is a corporation duly organized and existing under
and by virtue of the laws of the State of Missouri, with its principal executive office in the City of St. Louis, Missouri, and its registered office
within the State of Illinois in the Village of Monsanto, St. Clair County,
Illinois; it is a public utility within the meaning of Section 10, Article 1
of the Illinois Public Utilities Act; and is engaged in the business of
furnishing electric and gas utility services in the State of Illinois, electric
utility service in the State of Iowa, and electric and steam heating utility
services in the State of Missouri.

Upon petition filed by the Company in this proceeding on November 8,
1956, the Commission, by its original order herein, prescribed certain
accounting procedures to be followed with respect to deferred federal
income taxes resulting from accelerated depreciation on any of its properties
which the Company might elect to use accelerated depreciation under
Section 167 of the Internal Revenue Code of 1954. Briefly stated, such
accounting procedures provided (1) that the normal depreciation policies
of the Company for regulatory and general accounting purposes should not
be changed by reason of the adoption by it of accelerated depreciation for
federal income tax purposes; (2) that for each month as to which the Company determined that a deferral of federal income taxes results from the
use by it of accelerated depreciation, the Company should make provision
for its estimated future liability for additional federal income taxes by
debiting the amount of such provision to a new subaccount "Provision for
Deferred Federal Income Taxes — Accelerated Depreciation" and crediting
such amount to a new subaccount "Reserve for Deferred Federal Income

Taxes — Accelerated Depreciation''; and (3) in each month in which federal income taxes accrue as the result of the Company's prior use of accelerated depreciation for federal income tax purposes, a transfer should be made in amount equal to the Tax Addition (as defined in the original order) by debiting such amount to the subaccount "Reserve for Federal Income Taxes — Accelerated Depreciation" and crediting such amount to a new subaccount "Current Federal Income Taxes Deferred in Prior Years — Accelerated Depreciation".

Authority to account for such deferred federal income taxes in a manner similar to that authorized by this Commission, as outlined above, was also granted by the Missouri Public Service Commission by order dated December 13, 1956 in case No. 13531, with respect to properties of the Company subject to the jurisdiction of that Commission which might be made the basis of accelerated depreciation for federal income tax purposes. The State of Iowa has no regulatory commission with jurisdiction over the Company's accounts and accounting procedures.

The Company adopted the declining balance method of computing accelerated depreciation for federal income tax purposes effective as of January 1, 1955, and has followed, with respect thereto, the accounting procedures prescribed by the Missouri Public Service Commission and this Commission as above described. As of December 31, 1957, the Company had an accumulated credit balance in its subaccount "Reserve for Deferred Federal Income Taxes — Accelerated Depreciation" aggregating $1,545,000, of which the sum of $139,000 is applicable to properties within the State of Illinois. Between January 1, 1958 and July 31, 1958, the Company set up an additional $780,600 in such reserve, of which $72,300 is applicable to properties in Illinois.

In recent cases involving rate determinations, the Missouri Public Service Commission, which has jurisdiction over approximately 79% of the business of the Company, has announced a policy of allowing only the actual tax liability. In other words, for rate making purposes, the Missouri Public Service Commission does not recognize a deferral of federal income taxes as a result of claiming accelerated depreciation, and does not permit the utilities under its jurisdiction to include a component in their rates for utility services to provide a "Reserve for Deferred Federal Income Taxes — Accelerated Depreciation". However, since the Company commenced accumulating such reserves, the Company has not sought increased rates from either this Commission or the Missouri Public Service Commission and therefore the Company represents that the rates now being collected from its customers have not been affected in any way by the amounts debited to the "Provision for Deferred Federal Income Taxes — Accelerated Depreciation" and credited to the "Reserve for Deferred Federal Income Taxes — Accelerated Depreciation".

Deferrals result in greater future taxes

The Company by its original petition in this cause, and by the testimony of its witness and statements of counsel at the original hearing, very positively represented to the Commission that "the adoption of a method of accelerated depreciation for income tax purposes will result in deferring, with respect to the property affected, for a considerable period of time, substantial and increasing amounts of federal income taxes." The Company at that time requested authority to make a charge against income and a credit in corresponding amount to a reserve for deferred federal income taxes, to appear on the liability side of its balance sheet to reflect a future obligation for the payment of income taxes that would result by reason of future lesser depreciation deductions because of the greater current depreciation deductions. Petitioner's witness specifically recognized that the taking of accelerated depreciation in computing federal income taxes would have the result that "liability for payment of federal income taxes is decreased during the earlier years, and with decelerated deductions, such liability is increased during the later years as compared with straight-line depreciation." The said witness in speaking of the resulting current reductions in federal income taxes, said that "they are not a forgiveness of taxes" and further that "they merely constitute a deferral of taxes from the earlier to the later years." The Commission in its order authorizing the Company to establish certain accounts to record such deferral of taxes and in prescribing the rules for the use of such accounts, purposely used language to clearly establish that such accounting was specifically authorized to provide for actual liabilities, rather than merely a computed reduction of the current income tax. The Commission of course recognized that the amounts recorded would necessarily be estimates, but nevertheless the intent of the order is clear to the effect that such accounts were to be used (in the early years of the life of any unit of property) only to provide for real liabilities for taxes payable in the future.

Such language appears throughout the Commission's order of February 19, 1956 and is illustrated by the following portion of such accounting instructions pertaining to the initial (early period) accounting for deferred federal income taxes: "for each month as to which the Company <u>determines that any deferral of income taxes results</u> from the use by the Company for federal income tax purposes, of accelerated depreciation with respect to each year's property additions involved, the Company shall make a provision for <u>its estimated future liability</u> for additional federal income taxes due to the use of accelerated depreciation in such month". It appears, therefore, that the Company, by reason of its own definite statements and by reason of its acceptance of the Commission's order and the making of entries on its books in response to such order, has accepted as a basic fact, which appears to this Commission to be incontrovertible, the proposition, that, while federal income taxes in the earlier years of the use of accelerated depreciation will be smaller, <u>such taxes will be greater in the later years.</u>* (See Footnote)

Is This Problem Divisible by States? —
Uniformity Desirable

By its supplemental petition, filed herein, the testimony of its Vice President in support thereof, and a "Memorandum in re Supplemental Petition" submitted to the Commission on January 6, 1959 (subsequent to the hearing) summarizing its case, the Company takes the position that the approvals heretofore given by this Commission and the Public Service Commission of Missouri to the Company's original requests for amendment

---

*(Footnote)

In all of the representations by the Company and the discussions of this matter in the Commission's orders, it is assumed, for the purpose of clarity in reasoning, that the income tax rates remain the same. It is of course understood, in looking toward those future years, to which we here refer, that if the tax rates should be increased the aggregate effect would be to further increase the future liability resulting from the prior use of accelerated depreciation. A reduction in taxes would have the contra effect. We do not believe that we, here, need to discuss any problems related to variations in tax rates. The effect of changes in the income tax rates is a separate problem which has already been adequately provided for in the Commission's order of December 19, 1956.

and/or additions to the Uniform System of Accounts pertain, in each case, only to certain portions of its accounts as allocated in some manner to the respective states and coming under their respective jurisdictions. In this respect the supplemental petition differs from the Company's presentation in the original proceeding, in which no indication was made that the accounting for the deferred income taxes was a matter that was divisible by states but rather one that called for uniformity in the same manner that the System of Accounts, has been uniformly adopted by various states.

While this Commission recognizes divided jurisdiction as to rates of a public utility operating in two or more states and the necessity that, for the fixing of rates, the amounts recorded in accounts such as here under discussion, must properly be allocated to each state, the Commission is not convinced that the System of Accounts to be followed and the general financial reports to be issued by the utilities on the basis of which the utilities' stocks and bonds are offered to the public are matters on which two or more divergent rules can properly be applied. On such broad issues, vitally affecting the Company as a whole, it seems that there should be only one accounting rule which would be generally accepted in the accounting and financial world. The Company emphasizes the need for such uniformity.

In the present case substantial uniformity of the accounting requirements existed (until recently) by reason of the acceptance by the Public Service Commission of Missouri and this Commission, as logical and proper, the original views of the Company with respect to the accounts and accounting procedures substantially as expressed in this Commission's order of December 19, 1956. The Federal Power Commission has provided essentially identical accounts and procedures to be used if the utility records such deferred federal income taxes. The requirements of the Federal Power Commission differ from those of this Commission only in that the Federal Power Commission has not specifically required that such deferred taxes be recorded even through the utility uses accelerated depreciation for tax purposes.

The said three Commissions have also authorized substantially identical accounts and rules as desired by the Company for recording deferred federal income taxes resulting from accelerated amortization as elsewhere in this order set forth.

To date, this Commission has entered 25 orders for utilities prescribing the same accounting procedures as prescribed by this Commission's order of December 19, 1956 in this cause; 18 of them being for accelerated depreciation and 7 being for accelerated amortization.

This Commission concedes that unanimity is not infallible proof that the rule we have prescribed is the right one but such unanimity deserves serious consideration. Basically the propriety must be decided according to the correctness of the principles — as to whether the application of the rules prescribed will result in true statements of net income and the financial condition of the Company. After careful review of the underlying principles and logic of our several orders, we can only reaffirm the propriety thereof.

This uniformity, that has heretofore existed, has now been upset by the complete about-face of the Company, supported by an order entered by the Public Service Commission of Missouri (which the Company has interpreted in part as a permissive* order). By such reversal of position the Company would now denominate as "profits" and make available for dividends (to the extent not passed on to rate-payers) that which it previously claimed was an "expense"; and the cumulative amount which it previously stated was a real liability for future taxes would no longer appear on the balance sheet to warn future investors of deferred taxes. Furthermore, should the Company's present proposal result in the entire benefit of accelerated depreciation being either (a) effectively passed on to the public, or (b) only in part to the public and all the rest be distributed as dividends, there would remain no balance of such funds available for modernization and expansion of its property with resulting economic growth, increased production and a higher standard of living as contemplated by the Congress of the United States in the enactment of Sections 167 and 168 of the Internal Revenue Code of 1954.

The Company states that the reason for which it now repudiates the accounting principles previously so energetically supported is that the Public Service Commission of Missouri has adopted the rule of not recognizing deferred income taxes resulting from accelerated depreciation in

---

*Because of a variation proposed to be made by Company to agree with indicated objection by the staff of the Federal Power Commission

the process of fixing rates in that state. Thus the Company now definitely injects rate considerations into a problem which hitherto was specifically considered to be one of accounting, as clearly indicated by the orders entered by the Federal Power Commission, the Public Service Commission of Missouri and this Commission.

Matching of Current Expenses with Current Revenues

The Company represents that it has filed the supplemental petition herein and that it made a similar request of the Public Service Commission of Missouri (which request has been granted) because in its "opinion sound accounting principles require a matching of current expenses with current revenues and practices with respect to accelerated depreciation which would conform with the rate-making policies and requirements of the Commission." As already indicated these supplemental petitions were filed because of rate-making policies adopted by Missouri.

The Commission may agree with the general idea expressed by the Company as to matching expenses and revenues, but possibly such statement is not exactly correct. A more accurate statement would probably be that both revenues and expenses should be properly allocated to the period of time to which they pertain and that if that is done, the revenues and expenses would be properly matched. Thus the cost of generating and distributing electricity should be charged to the period in which it is generated, and the actual revenues earned from the sales thereof should be credited to the same period whether the regulatory commission has fixed the rates as requested by the utility or lower. This Commission does not believe that the simple fact that a Commission, in fixing rates lower than desired by the utility because it disregards some payments or charges found on the books of the utility in a certain period, necessarily means that such item should be charged to a different period of time. There may occasionally be expenditures made by utilities which the regulatory commission does not accept as a reasonable charge against the rate payer, but this does not shift the payment or the accounting therefor to another period which does not benefit from such item. By the present supplemental petition the Company proposes to omit the current accounting for income tax which would now be payable if accelerated depreciation were not taken, and then to charge the same to its expenses in a future period. This in our opinion does not match expenses properly to the period of time to which they relate.

Since the amount of the income tax in any period is conversely affected by the amount of the depreciation taken for income taxes rather than the charge for depreciation recorded on the books and reflected in the Company's financial statements, the Company by its suggested change, fails to match the proposed charge for income taxes with the book charge for depreciation. This failure to match two items of expense where the one is dependent upon the other, appears to us to be an unsound accounting principle and to result in misleading or inaccurate financial statements. The accounting prescribed by this Commission's order of December 19, 1956 in this cause does not entail such inconsistencies. Said order in our opinion properly matches costs and revenues.

As already mentioned, the Company in presenting its case, has made strong representations that it was seeking the proposed changes in, or cancellation of, the previous order of this Commission because in its opinion sound accounting principles require a matching of current expenses with current revenues. Such language is found in the Accounting Research Bulletin No. 44 (Revised) of July 1958, issued by the Committee on Accounting Procedure of the American Institute of Certified Public Accountants, which bulletin is referred to and partially quoted in the order of the Public Service Commission of Missouri, entered on August 29, 1958, dealing with the same matters now before this Commission, a copy of which order was submitted in evidence herein as the Company's Exhibit A. A careful reading of the entire bulletin indicates that in the main the Committee was of the opinion that "recognition of deferred income taxes in the general accounts is needed to obtain an equitable matching of costs and revenues, and to avoid income distortion even in those cases in which the payment of taxes is deferred for a relatively long period." The Committee however, appears to make a possible exception to such general rule but refers to such as "rare situations" and sets forth a condition that might be almost impossible to meet. The full paragraph from which the Missouri Commission has quoted a part, is as follows:

"Many regulatory authorities permit recognition of deferred income taxes for accounting and/or rate-making purposes, whereas some do not. The Committee believes that they should permit the recognition of deferred income taxes for both purposes. However, where charges for deferred income taxes are not allowed for rate-making purposes, accounting recognition need not be given to the deferment of taxes if it may reasonably be expected that increased future income taxes, resulting from the earlier deduction of declining-balance depreciation for income tax purposes only, will be allowed in future rate determinations.''

It appears to this Commission that it would be merely a hopeful guess by a utility that a Commission some time in the future would allow for rate-making the payment of income taxes in excess of otherwise normal income taxes resulting from savings in income taxes in earlier years, which may have been, in part or in whole, distributed as dividends. This Commission does not believe that it may reasonably be expected that such increased future income taxes will be allowed in future rate determinations.

Financial Statements Presented in Connection
With the Sale of Securities

This Commission is also very doubtful that the Securities and Exchange Commission will accept as a basis for the issuance of securities any financial statements which do not adequately reflect a liability for deferred income taxes in cases where the utility uses accelerated depreciation for income tax purposes. If the Securities and Exchange Commission should hold that such statements were misleading or inaccurate it would appear that the Company would be required to keep its books in the manner prescribed by this Commission's order of December 19, 1956 whether or not this Commission now grant the prayer of the Company to rescind such order.

Deferred Income Taxes — Amortization of
Emergency Facilities

Prior to the original application of the Company in this case, filed on November 8, 1956, the Company filed an essentially similar application (Docket 40815) for the establishment of certain accounts and accounting procedures in connection with the deferment of income taxes by reason of its availing itself for income tax purposes of accelerated amortization over a period of five years of certain emergency facilities designated by the Government to be in the interest of the common defense. A similar application was also filed with the Public Service Commission of Missouri.

Both that Commission and this Commission entered orders substantially alike granting the prayers of the Company. The accounting procedures in that matter are identical with those pertaining to accelerated depreciation, which is the subject of the present proceeding. Certain differences however exist which are entirely immaterial as far as the accounting procedures are concerned. Such differences include the fact that the cost of the emergency facilities may be completely amortized or written off in a period of five years, while the general property covered by accelerated depreciation must be depreciated over the estimated life thereof. It is interesting to note that every piece of property, acquired after 1953, which is involved under the program of amortization of emergency facilities is also depreciated under the provision for accelerated depreciation, for the reason that the Government granted the right of five year amortization only with respect to a certain percentage of the total cost of certain physical property. At the initial hearing on the Company's first application in this cause (Docket 43748) the Company's witness in comparing the then suggested accounting for the tax effect of acclerated depreciation with the accounting previously authorized for the tax effect of accelerated amortization stated that "the methods are generally similar. In each case there is a deferral of federal income taxes and the methods proposed are the same."

The Company by its supplemental petition herein is seeking the reversal only of this Commission's order pertaining to the accounting for the tax effect of accelerated depreciation. It is satisfied and desires to retain the similar accounting heretofore authorized with respect to the tax effect of the accelerated amortization. This Commission can see no sufficient reason for a difference in the accounting procedures as to the income tax effect of accelerated depreciation as against accelerated amortization.

The Company also requested authority from the Public Service Commission of Missouri to transfer the balance in its "Reserve for Federal Income Taxes — Accelerated Depreciation" as of December 31, 1957, to its earned surplus account, and to reverse all entries recorded in the year 1958 which shall have accounted for accelerated depreciation in accordance with the methods authorized by that Commission's order dated December 13, 1956 as above mentioned. Such authority was granted by the

Public Service Commission of Missouri by its supplemental order dated August 29, 1958, a copy of which was filed with the supplemental petition herein.

The Commission, having considered the supplemental petition and the evidence submitted in support thereof, and being fully advised in the premises, is of the opinion and finds:

(a) that the Commission has jurisdiction of the Company and of the subject matter of the verified supplemental petition herein;

(b) that the recitals of fact hereinabove set forth in this supplemental order are supported by evidence introduced in the record herein;

(c) that the use of the accounts and accounting procedures relating thereto prescribed by this Commission's order of December 19, 1956 will result in the charging of Federal Income Taxes to the appropriate period thus properly matching costs and revenues;

(d) that the adoption of the proposal of the Company as set forth in its supplemental petition herein would have the result that its accounts and financial statements would be misleading and inaccurate;

(e) that the principles involved in the accounting for the federal income tax effect of the use by the Company of accelerated depreciation are not different from the principles underlying the accounting for the federal income tax effect of the use by the Company of accelerated amortization as prescribed respectively by this Commission's initial orders in this cause, Docket 43748 and Docket 40815;

(f) that the prayers of the supplemental petition herein should be denied.

IT IS THEREFORE ORDERED by the Illinois Commerce Commission that the prayers of Union Electric Company as set forth in its supplemental petition herein filed on September 3, 1958, be, and they are hereby, denied.

By order of the Commission at Chicago, Illinois, this 28th day of January, 1959.

(Signed) SHERMAN H. CANTY

Secretary

(Seal)

STATE OF ILLINOIS
Illinois Commerce Commission

C E R T I F I C A T E

Re: 43748 - Supp.

I, SHERMAN H. CANTY, do hereby certify that I
am Secretary of the Illinois Commerce Commission
of the State of Illinois and keeper of the records
of said Commission.

I further certify that the above and foregoing
is a true, correct and complete copy of order made
and entered of record by said Commission on the
28th day of January, A. D. 1959.

Given under my hand and seal of said Illinois
Commerce Commission at Chicago, Illinois, this 29th
day of January, A. D. 1959.

/s/ SHERMAN H. CANTY

Sherman H. Canty
Secretary

SECURITIES AND EXCHANGE COMMISSION
Washington 25, D. C.

February 4, 1959

Honorable George R. Perrine
Chairman, Illinois Commerce Commission
160 North LaSalle Street
Chicago 1, Illinois

Dear Mr. Perrine:

Thank you very much for your letter of January 29, 1959, enclosing copies of your supplemental order in the matter of petition of Union Electric Company which relates to matters covered by our release No. 4010 under the Securities Act of 1933. Your comments and this material will be very helpful in our consideration of the problem.

Sincerely yours,

Andrew Barr
Chief Accountant

STATE OF NEW YORK
Public Service Commission
199 Church Street
New York 7

January 27, 1959

Mr. Orval L. DuBois, Secretary
Securities and Exchange Commission
Washington 25, D. C.

Dear Mr. DuBois:

Receipt is acknowledged of the release of
December 30, 1958 entitled "NOTICE OF INTENTION
TO ANNOUNCE INTERPRETATION OF ADMINISTRATIVE PO-
LICY" (Securities Act of 1933 Release No. 4010;
Securities Exchange Act of 1934 Release No. 5844;
Public Utility Holding Company Act of 1935 Re-
lease No. 13894; Investment Company Act of 1940
Release No. 2814). It is assumed that ample no-
tice will be given of public hearings on the sub-
ject when scheduled by your Commission.

Very truly yours,

/s/ ALTON G. MARSHALL

Alton G. Marshall
Secretary

STATE OF OREGON
Public Utility Commissioner
Salem

February 25, 1959

In Reply Please Refer
To File No. 15570

Securities and Exchange Commission,
Washington 25, D. C.

Re: Securities Act Release No. 4010.

Gentlemen:

It is our understanding that the new Interpretation of Administrative Policy proposed to be
made by the Commission, as noticed in its Securities Act Release No. 4010, dated December 30, 1958,
is predicated on a tentative finding that the inclusion in earned surplus of amounts representing
deferred income taxes which have been restricted
results in an "inaccurate and misleading" financial
statement. According to the release, this is the
Commission's position regardless of whether or not
the restriction is explained by an appropriate
footnote.

We have from time to time examined the Registration Statements of Pacific Power & Light Company
filed with your Commission under the Securities
Act of 1933, as amended. It is our opinion that
the financial statements and footnotes used to disclose that Company's treatment of deferred taxes
accurately and fully set forth all material facts.
It is our understanding that footnotes similar to
those used by the Pacific Company have been required to the balance sheets of other registrants
with similar situations. The jurisdiction of this
office extends to the issuance of securities by
privately owned electric utilities. We, too, are
concerned with adequate disclosure and seek to

protect against misleading financial statements.
In Oregon when we exercise this jurisdiction, we
perform with respect to utilities substantially
the same functions as would be performed by the Corporation Commissioner under the Oregon Securities
Act with respect to other issuers.

　　We have concluded that in the circumstances,
and so far as the utilities subject to the jurisdiction of this Commission are concerned, the present practice is not "inaccurate or misleading"
and, accordingly, this proposed new Interpretation
of Administrative Policy appears to us unnecessary
and inappropriate.

　　　　　　　　　　　Very truly yours,

　　　　　　　　　　　/s/ JONEL C. HILL

　　　　　　　　　　　JONEL C. Hill,
　　　　　　　　　　　Public Utility
　　　　　　　　　　　Commissioner of Oregon.

JCH:GH

STATE OF WASHINGTON
Washington Public Service Commission
Olympia

January 26, 1959

VIA AIR MAIL

Honorable Edward N. Gadsby
Chairman, Securities and Exchange Commission
Washington 25, D. C.

Dear Mr. Gadsby:

This is in reference to Security and Exchange
Commission release dated December 30, 1958, entitled "Notice of Intention to Announce Interpretation of Administrative Policy."

It is not entirely clear to this Commission
the full scope and intent of the interpretation set
forth in this release.

From the preliminary study by the staff of
this Commission, it appears that the interpretations
set forth in this release could have far-reaching
and significant effect on consumers of some of the
utilities under the jurisdiction of this Commission.
Due to the extraordinary work load at the present,
the staff of this Commission will not be able to
give this matter the thorough study it should have
by January 31, 1959.

Therefore, it is requested that an extension
of time of at least two (2) months, or until March
31, 1959, be given for interested parties to submit written views and comments on this matter.

Sincerely yours,

/s/ FRANCIS PEARSON

Francis Pearson
Chairman

FP:s

SECURITIES AND EXCHANGE COMMISSION
Washington 25, D. C.

January 30, 1959

Honorable Francis Pearson
Chairman, Washington Public Service Commission
Insurance Building
Olympia, Washington

Dear Mr. Pearson:

This is in reply to your letter of January
26, 1959, requesting an extension of time to submit written views and comments on our proposal
regarding the balance sheet treatment of the credit
equivalent to the reduction in federal income
taxes.

The enclosed release, published in response
to several requests, extends the time for comment
and announces a hearing on our proposal. It was
the staff's opinion that the time allowed for
written comment coupled with the additional time
to the date for the hearing should be ample for
all parties to prepare their responses to the proposals.

Your comments on the proposal will be appreciated and will be given careful attention.

Very truly yours,

Edward N. Gadsby
Chairman

Enclosure

STATE OF WASHINGTON
John J. O'Connell
Attorney General
Olympia, Washington

February 25, 1959

Securities & Exchange Commission
Washington 25, D. C.

   Attention: Orval L. DuBois, Secretary

   Re: Securities Act of 1933 Release Nos.
     4010 and 4023, Interpretation of
     Administrative Policy

Gentlemen:

   In accordance with Release No. 4023 dated
January 28, 1959, we wish to advise that the undersigned, Mr. David S. Black, Assistant Attorney
General of the State of Washington, intends to
appear on behalf of the Washington Public Service
Commission at the hearing beginning on March 25,
1959 in Washington, D. C., to present the views of
the Washington Public Service Commission relating
to the captioned matter. It is respectfully requested that twenty minutes' time be alloted for
such presentation.

   Enclosed herewith in triplicate and with
attachments is the statement of views of the Washington Public Service Commission relating hereto.

      Very truly yours,

      John J. O'Connell
      Attorney General

      /s/ DAVID S. BLACK

      David S. Black
DSB:iw   Assistant Attorney General
Enc

UNITED STATES OF AMERICA

Securities and Exchange Commission

SECURITIES ACT OF 1933
Release No. 4010 and 4023

STATEMENT OF VIEWS OF WASHINGTON PUBLIC
SERVICE COMMISSION RELATING TO NOTICE
OF INTENTION TO ANNOUNCE INTERPRETATION
OF ADMINISTRATIVE POLICY

The Washington Public Service Commission by
its orders Nos. U-8616 and U-8620 dated respectively January 30, 1953 and March 10, 1953, established
certain accounting procedures to be followed by
the Pacific Power & Light Co., a Maine corporation,
and the Washington Water Power Co., a Washington
corporation, both doing Washington intrastate
business as electric utility companies and under
regulatory jurisdiction of the Washington Public
Service Commission. The said orders, copies of
which are attached hereto and by this reference
incorporated herein, direct the accounting treatment to be followed by the respective utility companies with respect to tax deferment resulting
from the accelerated amortization of certain depreciable investments for Federal income tax purposes,
as permitted by Section 168 of the Internal Revenue
Code of 1954 and the defense production administration. It is the position of the Washington Public
Service Commission that this accounting treatment
is in all respects proper, and is not misleading
or inaccurate.

Also attached hereto and by this reference
incorporated herein is a copy of a letter from the
Washington Public Service Commission to Mr. Robert

D. Yeomans, Secretary of the Washington Water Power
Co. dated December 1, 1958, setting forth the procedure for an electric utility to account for reduced taxes due to liberalized depreciation as permitted by Section 167 of the 1954 Revenue Code.
It is the position of the Washington Public Serviee
Commission that the accounting treatment as set
forth in the said letter is in all respects proper
and is not misleading or inaccurate.

/s/ WESLEY L. BARCLIFT

Wesley L. Barclift
Executive Secretary

BEFORE THE WASHINGTON PUBLIC SERVICE COMMISSION

In the Matter of the Accounting Treatment for Pacific Power & Light Company to Record the Tax Deferment Resulting from the Accelerated Amortization of Certain Depreciable Investment for Federal Income Tax Purposes as Permitted by the Defense Production Administration per Necessity Certificate No. TA-NC-2617	CAUSE NO. U 8616 ORDER DIRECTING ACCOUNTING TREATMENT

Pacific Power & Light Company (company) was issued June 9, 1951, a Necessity Certificate No. TA-NC-2617 by the Defense Production Administration of the Federal Government under the terms of which the company was authorized to amortize over a 5-year period 75% of the depreciable cost of its Yale Hydroelectric Project for Federal tax on income purposes.

Recommendations have been made by the staff to this Commission relative to the accounting, particular to this situation, and after correspondence and conferences between members of the company and this Commission, agreement has been reached in the methods to be followed.

Substantially, the accounting treatment to be used by the company as will be ordered hereinafter is as follows:

I. During the 60-month period of rapid amortization:

    (a) Income statements and net income transfers to earned surplus shall reflect actual Federal tax on income liability which computes as applicable to net taxable income after the application of the tax benefit resulting from the accelerated amortization.

    (b) Federal taxes on income as stated actually on income statements shall be footnoted as per Appendix A-I attached hereto to reveal the estimated portion of tax deferment associated with the statement period due to the benefit of accelerated amortization.

(c) Transfers to earned surplus shall be divided as follows:

   (1) That portion which is equivalent to the estimated defer-
       ment of Federal tax on income due to accelerated
       amortization shall be credited to Account 271.1,
       "Earned Surplus — Restricted (Amount of Federal
       Income Taxes Deferred Due to Accelerated Amorti-
       zation of Certain Facilities)."

   (2) That portion which remains shall be credited to Ac-
       count 271, "Earned Surplus." The balance in Account
       271.1 is restricted as to distribution for dividends and
       to any other distribution except as will be set forth
       hereinafter. Financial statements prepared by the com-
       pany at any time a balance is reflected in Account 271.1
       shall set forth this balance separately and shall foot-
       note this account to read as indicated in Appendix A-II
       attached hereto.

II. After the expiration of the 60-month rapid amortization period:

   (a) Income statements and transfers of net income to earned sur-
       plus shall reflect actual Federal tax on income liability,
       which computes from the net taxable income having re-
       flected therein no benefit from the fully amortized invest-
       ment.

   (b) Federal taxes on income as reported actually for the state-
       ment period shall be footnoted as indicated in Appendix
       A-III attached hereto and shall reveal the estimated amount
       of the deferred Federal tax on income which is included
       within the statement, and which is an excess due to the
       earlier complete amortization of the depreciable investment.

   (c) Net income transfers to earned surplus shall be in total to
       Account 271. Further, an amount equal to 1/12 of 1/25 of
       the total balance accumulated in Account 271.1 at the
       expiration of the 60-month rapid amortization period shall
       be transferred each month to Account 271 until the total

accumulation in Account 271.1 is exhausted. The footnote as set forth in Appendix A-II attached, shall be continued with all financial statements rendered until the balance in Account 271.1 is exhausted.

The company has entered into agreement with this Commission, and has so stipulated as included in Appendix B hereof, that for each of the 25 years following the expiration of the 60-month period of accelerated amortization, in so far as such years may be involved in any proceeding before the Commission affecting the company's electric rates, the company will credit to its operating revenue deductions for Federal income taxes as shown on its books of account, one twenty-fifth (1/25) of the total amount by which its Federal income taxes were reduced by reason of such accelerated amortization.

FINDINGS

Being fully advised in the premises, and based upon the facts and the law, the Commission now concludes and finds as follows:

1. Pacific Power & Light Company, a Maine corporation, renders electric service for hire in the State of Washington as an electrical company and as a public service company, is subject to the jurisdiction of this Commission.

2. Section 80.04.080 RCW authorizes this Commission to establish uniform systems of accounts for public service companies, and permits thereby the jurisdiction of this Commission over special accounting treatment relative to special situations.

ORDER

IT IS THEREFORE ORDERED:

1. That Pacific Power & Light Company will proceed with the accounting for the deferment of Federal taxes on income due to the accelerated amortization of certain of its depreciable investment as outlined in the body of this order.

2. That Pacific Power & Light Company will afix footnotes as referred to in the body of this order and as attached hereto in Appendix A to all income and financial statements rendered during the effective period of this order.

3. That the effective period of this order shall commence with the first month during which the Pacific Power & Light Company avails itself of the tax benefit of the accelerated amortization, in its computation of Federal income tax liability, and shall continue for a period of thirty (30) years thereafter.

4. That Pacific Power & Light Company will submit in writing within sixty (60) days of the date of this order, a statement declaring the date upon which the company first availed itself of such tax benefits.

DATED at Olympia, Washington, and effective this 30th day of January, 1953.

WASHINGTON PUBLIC SERVICE COMMISSION

JEROME K. KUYKENDALL, Chairman

JOSEPH STARIN, Commissioner

E. W. ANDERSON, Commissioner

Explanatory Footnote to Income and Financial
Statements to be Rendered by the Company During the
Effective Period of this Order

I. Footnote Applicable to Income Statements During 60-month Amortization Period

The amount deducted for Federal income taxes reflects a deferred amount of Federal income taxes for the period covered by the statement, resulting from the application in such period of its prorated part of the accelerated amortization, over a period of 60 months beginning with the month of   , 1953, of approximately $ of the cost of the Yale Hydroelectric Project, as authorized by Necessity Certificate No. TA-NC-2617 issued by Defense Production Administration pursuant to Section 124A of the Internal Revenue Code. The amount of such deferred Federal income taxes applicable to the period covered by the income statement is estimated to be $, and the amounts shown on the income statement as a deduction for Federal income tax and as total operating revenue deductions are therefore less by said estimated amount, and the amounts shown on the statement as gross income and net income are therefore greater by said amount, than would have been shown in said statement had the company not elected to apply such accelerated amortization.

II. Footnote Applicable to Financial Statements

Surplus is also restricted by an order of the Washington Public Service Commission, dated January 30, 1953, which requires the company, (1) during the 60-month period when it claims accelerated amortization of 75% of the depreciable cost of its Yale Hydroelectric Project, to accumulate the amounts by which Federal income taxes are reduced by reason of said accelerated amortization in an account designated Account 271.1, Earned Surplus — Restricted (Amount of Federal Income Taxes Deferred Due to Accelerated Amortization of Certain Facilities) by bookkeeping entries to be made each month during said 60-month period, charging to Earned Surplus and concurrently crediting to said Earned Surplus — Restricted account the amount of such tax reduction pertaining to such month's operations; and (2) provides that the total of the Earned Surplus — Restricted, so accumulated in said 60-month period, may be transferred to Earned Surplus during the 25-year period immediately following said 60-month period by bookkeeping entries to be made each month during said 25-year period, charging to said Earned Surplus — Restricted, and crediting to Earned Surplus, one-twelfth (1/12th) of one twenty-fifth (1/25th) of the total amount by which Federal income taxes were reduced by reason of such accelerated amortization.

The amount so credited to earned surplus restricted for the current month is $, for the 12-month period ending with the current month is $, and the total accumulated amount to date is $

III. Footnote Applicable to Income Statements After Amortization Period

The amount deducted for Federal income taxes on the attached statement reflects a deferred amount of Federal income taxes for the period covered by the statement, resulting from the application in such period of its prorated part of the accelerated amortization, over a period of 60 months beginning with the month of   , 1953, of approximately $ of the cost of the Yale Hydroelectric Project, as authorized by Necessity Certificate No. TA-NC-2617 issued by Defense Production Administration pursuant to Section 124A of the Internal Revenue Code. The amount of such deferred Federal income tax applicable to the period covered by the income statement is estimated to be $, and the amounts shown on the income statement as a deduction for Federal income tax and as total operating revenue deductions are therefore more by said estimated amount, and the amounts shown on the statement as gross income and net income are therefore less by said amount than would have been shown in said statement had the company not elected to apply such accelerated amortization.

BEFORE THE WASHINGTON PUBLIC SERVICE COMMISSION

Accounting Treatment for Rate Making Purposes of Temporary Reductions in Federal Income Taxes Resulting from Accelerated Amortization of Yale Hydroelectric Project	STIPULATION OF PACIFIC POWER & LIGHT COMPANY

Pacific Power & Light Company (Pacific) is a public service company within the meaning of RCW 80.04.010. Pacific is engaged primarily in the business of generating, purchasing, transmitting, distributing, and selling electric energy in the states of Washington and Oregon. As a public service company operating within the State of Washington, its electric rates are subject to regulation by the Washington Public Service Commission. Because its accounting treatment for federal income tax purposes may have an important bearing on future proceedings before the Commission involving the Company's electric rates in the State of Washington, Pacific represents, agrees and stipulates as follows, namely:

(a) Pacific has substantially completed its 108,000 kilowatt Yale Hydroelectric Project on the Lewis River in the State of Washington. The Yale Project was financed at an estimated cost of $33,000,000 with proceeds, in part, from the issuance and sale of securities expressly authorized to be sold by the Washington Public Service Commission, namely:

$13,500,000 of the $16,100,000 in principal amount of 3½% notes under Credit Agreement dated May 18, 1951

Washington Commission Cause No. U-8448, Order dated June 1, 1951

250,000 shares of Common Stock, no par value, net proceeds $3,363,800

Washington Commission Cause No. U-8461, Order dated July 17, 1951

200,000 shares of Common Stock, no par value, net proceeds $3,095,000

Washington Commission Cause No. U-8502, Order dated January 7, 1952

$12,500,000 principal amount First Mortgage Bonds

Washington Commission Cause No. U-8504, Order dated January 30, 1952

$7,500,000 principal amount First Mortgage Bonds

Washington Commission Cause No. U-8565, Order dated August 20, 1952

(b) The issuance and sale of the foregoing securities, from which Pacific realized aggregate net proceeds of approximately $40,000,000 was in each case also expressly authorized by the Public Utilities Commissioner of Oregon, the Federal Power Commission; and all of the securities, except the notes, were registered with the Securities and Exchange Commission. The issuance of such securities increased the capitalization of Pacific by approximately 65%.

(c) The construction of the Yale Hydroelectric Project was undertaken as a defense project with the support and assistance of the Federal government to provide additional power for essential industries served by the Northwest Power Pool. The addition of the Yale Project to Pacific's facilities increased its plant account by approximately 40%.

(d) All the securities of Pacific issued subsequently to May 18, 1951, approximating $40,000,000, were sold on the basis and with the knowledge by the purchasers of such securities that a necessity certifi- under Section 124A of the Internal Revenue Code had been issued to Pacific and that Pacific would be permitted to realize all of the benefits of such certificate. Such a certificate, Necessity Certificate No. TA-NC-2617, was issued by the Defense Production Administration to Pacific on June 9, 1951. Under the terms of this certificate, Pacific is authorized for federal income tax purposes to amortize over a period of 5 years 75% of the total depreciable cost of the Yale Project. During each of these years Pacific estimates that, by applying such accelerated amortization on the Yale Project, its federal income taxes, assuming a continuance of present tax rates, will be temporarily reduced by approximately $2,000,000 per year. The cash made available from such temporarily reduced income taxes will be applied by Pacific toward the repayment of the $13,500,000 principal amount of notes, and so long as such notes are outstanding (until 1961) no part of such temporary reductions in taxes can be paid out in the form of dividends.

(e) Pacific realized that the sale of debt securities in connection with the financing of the Yale Project would temporarily lower its equity ratio, but that such ratio, however, would rapidly be restored through the retirement of the notes with funds made available from tax deferments. This necessarily assumed that the tax deferments would be reflected in Pacific's net income and carried through to its surplus. The temporary lowering of the equity ratio by any failure to carry such savings through net income to surplus would, by reason of certain provisions in Pacific's by-laws, probably make it impossible for Pacific to maintain a reasonable dividend rate on its Common Stock. Such a failure would be a serious breach of good faith with the purchasers and the owners of such stock, and would work to the serious disadvantage of Pacific's customers and the investors in its securities.

(f) It is realized that the effect of the proposed accounting for the tax deferrals will be to show an increase in Pacific's earnings as reflected on its income statements by the amount of such tax deferrals during the 60-month period of accelerated amortization and a decrease following the period of accelerated amortization because of resulting increased federal income taxes then to be payable. In the circumstances above mentioned, and particularly because of the necessity of using the cash thus made available to pay the notes under the loan agreement mentioned in paragraph (d), it is neither feasible nor equitable that electric customers during the 60-month period of accelerated amortization be favored at the expense of electric customers in the years following such 60-month period. The accounting treatment of such tax deferrals herein provided for will assure equity in respect thereof to electric customers in both periods.

(g) Based on the foregoing, PACIFIC HEREBY STIPULATES AND AGREES, that for each of the 25 years following the expiration of the 60-month period of accelerated amortization insofar as such years may be involved in any proceeding before the Commission affecting Pacific's electric rates, Pacific will credit to its operating revenue deductions for federal income taxes as shown on its books of account, one twenty-fifth (1/25) of the total amount by which its federal income taxes were reduced by reason of such accelerated amortization.

Portland, Oregon, January 28, 1953.

PACIFIC POWER & LIGHT COMPANY

By /s/ D. R. McCLUNG

D. R. McClung
Executive Vice President

ATTEST:

(Seal)

/s/ H. W. MILLAY

H. W. Millay
Secretary

BEFORE THE WASHINGTON PUBLIC SERVICE COMMISSION

In the Matter of the Accounting Treatment for The Washington Water Power Company to Record the Tax Deferment Resulting from the Accelerated Amortization of Certain Depreciable Investment for Federal Income Tax Purposes as Permitted by the Defense Production Administration per Necessity Certificate No. TA-NC-9077	CAUSE NO. U-8620 ORDER DIRECTING ACCOUNTING TREATMENT

The Washington Water Power Company (company) was issued December 7, 1951, a Necessity Certificate No. TA-NC-9077 by the Defense Production Administration of the Federal Government under the terms of which the company was authorized over a 5-year period 65% of the depreciable cost of its Cabinet Gorge Hydroelectric Project for Federal tax on income purposes.

Recommendations have been made by the staff to this Commission relative to the accounting, particular to this situation, and after correspondence and conferences between members of the company and this Commission, agreement has been reached in the methods to be followed.

Substantially, the accounting treatment to be used by the company as will be ordered hereinafter is as follows:

1. During the 60-month period of rapid amortization:

   (a) Income statements and net income transfers to earned surplus shall reflect actual Federal tax on income liability which computes as applicable to net taxable income after the application of the tax benefit resulting from the accelerated amortization.

   (b) Federal taxes on income as stated actually on income statements shall be footnoted as per Appendix A-I attached hereto to reveal the estimated portion of tax deferment associated with the statement period due to the benefit of accelerated amortization.

(c) Transfers to earned surplus shall be divided as follows:

(1) That portion which is equivalent to the estimated deferment of Federal tax on income due to accelerated amortization shall be credited to Account 271.1, "Earned Surplus — Restricted (Amount of Federal Income Taxes Deferred Due To Accelerated Amortization of Certain Facilities)."

(2) That portion which remains shall be credited to Account 271, "Earned Surplus." The balance in Account 271.1 is restricted as to distribution for dividends and to any other distribution except as will be set forth hereinafter. Financial statements prepared by the company at any time a balance is reflected in Account 271.1 shall set forth this balance separately and shall footnote this account to read as indicated in Appendix A-II attached hereto.

II. After the expiration of the 60-month rapid amortization period:

(a) Income statements and transfers of net income to earned surplus shall reflect actual Federal tax on income liability, which computes from the net taxable income having reflected therein no benefit from the fully amortized investment.

(b) Federal taxes on income as reported actually for the statement period shall be footnoted as indicated in Appendix A-III attached hereto and shall reveal the estimated amount of the deferred Federal tax on income which is included within the statement, and which is an excess due to the earlier complete amortization of the depreciable investment.

(c) Net income transfers to earned surplus shall be in total to Account 271. Further, an amount equal to 1/12 of 1/25 of the total balance accumulated in Account 271.1 at the expiration of the 60-month rapid amortization period shall be transferred each month to Account 271 until the total accumulation in Account 271.1 is exhausted. The footnote as set forth in Appendix A-II attached, shall be continued with all financial statements rendered until the balance in Account 271.1 is exhausted.

The company has entered into agreement with this Commission, and has so stipulated as included in Appendix B hereof, that for each of the 25 years following the expiration of the 60-month period of accelerated amortization, in so far as such years may be involved in any proceeding before the Commission affecting the company's electric rates, the company will credit to its operating revenue deductions for Federal income taxes as shown on its books of account, one twenty-fifth (1/25) of the total amount by which its Federal income taxes were reduced by reason of such accelerated amortization.

FINDINGS

Being fully advised in the premises, and based upon the facts and the law, the Commission now concludes and finds as follows:

1. The Washington Water Power Company, a Washington corporation, renders electric service for hire in the State of Washington as an electrical company and as a public service company, and is subject to the jurisdiction of this Commission.

2. Section 80.04.080 RCW authorizes this Commission to establish uniform systems of accounts for public service companies, and permits thereby the jurisdiction of this Commission over special accounting treatment relative to special situations.

ORDER

IT IS THEREFORE ORDERED:

1. That The Washington Water Power Company will proceed with the accounting for the deferment of Federal taxes on income due to the accelerated amortization of certain of its depreciable investment as outlined in the body of this order.

2. That The Washington Water Power Company will affix footnotes as referred to in the body of this order and as attached hereto in Appendix A to all income and financial statements rendered during the effective period of this order.

3. That the effective period of this order shall commence with the first month during which The Washington Water Power Company avails itself of the tax benefit of the accelerated amortization, in its computation of Federal income tax liability, and shall continue for a period of thirty (30) years thereafter.

4. That The Washington Water Power Company will submit in writing within sixty (60) days of the date of this order, a statement declaring the date upon which the company first availed itself of such tax benefits.

DATED at Olympia, Washington, and effective this 10th day of March, 1953.

WASHINGTON PUBLIC SERVICE COMMISSION

JEROME K. KUYKENDALL, Chairman

JOSEPH STARIN, Commissioner

E. W. ANDERSON, Commissioner

Appendix A-I

Note Applicable to Income Statements
During 60-Month Amortization Period

The amount deducted for Federal income taxes reflects a deferred amount of Federal income taxes for the period covered by the statement, resulting from the application in such period of its prorated part of the accelerated amortization, over a period of 60 months beginning with the month of January, 1953, of 65% of the depreciable cost of the Cabinet Gorge Project as determined by the Commissioner of Internal Revenue. The authorization is identified as Necessity Certificate No. TA-NC-9077 issued by the Defense Production Administration pursuant to Section 124A of the Internal Revenue Code. The amount of such deferred Federal income taxes applicable to the period covered by the income statement is estimated to be $, and the amounts shown on the income statement as a deduction for Federal income tax and as total operating revenue deductions are therefore less by said estimated amount, and the amounts shown on the statement as gross income and net income are therefore greater by said amount, than would have been shown in said statement had the company not elected to apply such accelerated amortization.

NOTES TO FINANCIAL STATEMENTS

Surplus is restricted by an order of the Washington Public Service Commission, dated March 10, 1953, which requires the company, (1) during the 60-month period when it claims accelerated amortization of 65% of the depreciable cost of its Cabinet Gorge Hydroelectric Project, to accumulate the amounts by which Federal income taxes are reduced by reason of said accelerated amortization in an account designated Account 271.1, Earned Surplus — Restricted (Amount of Federal Income Taxes Deferred Due to Accelerated Amortization of Certain Facilities), by bookkeeping entries to be made each month during said 60-month period, charging to Earned Surplus and concurrently crediting to said Earned Surplus — Restricted, account the amount of such tax reduction pertaining to such month's operations; and (2) provides that the total of the Earned Surplus — Restricted, so accumulated in said 60-month period may be transferred to Earned Surplus during the 25-year period immediately following said 60-month period by bookkeeping entries to be made each month during said 25-year period, charging to said Earned Surplus — Restricted, and crediting to Earned Surplus, one-twelfth (1/12th) of one twenty-fifth (1/25th) of the total amount by which Federal income taxes were reduced by reason of such accelerated amortization.

The amount of such restriction as at the date of this financial statement is $

Appendix A-III

Note Applicable to Income Statements
After Amortization Period

The amount deducted for Federal income taxes on the attached statement reflects a deferred amount of Federal income taxes for the period covered by the statement, resulting from the application in such period of its prorated part of the accelerated amortization, over a period of 60 months beginning with the month of January, 1953, of 65% of the depreciable cost of the Cabinet Gorge Project as determined by the Commissioner of Internal Revenue. The authorization is identified as Necessity Certificate No. TA-NC-9077 issued by Defense Production Administration pursuant to Section 124A of the Internal Revenue Code. The amount of such deferred Federal income tax applicable to the period covered by the income statement is estimated to be $, and the amounts shown on the income statement as a deduction for Federal income tax and as total operating revenue deductions are therefore more by said estimated amount, and the amounts shown on the statement as gross income and net income are therefore less by said amount than would have been shown in said statement had the company not elected to apply such accelerated amortization.

BEFORE THE WASHINGTON PUBLIC SERVICE COMMISSION

Accounting Treatment for Rate Making Purposes of Temporary Reductions in Federal Income Taxes Resulting from Accelerated Amortization of Cabinet Gorge Hydroelectric Project	STIPULATION OF THE WASHINGTON WATER POWER COMPANY

The Washington Water Power Company (Washington) is a public service company within the meaning of RCW 80.04.010. Washington is engaged primarily in the business of generating, purchasing, transmitting, distributing and selling electric energy in the states of Washington and Idaho. As a public service company operating within the State of Washington, its electric rates are subject to regulation by the Washington Public Service Commission. Because its accounting treatment for federal income tax purposes may have an important bearing on future proceedings before the Commission involving the Company's electric rates in the State of Washington, Washington represents, agrees and stipulates as follows:

(a) Washington has substantially completed its 200,000 kilowatt Cabinet Gorge Hydroelectric Project on the Clark Fork River in the State of Idaho. The Cabinet Gorge Project was financed at an estimated cost of $46,000,000 with proceeds in part from temporary bank loans, a portion of which were repaid out of the proceeds from the sale of $30,000,000 First Mortgage Bonds October 1, 1952. There will be outstanding and maturing June 30, 1953 additional bank loans amounting to $25,000,000. It is the present intention of the Company to issue $10,000,000 First Mortgage Bonds and the balance in debentures to repay these bank loans.

(b) The construction of the Cabinet Gorge Hydroelectric Project was undertaken as a defense project with the support and assistance of the Federal government to provide additional power for essential industries served by the Northwest Power Pool. The addition of the Cabinet Gorge Project to Washington's facilities increased its plant account by approximately 54%.

(c) A necessity certificate under Section 124A of the Internal Revenue Code was issued to Washington by the Defense Production Administration. The certificate is identified as Necessity Certificate No. TA-9077, dated December 7, 1951. Under the terms of this certificate, Washington is authorized for federal income tax purposes to amortize over a period of 5 years 65% of the total depreciable cost of the Cabinet Gorge Project. During each of these years Washington estimates that, by applying such accelerated amortization on the Cabinet Gorge Project, its federal income taxes, assuming a continuance of present tax rates, will be temporarily reduced by approximately $2,600,000 per year. The cash made available from such temporarily reduced income taxes will be applied by Washington toward the repayment of debt or used for the construction, extension or improvement of the Company's facilities in connection with its construction program. To the extent such cash is added to cash generated through the Company's retirement reserve and surplus funds to carry on its normal construction program, the Company will be relieved from incurring additional debt.

(d) Washington realizes that the sale of debt securities in connection with the financing of the Cabinet Gorge Project will temporarily lower its equity ratio, but that such ratio, however, will be restored through the retirement of the debentures with funds made available from tax deferments to approximately 55% at the end of the amortization period. This is a step toward correcting the high percentage of long term debt referred to in the Commission's Order No. U-8569, Granting Application to issue $30,000,000 of First Mortgage Bonds, October 1, 1952.

The purchasers of our bonds and investors in our common stock were informed through statements made by security analysts that the Company intended to credit the tax reductions from accelerated amortization to surplus.

(e) It is realized that the effect of the proposed accounting for the tax deferrals will be to show an increase in the Company's earnings as reflected on its income statements by the amount of such tax deferrals during the 60-month period of accelerated amortization and a decrease following the period of accelerated amortization because of resulting increased federal income taxes then to be payable. Inasmuch as the tax savings are not to be used for the payment of dividends but will be used to reduce outstanding debt or for construction, extension or improvement of the Company's facilities, it should not be considered that the benefits of such tax deferrals should be passed on to the Company's electric customers. Neither is it equitable to consider that customers should be burdened by the effect of the resulting increased federal income taxes payable after the period of accelerated amortization.

(f) Based on the foregoing, Washington hereby stipulates and agrees that for each of the 25 years following the expiration of the 60-month period of accelerated amortization insofar as such years may be involved in any proceeding before the Commission affecting Washington's electric rates, Washington will credit to its operating revenue deductions for federal income taxes as shown on its books of account, one twenty-fifth (1/25) of the total amount by which its federal income taxes were reduced by reason of such accelerated amortization.

Spokane, Washington, February 28, 1953.

The Washington Water Power Company

By /s/ J. E. E. ROYER

J. E. E. Royer
Vice-President & General Manager

ATTEST:

(Seal)

/s/ E. B. TALKINGTON

E. B. Talkington
Assistant Secretary

December 1, 1958

Mr. Robert D. Yoemans, Secretary
The Washington Water Power Company
P. O. Drawer 1445
Spokane 10, Washington

Gentlemen:

This is in reply to your letter of November 25, 1958, requesting an expression from this Commission as to whether your proposed accounting for income taxes, reduced by the use of liberalized depreciation permitted under section 167 of the 1954 Internal Revenue Code, is acceptable.

Under the Uniform System of Accounts for electric utilities adopted by this Commission in its Order No. 7081 dated December 10, 1937, and effective January 1, 1938, (which order is still in effect for electric utilities under the jurisdiction of this Commission) it is proper procedure for an electric utility to account for reduced taxes due to liberalized depreciation as permitted by section 167 of the 1954 Internal Revenue Code, by recording actual taxes that are paid, as tax expense, and also to show in like manner its tax expense on income statements and annual reports to this Commission. This method of accounting for reduced income taxes due to Section 167 of the 1954 Internal Revenue Code is commonly known as the "flow-through" method.

The Commission is of the opinion with respect, to a utility using said "flow-through" method that this method should also be followed for rate making purposes and consistantly applied to property additions on which liberalized depreciation is taken.

In view of the foregoing the Commission sees
no reason to take exception to your company's accounting for income taxes for the years 1956 and
1957 and your proposed accounting for 1958 and
thereafter with the understanding that this "flow-
through" accounting method will be followed consistantly in the future.

Very truly yours,

Wesley L. Barclift
Executive Secretary

PD:ba

AMERICAN GAS ASSOCIATION

C. S. STACKPOLE,
MANAGING DIRECTOR

420 Lexington Avenue
New York 17, N. Y.
MUrray Hill 3-8200

January 20, 1959

Securities and Exchange Commission
Washington 25, D. C.

Gentlemen: Attention: Mr. Orville L. DuBois,
                             Secretary

The member companies of the American Gas Association presently have under study and consideration the notice of intention to announce "an interpretation of administrative policy on financial statements regarding balance sheet treatment of credits equivalent to the reduction in income taxes", released by the Commission under date of December 30, 1958. (Securities Act of 1933 Release No. 4010; Securities Exchange Act of 1934 Release No. 5844; Public Utility Holding Company Act of 1935 Release No. 13894; Investment Company Act of 1940 Release No. 2814).

It is not clear whether the interpretation of administrative policy proposed by the Commission is directed solely to the balance sheet treatment of accumulations resulting from "normalizing" or deferred tax accounting procedures where such procedures are actually used by the affected companies, or whether it is intended also to require the adoption of "normalizing" or deferred tax accounting procedures with respect to "reductions in income taxes for various items including those under Sections 167 and 168 of the Internal Revenue Code of 1954", even where such procedures are not being used by the affected gas or pipeline companies. In these circumstances, it is submitted that the Commission should supply a more specific statement of the scope and application of the changes proposed, including an explanation of the words "various items".

In view of the difficulty of determining the scope and application of the proposed interpretation of administrative policy and its possible serious impact upon the gas industry, it is believed that the Commission would receive more informative statements if the time for submission of views and comments were extended.

We, therefore, request on behalf of the member companies of the American Gas Association that the Commission provide a more specific statement of the proposed changes and that the time for submission of views and comments be extended to March 31, 1959.

Respectfully submitted,

/s/ C. S. STACKPOLE

C. S. Stackpole
scj

SECURITIES AND EXCHANGE COMMISSION
Washington 25, D. C.

Mr. C. S. Stackpole   January 28, 1959
Managing Director
American Gas Association
420 Lexington Avenue
New York 17, N. Y.

Dear Mr. Stackpole:

The enclosed release published in response to
several requests extends the time for comment and
announces a hearing on our proposal with respect to
balance sheet treatment of amounts arising from
deferred tax accounting. It is believed that the
time allowed for written comment coupled with additional time to the date for the hearing should
be ample for all parties to prepare their responses
to the proposal.

We have assumed that utility companies which
will be affected by our proposal are familiar with
the Federal Power Commission Orders 203 and 204
referred to in Note 4 of our release. These Orders
provide for accounts to accommodate entries when
deferred tax accounting is applied to items other
than depreciation. Our "various items" wording is
intended to cover similar situations. The Civil
Aeronautics Board made a similar provision in its
Regulation No. ER-230 adopted March 12, 1958.

Our proposal is directed primarily to secure
uniformity in balance sheet treatment when deferred
tax accounting is adopted. Certifying accountants
and their clients we assume will consider how Accounting Research Bulletin No. 44 (Revised) (July
1958) issued by the Committee on Accounting Procedure of the American Institute of Certified Public Accountants applies in a particular case.

Your comments on the proposal will be given
careful consideration.

Very truly yours,

Andrew Barr
Enclosure   Chief Accountant

AMERICAN GAS ASSOCIATION

420 Lexington Avenue
New York 17, N. Y.
MUrray Hill 3-8200

C. S. STACKPOLE,
Managing Director

February 27, 1959

Hon. Orval L. DuBois, Secretary
Securities & Exchange Commission
425 Second Street, N. W.
Washington, D. C.

Dear Sir:

Enclosed are comments of the American Gas Association, Inc. with respect to Securities Act Release 4010, et al. In addition to the three copies required by Securities Act Release 4010, we enclose ten additional copies for the convenience of the Commission.

Cordially,

/s/ C. S. STACKPOLE

C. S. Stackpole
Encs.

UNITED STATES OF AMERICA
SECURITIES AND EXCHANGE COMMISSION

In the Matter	Securities Act of 1933 —
	Release Nos. 4010, 4023
of	Securities Exchange Act of 1934 —
	Release No. 5844
Proposed interpretation of adminis-	Public Utility Holding Company
trative policy on financial statements	Act of 1935 —
regarding balance sheet treatment of	Release No. 13894
credits equivalent to the reductions	Investment Company Act of 1940 —
in income taxes	Release No. 2814

COMMENTS OF
AMERICAN GAS ASSOCIATION, INC.

American Gas Association, Inc. (A.G.A.) is a nonprofit membership corporation organized for the advancement of the gas industry. The membership is composed of all segments of the gas industry, including gas pipe line companies, gas distribution companies and gas appliance manufacturers. Various of such members are subject to the jurisdiction of this Commission either because they make public offerings of securities as defined in the Securities Act of 1933; or because they have securities listed on national securities exchanges as defined in the Securities and Exchange Act of 1934; or because they are holding companies or holding company subsidiaries under the Public Utility Holding Company Act of 1935.

With the exception of the appliance manufacturer members, almost all of the members of A.G.A. are subject to the regulation of state or federal agencies with respect to rates and accounting. Due in large part to the diversity of state and federal accounting requirements with respect to treatment of tax reductions arising from rapid depreciation, the membership of A.G.A. utilizes varying procedures and forms of accounting for such tax reductions.

The A.G.A. is opposed to the proposed interpretation of administrative policy for the following reasons:

1. The Commission's notice of intention is ambiguous. It seems clear that the proposed interpretation of administrative policy would apply in those cases where deferred tax accounting has been adopted. In such cases, financial statements in which the resultant accumulated credits are designated as earned surplus or its equivalent, or included as a part of equity capital, would be deemed misleading despite disclosure made in footnotes or elsewhere. It is not clear, however, whether it is also the intention of the Commission to <u>require</u> the use of deferred tax accounting in connection with "reductions in income taxes for various items including those under Sections 167 and 168 of the Internal Revenue Code of 1954" (except in those cases referred to in footnote 3 of the Release), and, if so, what is comprised in the "various items". The "various items" other than Sections 167 and 168 are not defined in the release. However, in the light of correspondence between the A.G.A. and the Chief Accountant of this Commission with respect to the scope of the notice of intention, it appears not unlikely that the term would include tax reductions arising from the deduction for tax purposes of intangible drilling costs that are capitalized rather than expensed for corporate accounting purposes.

If, in fact, it is the intention of the Commission to deal with this matter so broadly, it is the view of A.G.A. that such intention should be publicized in a clear and unambiguous manner so as to assure that all interested parties may be put on notice as to the Commission's intentions.

2. If the proposed interpretation of administrative policy is to be construed as broadly as we have indicated, it is submitted that it would create substantial conflict with the accounting requirements of many state and federal regulatory agencies, some of which have accounting jurisdiction paramount to that of this Commission.* Such conflict would result in great difficulties for the regulated company and for the various Commissions involved.

---

* Public Utility Holding Company Act § 20(b) prohibits this Commission from prescribing accounting for any company inconsistent with that imposed on such company pursuant to any "law of the United States or of any State."

Securities and Exchange Act § 13(b) prohibits this Commission from prescribing accounting for any person inconsistent with that prescribed for such person under "any law of the United States."

Securities Act § 19(a) prohibits this Commission from prescribing accounting for any carrier inconsistent with that imposed on such carrier by the I.C.C. pursuant to § 20 of The Interstate Commerce Act.

3. This Commission has long adhered to the policy set forth in Accounting Series Release No. 4 of accepting variant accounting practices for which there is "substantial authoritative support", provided they are accompanied by full disclosure. As noted above, there is substantial authoritative support by various regulatory Commissions for each accounting practice which the proposed new policy would apparently proscribe. Without reviewing the accounting arguments with respect to the relative merits of the various practices, it is submitted that the proposed new policy is unnecessary to achieve adequate disclosure to the investor. Nor would such new policy achieve any substantial uniformity of accounting practice, in view of the exceptions created by footnote 3 of Release 4010 and by the statutory exceptions to this Commission's accounting jurisdiction.

CONCLUSION

American Gas Association, Inc. submits, therefore, that there is no valid purpose which would be served by the adoption of the proposed new policy and the consequent abandonment of the sound policy set forth in Accounting Series Release No. 4, and respectfully urges that this Commission not adopt the policy proposed by Release 4010.

Dated: New York, New York
February 27, 1959

Respectfully submitted,

AMERICAN GAS ASSOCIATION, INC.

EDISON ELECTRIC INSTITUTE

750 Third Avenue
New York 17
YUkon 6-4100

January 27, 1959

Securities and Exchange Commission
Washington 25, D. C.

           Attention: Honorable Orval L. DuBois,
                       Secretary

Dear Sirs:

     On January 5, 1959, we received a Release of
the Securities and Exchange Commission entitled,
"Notice of Intention to Announce Interpretation of
Administrative Policy," which Release was made under the several Acts administered by the Commission
(e.g., Release No. 4010 Securites Act of 1933). This
Release gave interested parties until January 31st
to submit their views and comments with respect to
its subject matter.

     The Edison Electric Institute is a trade as-
sociation having members which represent, on a customer basis, about 98% of the investor-owned electric utility companies. As recognized in the
Release itself, its subject matter, because of the
amounts involved, is of importance to the entire
electric industry. Although the Release appears
to deal primarily with accounting practice relating
to the treatment of liberalized depreciation and
accelerated amortization, its reference to "various
items" does not make it clear that it is so confined. It is also not clear whether "normalizing"
is to be construed as mandatory in all instances
except those referred to in Footnote 3 of the Release. In these and in other important respects

we feel that it would be helpful if the Commission would clarify the contents and scope of the Release.

The Edison Electric Institute is presently canvassing its members in order to ascertain their views on the subject matter of the Release. It will be impossible to effectively accomplish this by January 31, 1959, and therefore, we respectfully request, upon behalf of ourselves and our member companies, that an extension of time be granted for the expression of views until at least March 31, 1959.

Very truly yours,

/s/ EDWIN VENNARD

Edwin Vennard
Managing Director

SECURITIES AND EXCHANGE COMMISSION
Washington 25, D. C.

February 2, 1959

Mr. Edwin Vennard
Managing Director
Edison Electric Institute
750 Third Avenue
New York 17, N. Y.

Dear Mr. Vennard:

In response to your letter of January 27, 1959, I enclose a copy of the Commission's release extending the time for comment on its Release No. 4010. You will note that this release also announces a public hearing on the subject.

With respect to your comment on "various items," I am sure you and your members are familiar with the F.P.C. orders 203 and 204 which provide accounts for items other than depreciation. Similar provision is made by the Civil Aeronautics Board in its Regulation No. ER-230 adopted March 12, 1958. This point and any others may be discussed in your comments on the proposal.

Very truly yours,

Andrew Barr
Chief Accountant

Enclosure

EDISON ELECTRIC INSTITUTE

750 Third Avenue
New York 17
YUkon 6-4100

March 9, 1959

Securities and Exchange Commission
Washington 25, D. C.

Attention: Honorable Orval L. DuBois,
Secretary

Dear Sirs:

This refers further to Release No 4010 and
the proposed public hearing to be held on April 8.
We can appreciate that this hearing has already
been postponed twice and we hesitate to ask for another postponement. However, the Edison Electric
Institute's Annual Convention is scheduled to be
held in New Orleans on April 6, 7 and 8 and most
of the electric power company people who would normally attend your hearing will be in New Orleans.

We usually hold our annual meeting in June but
it was changed this year because of it being held
in New Orleans.

If you can see your way clear to setting another date for the hearing, I am sure it would be
greatly appreciated.

Very truly yours,

/s/ J. E. CORETTE

J. E. Corette
President

hm

March 12, 1959

Mr. J. E. Corette, President
Edison Electric Institute
750 Third Avenue
New York 17, N. Y.

Dear Mr. Corette:

Your letter of March 9, 1959, asking that the
Commission set another date for the hearing on Release No. 4010 was considered by the Commission
yesterday. In view of the number of requests for
appearance at the hearing the Commission concluded
that it would require more than the one day, April
8, to complete the hearing, and therefore concluded
that the hearing should resume at 2:30 p.m. on
April 9. This should permit you to attend to your
duties at the Edison Electric Institute's Annual
Convention and make your appearance here on the
9th.

Very truly yours,

Andrew Barr
Chief Accountant

ABarr:mag

REID & PRIEST

Two Rector Street - New York 6, N. Y.

41 Old Farm Road   March 23, 1959
Charlottesville, Va.

Mr. Orval L. DuBois, Secretary
Securities and Exchange Commission
Washington 25, D. C.

Re: Securities Act of 1933 Release No. 4010
    Securities Exchange Act of 1934 Release No. 5844
    Public Utility Holding Company Act of 1935
       Release No. 13894
    Investment Company Act of 1940 Release No. 2814

Dear Mr. DuBois:

    I enclose, on behalf of the Edison Electric
Institute, the trade association of the electric
utility industry, the original and ten copies of a
memorandum commenting on the Commission's "Notice of
Intention to Announce Interpretation of Administrative
Policy" dated December 30, 1958.

    The undersigned expects to participate in the
oral discussion of this problem and hereby requests
a time allowance of forty-five minutes for that
purpose. Representatives of a number of electric
utilities expect to meet in Washington next week to
attempt to work out a coordination of their presentation. It obviously will not be possible
to have that presentation made by one person,
but we hope at least to avoid duplication.

                        Very sincerely yours,

                        /s/ A. J. G. PRIEST

AJGP:MAC   A. J. G. PRIEST
Enc.

P.S. As you probably know, Mr. J. E. Corette, President
     of the Edison Electric Institute, who is much
     interested in this problem, will not be able
     to return to Washington from New Orleans until
     April 10th. I therefore request that I be per-
     mitted to participate in the discussion scheduled
     for that date.

                        /s/A. J. G. P.

                        A. J. G. P.

United States of America

Before the

Securities and Exchange Commission

Re: Securities Act of 1933
   Release No. 4010

   Securities Exchange Act of 1934
   Release No. 5444

   Public Utility Holding Company Act of 1935
   Release No. 13894

   Investment Company Act of 1940
   Release No. 2814

In the Matter

of

Notice of Intention to Announce
Interpretation of Administrative Policy

MEMORANDUM OF EDISON ELECTRIC INSTITUTE.

A. J. G. Priest
41 Old Farm Road
Charlottesville, Va.,
Special Attorney for
Edison Electric Institute

March 24, 1959

Pandick Press, Inc.,'22 Thames St., New York 6. N. Y., U. S. A.

TABLE OF CONTENTS.

ii

iii

TABLE OF CITATIONS.

iv

UNITED STATES OF AMERICA

BEFORE THE

Securities and Exchange Commission

Re: SECURITIES ACT OF 1933
Release No. 4010

SECURITIES EXCHANGE ACT OF 1934
Release No. 5844

PUBLIC UTILITY HOLDING COMPANY ACT OF 1935
Release No. 13894

INVESTMENT COMPANY ACT OF 1940
RELEASE No. 2814

IN THE MATTER

of

NOTICE OF INTENTION TO ANNOUNCE
INTERPRETATION OF ADMINISTRATIVE POLICY

MEMORANDUM OF EDISON ELECTRIC INSTITUTE.

On December 30, 1958, this Commission gave notice that it had under consideration the announcement of an interpretation of administrative policy as to the balance sheet treatment of credits "equivalent to the reductions in income taxes". After the issuance of that notice, a number of the member companies of this Institute (Edison Electric Institute, the trade association of the electric utility industry) filed comments with the Commission and some of them have corresponded with the Commission about the precise meaning of the interpretation proposed.

2

THE FACTUAL BACKGROUND.

All of the member companies of the Institute are engaged primarily in the business of producing and distributing electric power and energy. They serve approximately 97.6% of the customers of the nation's investor-owned electric utilities. With comparatively few exceptions, the rates, financing and accounting practices of all such member companies are regulated by State authorities and in some instances and in certain respects are also subject to the jurisdiction of the Federal Power Commission.

State Commission Action.

(a) Liberalized Depreciation.

Reports as of February 19, 1959 indicate that twenty-nine State Commissions had adopted formal orders or directions prescribing the accounting treatment which subject utilities must follow in connection with liberalized depreciation. These orders are tabulated in Appendix I.

Five states (Alabama, Colorado, Florida, Maryland and Virginia) have either authorized specific utilities, or have directed all subject utilities, to use a restricted or appropriated surplus method in recording the tax deferral. Arizona has provided for an actual-taxes-paid procedure.

Fourteen states (Arkansas, Georgia, Idaho, Illinois, Kansas, Louisiana, Maine, Massachusetts, Minnesota, Missouri, Nebraska, New Mexico, Tennessee and Vermont) have prescribed a tax reserve method.

Six other states (Kentucky, Michigan, New Jersey, Ohio, Oklahoma and South Carolina) have permitted, upon application by specific companies, the use of either restricted surplus or the reserve method. West Virginia, in addition to the restricted surplus and reserve procedures, has approved actual-taxes-paid procedure in two recent cases. The Indiana Commission, after approving restricted surplus procedure in four cases, issued an order on December 24, 1957, applicable to all utilities, providing for a reserve method. An appeal by Indiana & Michigan Electric Company from this order is now pending.

3

The Wisconsin Public Service Commission has approved an accounting method differing substantially from the techniques adopted by other State Commissions. Wisconsin provides for a charge to depreciation expense and a credit to depreciation reserve (in addition to depreciation computed on a straight-line basis) equal to the deferral of Federal income taxes resulting from the use of liberalized depreciation.

In its treatment of the tax effect of liberalized depreciation, the Pennsylvania Commission has disallowed the normalization of deferred income taxes in two recent rate proceedings and has said that the same treatment should be used for accounting purposes.

(b) Accelerated Amortization.

Thirty-six State Commissions, through formal orders or otherwise, have prescribed the accounting treatment for accelerated amortization. These accounting orders are tabulated in Appendix II.

Sixteen states (Alabama, Colorado, Florida, Kentucky, Maryland, Montana, New Jersey, Oklahoma, Pennsylvania, South Carolina, Utah, Vermont, Virginia, Washington, West Virginia, and Wyoming) have provided for a credit to restricted surplus.

Ten states (Arkansas, Connecticut, Georgia, Illinois, Kansas, Louisiana, Massachusetts, Missouri, Nevada and New Hampshire) have prescribed a reserve method.

The Idaho, Maine and North Carolina Commissions have each issued orders to two different utilities in their respective States authorizing a credit to restricted surplus in one case and to reserve in the other. California and New Mexico have each required two utilities to credit restricted surplus and one to credit reserve. Michigan has required two utilities to credit restricted surplus and two to credit reserve. Oregon has required two utilities to credit restricted surplus and one to credit reserve. Ohio has required six utilities to credit restricted surplus and one to credit reserve.

4

Wisconsin provides for a substantially unique accounting procedure, as recited under "Liberalized Depreciation." See also the reference to Indiana under "Liberalized Depreciation."

A recent rate case* before the Maine Public Utilities Commission involving Central Maine Power Company, which operates entirely within the State of Maine, sharply differentiates liberalized depreciation and accelerated amortization. The Maine Commission had previously permitted normalization of taxes for accounting purposes as to both accelerated amortization and liberalized depreciation. However, in this subsequent proceeding it distinguished between accelerated amortization and liberalized depreciation and held that for rate-making purposes "normalization" of tax deferments would be permitted as to the former but denied as to the latter.

Proceedings Before the Federal Power Commission.

On December 4, 1953, after oral argument, the Federal Power Commission, in Opinion No. 264, announced its policies on the treatment (under both the Federal Power Act and the Natural Gas Act) of the deferral of Federal income taxes resulting from accelerated amortization, for rate-making purposes only. The Commission stated that it would continue the depreciation policies previously followed: "Namely, to relate the annual depreciation charge to the service life of the facility being depreciated", and that accelerated amortization "should not affect the annual charge for depreciation for rate-making purposes." (Opinion No. 264, Mimeo ed., p. 7). The Opinion also said that the accounting phase would be dealt with at a later date.

Accounting treatment for natural gas companies only was subsequently directed by Orders Nos. 171 and 171-A, issued April 21 and May 17, 1954. Amendment of the Uniform System of Accounts prescribed for electric public utilities and licensees was specifically reserved for later disposition.

---

* *Re Central Maine Power Co.*, 17 P. U. R. 3d 452 (1957).

5

On February 8, 1957, the Federal Power Commission gave notice of its intention to amend its Uniform System of Accounts for Public Utilities and Licensees by adding a new Account 259, with appropriate sub-accounts, and new Accounts 507A and 507B. Views and comments were received from many electric utilities, regulatory agencies and accounting firms and oral argument was heard on September 17, 1957.

In its Order No. 204, dated May 29, 1958, the Federal Power Commission amended its Uniform System of Accounts for Public Utilities and Licensees, but departed somewhat from the techniques contemplated by the original notice of proposed rule-making. The first major change was that, in lieu of the original proposed balance sheet Account 259, "Reserve for Deferred Taxes on Income", the Commission adopted Account 266, captioned "Accumulated Deferred Taxes on Income", explaining (Order No. 204, Mimeo., pp. 4-6):

> "On consideration of the various aspects of this problem, we conclude that the congressional purposes which led to the enactment of Section 167 of the Tax Code can reasonably be achieved by employing the procedures contemplated in the proposed amendments described above, but providing a balance sheet treatment that *neither identifies the accumulated amounts as a reserve or as restricted surplus.*"

> * * * * * *

> "In view of the differences of opinion and conflicting considerations present, what is called for, in our judgment, is a separate balance sheet classification for accumulated deferred taxes. This will assure clear disclosure of this important item and lessen the possibilities of misunderstanding and misinterpretation of the nature and purposes of accumulated tax deferrals. It will meet the intent of Congress that the funds generated from the effect of accelerated amortization and liberalized depreciation be available to the utilities for plant expansion. And while making provision for future tax liability, it *will not foreclose financial analysts, investors and others from considering these amounts as part of equity capital* if they think proper, with

6

such consequential benefits to the rating of the company's securities and costs of financing as may result therefrom.''

*   *   *   *   *   *

"Under the circumstances, however, we see no reasonable solution to the problem for those utilities which are required by a state commission to report deferred taxes in a reserve or surplus account but to *classify the deferred taxes in accordance with state requirements for state purposes,* and to use the treatment specified by this order for the purposes of this Commission." (Emphasis added)

The second major provision of Order No. 204 (representing a departure from some of the accounting advice urged on the Commission) was that the deferred tax accounting provided for in the amendments to the System of Accounts is not mandatory, the Federal Power Commission saying (*ibid.* p. 6):

"This non-mandatory feature is desirable, among other reasons, to avoid to the extent possible conflict with requirements which may be prescribed by state regulatory authorities having major rate regulatory responsibilities, some of which may authorize and others deny deferred tax accounting."

Action by Other Federal Agencies.

On February 9, 1959, Division 2 of the Interstate Commerce Commission issued a statement of policy, *Notice To All Carriers Subject To Prescribed Accounting Rules—Accounting For Federal Income Taxes,* requiring that subject carriers should use only the actual taxes paid in connection with accelerated depreciation. That notice also stated that the actual-taxes method should be "disclosed by explanatory notes in reports filed with the Commission" and urged that all carriers "disclose this information in their reports to stockholders and in financial statements released to the press."

On March 12, 1958, the Civil Aeronautics Board, by Regulation No. ER-230, suspended a prior prohibition against deferred tax account-

7

ing and placed it on a voluntary basis, pending a final decision of the Board as to the rate treatment that should be given to any tax deferrals arising from either accelerated amortization or liberalized depreciation.

SUMMARY OF ARGUMENT.

In this instance, the Commission is not writing upon a fresh page. If the uniform accounting treatment of accelerated amortization and liberalized depreciation at the federal level had been attempted nine years, or even five years, ago, it might well have been made effective, but any such uniformity has now been made impossible by the widely varying conclusions of other federal agencies and of the several state commissions. We are confronted with an existing factual situation, not mere accounting theory. Without indicating any preference for a particular accounting technique, we suggest (1) that this Commission is not authorized, under any of the statutes which it administers, to reconstitute accounting practices of electric utilities which have been prescribed by other agencies having jurisdiction, (2) that the accounting interpretation here proposed is not consonant with the Commission's own rules of conduct and (3) that the adoption of such interpretation would, in the circumstances here presented, be arbitrary, would be neither necessary nor appropriate in the public interest and would not protect investors or consumers.

ARGUMENT.

I. THIS COMMISSION DOES NOT HAVE AUTHORITY UNDER ANY OF ITS ORGANIC STATUTES TO RECONSTITUTE THE ACCOUNTING PRACTICES OF THE ELECTRIC UTILITIES HERE INVOLVED AS IS NOW PROPOSED.

It was not the intent of Congress to permit this Commission to establish a uniform method of accounting under the Securities Act of 1933 or the Securities Exchange Act of 1934. Nor was it the intent of Congress to permit accounting regulation under these statutes

8

inconsistent with accounting regulations of competent state authorities or of other Federal agencies having supervening original jurisdiction over accounting matters.

The Commission's authority to promulgate rules regulating the reporting of accounting results under the Securities Act of 1933 and its authority to promulgate rules regulating accounting methods under the Public Utility Holding Company Act of 1935 are somewhat similar. Such points of similarity appear in Section 19(a) and paragraph 25 of Schedule A of the 1933 Act and in Section 20(a) of the 1935 Act. There is also similarity of purport in Section 19(a) of the 1933 Act and Section 13(b) of the Securities Exchange Act of 1934, which bear on the Commission's authority to prescribe regulations for the reporting of accounting results. Section 19(a) of the 1933 Act and Section 20(a) of the 1935 Act are set forth below for comparative purposes:

§19(a)

"(a) The Commission shall have authority from time to time to make, amend, and rescind *such rules and regulations as may be necessary to carry out the provisions of this title, including rules and regulations* governing registration statements and prospectuses for various classes of securities and issuers, and *defining accounting*, technical, and trade *terms* used in this title. Among other things, the Commission shall have authority, for the purposes of this title, *to prescribe the form or forms in which required information shall be set forth, the items or details to be shown in the balance sheet and*

§20(a)

"(a) The Commission shall have authority from time to time to make, issue, amend, and rescind *such rules and regulations and such orders as it may deem* **necessary** *or appropriate to carry out the provisions of this title, including rules and regulations defining accounting,* technical, and trade *terms* used in this title. Among other things, the Commission shall have authority, for the purposes of this title, *to prescribe the form or forms in which information required in any statement, declaration, application, report, or other document filed with the Commission shall be set forth, the items or details*

9

earning statement, and the methods to be followed in the preparation of accounts, in the appraisal or valuation of assets and liabilities, in the determination of depreciation and depletion, in the differentiation of recurring and nonrecurring income, in the differentiation of investment and operating income, and in the preparation, where the Commission deems it necessary or desirable, of consolidated balance sheets or income accounts of any person directly or indirectly controlling or controlled by the issuer, or any person under direct or indirect common control with the issuer; . . .'' (Emphasis added)

to be shown in balance sheets, profit and loss statements, and surplus accounts, the manner in which the cost of all assets, whenever determinable, shall be shown in regard to such statements, declarations, applications, reports, and other documents filed with the Commission, or accounts required to be kept by the rules, regulations, or orders of the Commission, *and the methods to be followed in the keeping of accounts and cost-accounting procedures and the preparation of reports,* in the segregation and allocation of costs, in the determination of liabilities, in the determination of depreciation and depletion, in the differentiation of recurring and nonrecurring income, in the differentiation of investment and operating income, and in the keeping or preparation, where the Commission deems it necessary or appropriate, of separate or consolidated balance sheets or profit and loss statements for any companies in the same holding-company system.'' (Emphasis added)

If, however, the above sections had been sufficient in themselves to give the Commission authority to promulgate a uniform system of accounts, there would have been no necessity for Congress to include

10

in the 1935 Act its Section 15(i), which expressly grants the power to prescribe uniform methods of accounting:

> §15(i) "The Commission, by such rules and regulations as it deems necessary or appropriate in the public interest or for the protection of investors or consumers may prescribe for persons subject to the provisions of subsections (a), (b), (c), or (d) of this section uniform methods for keeping accounts . . ."

Since Section 15(i) cannot be considered as surplusage, the absence of a similar section in the 1933 and 1934 Acts requires the conclusion that the Commission is not permitted to prescribe a uniform system of accounts under those statutes. This conclusion is strengthened by the remarks of Senator Barkley in debate preceding the enactment of Section 13 of the Securities Exchange Act of 1934, the section similar in import to Section 19(a) of the 1933 Act:

> "It does not seem to me it [Sec. 13] gives the commission any power to impose on a corporation any particular method of bookkeeping . . .
> "It does not require them to adopt a set of books to suit us or the commission. It authorizes the commission to require the company to advise it by what bookkeeping method of its own it has arrived at those conclusions." (78 Cong. Rec. 8282.)

A similar view has been expressed by the former Associate General Counsel of the Commission, Professor Louis Loss, in his outstanding work, *Securities Regulation* (1951). He says at p. 223:

> "So far as the other three acts are concerned—the 1933 and 1934 acts and the Investment Company Act—there are *no uniform systems of accounts,* but there is a single accounting regulation, Regulation S-X, which governs the form and content of financial statements." (Emphasis added)

The Holding Company Act is, without question, the most comprehensive and detailed regulatory statute which this Commission admin-

11

isters. Its sanctions have a continuous effect upon the operations of companies subject to it, while the Securities Act of 1933 has an essentially intermittent effect upon issuers. The powers conferred by the Securities Act are far more limited than those prescribed by the Holding Company Act. Yet the Holding Company Act itself provides in Section 20(b) that:

> "In the case of the accounts of any company whose methods of accounting are prescribed under the provisions of any law of the United States *or of any State,* the rules and regulations or orders of the Commission in respect of accounts *shall not be inconsistent with the requirements imposed by such law or any rule or regulation thereunder;* nor shall anything in this title relieve any public-utility company from the duty to keep the accounts, books, records, or memoranda which may be required to be kept by the law of any State in which it operates or by the State Commission of any such State. But this provision shall not prevent the Commission from imposing such additional requirements regarding reports or accounts as it may deem necessary or appropriate in the public interest or for the protection of investors or consumers." (Emphasis added).

The Commission's Rule U-27, promulgated under the Holding Company Act, italicized the limited character of its accounting authority. That Rule provides, in part:

> "(a) Every registered holding company, and subsidiary thereof, which is a public-utility company and which is *not required* by either the Federal Power Commission or *a State commission to conform to a classification of accounts,* shall keep its accounts insofar as it is an electric utility company in the manner currently prescribed for similar companies by the Federal Power Commission and insofar as it is a gas utility company in the manner recommended by the National Association of Railroad and Utilities Commissioners, except any company whose public utility activities are so limited that the application to it of such system of accounts is clearly inappropriate * * *."
> (Emphasis added).

12

The Commission's general authority as to reports and accounting matters is further limited by Section 13(b) of the 1934 Act, which provides:

> " * * * but in the case of the reports of any person whose methods of accounting are prescribed under the provisions of any law of the United States, or any rule or regulation thereunder, the rules and regulations of the Commission with respect to reports shall not be inconsistent with the requirements imposed by such law or rule or regulation in respect of the same subject matter, and in the case of carriers subject to the provisions of section 20 of the Interstate Commerce Act, as amended, or carriers required pursuant to any other Act of Congress to make reports of the same general character as those required under such section 20, shall permit such carriers to file with the Commission and the exchange duplicate copies of the reports and other documents filed with the Interstate Commerce Commission, or with the governmental authority administering such other Act of Congress, *in lieu of the reports, information and documents required under this section and section 12 in respect of the same subject matter.*" (Emphasis added).

Similarly, Section 19(a) of the 1933 Act limits the Commission's authority under that statute, providing:

> " * * * insofar as they relate to any common carrier subject to the provisions of section 20 of the Interstate Commerce Act, as amended, the rules and regulations of the Commission with respect to accounts shall not be inconsistent with the requirements imposed by the Interstate Commerce Commission under authority of such section 20 * * *."

If the most comprehensive of the Acts which the Commission administers prevents the adoption of accounting rules inconsistent with State regulation, how may more stringent requirements be imposed under the less-comprehensive and non-regulatory "Federal Blue-sky" law? *A fortiori*, the Commission may not, under the 1933

13

or the 1934 Act,* impose accounting (reporting) methods which do violence to existing state regulation.

Furthermore, the proposed interpretation does not fall within the requirement of Section 19(a) of the Securities Act of 1933 that rules adopted be "* * * *necessary* to carry out the provisions * * *" of said Act. The interpretation now proposed clearly is not indispensable. Alternative accounting methods have been applied and have been found acceptable by this Commission, among other regulatory agencies, for many years.

Tests of legislative authority to promulgate rules require the action be necessary, and also demand that the rule of *reason* be followed by administrative agencies. For example, in *United States v. Goldsmith,* 91 F. 2d 983, 985 (2d Cir. 1937), cert. denied, 302 U. S. 718 (1937) it was held:

> "* * * such rules and regulations as are fairly within such defined scope and are *reasonably necessary* to the proper administration of the law are to be upheld as lawful incidents of administration." (Emphasis added)

See also *Frahn* v. *Tennessee Valley Authority,* 41 F. Supp. 83 (N. D. Ala. 1941) in which the court indicated that administrative rules must be *reasonably* consonant with the enabling statute. It is at best doubtful whether, in view of the Commission's acceptance of registration statements (1) covering more than a billion dollars of securities** and (2) containing what the Commission now suggests are "misleading" statements of surplus, the proposed interpretation falls within the rule of reason.

Again where any question of ambiguity exists, a long and consistent administrative interpretation is of great weight in determining

---

* The 1934 Act, of course, is purely a reporting statute so far as electric utility companies are concerned.

** See infra p. 21.

14

its meaning. In *Walling* v. *Baltimore Steam Packet Co.*, 144 F. 2d
130, 135 (4th Cir. 1944) it was held:

> "* * * It is well settled that, in case of ambiguity, great
> weight is given to an administrative interpretation of a statute
> long and consistently followed; * * *"

It is submitted that the administrative approval of the current
accounting practice is such a long and settled interpretation as to raise
serious doubts whether this Commission can, as a matter of sound
regulation, abandon that practice. Certainly its retroactive abandonment would be shockingly arbitrary and capricious.

As early as 1938, the Commission recognized appropriate cross-
reference to other portions of the registration statement as adequate for
the protection of investors, *In Matter of Ypres Cadillac Mines*, 3 S. E. C.
41 (1938). Again in *Matter of Missouri Pacific Railroad Company*, 6
S. E. C. 268, 277 (1939) the Commission held as to questions of balance-
sheet disclosure:

> "We have heretofore held that it is necessary, in order to
> diminish the possibility of erroneous conclusions, that all infor-
> mation required in answer to each item in a registration state-
> ment be complete and accurate in itself, either through a full
> statement of the relevant facts or by appropriate cross-reference
> to other portions of the registration statement where the facts
> are stated."

As Professor Louis Loss observes*, "Footnote explanations will
be accepted only where alternative accounting practices are generally
recognized by the profession; otherwise the body of the financial statement must be conformed to what the Commission regards to be generally
accepted accounting principles." And in this instance, alternative
accounting practices *are* generally recognized by the profession.

---

* Loss, *Securities Regulation*, p. 227, *supra*.

15

II. THE PROPOSED INTERPRETATION IS INHIBITED BY THE COMMISSION'S OWN RULES FOR ITS OWN CONDUCT.

The power of the Commission to make rules is limited by its own recognition that its responsibility is to promote the economic strength of legitimate business enterprise. And the interpretation here proposed clearly is not consonant with that declared objective.

The preamble of the Commission's "Canons of Ethics for Members of the Securities and Exchange Commission" (July 22, 1958), states:

> "It is their task to regulate varied aspects of the American economy, within the limits prescribed by Congress, to insure that our private enterprise system serves the welfare of all citizens. Their success in this endeavor is a bulwark against possible abuses and injustice which, if left unchecked, might jeopardize the strength of our economic institutions."

The rule-making power is dealt with under Canon 2 and Canon 14:

> "2. Statutory Obligations.
>
> ". . . In the exercise of the rule-making powers delegated this Commission by the Congress, members should always be concerned that the rule-making power be confined to the proper limits of the law and be consistent with the statutory purpose expressed by the Congress."

* * * * * *

> 14. The Power to Adopt Rules.
>
> In exercising its rule-making power, this Commission performs a legislative function. The delegation of this power by the Congress imposes the obligation upon the members to adopt rules necessary to effectuate the stated policies of the statute in the interest of all of the people. *Care should be taken to avoid the adoption of rules which seek to extend the power of the Commission beyond proper statutory limits. Its rules should never tend to stifle or discourage legitimate business enterprise or activities, nor should they be interpreted so as unduly and unnecessarily to burden those regulated with onerous obligations.* * * *" (Emphasis added)

16

It may be said, without considering its merits as an accounting regulation, that the proposed interpretation may tend to stifle and discourage legitimate business enterprise and activities. If it were adopted, the removal of the tax deferrals from surplus accounts might have the effect of making financing more difficult and more costly for the utilities affected. In a regulated industry, this cost can only be borne by those having the least benefit from the proposed interpretation—the consumers of electric energy. And the adoption of the proposed interpretation might affect the capacity of the utility industry to attract capital. The charters of many electric utility operating companies, as the Commission knows, contain provisions restricting payment of dividends if, after their payment, the surplus remaining would be less than a stated percentage of capitalization (usually 25%). Removal of tax deferrals from surplus might reduce the base of calculation to a point where a steady record of dividends could be jeopardized. Similar problems may well arise under indentures pursuant to which securities have been issued.

Investors comparing a utility's previous prospectuses with those issued following the adoption of the proposed interpretation may not be able to distinguish between a new accounting method reflecting a reduction in surplus and what might, on its surface, appear to be a capital loss. Reluctance to invest could be the result. Further, when required to issue statements complying with contrary state regulation, such companies will be faced with the possibility of issuing information which will be "misleading" under the proposed interpretation, but they nevertheless will have to "mislead".

We do not suggest that the past reliance of much of the utility industry on this Commission's previous acceptance of the crediting of tax deferrals to surplus as not misleading necessarily estops the Commission from changing its mind, but it is submitted that such a change would be an unreasonable and arbitrary application of the Commission's rule-making power, completely out of consonance with its Canons of Ethics and the view of many reputable accountants.

17

Furthermore, the adoption of such a rule would not accomplish the result desired. For example, companies subject to state regulation of accounting practices and to the Holding Company Act would be exempt, and would be permitted to continue to "mislead".

III. EVEN ASSUMING, BY WAY OF ARGUMENT, THAT THE COMMISSION HAS THE NECESSARY ADMINISTRATIVE AUTHORITY, ITS EXERCISE IN THE MANNER PROPOSED WOULD BE ARBITRARY, AN UNWISE USE OF ADMINISTRATIVE DISCRETION, AND WOULD NOT PROMOTE UNIFORMITY OF ACCOUNTING.

A. Regulation of the Operations of Electric Utility Companies Has Traditionally Been Subject to the Control of the States.

Today all but six States (Alaska, Iowa, Minnesota, Nebraska*, South Dakota and Texas) have public service commissions which possess broad regulatory authority over the accounts of electric public utility companies: *Federal Power Commission* "State Commission Jurisdiction and Regulation of Electric and Gas Utilities—1954", p. 26, and *The Council of State Governments,* "The Book of the States (1958-59"), p. 457. In this connection, the Supreme Court pointed out in *First Iowa Hydro-Elec. Coop.* v. *Federal Power Commission,* 328 U. S. 152, 171 (1946):

> "We find that when that [Federal Power] Act is read in the light of its long and colorful legislative history, it discloses both a vigorous determination of Congress to make progress with the development of the long idle water power resources of the nation and a determination to avoid unconstitutional invasion of the jurisdiction of the states. The solution reached is to apply the principle of the division of constitutional powers between the state and Federal Governments. This has resulted in a dual system involving the close integration of these powers

---

* There are no investor-owned electric utility companies in Nebraska.

18

rather than a dual system of futile duplication of two authorities over the same subject matter.''

Sound administration of any Federal statute not clearly designed to supplant state regulation plainly calls for restraint as frequently as it does for action. It must have been precisely this thought that compelled a number of state utility commissions to urge restraint upon the Federal Power Commission (the state and local commissions regulate the rates which produce more than 94 percent of the revenues of electric utility companies; rates regulated by the Federal Power Commission produce less than 6 percent of such revenues) in the course of prior proceedings before it dealt with this subject matter.

The Virginia State Corporation Commission, in a Petition for Intervention in Docket No. R-126, dated July 31, 1953, noted that it had prescribed normalization accounting with the use of a restricted surplus account for companies subject to its jurisdiction. Urging that no action be taken by the Federal Power Commission which would conflict with its orders, the Virginia Commission said:

> "This Commission believes that the view that it has taken is the proper view. It further believes that conflict of regulation between the Federal Power Commission and the State commissions is of material importance in this matter. Finally, it believes that insofar as the electric utilities are concerned, this is a field where State regulation is of greater importance than Federal regulation, where there is no need of uniformity throughout the country and where the views of the respective States should not be overridden by the Federal Power Commission. That is what the Federal Power Commission proposes to do in this proceeding and the State Corporation Commission of Virginia protests against such action.''

The Ohio Public Utilities Commission, in a letter (dated March 5, 1953) to the Federal Power Commission in the same proceeding also noted that it had prescribed accounting regulations for companies

19

subject to its jurisdiction. Urging that an overriding Federal accounting rule was uncalled for, the Ohio Commission said:

" * * * We suggest that if your Commission is to promulgate any rule that it be confined to a rule with respect to rate making and then in accord with the principles expressed above. *We sincerely submit that a rule is not required with respect to the accounting treatment.*" (Emphasis added)

Along these same lines the Michigan Public Service Commission, in a letter to the Executive Committee of the NARUC, dated July 23, 1953, stated:

" * * * The individual commissions are entirely competent to deal with this matter and *nothing will be gained by attempting to establish a uniform accounting approach to the problem.*

'We have taken the same position before the Federal Power Commission in its recent proceedings in this matter (Docket R-126) * * * The adoption of any general rule or policy by the Federal Power Commission, prescribing accounting treatment for accelerated amortization would be in conflict with the treatment prescribed in the orders of the state commission. Such *action by the FPC would infringe upon the regulatory jurisdiction of the state commissions and, moreover, would be wholly unwarranted.*" (Emphasis added)

Also indicative of the views of the State Commissions is this resolution adopted by the Executive Committee of the NARUC on March 6, 1953:

"WHEREAS, The Federal Power Commission has initiated an investigation to determine whether it should establish rules as to the accounting and rate-making treatment of accelerated amortization of defense facilities for Federal income tax purposes in accordance with Section 124A of the Internal Revenue Code; and

'WHEREAS, Many of the public utility commissions of the several States have established policies in this regard as best fit the needs of the particular States while others have the matter

20

under consideration or propose action in the immediate future; and

'WHEREAS, There is no need for Federal action in this matter under the Federal Power Act since uniformity is not required; now, therefore, be it

'RESOLVED, That, *in the judgment of this committee, the proper accounting treatment of accelerated amortization of defense facilities for federal income tax purposes is properly a matter for determination by the public utility commissions of the several States and not a matter requiring uniform action under an order of a Federal regulatory agency;* and further

'RESOLVED, That a copy of this resolution be filed with the Secretary of the Federal Power Commission.' " (Emphasis added)

Similar expressions of views by State Commissions have been made to this Commission in this proceeding. We are informed that the Idaho Public Utilities Commission in a letter dated February 27, 1959, advised this Commission that the adoption of the proposed interpretation would put electric utility companies in an "untenable position" and that accounting regulations which would result in "changing the effect of a past transaction which was properly accounted for at the time the transaction took place" should not be adopted.

The Washington Public Service Commission in a letter dated February 27, 1959 to the Commission stated that the accounting treatment prescribed by the Washington Commission is "in all respects proper, and is not misleading or inaccurate." Similarly under date of March 2, 1959 the Oregon Public Utility Commissioner wrote the Commission saying:

"We have concluded that in the circumstances, and so far as the utilities subject to the jurisdiction of this Commission are concerned, the present practice is not 'inaccurate or misleading' and, accordingly, this proposed new Interpretation of Administrative Policy appears to us unnecessary and inappropriate".

21

B. The Proposed Action By The Commission At This Late Date Would Be Unfair To The Holders of Utility Securities Purchased On The Basis of Established Accounting Requirements, As Well As To The Holders of Securities Heretofore Approved By This Commission Under The Public Utility Holding Company Act.

No position is taken in this memorandum urging any particular method of accounting for accelerated amortization or liberalized depreciation. But to the extent that the Commission's current proposal may be interpreted as proscribing any of the methods for which there is substantial authoritative support, financial statements of many electric utility companies may be questioned.

For example, since the companies listed in our Appendices first began to take advantage of the tax deferrals authorized by accelerated amortization, and subsequently by liberalized depreciation, those which use the restricted surplus method have issued securities in an aggregate amount exceeding $2,200,000,000. We are advised that none of the independent public accountants concerned has taken exception to the restricted surplus technique in any certification of the accounts of a public utility which has used that technique. Financial representations made by the companies concerned plainly have been relied upon by the purchasers of those securities and it is submitted that such representations should not be required to be modified, either directly or indirectly, at this late date.

Perhaps even more serious questions of civil liability might arise if this Commission should now interpret its accounting regulations so that the employment of the restricted surplus method might be regarded as *per se* "misleading". Even though no liability under any of the Commission's organic statutes might eventually be imposed against any company, or its officers or directors, the Commission's declaration that particular accounting statements were "misleading" might subject many companies to the expense and hazard of litigating such claims. Furthermore, as has been pointed out in other memoranda filed with the Commission, such a declaration might impose serious

22

problems in connection with the certification by public acountants of financial statements relating to the past transactions of a particular company, as well as in connection with opinions of counsel given in connection with prior security issues.

C. The Present Proposal Does Violence to What Has Been the Basic Accounting Policy of This Commission for the Past Twenty-One Years of Accepting Methods of Accounting Treatment for which There Is Substantial Authoritative Support.

As is apparent from our discussion under the caption "The Factual Background", *supra,* there is substantial diversity of opinion among the State Commissions as to the accounting treatment of accelerated amortization and liberalized depreciation. Almost equal diversity is to be found in the views of other federal regulatory agencies.

For example, the Federal Power Commission does not make deferred tax accounting mandatory and has adopted a balance sheet account which is neither a part of earned surplus nor a reserve. On the other hand, the Interstate Commerce Commission requires that all carriers subject to its jurisdiction use only actual-taxes-paid accounting, *I. C. C. Notice to All Carriers Subject To Prescribed Accounting Rules, February 9, 1959.* Similarly, the Civil Aeronautics Board on March 12, 1958, by Regulation No. ER-230, suspended its prior prohibition against deferred tax accounting and placed it on a voluntary basis, pending a final decision of the Board as to the rate treatment that should be given to any tax deferrals arising from either accelerated amortization or liberalized depreciation.

Some of those taking the extreme view that the "normalization" of tax deferrals is improper have gone so far as to claim (*"The Treatment of Accelerated Depreciation For Rate Making Purposes",* NARUC Panel discussion, Phoenix, Arizona, November 20, 1958, p. 27) that "inconsistencies" in deferred tax accounting theories "remind one of the philosophy of Doublethink, a characteristic of the rulers of Oceania in George Orwell's 'Nineteen Eighty-Four'."

23

Similarly, the Committee on Concepts and Standards Underlying Corporate Financial Statements of The American Accounting Association in its "Accounting and Reporting Standards for Corporate Financial Statements, 1957 Revision" (p. 7) takes the position that "disclosure by accrual may be more confusing than enlightening and is therefore undesirable."

From the foregoing, it is evident that there is "substantial authoritative support" for virtually all of the various methods of accounting for tax deferrals presently used by regulated industry. To single out any particular method, or combination of methods, as the only approach which is not "misleading" to investors is patently arbitrary and capricious. Even if such a selection of the one "correct" method were made by counting heads, validity could hardly be claimed for it.

Sharp diversity of opinion prevails among leading members of the accounting profession in this country, as indicated by the memoranda filed and oral presentations made by outstanding firms in the Federal Power Commission proceedings (Docket R-159) referred to above, and in the memoranda filed in the present proceeding before this Commission.

In sum, there is substantial agreement throughout all this diversity of opinion that deferred tax accounting should not be made mandatory. And if deferred tax accounting *is* adopted, there is an abundance of "substantial authoritative support" both for a credit to a reserve or other special account and for a credit to restricted surplus.

Furthermore, there seems to be substantial agreement that any statement of accounting policy adopted by the Commission in these circumstances should not require the revision or reclassification of prior financial statements made in reliance upon then accepted accounting practices. To apply revised standards retroactively in the teeth of genuine conflict among both regulatory agencies and accounting experts would do serious violence to our normal standards of fair play.

24

We obviously cannot suggest to the Commission what it should do with all of the 3,169 issuers of securities now required to file reports with the Commission pursuant to the Securities Exchange Act of 1934 and the Securities Act of 1933 (S. E. C. Statistical Release No. 1590, March 16, 1959). But it is suggested that application of the proposed standard accounting treatment to the more than 500 companies presently su' ject to regulation by the Federal Power Commission, the Interstate Commerce Commission, the Civil Aeronautics Board and the various State Commissions would produce distressing conflict rather than uniformity, and therefore could not be looked upon as sound regulation administered in the public interest.

Respectfully submitted,

A. J. G. PRIEST,
41 Old Farm Road,
Charlottesville, Va.

*Special Attorney for
Edison Electric Institute*

25

APPENDIX I

(See explanation of symbols following Appendix II)

LIBERALIZED DEPRECIATION

State	Company	Date of Order	Procedure Approved
Alabama	Alabama Power Co., Non-dkt #1679	2/28/55	RS
	Mobile Pub. Serv. Corp., Non-dkt #1691	8/16/55	RS
	Alabama Gas Corp., Non-dkt #1704	1/27/56	RS
Arizona	Letter from Tucson Gas, Elec. Lt. & Pr. Co. to State Corporation Commission, advising of company's procedure; no adverse reply received	4/13/57	RT
	Ariz. Pub. Serv. Co., Ded. No. 31345	1/26/59	AT
Arkansas	Gen. Tel. Co. of S. W. (17 PUR 3d 511)	9/17/56	RT*
California	Calif. Water & Tel. (ULR 17,714)	8/ 5/57	3
	Southern Counties Gas Co. of Calif., Dec. No. 55579	9/17/57	10
	Southern Calif. Edison Co., Dec. No. 55703	10/15/57	10
	Pac. Gas & Elec. Co., Dec. No. 55720	10/22/57	10
	Citizens Utilities Co. of Calif. (22 PUR 3d 482)	3/11/58	10
	Calif. Elec. Power Co. (23 PUR 3d 275)	4/ 8/58	10
	Pac. Gas & Elec. Co., Dec. No. 56967	7/ 9/58	10
	Citizens Utilities Co. of Calif., Dec. No. 57177	8/14/58	10
	Southern Calif. Water Co., Dec. No. 57263	8/26/58	10
	Citizens Utilities Co. of Calif., Dec. No. 57471	10/15/58	10
	San Diego Gas & Elec. Co., Dec. No. 57509	10/21/58	10
	Citizens Utilities Co. of Calif., Dec. No. 57724	12/16/58	10
Colorado	Pub. Serv. Co. of Colo. (12 PUR 3d 158)	1/ 5/56	RS*
	Colo. Central Power Co. (12 PUR 3d 163)	1/16/56	RS*
	So. Colo. Power Co. (12 PUR 3d 163)	1/16/56	RS*
	Home Lt. & Power Co. (18 PUR 3d 1)	4/ 5/57	RS*
Connecticut	Housatonic Pub. Serv. Co. (22 PUR 3d 1)	1/22/58	3a
Florida	Gulf Power Co.; Tampa Elec. Co. (10 PUR 3d 273)	9/ 1/55	RS
	All utilities except RRS and motor carriers, Dec. No. 2422 (NARUC-Util. Reg. (1957) p. 12) (digest, 16 PUR 3d 529)	12/12/56	RS
	Florida Power & Lt. Co., Order No. 2515	8/22/57	2a
Georgia	Georgia Power Co. (10 PUR 3d 259)	8/16/55	RT1
	Georgia Continental Tel. Co., Dkt. No. 865-U	12/ 1/55	RT1
	Georgia Gas Co., Letter authorization	12/14/56	RT1
	Atlanta Gas Lt. Co.	4/18/58	
Idaho	Idaho Power Co.	5/18/56	RT

26

State	Company	Date of Order	Procedure Approved
Illinois	Central Ill. Elec. & Gas Co.	1/ 1/55	RT
	Central Ill. Lt. Co.	1/29/55	RT
	Commonwealth Edison Co., Dkt. No. 42105	6/13/55	RT*
	No. Ill. Gas Co., Dkt. No. 42106	6/13/55	RT*
	Ill. Power Co.	8/ 3/55	RT
	Cent. Ill. Pub. Serv. Co., Dkt. No. 42669	10/11/55	RT
	Iowa-Ill. Gas & Elec. Co., Dkt. No. 42600	10/11/55	RT*
	Cent. Ill. Elec. & Gas Co., Dkt. No. 42804	12/ 1/55	RT*
	Ill. Tel. Co., Dkt. No. 42928	12/29/55	RT*
	General Tel. Co. of Ill., Dkt. No. 42885	12/29/55	RT*
	Ill. Cent. Tel. Co., Dkt. No. 42927	12/29/55	RT*
	No. Ill. Gas Co., Dkt. No. 42106	6/13/55	RT*
	Cent. Ill. Lt. Co., Dkt. No. 42869	12/29/55	RT*
	Middle States Tel. Co. of Ill., Dkt. No. 43262	6/28/56	RT*
	S.E. Ill. Gas Co., Dkt. No. 43753	12/19/56	RT*
	Peoples Gas Lt. & Coke Co., Dkt. No. 43800	3/14/57	RT*
	Alton Water Co., Dkt. No. 43978	4/ 9/57	RT*
	Alton Water Co., Dkt. No. 43950 (22 PUR 3d 358)	12/18/57	2
	Peoples Gas Lt. & Coke Co., Dkt. No. 44293 (62 PUF 39)	5/23/58	2
	Commonwealth Edison Co., (24 PUR 3d 209)	6/18/58	2a
Indiana	Ind. & Mich. Elec. Co., et al., (7 PUR 3d 26)	12/23/54	RS*
	Central Ind. Gas Co. (ULR 16837)	7/29/55	RS*
	Home Tel. & Teleg. Co. (ULR 16903)	10/14/55	RS*
	Citizens Indepen. Tel. Co., Cause No. 26460	11/18/55	RS*
	Ind. Gas & Water Co. (ULR 17046)	12/22/55	RS*
	General Tel. Co. of Ind. (ULR 17045)	1/13/56	RS*
	Natural Gas Serv. Co. (12 PUR 3d 365)	2/10/56	RS*
	Pub. Serv. Co. of Ind. (12 PUR 3d 509) Affmd. by Ind. Circ. Ct., Hendricks County, 12/19/57 (22 PUR 3d 13)	3/ 9/56	2
	Greenfield Gas Co. (ULR 17266)	8/31/56	RS*
	Hoosier Gas Co. (ULR 17287)	8/31/56	RS*
	Lawrenceburg Gas Co., Cause No. 26614	8/31/56	RS*
	Lawrenceburg Gas Transmission Corp., Cause No. 26613	8/31/56	RS*
	All Utilities (ULR 17794) (21 PUR 3d 414) [Appealed by Ind. & Mich. Elec. Co., 1/13/58, Dkt. No. 19149; case still pending]	12/24/57	RT*8

27

State	Company	Date of Order	Procedure Approved
Kansas	Kansas City Power & Lt. Co. (14 PUR 3d 246)	5/16/56	RT*
	Empire District Elec. Co., Dkt. No. 52, 135-U (cited 23 PUR 3d 50)	7/11/56	RT*
	Kansas Power & Lt. Co., Dkt. No. 52, 754-U	8/ 1/56	RT*
	Empire District Elec. Co. (ULR 17,964) (23 PUR 3d 45)	2/11/58	2
Kentucky	Kentucky Utilities Co. (cited 22 PUR 3d at 116)	1/ 6/54 & 9/28/55	RS*
	Kentucky Power Co., Case No. 2989	8/16/55	RS*
	Union Light, Heat & Power Co., Case No. 3011	9/27/55	RS*
	Southern Continental Tel. Co., Case No. 3039	11/15/55	RT*
	Western Kentucky Gas Co. (cited 21 PUR 3d 399)	11/15/55	RT*
	General Tel. Co. of Ky., Case No. 3087	1/31/56	RT*
	Central Ky. Natural Gas Co. & United Fuel Gas Co., Case No. 3196	9/14/56	RT*
	Western Ky. Gas Co. (21 PUR 3d 394)	10/27/57	2a
	Union Lt., Heat & Power Co., Case No. 3271	12/27/57	2
	Kentucky Utilities Co. (22 PUR 3d 113)	1/15/58	2a
	Central Ky. Natural Gas Co.	3/14/58	
	United Fuel Gas Co.	3/14/58	
Louisiana	All Utilities General Order No. 6172	6/13/55	RT
Maine	Bangor Hydroelec. Co., No. U-2164 (cited 21 PUR 3d 337)	1/12/55	RT
	Maine Pub. Serv. Co. (ULR 17001) (12 PUR 3d 349)	1/26/56	RT
	Central Maine Power Co. (17 PUR 3d 452) [Affirmed, Maine Supreme Court, 11/7/57 (ULR 17749) (21 PUR 3d 321)]	3/15/57	3
	Central Maine Power Co. (ULR 17,792) (21 PUR 3d 337)	12/ 4/57	7
	New England Tel. & Tel. Co. (EIS 1271—5/9/58)	4/30/58	3a
	Bangor Hydroelec. Co., F. C. No. 1564 (NARUC-Bull. No. 17-1959, 2/18/59)	12/30/58	2
Maryland	Potomac Edison Co.	8/22/56	RS
	Cumberland & Allegheny Gas Co.	4/24/58	**

28

State	Company	Date of Order	Procedure Approved
Massachusetts.............	Negea Serv. Co. (letter from Chief Accountant)........	7/17/56	RT
	Berkshire Gas Co. (17 PUR 3d 515) [Applicable to all gas and electric utilities—1/1/54]....................	12/31/56	RT*
	Plymouth County Elec. Co.....................................	2/28/58	**
Michigan......................	Detroit Edison Co., D-1282-A-54.2 (digest, 8 PUR 3d 545)	11/ 5/54	RT*
	S. E. Mich. Gas Co., D-3769-55.2.....................	7/28/55	RT
	Edison Sault Elec. Co., D-500-55.1...........................	8/ 3/55	RT
	Mich. Gas Utilities Co., D-2320-55.2.......................	8/ 3/55	RT
	Mich. Gas & Elec. Co., D-1103-55.2.....................	8/ 3/55	**RT**
	Consumers Power Co., D-875-A-55.1 (cited 11 PUR 3d 471)	8/ 3/55	RT*
	Indiana & Mich. Elec. Co. (Trans't D-668)...............	8/31/55	
	Indiana & Mich. Elec. Co., (11 PUR 3d 470)...........	9/12/55	RS*
	Union Tel. Co., D-207-55.2...........................	12/ 9/55	RT
	Upper Peninsula Power Co...........................	12/ 9/55	RT
	Mich. Consolidated Gas Co. (ULR 17,851) (22 PUR 3d 369)......................................	2/ 6/58	2a
	Mich. Gas & Elec. Co., D-2932-58.1...........................	6/19/58	2a
Minnesota	Letter to Minn. Railroad & Warehouse Comm. advising of company's procedure; no adverse reply received, Minnesota Community Tel. Co....................	4/ 7/55	RT
	Fairmont Tel. Co................................	11/ 8/55	RT
Missouri	Kansas City Power & Lt. Co. (12 PUR 3d 472)........	2/28/56	RT*
	Andrew County Mutual Tel. Co., No. 13,289............	3/29/56	RT*
	Central States Tel. Co., No. 13,290............................	3/29/56	RT*
	Missouri Tel. Co., No. 13,291................................	3/29/56	RT*
	Middle States Utilities Co. of Mo., No. 13,292 (cited 12 PUR 3d 477).....................................	3/29/56	RT*
	Empire District Elec. Co. (14 PUR 3d 103).............	6/20/56	RT*
	Laclede Gas Co., No. 13,486......................................	9/ 7/56	RT*
	Union Elec. Co., No. 13,531.................................	12/13/56	RT*
	Missouri Edison Co., No. 13,544................................	12/14/56	RT*
	Missouri Natural Gas Co., No. 13,561.......................	12/13/56	RT*
	Missouri Power & Lt. Co., No. 13,545.......................	12/17/56	RT*
	Joplin Water Works Co., No. 13,618 (digest, 17 PUR 3d 530) (NARUC-Util. Reg. (1957) p. 10)	2/26/57	RT*

29

State	Company	Date of Order	Procedure Approved
Missouri	United Tel. Co. of Mo., No. 13,608 (digest, 17 PUR 3d 530) (NARUC-Util. Reg. (1957) p. 10)	2/ 8/57	RT*
	Joplin Water Works Co., (20 PUR 3d 195) (ULR 17,759)	9/ 4/57	3
	Missouri Power & Lt. Co. (21 PUR 3d 404)	12/17/57	3
	Empire District Elec. Co. (22 PUR 3d 399)	1/24/58	3
	Union Elec. Co., No. 13,531	8/29/58	3
	Kansas City Power & Lt. Co., No. 13,822	9/15/58	3
Nebraska	Letter from Nebraska Continental Tel. Co. to State Railway Comm., advising of company's procedure; no adverse reply	11/23/55	RT
	United Tel. Co. of the West, No. A-20745	3/ 5/57	RT
Nevada	Southern Nevada Power Co., I & S Dkt. No. 195	3/20/58	2
New Hampshire	Pub. Serv. Co. of N. H. (18 PUR 3d 523)	4/16/57	3
	All Utilities, No. 6971 (I-F 10,382)	4/16/57	7
New Jersey	Letter from Dept. of Pub. Util. to Pub. Serv. Elec. & Gas Co.	12/ 8/55	RS*
	Letter from Dept. of Pub. Util. to Elizabethtown Consol. Gas Co.	3/29/56	RT
	Bernards Water Co. (18 PUR 3d 92)	4/24/57	3
	Commonwealth Water Co. (18 PUR 3d 445)	5/ 8/57	3
	Frenchtown Water Co. (digest, 18 PUR 3d 558) (ULR 17,564)	5/ 8/57	3
New Mexico	Lea County Gas Co. (10 PUR 3d 279)	9/22/55	3
	General Tel. Co. of the S. W. (14 PUR 3d 243)	5/28/56	RT4
New York	N. Y. Water Serv. Corp.	1/13/58	**
North Dakota	Montana-Dakota Utilities Co., No. 5576	1/24/58	3
Ohio	Ohio Power Co., No. 25,638 (Denied)	9/ 9/55	RS*
	Cleveland Elec. Illum. Co. (11 PUR 3d 465)	12/29/55	RT*
	Ohio Consol. Tel. Co., No. 26,009 (cited 12 PUR 3d 530)	2/24/56	RT*
	Cincinnati Gas & Elec. Co., No. 26,010	3/ 6/56	RT
	General Tel. of Ohio, No. 26,027	3/ 6/56	RT*
	Ohio Power Co., No. 26,190	4/ 6/56	RT
	Toledo Edison Co., No. 26,378	7/10/56	RT*

30

State	Company	Date of Order	Procedure Approved
Ohio	Columbus & So. Ohio Elec. Co., No. 26,406	8/ 6/56	RT*
	Ohio Edison Co., No. 26,439	8/ 6/56	RT*
	Ohio Fuel Gas Co., et al, Formal Case No. 26,494	9/14/56	RT*
	Marietta Elec. Co.	12/20/56	RS
	Ohio Fuel Gas Co., No. 26,371	6/11/58	2
Oklahoma	Okla. Nat. Gas Co. (12 PUR 3d 293)	6/29/55	2
	Pub. Serv. Co. of Okla. (12 PUR 3d 296)	7/18/55	RS
	Okla. Tel. Co., No. 21,135	1/19/56	RT
	Okla. Nat. Gas Co. (ULR 17,816)	12/24/57	2
Pennsylvania	Citizens Water Co. of Wash., Pa. (13 PUR 3d 189)	12/12/55	3
	Manufacturers Lt. & Heat Co. (No. 16,330); [affirmed by Penn. Superior Ct. in City of Pittsburgh v. Penn. PUC, 12/28/56—(ULR 17,388) (17 PUR 3d 249)]	1/ 3/56	3
	So. Pittsburgh Water Co., No. 16,266 (ULR 17,508)	1/ 7/57	3
	Penn. Power & Lt. Co. (14 PUR 3d 438) (ULR 17355)	7/16/56	3
	Penn. Gas Co. (18 PUR 3d 552) (ULR 17554)	2/26/57	3
	Penn P. U. C. v. Northumberland Water Co. (digest, 20 PUR 3d 548)	10/ 7/57	3
	Manufacturers Lt. & Heat Co., et al. C. 16,719, appealed 9/11/58	2/10/58	3
South Carolina	So. Car. Elec. & Gas Co., et al., Order No. E-754	12/20/55	RS*
	Sumter Tel. Co.	12/20/55	RT
	So. Car. Continental Tel. Co. (ULR 17049)	1/11/56	RT
	Sumter Tel. Co., Order No. 9850	1/11/56	RT
	So. Car. Gas Co., (ULR 17,350)	11/14/56	RT*
	United Tel. Co. of the Carolinas (ULR 17473)	2/27/57	RT*
	Lockhart Power Co. (ULR 17562)	5/ 2/57	RS
Tennessee	Letter from Tax & Rate Consultant (Tenn. PSC) to Southern Continental Tel. Co.	12/30/55	RT*
Vermont	All Utilities—Temporary Order	3/ 5/56	RT*1
Virginia	Appalachian Elec. Power Co., Case No. 12665	6/ 6/55	RS*
	General Tel. Co. of the S. E. (14 PUR 3d 239)	12/19/55	RS*
	Virginia Tel. & Tel. Co., Case No. 12958	3/13/56	RS*
	Eastern Shore Pub. Serv. Co., Case No. 12990	4/ 4/56	RS*

31

State	Company	Date of Order	Procedure Approved
Virginia	Old Dominion Power Co., Case No. 12954	8/ 7/56	RS*
	Virginia Gas Distrib. Corp., Case No. 13173	9/ 6/56	RS*
	No. Va. Power Co.	12/28/56	RS
West Virginia	Appalachian Electric Power Company, Case No. 4289	5/26/55	RS*
	Wheeling Electric Company, Case No. 4305	6/30/55	RS*
	Hope Natural Gas Company, Case No. 4462	9/ 7/56	RT*
	General Telephone Company of the Southeast, Case No. 4478	11/ 9/56	RS*
	United Fuel Gas Company, Case No. 4492	12/ 3/56	RT*
	Amere Gas Utilities Company, Case No. 4493	12/ 3/56	RT*
	Monongahela Power Company, Case No. 4490	12/ 4/56	RS*
	Potomac Light and Power Company, Case No. 4499	12/21/56	RS*
	Cumberland and Allegheny Gas Company, Case No. 4535	3/ 8/57	RT*
	Manufacturers Light and Heat Company, Case No. 4536	3/11/57	RT*
	Hope Natural Gas Company (23 PUR 3d 394)	4/18/58	3
	Appalachian Elec. Power Co., Case No. 4867, modifying Case No. 4289 above	12/22/58	AT
	Wheeling Elec. Co., Case No. 4868, modifying Case No. 4305 above	12/22/58	AT
Wisconsin	Wisconsin Fuel and Light Company (12 PUR 3d 254)	1/27/56	DR4
	Wisconsin Power and Light Company, 2-U-4177 (digest, 14 PUR 3d 558, 75)	8/ 7/56	DR4
	Wisconsin Public Service Corporation, 2-U-4164 (digest, 14 PUR 3d 558, 75)	8/10/56	DR4
	Lake Superior District Power Company, 2-U-4169 (digest, 14 PUR 3d 558, 75)	8/10/56	DR4
	Milwaukee Gas Light Company (15 PUR 3d 170)	8/30/56	DR4
	Mississippi Valley Public Service Company, 2-U-4188	12/21/56	DR4
	Wisconsin Hydro Electric Company, 2-U-4148	1/ 3/57	DR4
	Rhinelander Telephone Company, 2-U-4530	1/10/57	DR4
	Wisconsin Southern Gas Company, Inc., 2-U-4206	1/10/57	DR4
	Madison Gas & Electric Company, 2-U-4173	1/22/57	DR4
	La Crosse Telephone Corporation (20 PUR 3d 94)	7/23/57	DR4
Wyoming	United Telephone Co. of the West (23 PUR 3d 68)	3/24/58	2

32

APPENDIX II
ACCELERATED AMORTIZATION

State	Company	Date of Order	Procedure Approved
Alabama	Alabama Power Co. (letter)	7/24/52	RS
Arkansas	Arkansas Power & Light Co. (cited, 13 PUR 3d 22)	11/19/53	RT
	Arkansas Power & Light Co. (13 PUR 3d 1)	3/ 7/56	5
California	Pacific Gas & Elec. Co.	4/27/54	RS
	Calif. Elec. Power Co., Dec. No. 50694 (digest, 9 PUR 3d 529)	10/26/54	RT
	So., Calif. Edison Co., Dec. No. 50723 (cited, 21 PUR 3d 21)	11/ 3/54	RT*
	So. Calif. Edison Co. (21 PUR 3d 15)	10/15/57	5
	Pacific Gas & Elec. Co. (ULR 17757) (21 PUR 3d 48)	10/22/57	5
Colorado	Public Services Co. of Colo. (3 PUR 3d 161)	12/15/53	RS
	Colorado Central Power Co. (21 PUR 3d 491)	12/30/57	RS*
Connecticut	Connecticut Light & Power Co.	4/23/53	RT
	United Illuminating Company	4/23/53	RT
Florida	Gulf Power Co. (letter)	9/12/52	RS
	Florida Power & Light Co. (4 PUR 3d 91)	6/ 7/54	RS
	Florida Pr. Corp., 3902-EU, Order #1982	3/ 5/54	RS
Georgia	Georgia Power Co. (97 PUR NS 88)	12/23/52	RT
Idaho	Idaho Power Co.	3/18/53	RT
	Washington Water Power Co.	3/18/53	RS
Illinois	Iowa-Ill. Gas & Elec. Co. (ULR 17286)	9/13/56	RT
	Central Illinois Light Company	12/17/53	RT
	Union Electric Power Co.	12/17/53	RT
	Central Ill. Elec. & Gas Co.	2/17/54	RT
Indiana	Indiana & Mich. Elec. Co. (96 PUR NS 51) (ULR 16503)	10/ 7/52	RS*
	Indianapolis Pr. & Lt. Co. (2 PUR 3d 437)	11/12/53	RS*
	Southern Ind. Gas & Elec. Co. (#25126) (cited 12 PUR 3d 368)	3/16/54	RS*
	Public Service Co. of Indiana (#25311) (cited 12 PUR 3d 368)	6/17/54	RS*

33

State	Company	Date of Order	Procedure Approved
Indiana	All utilities (ULR 17794) (21 PUR 3d 414) .... [Appealed by Ind. & Mich. Elec. Co., 1/13/58, Dkt. No. 19149; case still pending.]	12/24/57	RT*8
	Pub. Serv. Co. of Ind. (12 PUR 3d 509), Affirmed (22 PUR 3d 13)	3/ 9/56	5
Kansas	Kansas Power & Light Company	10/28/53	RT
	Kansas City Power & Light Co., #46461-U	12/23/53	RT
Kentucky	Kentucky Utilities Co. (case #2493)	11/25/52	RS
	Kentucky & West Virginia Pr. Co. (case #2517)	2/26/53	RS
	Kentucky Utilities Co. (cited 22 PUR 3d 116)	1/ 6/54 & 9/28/55	RS*
	Union Light, Heat & Power Co.	12/30/55	RS
	Kentucky Utilities Co. (22 PUR 3d 113)	1/15/58	2a
Louisiana	Louisiana Power & Light Co.	5/ 2/52	RT
	All utilities (Order #6172) (ULR 16547) (100 PUR NS 247)	2/25/53	RT
Maine	Central Maine Power Co., U-2068	8/11/52	RS
	Maine Public Service Co. (ULR 17002) (12 PUR 3d 352)	1/26/56	RT
	Central Maine Power Co. (17 PUR 3d 452), affirmed in *Central Maine Power Co. v. Maine P. U. C.*, 136 A 2d 726, 21 PUR 3d 321, 11/7/57	3/15/57	5
Maryland	Potomac Edison Co.	4/24/53	RS
Massachusetts	Boston Edison Co. (ULR 16640) (2 PUR 3d 137)	12/29/53	RT
	Western Mass. Elec. Co., No. 10779 (cited 17 PUR 3d 516)	1/ 8/54	RT
	Berkshire Gas Co. (17 PUR 3d 515) (Applicable to all electric and gas utilities as of 1/1/54)	12/21/56	RT*
Michigan	Detroit Edison Co. (90 PUR NS 76)	8/ 8/51	RT
	Consumers Power Co. (D-875-A-52.3)	4/ 3/52	RS
	Ind. & Michigan Elec. Co. (D-668-52.4)	10/17/52	RS
	Michigan Gas & Elec. Co.	8/11/55	RT
Mississippi	Miss. Power Co.	12/16/58	{ FPC Order 204
	Miss. Power & Lt. Co.	12/16/58	{ FPC Order 204

34

State	Company	Date of Order	Procedure Approved
Missouri	Union Elec. Co. of Mo. (2 PUR 3d 427)	11/ 9/53	RT
	Kansas City Power & Lt. Co. (#12,735) (cited 12 PUR 3d 475)	12/22/53	RT
	Missouri Public Serv. Co. (#12,964) (digest, 7 PUR 3d 686)	3/ 4/55	RT
Montana	Montana Power Co.	1/19/59	RS
Nevada	So. Nevada Power Co.	4/16/56	RT
New Hampshire	Public Service Co. of N. H. (Order #6072)	5/20/52	RT9
New Jersey	Public Service Elec. & Gas Co. (letter)	1/16/53	RS*
New Mexico	General Order #18	6/ 9/52	RT
	General Tel. Co. of S.W. (14 PUR 3d 243)	5/28/56	RT4
	New Mexico Pub. Ser. Co.	12/28/54	RS
N. Carolina	Carolina Power & Light Co. (97 PUR NS 111)	1/26/53	RS
	Nantahala Pr. & Lt. (17 PUR 3d 517)	3/20/57	RT*
	Virginia Elec. & Pr. Co., Docket E-22, sub 20	7/20/54	RS
N. Dakota	Montana-Dakota Utilities Co. (22 PUR 3d 505)	1/24/58	6
	N. Dakota Utilities Co. (22 PUR 3d 505)	1/24/58	6
Ohio	Cleveland Elec. Illum. Co., #23,017	3/13/52	RS
	Cincinnati Gas & Elec. Co., #23,090	4/18/52	RS
	Ohio Edison Co., #23,297	7/28/52	RS
	Ohio Power Co., #23,321 (cited 10 PUR 3d 277)	8/27/52	RS
	Toledo Edison Co., #25,672	9/ 9/55	RS
	Marietta Elec. Co.	12/20/56	RS
	Columbus & So. O. Elec. Co.	11/18/57	RT
Oklahoma	Pub. Serv. Co. of Okla. (cited 12 PUR 3d 298)	1/28/53	RS
	Okla. Nat. Gas Co. (12 PUR 3d 293)	6/29/55	5
	Okla. Gas & Elec. Co.	7/22/57	RS
Oregon	Pacific Power & Light Company	12/23/53	RS
	Calif. Oregon Power Co. (ULR 16711)	5/24/54	RT
	Portland General Elec. U-F-1790	2/19/54	RS
Pennsylvania	Philadelphia Elec. Co. (letter)	2/24/53	RS
	Penn. Pr. & Lt. Co. (14 PUR 3d 438) (Restricted Surplus Deducted from Rate Base)	7/16/56	5
	Duquesne Light Co.	2/24/53	RS
	Penn Elec. Co.	12/22/54	RS
	Penn Power Co.	2/25/53	RS

35

State	Company	Date of Order	Procedure Approved
Pennsylvania	South Penn Power Co.	2/24/53	RS
	West Penn Power Co.	2/24/53	RS
S. Carolina	Carolina Power & Light Co., Order #E-707	1/27/53	RS
	S. Carolina Elec. & Gas Co., S. Carolina Generating Co., E-742	3/23/55	RS
Utah	Utah Power & Light Co. (11 PUR 3d 477)	12/29/55	RS
Vermont	Central Vermont Pub. Serv. Co.	12/ 3/58	RS
Virginia	Virginia Elec. & Pr. Co., #11347 Va. S.C.C. Rep. p. 228	11/26/52	RS
	Appalachian Elec. Pr. Co., #11343	11/25/52	RS
	Board of Supervision of Arlington County v. Virginia Elec. & Power Co., 196 Va. 1102	4/25/55	5
	No. Virginia Power Co.	3/12/57	RS
Washington	Pacific Pr. & Lt. Co. (ULR 16,469)	1/30/53	RS6
	Wash. Water Pr. Co. (98 PUR NS 526)	3/10/53	RS6
	Washington Water Power Co., #U-8398 (98 PUR NS 12)	1/23/53	RS6
West Virginia	Appalachian Elec. Pr. Co., Case #3894	2/ 6/53	RS
	Monongahela Power Co.	1/22/57	RS
	Potomac Lt. & Pr. Co.	2/27/57	RS
Wisconsin	Wisc. Power & Light Co., 2-U-4177 (digest, 14 PUR 3d 558, 575)	8/ 7/56	DR4
Wyoming	Utah Pr. & Lt. Co. (ULR 17067) (12 PUR 3d 489)	3/ 8/56	RS*

36

SYMBOLS USED IN BOTH APPENDICES

AT	Actual-taxes-paid.
RS	Restricted Surplus.
RT	Reserve for Taxes.
DR	Depreciation Reserve.
( )	Order Revoked.
*	Order expressly excludes consideration of procedure to be followed in rate cases.
ULR	CCH Utilities Law Reports.
PUR	Public Utilities Reports.
EIS	P. U. R. Executive Information Service.
PUF	Public Utility Fortnightly.
N. A. R. U. C. Util.	Reg.—National Association of Railroad and Utilities Commissioners—*Report of the Committee on Progress in the Regulation of Public Utilities.* (1957)
N. A. R. U. C. — Bull.	—National Association of Railroad and Utilities Commissioners—*Bulletin to Member Commissioners.*
r	Reserve to be deducted from rate base.
1	Temporary orders.
2	Rate Case—normalization of taxes permitted for liberalized depreciation.
2a	Rate Case—normalization of taxes permitted for liberalized depreciation but deferral deducted from rate base.
3	Rate Case—normalization of taxes disallowed for liberalized depreciation.
3a	Rate Case—State Commission said that if company should change from straight-line to liberalized depreciation, it would have to pass on savings to customers.
4	Order states that same procedure would be applied for rate-making purposes.
5	Rate Case—normalization of taxes permitted for accelerated amortization.
6	Rate Case—normalization of taxes disallowed for accelerated amortization.

37

7	Revoked previous accounting order permitting normalization.
8	Reversed all prior accounting orders which had permitted use of restricted surplus.
9	Order indicates that Commission would approve this treatment if situation arose.
10	Rate Case—Normalization discussed but matter not resolved.
**	Not on file. According to the testimony of F. Merrill Beatty presented in Case No. 6148 these orders were silent as to the treatment of the tax effect of accelerated depreciation. However, from analysis of exhibits showing cost of service and rate base determinations, and the order, it has been ascertained that the companies were allowed to defer the tax effect of accelerated depreciation.

SECURITIES AND EXCHANGE COMMISSION
Washington 25, D. C.

March 25, 1959

Mr. A. J. G. Priest
Reid & Priest
Two Rector Street
New York 6, N. Y.

Dear Mr. Priest:

Receipt is acknowledged of ten copies of your memorandum on behalf of the Edison Electric Institute commenting on our Securities Act Release No. 4010. Your request for 45 minutes time at the public hearing on April 10, 1959, has been noted.

The Commission appreciates your efforts to work out a coordination of the presentation by the industry.

Very truly yours,

Andrew Barr
Chief Accountant

UNITED STATES INDEPENDENT
TELEPHONE ASSOCIATION

438 Pennsylvania Building
Washington 4, D. C.
National 8-6512

January 30, 1959

Mr. Orval L. DuBois
Secretary
Securities and Exchange Commission
Washington 25, D. C.

Dear Mr. Dubois:

This refers to the Commission's Notice of
Intention to Announce Interpretation of Administrative Policy of December 30, 1958 which contemplates announcement of administrative policy
on financial statements regarding balance sheet
treatment of credits equivalent to the reductions
in income taxes.

We have solicited the views of our Accounting
Committee with regard to the Commission's intention
in this respect. It is the view of the Committee
that it would appear that there would be no objection generally to the proposed interpretation.
However, the Committee has also suggested that the
Commission would want to have the benefit of the
following additional information relating to this
matter.

"One sentence in the interpretation could
create some concern among our rate case
people. That sentence reads, 'The cash
working capital is thus temporarily
increased by an amount equal to the
current tax reduction resulting from the
excess depreciation deductions taken for
tax purposes in earlier years.' The
inclusion of this statement in the interpretation would probably mean little to

other than utility companies whose rates
are keyed to a rate base which usually
includes an allowance for working
capital. Our concept of working capital
is that it represents the amount of
material and supplies and cash which is
required to carry on current operations;
I doubt if anyone would object to this
definition. The words current operations
mean just that--this does not include
either cash or supplies required for
plant construction and this distinction
is important to us. You will recall that
when we were under accelerated depreciation estimated amounts of taxes to be
deferred were included in our budgets as
decreases in amounts necessary to finance
our construction programs. On this basis
then, the cash available as a result of
adopting accelerated depreciation was
immediately committed to construction and
was not available as working capital if
the definition of that term above is
sound. The importance of this distinction in regard to a rate case is that if
a commission considered a tax deferral
to be an increase in available cash, it
might reduce the working capital requirement in the rate base determination."

We hope the comments of our Committee will be
helpful to the Commission in its consideration of
this matter.

Very truly yours,

/s/ CLYDE S. BAILEY

Clyde S. Bailey
Executive Vice President

CSB:ha

ALABAMA POWER COMPANY

WALTER BOULDIN
PRESIDENT

Birmingham 2, Alabama
January 21, 1959

Mr. Orval L. DuBois, Secretary
Securities and Exchange Commission
Washington 25, D. C.

Dear Mr. DuBois:

Referring to the Commission's "Notice of Intention to Announce Interpretation of Administrative Policy" relating to deferred income taxes as set forth in release dated December 30, 1958, we submit below for the consideration of the Commission the reasons which make it appear undesirable, in our opinion, for the Commission to make an interpretation of administrative policy as set forth in such release.

Alabama Power Company is subject to regulation, including accounting regulation, by the Alabama Public Service Commission. The Commission has prescribed that provisions shall be made, by credits to "Earned Surplus Restricted for Future Income Taxes," of amounts equivalent to the reduction in Federal and State income taxes resulting from accelerated amortization and depreciation for income tax purposes under Sections 167 and 168 of the Internal Revenue Code of 1954. The company has been so accounting and reporting, in accordance with the treatment prescribed by such Commission, since 1952 without objection by the Securities and Exchange Commission or any other body having jurisdiction or, for that matter, by any other persons whatsoever.

Since 1953, in balance sheets contained in reports to stockholders and in filings with the Securities and Exchange Commission, "Earned Surplus Restricted for Future Income Taxes" has been carried, not as a part of "Capitalization," but as a wholly separate and correlative item. The basis and nature of the accounting has also been described in an appropriate footnote.

In other words, as authorized by and in accordance with the prescription of the duly constituted public utility regulatory authority of the

State of Alabama having jurisdiction over such matters, and without objection or adverse comment by any others, the company for many years has been uniformly accounting for and reporting for all purposes the accumulated credit for deferred income taxes in a separate account entitled "Earned Surplus Restricted for Future Income Taxes." Substantially all of the revenues of the company are derived under rates subject to regulation by the State commission and the company is primarily subject to such State commission's regulation in most other respects. There is, therefore, clearly substantial authoritative support for such accounting treatment.

The Federal Power Commission, it its Order No. 204, referred to in the Commission's Notice, states that where there is inconsistency between the requirements of such order and the accounting requirements of a State commission having jurisdiction, a reasonable solution of the problem is "to classify the deferred taxes in accordance with state requirements for state purposes, and to use the treatment specified by this order for the purposes of this Commission." Pursuant to this suggestion, the company has, since the adoption by such order of appropriate amendments to the Federal Power Commission's Uniform System of Accounts providing for the accounting treatment of amounts so accumulated for deferred income taxes, entitled the account in which such amounts have been recorded as "Account 266, Accumulated Deferred Taxes on Income" for the purposes of the Federal Power Commission and "Account 271A, Earned Surplus Restricted for Future Income Taxes," for the purposes of the State commission, and it proposes to report to the commission in accordance with its own requirements.

The company desires, and in the absence of an announcement such as set forth in the Commission's Notice, proposes to continue its established practice in reports to stockholders and in filings with the Commission, of reporting the accumulated credit for deferred taxes in accordance with the accounting prescribed by the State commission, as a separate item on the balance sheet, not a part of "Capitalization" and with an appropriate footnote describing the requirements of the Federal Power Commission's order.

It is submitted with all respect that there can be nothing in such procedure which can fairly be described as "misleading or inaccurate."

Moreover, in the Public Holding Company Act of 1935, one of the laws cited in the Commission's Notice, it is specifically required of the Commission that the rules, regulations and orders of the Commission in respect of accounts "shall not be inconsistent with the requirements imposed by the law of any State or any rule or regulation thereunder." It can hardly be considered consistent with this statutory injunction to make the proposed announcement and thereby characterize as "misleading or inaccurate" the method of accounting prescribed by the duly constituted regulatory authority of this sovereign State.

Since the method of accounting and reporting in published statements followed by the company has been so followed for many years, in accordance with requirements prescribed by regulatory commissions having jurisdiction, without objection by anyone and without any evidence that the procedure has been misleading to any security holder (as it could hardly be since the origin and nature of the items are fully described in the published financial statements), the proposed interpretative announcement, particularly in its apparent prohibition against captioning, in accordance with the requirements of a State utility commission, the accumulated credit "Earned Surplus Restricted for Future Income Taxes," even when accompanied by a fully explanatory footnote, goes far beyond anything required for the protection of investors or consumers and appears to be contrary to the policy prescribed for the Commission in the Public Utility Holding Company Act of 1935.

Yours very truly,

ALABAMA POWER COMPANY

By /s/ WALTER BOULDIN

President

WB/w

ALABAMA POWER COMPANY

Birmingham 2, Alabama

January 28, 1959

Walter Bouldin
   President

          AIR MAIL

Mr. Orval L. DuBois, Secretary
Securities and Exchange Commission
Washington 25, D. C.

Dear Mr. DuBois:

     On January 21, a letter was submitted for
the consideration of the Commission which set
forth reasons that make it appear undesirable, in
our opinion, for the Commission to make an interpretation of administrative policy as set forth
in the Commission's "Notice of Intention to
Announce Interpretation of Administrative Policy."

     Inadvertently, only the original letter was
sent to the Commission on January 21. Attached are
three copies of our original letter as requested
in the notice.

                    Sincerely,

                    ALABAMA POWER COMPANY

                    By /s/ WALTER BOULDIN

                    President

WB-1:ny
Attachments

AMERICAN ELECTRIC POWER COMPANY, INC.
(FORMERLY AMERICAN GAS AND ELECTRIC COMPANY)

30 Church Street
New York 8, N.Y.
Cortlandt 7-5920

January 20, 1959

Securities and Exchange Commission
Washington 25, D. C.

Re: Securities Act of 1933, Release No. 4010
Securities Exchange Act of 1934, Release
No. 5844
Public Utility Holding Company Act of
1935, Release No. 13894

Gentlemen:

By your Notice of Intention to Announce Interpretation of Administrative Policy, dated December
30, 1958 (received by us on January 5, 1959), you
stated that you had under consideration the announcement of an interpretation of administrative
policy on financial statements regarding balance
sheet treatment of credits equivalent to the reduction in income taxes, as set forth in said Notice. You also pointed out that, in view of the
importance of the amounts involved, interested persons might file comments on or before January 31,
1959.

The undersigned, American Electric Power Company, a registered holding company, and its six
major operating companies, Appalachian Power Company, Indiana & Michigan Electric Company, Kentucky
Power Company, Kingsport Utilities, Incorporated,
Ohio Power Company, and Wheeling Electric Company,
believe this matter has the most serious implications for each of them and, therefore, are most
anxious to present a full statement of their views.

Because of the importance with which they regard
the proposed interpretation and the very serious
adverse effects upon them of such interpretation,
and because of the short period of time in which
to make comments, they respectfully request that
the time for comments by interested parties be extended for at least thirty days, and that, thereafter, a public hearing be held at which those interested may present oral arguments and file briefs.

   If the Commission is not disposed to grant
the requested extension of time on the basis of
this request, the undersigned would appreciate an
opportunity to appear before the Commission to
state in greater detail the reasons for such request.

                    Very truly yours,

                    AMERICAN ELECTRIC POWER COM-
                       PANY
                    APPALACHIAN POWER COMPANY
                    INDIANA & MICHIGAN ELECTRIC
                       COMPANY
                    KENTUCKY POWER COMPANY
                    KINGSPORT UTILITIES, INCORPO-
                    RATED
                    OHIO POWER COMPANY
                    WHEELING ELECTRIC COMPANY

                    By /s/ W. J. ROSE

SECURITIES AND EXCHANGE COMMISSION
Washington 25, D. C.

January 28, 1959

American Electric Power Company, Inc.
30 Church Street
New York 8, N. Y.

Attention Mr. W. J. Rose

Gentlemen:

The extension of time granted in the enclosed announcement adopted in response to several requests similar to that in your letter of January 20, 1959, should afford ample time for comment and presentation of your views on our proposed statement on balance sheet treatment of credits equivalent to reduction of income taxes.

Very truly yours,

Andrew Barr
Chief Accountant

Enclosure

AMERICAN ELECTRIC POWER COMPANY, INC.
(FORMERLY AMERICAN GAS AND ELECTRIC COMPANY)

30 Church Street,
New York 8, N. Y.
February 20, 1959

Securities and Exchange Commission
Washington 25, D. C.

Re: Notice of Intention to Announce
Interpretation of Administrative
Policy
Securities Act of 1933
Releases Nos. 4010 and 4023, etc.

Dear Sirs:

The subject Notice refers to the proposed announcement of an interpretation of administrative policy on financial statements regarding balance sheet treatment of credits equivalent to the reduction in income taxes. Release No. 4023 provides that interested persons may comment in writing by February 28, 1959, and provides for a public hearing on March 25, 1959. The undersigned companies have heretofore indicated that the proposed interpretation is of the highest importance to them and can have very serious adverse effects upon them.

From our analysis to date of the problems raised by the proposal, one of the very important matters which needs clarification is the intended meaning of the phrase "various items" as used in the portion of said Notice reading:

". . . any financial statement which designates as earned surplus or its equivalent or includes as a part of equity capital (even though accompanied by words of limitation such as 'restricted' or 'appropriated') the accumulated credit arising from accounting for reductions in income taxes for various items including those in sections 167 and 168 of the Internal Revenue Code . . . will . . . be presumed . . . 'to be misleading or inaccurate' . . . "

Our analysis to date has indicated that there are a number of different situations in which a taxpayer may take deductions of depreciation or amortization for tax purposes in excess of said deductions for book purposes. It appears that the Commission's proposal would establish as a rigid accounting principle the proposition that in this situation a provision should be made on the books for additional charges against net income equal to the resulting tax reduction, followed in later years by substantially equal aggregate credits to income when the reverse situation obtains. In order for us to determine the nature and extent of our comments, it is necessary for us to know whether, as a fact, the proposal is intended to establish such a rigid accounting principle, or, if not, to know the character, extent and basis of any exceptions from such a principle.

Disparity between tax and financial accounting is not an unusual phenomenon. Accounting for accelerated amortization is itself an illustration of long standing, having been followed for a period of almost twenty years. Accounting for liberalized depreciation is merely a more recent illustration.

The generally accepted method of accounting for intangible well-drilling expenses in the oil and gas field is an outstanding example of disparity between tax and book accounting, such disparity being many times greater than that produced by the methods of accounting for either accelerated amortization or liberalized depreciation. In such cases, the entire amount of the expense is taken as a tax deduction in the year in which it is incurred. This is equivalent to writing off in one year 100% of the cost of plant or property. But, for book accounting, the amount is capitalized as plant and property and is amortized over a period of years. This practice is widespread throughout the oil and gas industry and is reflected in many registration statements on file with the Commission. As indicated above, the practice has a far greater effect upon income statements than does the accounting for liberalized depreciation and accelerated amortization.

A simple illustration of this follows:

A. Utility Company "A" acquires depreciable plant in 1958 for $100,000, depreciable over a 20-year period. Declining balance depreciation is used for tax purposes and straight line for book purposes. In 1958 the results will be:

Book depreciation	— $	5,000
Tax deduction for liberalized depreciation	—	10,000
Current tax reduction because of liberalized depreciation ($5,000 times 52%)	—	2,600
Increase in current net income if income statement is not normalized	—	2,600

B. Oil Company "B" incurs $100,000 of intangible well-drilling expenses in 1958 which it capitalizes on its books and amortizes over a 20-year period. We then have:

Book amortization	—	5,000
Tax deduction for intangible well-drilling expenses	—	100,000
Current tax reduction resulting from taking entire drilling expense as a deduction ($95,000 times 52%)	—	49,400
Increase in current net income if income statement is not normalized	—	49,400

This practice also produces a much greater year-to-year distortion of income. Thus, for Company "A" in 1959, the following year, the book depreciation will remain $5,000. Its tax depreciation deduction will be $9,000 and its additional tax reduction and increase in net income will be $4,000 times 52%, or $2,080. On the other hand, the book amortization of Oil Company "B" will be $5,000, the tax deduction for intangible well-drilling expense will be zero, and the resultant tax increase and reduction in net income will be $5,000 times 52%, or $2,600. Thus, between 1958 and 1959, the utility's income will have decreased by $520 but the oil company's income will have decreased by $52,000, or 100 times as much.

If the proposed accounting principle is intended as a general accounting principle requiring tax equalization wherever there is a material difference between tax and book accounting with offsetting credits to a non-equity account, it will be of the greatest importance to consider the revolutionary nature of the new principle and to examine the breadth of its implications. On the other hand, if the proposal is limited to accounting for liberalized depreciation and accelerated amortization, it will be relevant to discuss whether there is a solid basis for such limitation, and, even more important, to analyze the basic reasons for normalization in the cases where the principle is to be applied.

For the reasons indicated, clarification of the intention of the proposal in the respects indicated is, therefore, indispensable to the preparation of our comments on this proposal.

Because of the complex nature of the problem as it affects the AEP System, particularly since the operating subsidiaries have accounting orders in six different states requiring an accounting treatment different from that set forth in the proposal, we will need additional time to prepare comprehensive comments and, therefore, request extension of the time for comments beyond February 28 by at least thirty days, and that the date of the public hearing be changed from March 25 to a date about thirty days thereafter.

In addition, March 25 is one of the days of the annual meeting, set many months ago, of the Southeastern Electric Exchange of which two of our companies and many others interested in this matter are members. In the case of ourselves, some of those who plan to be present and to represent us at the public hearing before the Commission have made long-standing arrangements to attend and deliver papers before the Southeastern Electric Exchange annual meeting.

Very truly yours,

AMERICAN ELECTRIC POWER COMPANY, INC.
APPALACHIAN POWER COMPANY
INDIANA & MICHIGAN ELECTRIC COMPANY
KENTUCKY POWER COMPANY
KINGSPORT UTILITIES, INCORPORATED
OHIO POWER COMPANY
WHEELING ELECTRIC COMPANY

By /s/ W. J. ROSE

mvs

SECURITIES AND EXCHANGE COMMISSION
Washington 25, D. C.

March 2, 1959

Mr. W. J. Rose
American Electric Power Company, Inc.
30 Church Street
New York 8, N. Y.

Dear Mr. Rose:

This is in reply to your letter of February 20, 1959, in which you request clarification of the term "various items" and inquire as to whether the proposal is intended to establish as a rigid accounting principle the proposition that a provision should be made on the books for additional charges against net income equal to the resulting tax reduction in all situations where depreciation and amortization for tax purposes is in excess of said deduction for book purposes.

The words "various items" I think you recognize as necessary to cover matters other than those growing out of Sections 167 and 168 of the Internal Revenue Code. The Federal Power Commission Orders 203 and 204 include accounts to take care of "other items," and the Civil Aeronautics Board's recent Regulation ER-230, adopted March 13, 1958, provides for such items as pre-operating, new aircraft integration, or extension and development expenses. I believe you would agree that it would be impracticable for us to enumerate all of the items which some registrants and their accountants might feel material enough to warrant deferred tax accounting. These matters, except for the special attention given to depreciation in Accounting Research Bulletin No. 44 (Revised), are deemed to be covered by the Institute's bulletins on tax allocation.

With respect to your example from the oil industry, it is a matter of public record that the American Petroleum Institute has suggested clarification of the release and that their organization will be represented at the hearing.

Any suggestions you have should be included in your comments on the proposed release.

I understand that you are aware of the postponement to March 25 for filing comments and to April 8 for the hearing.

Very truly yours,

Andrew Barr
Chief Accountant

cc: Commissioners
    Mr. J. A. Pines

AMERICAN ELECTRIC POWER COMPANY, INC.
(FORMERLY AMERICAN GAS AND ELECTRIC COMPANY)

30 Church Street
New York 8, N.Y.
Cortlandt 7-5920

March 18, 1959

Securities and Exchange Commission
Washington 25, D. C.

Dear Sirs:

Re: Securities Act of 1933 Release No. 4010
and related Releases under the other
Acts Administered by the Securities and
Exchange Commission

The undersigned companies (AEP Companies) desire to be heard at the public hearing to be held
commencing April 8 in connection with the Interpretation of Administrative Policy regarding balance
sheet treatment of financial statements set forth
in the subject Releases.

The AEP companies intend to have Mr. Philip
Sporn, President of the AEP Companies, and Mr.
Donald C. Cook, Vice President of certain of the
AEP Companies, make the oral presentation on their
behalf. As you know, the Edison Electric Institute
Convention meets in New Orleans on April 6-8, in-
clusive. This makes it impossible for the AEP Companies to make their oral presentation to the Commission on April 8 or 9. The AEP Companies have
been advised, however, that the hearings will be
continued through April 10 and that it is the intention to hear the oral presentation of Edison
Electric Institute at 2:00 p.m. on April 10. The
AEP Companies desire that they be heard on April
10 immediately following the presentation to be
made by Edison Electric Institute.

The complexity of the problem, resulting from the fact that the AEP Companies include a public utility holding company, six operating electric utilities and a common carrier, and that the AEP Companies are subject to the jurisdiction, in various respects, of seven State and three Federal commissions, makes necessary an extensive oral presentation by the AEP Companies. It is desired that one hour be allocated for their presentation. A written statement will be made on behalf of the AEP Companies not later than March 25.

Very truly yours,

AMERICAN ELECTRIC POWER COMPANY, INC.
APPALACHIAN POWER COMPANY
INDIANA & MICHIGAN ELECTRIC COMPANY
KENTUCKY POWER COMPANY
KINGSPORT UTILITIES, INCORPORATED
OHIO POWER COMPANY
TWIN BRANCH RAILROAD COMPANY
WHEELING ELECTRIC COMPANY

By /s/ W. J. ROSE

Vice President

mc

SECURITIES AND EXCHANGE COMMISSION
Washington 25, D. C.

March 20. 1959

Mr. W. J. Rose, Vice President
American Electric Power Company, Inc.
30 Church Street
New York 8, N. Y.

Dear Mr. Rose:

Your request of March 18, 1959, for one hour's time for Messrs. Philip Sporn and Donald C. Cook at the public hearing on Securities Act Release No. 4010 on April 10, 1959, has been noted. When all of the requests for appearances have been received, the Commission will make an appropriate allocation of time among those who appear at the public hearing.

Since it is assumed that the Commission will be particularly interested in your comments, if convenient it would be helpful to have enough copies of your written statement for use of the Commission and the staff. Ten copies should be sufficient.

Very truly yours,

Andrew Barr
Chief Accountant

AMERICAN ELECTRIC POWER COMPANY, INC.
(FORMERLY AMERICAN GAS AND ELECTRIC COMPANY)

30 Church Street
New York 8, N.Y.
Cortlandt 7-5920

March 24, 1959

Mr. Andrew Barr
Chief Accountant
Securities and Exchange Commission
Washington 25, D. C.

  Re: Securities Act of 1933 Release No. 4010
    and Related Releases Under the Other Acts
    Administered by the Securities and Ex-
    change Commission

Dear Mr. Barr:

  Attached is a copy of Herbert B. Cohn's letter
to the Secretary of the Commission making the formal filing in the above matter.

  As requested in your letter of March 20, enclosed are ten additional copies for your use.

       Very truly yours,

       /s/ W. J. ROSE

       W. J. Rose
       Vice President

Enclosures

AMERICAN ELECTRIC POWER SERVICE CORPORATION
(FORMERLY AMERICAN GAS AND ELECTRIC SERVICE CORPORATION)

30 Church Street
New York 8, N. Y.
Cortlandt 7-5920

March 24, 1959

Honorable Orval L. DuBois
Secretary
Securities and Exchange Commission
Washington 25, D. C.

> Re: Securities Act of 1933 Release No. 4010
> and Related Releases Under the Other
> Acts Administered by the Securities
> and Exchange Commission

Dear Sir:

I enclose in triplicate a Memorandum which
is being filed in the subject proceeding on
behalf of American Electric Power Company, Inc.,
Appalachian Power Company, Indiana & Michigan
Electric Company, Kentucky Power Company,
Kingsport Utilities, Incorporated, Ohio Power
Company, Twin Branch Railroad Company and Wheeling
Electric Company.

Mr. W. J. Rose's letter of March 18 sets
forth the request of these companies for time at
the hearings to be held in this proceeding.

Very truly yours,

/s/ HERBERT B. COHN

Herbert B. Cohn
Vice President and
Chief Counsel

Enclosures
mvs

United States of America

SECURITIES AND EXCHANGE COMMISSION

In the Matter

of

Interpretation of Administrative Policy
on Financial Statements Regarding
Balance Sheet Treatment of Credit
Equivalent to Reduction of Income
Taxes

MEMORANDUM IN OPPOSITION TO PROPOSED INTERPRETATION ON
BEHALF OF AMERICAN ELECTRIC POWER COMPANY, INC., APPA-
LACHIAN POWER COMPANY, INDIANA & MICHIGAN ELECTRIC
COMPANY, KENTUCKY POWER COMPANY, KINGSPORT UTILITIES,
INCORPORATED, OHIO POWER COMPANY, TWIN BRANCH RAIL-
ROAD COMPANY AND WHEELING ELECTRIC COMPANY (HEREIN-
AFTER COLLECTIVELY CALLED "AEP COMPANIES").

By Notice of Intention to Announce Interpretation of Administrative
Policy dated December 30, 1958, the Securities and Exchange Commission
invited interested persons to submit their views on the proposed Interpretation of Administrative Policy set forth therein. The AEP Companies,
consisting of American Electric Power Company, Inc., a registered public
utility holding company, and the seven operating utility companies in the
American Electric Power System submit this memorandum in response to
this Notice.

INTRODUCTION

A. General Background

Section 168 (formerly Section 124A) and Section 167 of the Internal
Revenue Code authorize accelerated tax amortization of certified emergency facilities and the use for tax purposes of certain methods of lib-

eralized depreciation, as for example declining balance depreciation, in which the depreciation deduction is greater in early years of service life than if straight line depreciation had been used.

There are at least three ways in which the increased tax deductions and decreased income tax arising therefrom may be treated. One way, a common industrial practice, is to use book depreciation identical to the tax depreciation. Utilities' depreciation, however, involves regulatory considerations since their book depreciation is an operating expense chargeable to rate-payers and may not be increased merely because of the use of Sections 167 and 168 of the Internal Revenue Code.* In a number of states, however, utilities have been authorized to provide for an additional operating expense equal to the amount by which the income tax would have been greater if straight line tax depreciation were used. This is a form of equalizing or normalizing which has been permitted despite the usual interdict against such accounting, in order that present and future rate-payers will have a proportionately constant cost. In other states, and in the case of the Interstate Commerce Commission, only actual taxes are allowed to be charged as an operating expense, and, thus, the tax reduction serves to increase net income. This is sometimes referred to as the flow-through method.

Tax depreciation, particularly in the utility area, differed from book depreciation long before the enactment of Sections 167 and 168. Many regulatory commissions have required a longer period of depreciable life than that suggested by Bulletin F of the Treasury Department. California has required sinking fund book depreciation, which results in greater depreciation expense in the later years than in the case of straight line depreciation.

Moreover, because utility plant is recorded at "original cost" and the tax base of a plant is actual cost, total available tax deductions for depreciation differ markedly from total available book depreciation. If, for example, utility assets have been purchased rather than constructed the tax base is likely to be considerably in excess of book cost and thus

---

* An exception to this principle exists in Wisconsin where by orders of the Wisconsin Public Service Commission an amount equal to the reduction in Federal income taxes is added to book depreciation.

total tax depreciation will exceed total book depreciation. On the other hand, where facilities are constructed by a utility, in accordance with approved regulatory practice, there is included in original cost an amount for interest during construction and for taxes paid during construction. Neither of these elements is included in the tax base. Thus, the book cost and total available book depreciation will exceed the tax cost and the total available tax depreciation. Another situation where this will occur is where the Securities and Exchange Commission has ordered the utility to dispose of certain properties under the Public Utility Holding Company Act. Under Part VI of Subchapter O, Chapter 1 of the Internal Revenue Code of 1954 (formerly Supplement R of Chapter 1 of the Internal Revenue Code of 1939) the utility would for tax purposes reduce the tax base of its remaining plant by the amount of profit realized from the properties sold. For book purposes, however, the remaining properties would be carried at their original cost. Here again total available tax deductions for depreciation will be less than available book depreciation. These differences are not minor or insignificant; in particular cases they may be, and frequently are, very substantial. .

That tax and book depreciation are not equal in amount is not unusual. "Tax accounting is not, and is not intended to be, the same as other accounting. The courts frequently have held that particular transactions have tax consequences different from their corporate intendment and their bookkeeping treatment." (Hills, "The Law of Accounting and Financial Statements" (1957) page 48).

Income tax deductions are a matter of Congressional grace. Comm'r v. Sullivan 356 U.S. 27 (1958). Tax depreciation is not any different from other deductions from gross income which the legislature may of grace allow. Jefferson and Clearfield Coal and Iron Co. v. U. S. 14 F. Supp. 918 (Ct. Claims 1936) cert. denied, 299 US 581 (1936). "The fact that greater charges were taken for income tax purposes than were actually made per books does not necessarily demonstrate the insufficiency of the latter figures. . . " In re Electric Power & Light Corp. et al. 29 SEC 52, 149 (1949). Tax depreciation is a right to reduce taxable income. It does not and need not bear any precise relation to the actual rate of using up of useful life. As the familiar example of statutory depletion (under which a cumulative depletion deduction equal to many times the cost of the property is possible) demonstrates, rights to reduction of taxable income need have no inherent or logical relationship to book costs.

Nor is this difference between book and tax depreciation and amortization an isolated phenomenon in the utility field. Long before Section 168 and Section 167 existed, and continuing on to the present, oil and gas companies have followed the practice for book purposes of capitalizing intangible well drilling expenses as plant and amortizing them over an extended period. For tax purposes they are deducted in the year the drilling is done. This often results, for a particular year, in an oil or gas company's having book income in the millions and no income at all for tax purposes. This is analogous to allowing a form of tax depreciation or amortization in which the entire assets are depreciable or amortizable for tax purposes in one year and the book depreciation is taken over their entire useful life. No one, certainly no accountant, appears to have taken exception to this common oil and gas company practice sanctioned time and again by the SEC and which exaggerates the disparities between books and taxable deductions to a degree which far exceeds that resulting under Sections 167 and 168.

The subject matter of the Notice relates then to only one of a variety of forms of a common phenomenon, book and tax differences, all of which have been with us for a long time and which can never be eliminated.

B. Differences Between Utility Accounting and Non-utility Accounting

Preliminarily, we urge upon the Commission the necessity for separating in its thinking the very different problems created by application of the proposal to regulated utilities on the one hand and to non-utilities on the other. The treatment of accounting in connection with regulated utility companies differs in many respects from accounting by unregulated industrial companies. This arises primarily because of the relation between utility accounting and the rate-making or rate-setting problem. Accounting, in the utility field, not only reflects substantive results but it produces them as well.

By way of illustration, reference is made to two important accounting concepts which are found only in the requirements and practices of public utility accounting and reflect the regulatory purpose and point of view. The first is the original cost basis of accounting for utility plant and the second is the concept of above and below the line. *

---

* See Foster and Rodey, "Public Utility Accounting", published by Prentice Hall, Inc. (1951), page 27.

Cost of plant is the cost to the accounting company. Original cost, which is the cost of plant used in utility accounting, means, however, the cost of such property to the person first devoting it to the public service. The actual cost to a public utility company may be, and is frequently, well in excess of "original cost" where plant has been purchased. On the other hand, where plant is constructed by a utility, interest during construction and taxes during construction are made part of "original cost" so that in this case original cost of a public utility may exceed, and usually does exceed, cost in ordinary industrial accounting.

The specialized accounting of above the line and below the line in the utility field relates to whether expenses are of such a nature that they are to be considered chargeable against consumers for the services received, i.e., operating expenses. Operating expenses are charged above the line and are a deduction from gross revenues in order to determine gross operating income. Gross operating income is the amount available for return on the aggregate capital used in rendering the utility service. Deductions for the use of capital and the like are below the line items, i.e., deductions from gross operating income. They are not expenses chargeable to consumers. Income taxes in utility accounting are above the line expenses since they are expenses chargeable against power consumers. Galveston Electric Co. v. Galveston 258 U.S. 388 (1922). In normal industrial practice, on the other hand, income taxes do not represent operating expenses.

Since utility accounting is different from non-utility accounting, what may be as a general matter an accepted accounting treatment may be wholly irrational when applied to regulated utilities. This difference between regulated utility accounting practice and ordinary industrial accounting practice has heretofore been entirely recognized by the accounting profession.

This difference has also been recognized and approved by the Securities and Exchange Commission. Thus, Rule 5.02 under Regulation S-X provides in the case of fixed assets that for utility companies plant must be shown in balance sheets at original cost as required by the system of accounts prescribed by the applicable regulatory authorities. This is not the rule for unregulated companies. Similarly, as permitted by Rule 5.03, utility companies follow the segregation of operating revenues and operating expenses in income statements as required by regulatory authorities. In the case of unregulated companies, on the other hand, it is clear that Federal income taxes must be stated as an income deduction and not as an operating expense.

All of the foregoing indicates the importance of separate consideration as between regulated utilities and non-utilities -- in applying any new accounting concept. The comments in this memorandum are directed primarily to the specialized accounting problems of public utility companies and public utility holding company systems. The memorandum is not intended as a general comment on accounting requirements by unregulated companies.

SUMMARY OF ARGUMENT

We contend that the proposal set forth in the Notice, insofar as it relates to regulated utilities, should not be adopted because

1. This Commission should not prescribe any accounting requirement for a regulated utility which is inconsistent with the requirements imposed by the state commission having jurisdiction;

2. Public utility subsidiaries of registered holding companies must be permitted to account as commissions having primary jurisdiction over rates require;

3. Where normalizing is followed, the use of restricted surplus in the balance sheet as the contra credit to the normalizing charge is proper accounting and indeed, if a choice had to be made, would be the preferred treatment.

4. The use of restricted surplus as the contra credit to the normalizing charge is more beneficial to investors and consumers than the use of a reserve account of any kind.

5. The proposed announcement would improperly brand as misleading and inaccurate accounting procedures which are in accord with accepted principles of accounting.

6. The proposed interpretation purports to make retro-active an accounting policy different from that heretofore adopted by the SEC and to brand the use of methods in accordance with the present policy misleading and inaccurate.

7. The requirements of full and fair disclosure of the Securities Act of 1933 and of the Securities Exchange Act of 1934 can adequately be met without any need for adoption of the proposed interpretation.

POINT I

THIS COMMISSION SHOULD NOT PRESCRIBE ANY ACCOUNTING REQUIREMENT FOR A REGULATED UTILITY WHICH IS INCONSISTENT WITH THE REQUIREMENTS IMPOSED BY THE STATE COMMISSION HAVING JURISDICTION.

Regulation of the business of electric utility companies is primarily under the jurisdiction of state public utility commissions. The single exception is the relatively minor sale of electricity for resale in interstate commerce which is regulated by the Federal Power Commission. The Federal Power Commission has recognized this predominance of state regulation. In considering the rate treatment the FPC should apply in connection with accelerated amortization, it stated "we realize that the electric public utilities are governed almost wholly in this regard by state commissions" (emphasis added). FPC Opinion No. 264 dated December 4, 1953 in Docket No. R-126. Indeed, the Federal Power Act, from which the Federal Power Commission derives its jurisdiction, was conceived as a supplement to the basic state regulation. Connecticut Light & Power Company v. FPC 324 U.S. 515, 525 (1945).

The AEP Companies which are electric utilities are subject to orders regulating accounting for accelerated amortization and liberalized depreciation issued by six state commissions in states where the AEP Companies operate, namely, Indiana, Kentucky, Michigan, Ohio, Virginia and West Virginia. SEC requirements should certainly not be inconsistent with the accounting treatments required by the orders of these state commissions. The majority of these commissions have required that the deferred taxes arising from accelerated amortization and liberalized depreciation be charged as operating expenses and that the contra credit be carried to a restricted surplus account. In West Virginia the commission has required, both for accounting and rate-making purposes, insofar as liberalized depreciation is concerned, that no charge shall be made as an operating expense for any deferred taxes with the necessary result that an amount equal to the deferred taxes augments net income and therefore unrestricted earned surplus.

Since the basic regulatory considerations are those of state regulatory commissions and since the utility investor is primarily concerned with the rate of return which will be afforded, the most useful accounting to the utility investor will be the accounting which reflects the attitudes and requirements of the state regulatory commissions. To compel an accounting requirement which is inconsistent with the state requirements for rate-making purposes would, in our opinion, be a disservice to investors.

POINT II

PUBLIC UTILITY SUBSIDIARIES OF REGISTERED HOLDING COMPANIES MUST BE PERMITTED TO ACCOUNT AS COMMISSIONS HAVING PRIMARY JURISDICTION OVER RATES REQUIRE.

There is a reason beyond policy why the SEC must permit the AEP Companies to account as required by state regulatory bodies having jurisdiction. This is the legal requirement to be found in Section 20(b) of the Public Utility Holding Company Act of 1935. Section 20(b) provides in relevant part:

"In the case of the accounts of any company whose methods of accounting are prescribed under the provisions of any law of the United States or of any State, the rules and regulations or orders of the Commission in respect of accounts shall not be inconsistent with the requirements imposed by such law or any rule or regulation thereunder;"

Congress incorporated Section 20(b) in the 1935 Act precisely because it wanted to avoid any encroachment on the jurisdiction of state commissions. The Senate Report on the Bill (Report No. 621, 74th Congress, 1st Session) provides at page 9:

"With regard to the accounts of public utility companies the committee has added an express provision in Section 20 to prevent any possible encroachment upon the practice and jurisdiction of State commissions."

Section 20(b) limits the SEC to accounting requirements which are consistent with the rules of state commissions and with the rules of the other Federal regulatory commissions, as ICC, FCC and CAB, with the exception of the Federal Power Commission. The exception in the case of the Federal Power Commission derives from Section 318 of the Federal Power Act, which was passed together with the Public Utility Holding Company Act of 1935, and which provides, as a part of the Federal Power Act, that the SEC has paramount jurisdiction in the case of holding company subsidiaries. Therefore, the requirement of consistency between accounts prescribed by the SEC and those prescribed under any law of the United States does not include accounts prescribed by the Federal Power Commission.

With respect to the paramount nature of ICC jurisdiction the provisions of Section 20(b) are bolstered by the provisions of two prior pieces of legislation, Section 19(a) of the Securities Act of 1933 which provides that the SEC may not require financial statements of common carriers inconsistent with the ICC rules, and Section 13(b) of the Securities Exchange Act of 1934 barring a similar inconsistency with respect to reports filed under that Act. In addition, Section 20 of the Interstate Commerce Act bars common carriers from keeping accounts, records or memoranda contrary to the ICC rules.

Because of the limitations of Section 20(b) the SEC may not prescribe accounting for the AEP Companies which are electric utilities inconsistent with the orders of their respective state commissions and, insofar as that AEP Company which is a common carrier, with the Federal commission having jurisdiction. The SEC requirements must comport with state commission requirements for the operating electric utility companies.

In the case of Twin Branch Railroad Company, an AEP Company regulated by the Interstate Commerce Commission under the Interstate Commerce Act, the accounts must comport with ICC requirements. The

ICC expressly forbids deferred tax accounting either for liberalized depreciation or accelerated amortization. It requires that only actual taxes be charged as an operating expense and that the amounts of any tax reduction flow through to net income and earned surplus. *

Section 20(b) presents a legal barrier to the proposed interpretation. Even if it did not, Section 20(b) would certainly demonstrate a Congressional policy to accord great weight to state accounting regulations and to dissuade this Commission from requiring a utility to follow accounting procedures differing from those prescribed by the regulatory commission having primary jurisdiction over its rates.

POINT III

WHERE NORMALIZING IS FOLLOWED, THE USE OF RESTRICTED SURPLUS IN THE BALANCE SHEET AS THE CONTRA CREDIT TO THE NORMALIZING CHARGE IS PROPER ACCOUNTING AND INDEED, IF A CHOICE HAD TO BE MADE, WOULD BE THE PREFERRED TREATMENT.

The subject Notice would establish a policy that would preclude the use of restricted surplus as the contra credit to the normalizing charge. Thus, Footnote 4 of Release No. 4010 states in part "Other companies may use the same or other appropriate captions and classifications pro-

---

* This requirement was only recently reaffirmed by the ICC in a notice to all carriers dated February 9, 1959 in which the Commission said "When an available depreciation allowance produces a reduction in Federal income taxes, no matter how temporary the benefit may be the effect on net income should be the same as a reduction in taxes produced by lower tax rates. Possible income taxes to be assessed in the future are not an element of tax expense for the current year. As to depreciable property with an expected life of thirty years, or even less, it is illogical to expect that tax reductions resulting from accelerated depreciation allowances can be matched with tax increases of the future. New property units acquired in the future will provide increased depreciation allowances to offset decreasing allowances for older units. Furthermore, income tax rates and tax procedures are subject to change from year to year, and the computation of income taxes differs as between carriers, and for any carrier differs as between years, in too many respects to justify special provision for a fluctuation in taxes resulting only from depreciation allowances."

vided they avoid any implication that the credit balance in question <u>is a part of earned surplus or of equity capital</u>" (emphasis added).

We see no justification whatever for such a proposal.

The Federal Power Commission in imposing its requirements as to the nature of the contra credit stated expressly, in justifying the caption it chose, that "while making provision for future tax liability, it will not foreclose financial analysts, investors and others from considering these amounts as part of equity capital if they think proper, with such consequential benefits to the rating of the company's securities and costs of financing as may result therefrom". See FPC Order No. 204 issued May 29, 1958 in Docket R-159. In addition, the Federal Power Commission requirements promulgated in Order 204 specifically permit electric public utilities "which are required by a state commission to report deferred taxes in a . . . surplus account . . . to classify the deferred taxes in accordance with state requirements for state purposes . . . "

The fact of the matter is that the use of restricted surplus has been certified as a generally accepted principle of accounting by the most eminent accounting firms in the country and is required by many state commissions.

The use of a restricted surplus is clearly permitted as a generally accepted principle of accounting. Although there appear to have been some unsupported assertions to the contrary, neither Bulletin 43 of the American Institute of Certified Public Accountants, which covers the Institute's views on accelerated amortization, nor Bulletin 44 which covers its views on liberalized depreciation, imposes any restriction on denoting the contra credit "restricted surplus". *

---

* In testimony before the Public Utilities Commission of the State of California on October 9, 1958, William W. Werntz, Chairman of the Committee on Accounting Procedure of the American Institute of Certified Public Accountants, the Committee which promulgated Bulletin 44, in answer to the question "Would it be fair to say then that your Committee and the American Institute has not designated the proper account for the deferral?" replied "We have not designated the classification, that is correct". (Transcript p. 1173)

Instead, the fact is that every outstanding public accounting firm in the United States has certified, without qualification, to financial statements which provided for deferred tax accounting for accelerated amortization and/or liberalized depreciation and in which the contra credit was carried to some form of earned surplus. *

The regulatory commissions of at least twenty-four states have authorized the use of a restricted earned surplus for the contra credit in respect of deferred tax accounting for accelerated amortization and at least thirteen state commissions have authorized such treatment in respect of liberalized depreciation. This, incidentally, compares with approximately eighteen states in which the commissions have authorized the use of a reserve treatment in respect of accelerated amortization and twenty-two states in which the commissions have authorized a reserve treatment in respect of liberalized depreciation. **

---

* Specific examples are contained in Appendix I hereof.

** Commissions in the following states have issued orders authorizing the following treatments:

LIBERALIZED DEPRECIATION:

RESTRICTED SURPLUS		RESERVE	
ALABAMA	MICHIGAN	ARIZONA	MICHIGAN
COLORADO	NEW JERSEY	ARKANSAS	MINNESOTA
FLORIDA	OHIO	GEORGIA	MISSOURI
INDIANA	OKLAHOMA	IDAHO	NEBRASKA
KENTUCKY	SOUTH CAROLINA	ILLINOIS	NEW JERSEY
MARYLAND	VIRGINIA	INDIANA	NEW MEXICO
	WEST VIRGINIA	KANSAS	OHIO
		KENTUCKY	OKLAHOMA
		LOUISIANA	SOUTH CAROLINA
		MAINE	VERMONT
		MASSACHUSETTS	WEST VIRGINIA

ACCELERATED AMORTIZATION:

RESTRICTED SURPLUS			RESERVE	
ALABAMA	MARYLAND	PENNSYLVANIA	ARKANSAS	MAINE
CALIFORNIA	MICHIGAN	SOUTH CAROLINA	CALIFORNIA	MASSACHUSETTS
COLORADO	NEW JERSEY	UTAH	CONNECTICUT	MICHIGAN
FLORIDA	NEW MEXICO	VERMONT	GEORGIA	MISSOURI
IDAHO	NORTH CAROLINA	VIRGINIA	IDAHO	NEVADA
INDIANA	OHIO	WASHINGTON	ILLINOIS	NEW MEXICO
KENTUCKY	OKLAHOMA	WEST VIRGINIA	INDIANA	NORTH CAROLINA
MAINE	OREGON	WYOMING	KANSAS	OHIO
			LOUISIANA	OREGON

The use of a restricted earned surplus account for the contra credit arising from the normalizing charge to income in connection with accounting for accelerated amortization and liberalized depreciation is a proper accounting treatment. Indeed it is the preferred accounting treatment.

The accumulated body of generally accepted accounting principles is rooted in the concept of matching costs and revenues in fiscal periods. But in the case of public utilities, a sterile adherence by the accountants to old concepts in dealing with new phenomena -- such as accelerated amortization and liberalized depreciation -- might not only have frustrated the Congressional purposes, as clearly disclosed by the legislative history of the applicable statutes, but might also have produced inequities as between present and future generations of customers.

Thus, as has been the case in other aspects of regulatory accounting (e.g. the use of "original cost" to take the place of actual cost), a new accounting procedure had to be devised. This new procedure, clearly an exception to the cost concept and to the general rule against equalizing, was found in "normalizing" the income account. The use of the normalizing technique has been approved by the American Institute of Certified Public Accountants.

The normalizing process consists merely of making a charge to income, with which no actual cost in the current fiscal period is associated, and carrying the offsetting credit directly to a balance sheet account. The amount of the charge is measured by the difference between actual income taxes and the amount such taxes would have been if the larger deduction for accelerated amortization and liberalized depreciation had not been taken. It is called a "provision for deferred taxes" because, in the future, income taxes may be larger than otherwise as a result of the then reduced available deductions.

But the way it is measured and what it is called cannot obscure what it actually is -- a charge to expense with which no <u>current</u> cost is associated. And since no cost is then involved it in fact is income in the period received. Accepted principles of accounting require that income be credited to earned surplus.

It is true that the taking of accelerated amortization and liberalized depreciation may result in higher taxes in the future but this prospect of future increased costs is also true in respect of labor contracts calling for increased wages in future fiscal periods, or leases calling for increased rentals in future fiscal periods, or long term purchase contracts for natural gas at increasing prices in future fiscal periods. And no one contends that as a matter of accounting principle such items, all representing much stronger cases, either give rise to current costs or existing liabilities.

Further, utilities may take liberalized depreciation for tax purposes but not normalize income. Many state commissions require this. F.P.C. Order No. 204 expressly permits it. Bulletin 44 of the American Institute of Certified Public Accountants permits such a flow-through under the conditions of Paragraph 8. Utilities which do not normalize charge regular book depreciation as an operating expense and the increased income resulting from the reduced Federal income taxes flows on through to net income. It is then credited to earned surplus as it should be. Everyone, including regulatory bodies both state and Federal, recognizes this as income and earned surplus when there is no normalization. This increased income and earned surplus cannot become something different when there is normalization. Their character cannot be changed by the normalizing process and they remain what they have always been -- an accretion to equity.

In sum: income equal to the normalizing charge has actually been received. But no expense has been incurred in the current fiscal period in connection with the receipt of the income. The income has been retained for use in the business. During the fiscal period no presently existing liability of any kind to anyone whomsoever has been created. There is no debt, no debtor and no creditor.

Since income has been received without any offsetting expense in the current fiscal period and the income has been retained in the business with no existing liability of any kind having been created, earned surplus must have been increased.

If any further demonstration of this were necessary, it need only be pointed out that when amortization deductions have ended and depreciation deductions have become less than those under straight line, a charge is made to restricted earned surplus and a credit is made to income. This increases stated current income and the stated income, as increased, is credited to earned surplus. Hence, in this final stage of the normalizing process, earned surplus restricted becomes earned surplus without restriction. Thus, earnings of an earlier period are treated as if received in the current later period.

Thus, the real effect of the normalizing charge is merely to delay the recognition of earnings in the income statement. But the earnings have been received and the preferred treatment is to show them as such by normalizing and carrying the offsetting credit to a restricted earned surplus account.

Many advocates of the liability treatment derive their argument from an overly literal interpretation of the metaphor "tax-free loan" as applied to the results of accelerated amortization or liberalized depreciation. But as has been stated there is no loan, there is no debtor, there is no creditor and there is no debt. The misconception can be dispelled if one considers a situation where sinking fund depreciation is used for tax purposes and straight line depreciation for book purposes. The depreciation for tax purposes will be less in the earlier years and will be greater in the later years. No one has ever suggested that the difference between the taxes actually paid and the lesser amount that would have been paid under straight line tax depreciation creates an asset, i.e., a receivable from the United States. Similarly, in the case of a utility whose tax cost of plant exceeds then recorded original cost (a common situation where plant has been purchased), its books will show an available depreciation based on the lower original cost, but it will in fact have a greater available tax depreciation. It has never been suggested that such a case creates a book asset.

The spurious nature of the liability may also be illustrated by the situation in which the shares of a utility are sold to a tax exempt entity, such as a Public Utility District, which then liquidates the utility and acquires the assets. If the utility actually had had a liability for future taxes the tax exempt entity would have to satisfy it. No such liability exists and the tax exempt entity owes no taxes. Nor is it otherwise penalized by the earlier consumption of tax base by its predecessor in interest. This demonstrates that there never has been a liability.

No provision needs to be made for a liability which does not exist and will not arise, if ever, except in the future. Moreover, as the SEC has long since pointed out (see SEC Accounting Series Release No. 53), a potential income tax expense is quite different from ordinary expense. "Unlike most expenses they exist if, and only if, there is net taxable income before any deduction for such taxes." Without income there can be no income tax liability.

So far as investors and creditors are concerned any amounts in restricted surplus are immediately there and represent an actual cushion protecting creditors. If a utility were to go bankrupt, or otherwise be liquidated, assets measured by the amounts in restricted surplus would be available for the payment of claims; there could be no claim by the United States for future tax liability based on future income. The real effect of the tax reductions from accelerated amortization and liberalized depreciation is not to create any liability for future taxes but rather to make accretions to equity in later years smaller.

POINT IV

THE USE OF RESTRICTED SURPLUS AS THE CONTRA CREDIT TO THE NORMALIZING CHARGE IS MORE BENEFICIAL TO INVESTORS AND CONSUMERS THAN THE USE OF A RESERVE ACCOUNT OF ANY KIND.

The use of restricted surplus as the contra credit to the normalizing charge has been, and will be, of substantial help to utilities in maintaining their equity ratios at a reasonable level. Such restricted surplus has served the same purpose as would have been served by selling additional amounts of equity securities. It has enabled utilities to sell more low cost debt securities than would otherwise have been possible and has served to reduce Federal income taxes and capital costs. This substantial help in financing has redounded to the benefit of both investors and consumers.

The chart on page 28[1] shows the pronounced effect of the debt ratio on annual costs or charges required to carry investment in plant and property. Based on the assumptions shown in the chart, which are conservative, annual costs decline from 9.77% to 9.32% when the debt ratio increases from 45% to 50% and from 9.32% to 8.86% when the debt ratio increases from 50% to 55%. Thus a change of 5 percentage points in the debt ratio increases annual carrying charges about $4,500 for each $1,000,000 of invested capital. In the case of the AEP Companies with about $1,200,000,000 of invested capital, 5 percentage points change in the amount of debt in the capital structure would mean increased annual costs of over $5,400,000.

As of December 31, 1958, the AEP Companies on a consolidated basis had restricted surplus due to deferred Federal taxes totaling some $66,000,000. If this amount had to be replaced by common stock, that common stock would not only have to have earnings at a rate sufficient to satisfy the requirements of the market place, but would also have to be supported by an additional 110% of such earnings (in the ratio of 52 over 48) to furnish the Federal income tax component. Our customers represent the only source of income to produce these earnings.

On the assumption that common stock can be sold at the present time to net a price equal to about 18 times earnings, which is certainly a very favorable assumption*, the capital cost would be on about a 5.50% basis. The Federal income tax component would therefore be 6.05% (110% of 5.5%) or a total common capital cost of 11.55%. The difference between this common capital cost of 11.55% and the cost of debt capital at 4.75% is 6.80%. If the approximately $66,000,000 now in the restricted surplus accounts of the AEP Companies had to be replaced by new common stock, it would involve additional Federal income taxes charged to operating expenses (6.05%) and additional capital costs (.75%) of approximately $4,500,000 a year.

The Holding Company Act provides that holding company systems be regulated by the SEC to protect "investors, consumers, and the general

---

* The average long-term common capital cost of the AEP Companies is 6.67% or 15 times earnings. (See chart)

[1] Page 341 in this volume.

public". The subject Notice fails to include "consumers" in stating that "The Commission considers that the action thus taken is necessary or appropriate in the public interest or for the protection of investors . . .". The consumers have apparently been overlooked in this instance.

Holders of debt securities cannot be prejudiced in any way whatsoever by accounting for deferred taxes using the restricted earned surplus method. The cash generated will have been used to increase assets, affording security to the debt holders. Further, the interest charges on debt are deductible for tax purposes and therefore are payable out of net income before income taxes. Thus any possible higher future income taxes cannot have any adverse effect on debt holders. So far as holders of equity securities are concerned this accounting method serves to reduce capital costs and avoids dilution. Thus no prejudice of any kind can result to investors. On the contrary their interests are enhanced.

Inasmuch as income taxes are an operating expense for utilities, the resulting reduction in operating expenses redounds entirely to the consumers. The reduction in capital costs also benefits the consumers. Further, in our opinion, the avoidance of conflicting requirements as between State and Federal regulatory bodies is in the public interest.

It is clear, therefore, that far from being detrimental to the interests of investors or consumers or to the general public interest, the restricted earned surplus method of accounting for deferred taxes protects and enhances such interests.

We submit, therefore, that the Commission cannot appropriately take the proposed action which, as we have shown, would adversely, and in material respects, affect both consumers and investors.

AEP Companies
EFFECT OF DEBT RATIO ON ANNUAL CHARGES
REQUIRED TO CARRY INVESTMENT
IN PER CENT OF ORIGINAL INVESTMENT

9.77%
9.32%
8.86%
8.41%

| 3.97 | 3.61 | 3.25 | 2.89 | ◀ FEDERAL INCOME TAX |

| 3.66 | 3.33 | 3.00 | 2.67 | ◀ EARNINGS ON EQUITY |

| 2.14 | 2.38 | 2.61 | 2.85 | ◀ INTEREST |

45%   50%   55%   60%
DEBT RATIO

BASED ON 4¾% BONDS,
6⅔% EARNINGS ON EQUITY
AND 52% FEDERAL INCOME TAX RATE

MARCH 1959

POINT V

THE PROPOSED ANNOUNCEMENT WOULD IMPROPERLY BRAND AS MISLEADING AND INACCURATE ACCOUNTING PROCEDURES WHICH ARE IN ACCORD WITH ACCEPTED PRINCIPLES OF ACCOUNTING.

The Notice of Intention to Announce Interpretation of Administrative Policy of December 30, 1958 states that financial statements not filed in accordance with such Notice will be presumed by the Commission "to be misleading or inaccurate despite disclosure contained in the certificate of the accountant or in footnotes to the statements provided the matters involved are material".

This memorandum has already demonstrated that the use of restricted surplus is in accordance with accepted principles of accounting and indeed is to be preferred. It has shown, moreover, that material benefits to investors and consumers of power are derived from its use.

SEC Accounting Release No. 4, which sets forth the administrative policy of the Commission on financial statements, provides that financial statements will be presumed to be misleading where they are prepared in accordance with accounting principles for which there is no substantial authoritative support. This cannot be the case in regard to financial statements which show the contra credit to the normalizing charge as restricted earned surplus.

Release No. 4 also provides that where there are choices as to methods of accounting and where there is substantial support for alternative methods, disclosure will be acceptable even though the Commission may not prefer the method of accounting used by the accounting company unless the Commission has adopted contrary rules or regulations.

Release No. 4, however, does not, and the Commission has not heretofore ever attempted to, claim that where there is a choice of methods of accounting and one is preferred by the Commission, that the use of another method would be misleading or inaccurate.

That the SEC may adopt rules and regulations under certain circumstances favoring a choice for its own purposes is one thing, but to brand as misleading and inaccurate statements made in accordance with accepted accounting principles is improper and unjust.

POINT VI

THE PROPOSED INTERPRETATION PURPORTS TO MAKE RET-
ROACTIVE AN ACCOUNTING POLICY DIFFERENT FROM THAT HERE-
TOFORE ADOPTED BY THE SEC AND TO BRAND THE USE OF METH-
ODS IN ACCORDANCE WITH THE PRESENT POLICY MISLEADING AND
INACCURATE.

The Notice of Intention to Announce Interpretation of Administrative
Policy of December 30, 1958 proposes that statements as of December 31,
1958 not complying with the proposed policy would be presumed to be
misleading or inaccurate. The time for comments as provided in the original notice would not have terminated until January 31, 1959 and has in
fact been extended to March 25, 1959. Public hearing is to be held commencing April 8, 1959. Thus, whether or not the Proposed Interpretation
of Administrative Policy will be implemented, such implementation will
not and cannot take place until long after December 31, 1958. If, therefore, it is to be made applicable to financial statements as of that date,
it will be applied retroactively over a considerable period.

The SEC has regularly, under the Acts it administers, approved the
use of the restricted surplus method of accounting under the very circumstances where it would now label such use misleading or inaccurate.

Since the subject Notice was promulgated on December 30 large
amounts of securities have been sold under registration statements which,
if the proposed interpretation were to be applied, would be branded
as false and misleading even though such registration statements had
been prepared and filed in accordance with principles of accounting approved by the Commission.

POINT VII

THE REQUIREMENTS OF FULL AND FAIR DISCLOSURE OF THE SECURITIES ACT OF 1933 AND OF THE SECURITIES EXCHANGE ACT OF 1934 CAN ADEQUATELY BE MET WITHOUT ANY NEED FOR ADOPTION OF THE PROPOSED INTERPRETATION.

The Securities Act of 1933 and the Securities Exchange Act of 1934, insofar as the latter Act pertains to reporting requirements, have as their primary purpose full and fair disclosure. The primary standard, therefore, by which regulations and interpretations pertaining to financial statements promulgated under these Acts should be measured is whether the purpose of full and fair disclosure has been served.

We have seen that the use of restricted surplus to reflect the contra credit to the normalizing charge is in accordance with generally accepted principles of accounting and indeed may be said to be the preferred method. Certainly the use of restricted surplus can create no disclosure problem under the Securities Act or the Securities Exchange Act. If the financial statements are in sufficient detail, investors will receive full disclosure of all the relevant facts.

The AEP Companies, as even a cursory examination of their filings under these two Acts will show, heretofore have presented, and intend to continue to present, full, adequately annotated statements which make clear the accounting methods which the AEP Companies are using, and which fully and clearly disclose all the material facts.

Moreover, as has been pointed out in POINT I of this memorandum, there is a greater chance that an investor may be misled if regulated utilities are forced, as they would be by the proposed interpretation, to follow accounting concepts inconsistent with the substantive effects of orders of state commissions having primary jurisdiction over them.

CONCLUSION

The proposed interpretation of administrative policy would be in violation of Section 20(b) of the Public Utility Holding Company Act of 1935.

The use of restricted surplus accounting, which would be barred by the proposed interpretation, is in accordance with generally accepted principles of accounting and is the preferred method.

The use of restricted surplus accounting affords great benefits to utility investors and to consumers.

THE PROPOSED INTERPRETATION OF ADMINISTRATIVE POLICY SHOULD NOT BE ADOPTED.

Respectfully submitted,

Herbert B. Cohn,
Chief Counsel for the AEP Companies

Wallace J. Borker,
Of Counsel

Dated March 23, 1959

AMERICAN NATURAL GAS SERVICE COMPANY
Affiliate of
Michigan Consolidated Gas Company
Milwaukee Gas Light Company
Michigan Wisconsin Pipe Line Company
American Louisiana Pipe Line Company

Penobscot Building
Detroit 26

February 26, 1959

Securities and Exchange Commission
425 Second Street, N. W.
Washington 25, D. C.

Gentlemen:

Pursuant to your Notice of Intention to Announce Interpretation of Administrative Policy dated December 30, 1958, as extended by securities Act of 1933 Release No. 4023 dated January 28, 1959, American Natural Gas Service Company, on behalf of its affiliates in the American Natural Gas system, hereby advises you of its intention to appear at the public hearing to be held on March 25, 1959.

In accordance with your request, we are submitting herewith a written statement of our views, in triplicate, which are in support of the proposed announcement, and request 15 minutes in which to make our oral presentation.

Very truly yours,

/s/ ROBERT M. HOFFER

Robert M. Hoffer
Controller

Encl.

AMERICAN NATURAL GAS SERVICE COMPANY

Treatment of Credits
Equivalent to Reduction of Taxes Resulting from
Liberalized Depreciation and Accelerated Amortization

Under the proposed announcement of the Securities and Exchange Commission, as set forth in its release dated December 30, 1958, the accumulated credits resulting from accounting for deferred taxes arising from various items including liberalized depreciation and accelerated amortization (Sections 167 and 168 of the Internal Revenue Code of 1954) would be excluded from the equity capital section of the balance sheet.

The American Natural Gas system companies concur in the proposed announcement. This treatment is consistent with that followed by those system companies which have elected to deduct liberalized depreciation and/or accelerated amortization for Federal income tax purposes; is in accordance with accounting orders from regulatory commissions having jurisdiction over the various system companies; and is in agreement with the recommendations of the independent public accountants certifying the system companies' financial statements.

It is clear that deduction of items such as liberalized depreciation and accelerated amortization for Federal income tax purposes in periods prior to those in which they are charged to expenses for book purposes results in a tax deferment--not a tax saving. The effect is merely to shift the deductions between years and to defer the tax, as is pointed out in the comments in the report of the Ways and Means Committee of the House of Representatives (House Report No. 1337 83d Congress, 2d Session, page 25):

> "The changes made by your committee's bill merely affect the timing and not the ultimate amount of depreciation deductions with respect to a property."

This being true, it is necessary to provide for deferred taxes on the difference between liberalized depreciation and/or accelerated amortization and normal straight-line depreciation. Not to do so would be to disregard a current cost--namely the expiration of the valuable right of deducting depreciation for tax purposes. This would result in an improper matching of revenues and expenses, frequently in material amounts, and would therefore not be in accordance with generally accepted accounting principles.

It would appear that the Securities and Exchange Commission is in general agreement with this position, although it should be noted that the proposed announcement does not deal specifically with the special provision for public utility companies contained in paragraph 8 of Accounting Research Bulletin No. 44 (Revised) issued in July 1958 by the Committee on Accounting Procedure of the American Institute of Certified Public Accountants. This paragraph provides that "where charges for deferred income taxes are not allowed for rate-making purposes, accounting recognition need not be given to the deferment of taxes if it may be reasonably expected that increased future income taxes, resulting from the earlier deduction of declining-balance depreciation for income-tax purposes only, will be allowed in future rate determinations" (underscoring supplied). The bulletin refers to these as "rare cases," and it appears to the American Natural Gas system companies that this paragraph should be followed only in the most unusual circumstances where it is clear that such increased taxes can and will be allowed in the future and that economic circumstances will make it possible for the company to recover them, if allowed.

When provision is made for deferred taxes, as recommended herein, the conclusion is inescapable that the contra credit should be classified outside the equity capital section of the balance sheet, irrespective of what captions, notes with respect to restrictions, etc. are used in describing the item. It is difficult to follow a line of reasoning under which recognition of a cost produces an increment in equity capital. The credit constitutes a reserve against which increased future taxes resulting from higher current depreciation deductions are to be charged; and such a reserve is no more a part of equity capital than is the reserve for depreciation.

Furthermore, it is misleading to investors and the general public to permit materially diverse treatment among companies of a comparable item. Capitalization ratio comparisons are distorted, and persons who rely on the equity capital shown in the balance sheets of those companies which classify the credit therein are misled.

Based on the reasons summarized herein, the American Natural Gas system concurs in the proposed announcement and recommends adoption of the policy as set forth therein.

AMERICAN TELEPHONE AND TELEGRAPH COMPANY

195 Broadway,
New York 7, N. Y.
Exeter 3-9800

ALEXANDER L. STOTT
COMPTROLLER

February 26, 1959

Mr. Orval L. DuBois, Secretary
Securities and Exchange Commission
Washington 25, D. C.

Dear Mr. DuBois:

This is in reference to the Notice of
Intention to Announce Interpretation of Administrative Policy released by the Commission on
December 30, 1958, relative to "interpretation of
administrative policy on financial statements
regarding balance sheet treatment of credits
equivalent to reductions of income taxes".

While none of the Bell System telephone
companies in the United States have adopted the
provisions of Sections 167 and 168 of the Code in
preparing their Federal income tax returns, and
do not plan to do so, the American Telephone and
Telegraph Company as an interested party submits
the following comments on behalf of the Bell
System telephone companies.

The proposed announcement deals with financial
statements of companies which have adopted the
liberalized depreciation or accelerated amortization procedures set forth in Sections 167 and 168,
respectively, of the Internal Revenue Code of 1954.
It states that, except in rare cases, it is
necessary for a corporation which deducts liberalized depreciation or accelerated amortization for
tax purposes but only normal depreciation in its
books of account, to charge current income with
an amount equal to the tax reduction in order that

its net income be not overstated in the earlier
years and understated in the later years. The
exception to this procedure is found, according
to the Notice, in those cases described in
paragraph 8 of Accounting Research Bulletin No. 44
(Revised) which provides that where charges for
deferred income taxes are not allowed for rate-
making purposes, accounting recognition need not
be given to the deferment of taxes if it may
reasonably be expected that increased income taxes
will be allowed in the future.

We are in complete agreement with the general
rule that where normal depreciation is used in the
books of account it is essential to give deferred
tax treatment to the differentials arising from the
use of accelerated depreciation or amortization for
tax purposes. Our belief is based on the following
reasons:

When straight line depreciation (which
communication carriers are required to use under
the Federal Communications Commission's Uniform
Systems of Accounts) is used for both the books of
account and tax purposes, the net cost of depreciation after taxes is distributed equitably over
the service life of the property and, in the case
of a utility, over the generations of ratepayers.
However, use of straight line depreciation for the
books of account and accelerated depreciation for
tax purposes, as permitted under the Internal
Revenue Code, has the effect of borrowing tax
deductions from the future to reduce current
taxes. If a tax deduction, arising from use of
depreciation accruals applicable to future years,
is used in the current year, the benefit of the
right to such deduction, which is a valuable right
granted by Congress, is lost for the future.
Under such conditions if deferred tax accounting
is not used the reduction in taxes in the early
years of the life of the property would flow
through to net income and result in an overstatement of earnings during that period. If deferred
tax treatment is used, there is synchronization
in the accounts of the depreciation expense shown

and the related tax deduction over the life of the
related plant with no distortion of net income at
any time.

Deferred tax treatment also provides protection against the possibility that the Internal
Revenue Code may change. At some time the Code
may not permit any tax deductions arising from the
use of accelerated depreciation or may limit the
deductions to a greater extent than is now the
case. If such deductions are no longer permitted
or are limited, and deferred tax treatment has not
been used, it becomes apparent immediately that net
income has been overstated in the interim and that
a company is then faced with carrying the burden
of taxes properly applicable to past periods, in
addition to the burden of current taxes.

Deferred tax treatment permits public
utilities to obtain the benefits intended by
Congress for all corporations as clearly stated
in the Notice of Intention. Public utilities which
adopt accelerated depreciation can obtain such
benefits only if they are permitted to charge as
an expense for rate-making purposes the difference
between normal taxes and taxes currently paid. If
such utilities are allowed only taxes currently
paid, the entire benefit of Sections 167 and 168
will be passed on to present ratepayers and the tax
deferment will not be available to aid the utilities
in their expansion programs, as intended by
Congress. The benefit to present ratepayers would
require future ratepayers to bear the burden of
higher taxes if taxes currently paid are also
allowed in the future.

For these reasons, and others set forth in
your announcement, we strongly advocate use of the
deferred tax treatment where normal depreciation
is used in the accounts and, except for the
reference to paragraph 8 of Accounting Research
Bulletin No. 44 (Revised), we are in agreement with
the principles and proposed accounting treatment of
material matters of this nature as presented in
your announcement.

With respect to paragraph 8 of Bulletin 44 (Revised), we concur in the belief expressed in the second sentence of that paragraph to the effect that regulatory authorities should permit the recognition of deferred income taxes for both book and rate-making purposes, inasmuch as both accounting and rate-making concepts are concerned with reflecting true costs in any period of operation. However, we cannot concur with respect to the third sentence of that paragraph which states that where charges for deferred income taxes are not allowed for rate-making purposes, accounting recognition need not be given to the deferment of taxes if it may reasonably be expected that increased future income taxes, resulting from the earlier deduction of declining-balance depreciation for income tax purposes only, will be allowed in future rate determinations. First, we have not been able to understand why regulatory policy with respect to rate-making should determine generally accepted accounting principles. Furthermore, we doubt that any regulatory authority can give reasonable assurance of increased future taxes being allowed in subsequent rate-making procedures by the regulatory authority as constituted at a future date. Despite the often repeated statement that commissions will allow taxes actually paid, it has been our experience that, in situations unrelated to accelerated depreciation, many regulatory authorities have made disallowances of current income taxes actually paid. Also, other utilities have experienced commission disallowances of depreciation accruals to amortize past deficiencies in depreciation caused by the application of depreciation theories accepted by the same commission at a previous time. Accordingly, we do not see any practical means for implementing the treatment referred to in paragraph 8 of Bulletin 44 (Revised).

As required by the Notice, two additional copies of this letter are enclosed.

Very truly yours,

/s/ A. L. STOTT

Comptroller

Enclosures

ARIZONA PUBLIC SERVICE COMPANY

P. O. Box 2591
Phoenix

February 27, 1959

Securities and Exchange Commission
Washington, D. C.

Attention: Mr. Orval L. DuBois, Secretary

Gentlemen:

In accordance with your notice dated
December 30, 1958, on the subject of the interpretation of administrative policy on financial
statements regarding balance sheet treatment of
credit equivalent to reduction of income taxes,
Arizona Public Service Company submits in book
form in triplicate its views and comments on the
said matter. It is this Company's intention to
appear at the hearing on March 25, 1959.

The Company has made extensive studies of
the effect of using so-called liberalized depreciation for income tax purposes as allowed under
Section 167 of the 1954 Internal Revenue Code.
As a result of these studies, the Company has
concluded, among other things:

1. Both customers and stockholders are
   better served where so-called
   liberalized depreciation is used for
   computing depreciation for income tax
   purposes;

2. Conversely, the adoption of liberalized depreciation for income tax
   purposes cannot have an adverse effect
   on either customers or stockholders,
   even if the code is changed to rescind

this provision, unless, of course, it be rescinded retroactively--an action which historically has never been taken;

3. Liberalized depreciation for income tax purposes and "flow through" accounting result in better matching of revenues and costs, a more even distribution of and lower total fixed charges;

4. "Normalizing" the income tax account (i.e., charging or crediting the income tax account, as the case may be, with the difference in income taxes arising from the use of liberalized rather than straight-line depreciation in the computation of income taxes) is misleading and inaccurate in that such procedure ignores time value of money and, hence, understates net income when total fixed charges are considered;

5. By crediting the differences described in (4) above to a balance sheet reserve, a Frankenstein monster will be created--compounding in growth each year into the foreseeable future and absorbing money from customers or stockholders--or both-- which by right should be their's.

The Arizona Corporation Commission has recently issued to this Company its decision No. 31345 pertaining to the Company's method of accounting for income tax liability. The Commission is of the opinion that the Company has properly accounted for its tax liability in its gross and net income, as recorded in its books of account by there reflecting only that amount of taxes that are actually payable each year under applicable statutes and regulations and in accordance with lawful elections made thereunder by the Company. The Commission

further orders "that the Company so continue to
reflect such tax liability in its books of
account and that this method be used in any book
cost computation that is used as an element in
rate determination of the Company, until further
order of the Commission for good cause shown".
It is the contention of the Company that its
accounting practices, with respect to income
taxes, conform to the exceptions referred to in
Bulletin 44 (revised) of the American Institute
of Certified Public Accountants and to the
requirements of Orders 203 and 204 of the Federal
Power Commission.

In view of the above, it is respectfully
suggested that financial statements for registration purposes should conform to orders of the
State Commission having jurisdiction and rules
of the Federal Power Commission in order to
avoid confusion and misleading and inaccurate
interpretation.

Respectfully submitted,

/s/ JOHN L. LIECTY

JLL:ks
Enclosures

THE EFFECT OF USING VARIOUS METHODS

OF COMPUTING DEPRECIATION FOR INCOME TAXES

AS ALLOWED UNDER SECTION 167 OF THE

1954 INTERNAL REVENUE CODE

* * * *

A STUDY PREPARED FOR PRESENTATION BY

ARIZONA PUBLIC SERVICE COMPANY

BEFORE THE

SECURITIES AND EXCHANGE COMMISSION

* * * *

CONTENTS

A. Discussion

B. Exhibits:

THE EFFECT OF USING VARIOUS METHODS OF
COMPUTING DEPRECIATION FOR INCOME TAXES
AS ALLOWED UNDER SECTION 167 OF THE 1954
INTERNAL REVENUE CODE
* * *
A STUDY PREPARED FOR PRESENTATION BY
ARIZONA PUBLIC SERVICE COMPANY
BEFORE THE
SECURITIES AND EXCHANGE COMMISSION

Let us start off by examining what occurs when we consider a single unit of property or vintage of mass property. First, a set of assumptions:

1. An installation costing $100

2. 30-year life

3. Capitalization at 50% debt at 4.75% and 50% equity

4. Total return of 6% on net plant

5. Composite Federal and State Income Tax Rate of 53.125% (current rate for my Company)

Fixed charges equal book depreciation plus total return (interest plus equity return) plus income taxes. It should be noted that, in Exhibit I, the numbers but not the pattern would change under the Fair Value concept. Let us refer now to Exhibit I and view arithmetic at work under the three main provisions of Section 167 -- namely, straight line; declining balance (using double the straight-line rate), and sum-of-the-years digits computations for determining the depreciation deduction.

First, what happens to Income Taxes? Under the straight-line computation of depreciation, Income Taxes drop evenly from a high of 4.108 the first year to a low of 0.137 the 30th year. Under the declining balance computation, Income Taxes rise from 0.330 in the first year to a high of 3.148 in the 16th year and then decline to 1.231 in the 30th year. Under the sum-of-the-years digits computation, Income Taxes rise from a low of 0.573 the first year to a high of 3.671 in the 30th year. In each case, the arithmetical average of the Income Taxes is the same--namely, 2.123. However, the uniform annual equivalent of the present worth (@ 6%) of the Income Taxes shows a very interesting situation. Under straight-line, it is 2.692; under declining balance, 1.989 (a drop of 26%), and under sum-of-the-years digits, 1.681 (a further drop of 12%).

Now for the nub of the situation: What happens to Fixed Charges? Under the straight-line computation of depreciation, Fixed Charges drop from a high of 13.441 in the first year to a low of 3.670 in the 30th year. Under the declining balance computation, Fixed Charges rise from 9.663 in the first year to a high of 10.202 in the 7th year and then decline to a low of 4.764 in the 30th year. Under the sum-of-the-years digits computation, Fixed Charges drop evenly from a high of 9.906 in the first year to a low of 7.204 in the 30th year. In each case, the arithmetical average of the Fixed Charges is the same--namely, 8.556. Again, however, the uniform annual equivalent of the present worth (@ 6%) of the Fixed Charges gives the key to the situation. Under straight-line, it is 9.957; under declining balance, it is 9.254 (a drop of 7%), and, under sum-of-the-years digits, it is 8.946 (a further drop of 3%).

What conclusions may be drawn from this?

First, present worth computations--the only true equalizer--show, in regard to Income Taxes, that depreciation deductions for income tax purposes are

least beneficial on a straight-line basis (2.692),

more favorable on a declining balance basis (1.989),

most favorable on a sum-of-the-years digits basis (1.681).

Second, present worth computations show, in regard to Fixed Charges, that depreciation deductions for income tax purposes are

least evenly distributed (73% spread) and highest (9.957) on a straight-line basis;

more evenly distributed (53% spread) and lower (9.254) a declining balance basis;

most evenly distributed (26% spread) and lowest (8.946) on a sum-of-the-years digits basis; therefore,

Third, both customers and stockholders are better served where so-called liberalized depreciation is used for computing depreciation for income tax purposes; and

Lastly, the adoption of liberalized depreciation for income tax purposes today cannot have an adverse effect on either customers or stockholders even if the code is changed to rescind this provision, unless, of course, it be rescinded retroactively--an action which historically has never been taken.

If the use of so-called liberalized depreciation for income tax purposes is beneficial to customers and company when applied to a "wasting" asset, it would seem it could do no harm with a stable or growing asset. So let's continue with Exhibit II(a), where the assumptions are the same as in Exhibit I, except that the original $100 asset grows at a constant rate of $10 per year with retirement after each 30-year life cycle. Also, for simplicity, only the two extremes--namely, straight-line and sum-of-years digits computations--have been shown. In this situation, three main items are noteworthy. First, gross plant stabilizes and remains constant after the 30th year. Second, by relating fixed charges to gross plant, we find that the pattern of these fixed charges under the two methods is the same as was the case in Exhibit I through year 30, except that maximum to minimum spreads are improved--from 73% to 45% for straight-line and from 26% to 17% for sum-of-the-years digits. After year 30, however, the annual fixed charges stabilize and become equal under the two methods. Third, in the case of income taxes, we do have a change. Notice that, from the first through the 30th year, they rise in both cases--considerably faster, to be sure, under sum-of-the-years digits--but, from year 31 on, they become equal under the two methods. Notice, too, that the sum of the income taxes for the first thirty years under the straight-line computation is 186.695, while, under the sum-of-the-years digits computation, it is 131.952--a reduction of 54.743, or 29.3% at this juncture. The amount of this difference remains constant thereafter, producing a permanent saving. A similar computation for a single asset with a 5% annual compound rate of growth is shown in Exhibit II(b), indicating that a like pattern exists.

This discussion could be stopped right here since it is hoped that the economic benefits to both customers and company of using so-called liberalized depreciation for income tax purposes has been demonstrated.

However, there are some who appear, for one reason or another, to leave out of consideration total fixed charges and time value of money and concentrate only on income taxes, which are but a single component of fixed charges. As a matter of completeness, therefore, let us show income tax effects only in the case of a growing combination utility--Arizona Public Service Company.

In the past thirty-eight years, the population of Arizona has been growing at a compound rate of 4.2%, approximately two and one-half times greater than the rate of growth for the entire United States. For the past eighteen years, the compound rate of growth has been even higher. Take the population of 1940--Arizona had approximately half a million people. Today, according to the Valley National Bank estimates, the population stands somewhere around 1.2 million. For the years to come the Valley National Bank forecasts a population of 2.047 million in 1975. The Stanford Research Institute estimates that it will be 2.327 million. Our own estimate indicates that the population will be even higher, reaching 2.6 million by that time, based on the growth trend for the recent two decades, as shown in Exhibit III.

In view of the rapid growth of Arizona population and the resultant increase in demand for electric and gas services, the need for the expansion of our utility plant is a foregone conclusion.

In recent years, the growth of our Company has exceeded the growth of the whole industry. This is readily understandable in that the Arizona population has outgrown that of the entire United States during the same period.

Our total capital expenditures in electrical plant facilities for the past decade, as well as those for the few years to 1962, have been increasing at a compound rate of 12.1%--far exceeding the 5.2% for the whole industry. (Exhibit IV (a))

Our electric plant capabilities for the same period have outgrown that for the whole industry at approximately the ratio of 2 to 1. (Exhibit IV (b))

Lastly, our kilowatt-hour sales for the same period indicate the same performance as that stated above. (Exhibit IV (c))

In all three cases the comparison is made on a relative basis, using 1950 figures as 100.

Following what we have seen in the growth of Arizona population as compared to the entire United States, and the growth in our electric plant as compared with the entire industry, it is only fair to say that, for many years to come, we expect the same trend to materialize. In any event, it would be difficult to conceive that our requirements would be lower than national averages.

After the second World War, Arizona Public Service Company started to enjoy a rapid expansion in its plant facilities. Total utility plant in service jumped from $31 million in 1945 to $190 million in 1958. Forecasts made by the Company in April 1958 indicated that total utility plant, taking into consideration both its budgeted and committed expenditures, will reach $353 million in 1962. This is a compound growth of approximately 14.7%.

While there is no forecast of our plant growth beyond 1962, we can project our total plant at various rates of growth. Taking the 15% compound rate of growth, we will have $2.17 billion in total utility plant by 1975. This, of course, is based on the trend of growth that we have had for the past decade as well as for the few years to come. Taking a less optimistic view, a 10% compound rate of growth will result in a total utility plant of $1.2 billion by that time. Should we be very conservative and say that the growth in our utility plant for the years beyond 1962 will parallel that for the projected growth in Arizona population, then a 5% compound rate will expand our plant to $666 million.

Taking a very pessimistic view by assuming that we have no physical growth in plant beyond 1962 except for complete replacements at higher costs due to inflation, our total utility plant will reach $439 million in 1975. This is based on the assumption that inflationary trends for 1962-1975 will be the same as that for 1950-1957, using 1947-1949 as a base period.

For a picture of the growth in our plant, as stated above, see Exhibit V.

Exhibit VI (a) pictures the trend of income tax differential resulting from using the declining balance depreciation method instead of the straight-line method. Assuming that the liberalized method was in force for all additions subsequent to December 31, 1925, the income tax differential accumulates at an increasing rate to an estimated $8.8 million by 1958. From there on, the increase in the tax differential will never stop if we continue to have a certain rate of growth, thus resulting in a permanent tax differential in the form of tax savings.

Exhibit VI (b) tabulates our computation of the accumulated income tax differential, supporting Exhibit VI (a). It is to be noted that various composite income tax rates, for both Federal and State, were used in our computation, based on the actual Federal and State rates that were in force for the respective years, the most recent composite rate being 53.125%. Had we used 53.125% for all the years, our accumulated tax differential would have reached $10.1 million at the end of 1958. Also, the depreciation rate used is a composite rate for our electric and gas plant.

Exhibit VI (c) states the assumptions we made in our computation. The reason for our making certain assumptions is stated therein.

Having illustrated the results of using liberalized depreciation instead of the straight-line method and the possible tax savings, we now come to the question of what actually happened since we began using the declining balance method of depreciation at twice the straight-line rates for all additions since December 31, 1953 (as provided under Section 167 of the Internal Revenue Code).

Exhibit VII (a) indicates in graph form the extent of income tax differential accumulated from 1954 to 1958, the estimated accumulated tax differential to 1962, and projections beyond 1962 to 1975, based on a minimum growth of 5% and a maximum growth of 15%. Also shown is a projection of tax differential based on no physical growth from 1962, except for taking into consideration the inflationary trends we mentioned earlier. All these are after deducting tax reversals from our using the accelerated amortization in the early years (as provided under Section 168 of the Revenue Code).

From computations made, it was determined that, in our situation, a compound rate of growth of 4.5% would yield a tax differential curve that would never curve downward. In other words, the tax differential so accumulated will become a permanent tax savings. Where no growth existed, except for inflationary trends, the curve started to bend down after 1975 at a very slow rate.

Exhibit VII (b) illustrates part of the computation involved under a 5%, 15% and no-growth situation. Detailed computations supporting these figures are not shown since they are more or less obtained in the same manner as we have shown in our Exhibit VI (b).

Let us now take a look at what will possibly happen to our balance sheet if we follow normalization and set up a reserve for deferred income taxes. For illustration purposes, let us assume that net plant is approximately equal to total capitalization plus earned surplus, and that thirty per cent of our net plant is financed by common equity and retained earnings.

In the case of Arizona Public Service Company, we have estimated that by 1975 we will have a gross plant of $666 million based on a 5% compound rate of growth. On the basis of an 85% net plant after depreciation reserve, we will have a $566 million net plant at that time. Our common equity and earned surplus before deducting tax reserves will then be $170 million. Earlier, we have shown that total accumulated tax differential will be approximately $49 million under the 5% growth situation. Crediting this amount of tax differential to a reserve for deferred income taxes account will leave a total balance of $121 million in our common equity and earned surplus accounts. The deferred taxes reserve is then approximately 40% of our common equity and earned surplus balances. On the other hand, a 15% compound growth situation would result in a tax differential of $439 million, approximately 27% of our common equity and earned surplus balances. If such a picture is visualized, what action would our commissioners take--especially when it is shown that there probably will never be a charge against this tax reserve?

Let us take a pessimistic view and ask, what if, all of a sudden, the growth trend stopped, with our plant being slowly retired without replacement, would there be charges against the reserve for deferred taxes? There certainly would be charges that would slowly extinguish the tax reserve we had accumulated at the time our growth ceased, but not until roughly fifteen years later. This is based on repeated studies of the arithmetic of the declining balance method by various concerned personnel.

In the last Congress, legislation was introduced (H.R. 13289) proposing the allowance of depreciation on a reinvestment basis. "This method, briefly, permits the taxpayer to deduct at the time of retirement the difference between the current value of the property and its original historical cost. It thus recognizes the additional depreciation which should have been provided during the life of the property in order to replace it at the end of its life". (Journal of Accountancy, December 1958, p. 76) And then talks or plans to reduce tax rates were heard constantly. While we cannot tell what courses of action will eventually be taken by the Congress, it is easily seen that any reduction in tax rates will result in permanent tax savings on a portion of our accumulated tax differential prior to date of reduction. Furthermore, allowing depreciation on a reinvestment basis will tend to widen the tax gap between the liberalized and straight-line methods of depreciation.

It has been emphasized that the intent of Sections 167 and 168 is to permit the tax-free recovery from operations of capital invested in plant at a faster rate than would be possible by depreciation methods previously permitted for income tax purposes. In our opinion, the loss in tax revenue due to these provisions is substantially offset by the additional tax revenue that would arise from the use of this tax-free recovery of capital. So long as this situation prevails, the Congress will never reverse its intention as previously disclosed in committee reports and seek to introduce new legislation to repeal these provisions.

Arizona Public Service Company believes in rendering an adequate service to its customers at reasonable and just rates. The Company further believes in earning a fair rate of return for its investors. Tax savings resulting from the use of liberalized depreciation should therefore be passed on to its investors and to its customers. Any provision for a tax differential which is in all probability a permanent tax saving would defeat its purpose.

1/20/59

EXHIBIT I

FIXED CHARGES ON INSTALLATION OF $100

Based on: Debt 50% @ 4.75%
Equity 50%
Total Return 6.00%

30-Year Life
Income Tax Rate 53.125% (Fed. & State)

Year	Net Plant	Book Dep'n 3-1/3%	Return	Equity Return	Straight Line Inc. Tax	Straight Line Fixed Chg.	Declining Balance Dep'n	Declining Balance Excess	Declining Balance Inc. Tax	Declining Balance Fixed Chg.	SYD Method Dep'n	SYD Method Excess	SYD Method Inc. Tax	SYD Method Fixed Chg.
1	100.000	3.333	6.000	3.625	4.108	13.441	6.667	3.334	0.330	9.663	6.452	3.119	.573	9.906
2	96.667	3.333	5.800	3.504	3.971	13.104	6.222	2.889	0.697	9.830	6.237	2.904	.680	9.813
3	93.333	3.333	5.600	3.383	3.834	12.767	5.807	2.474	1.030	9.963	6.022	2.689	.786	9.719
4	90.000	3.333	5.400	3.263	3.698	12.431	5.420	2.087	1.333	10.066	5.806	2.473	.895	9.628
5	86.667	3.333	5.200	3.142	3.561	12.094	5.059	1.726	1.605	10.138	5.591	2.258	1.002	9.535
6	83.333	3.333	5.000	3.021	3.424	11.757	4.722	1.389	1.850	10.183	5.376	2.043	1.108	9.441
7	80.000	3.333	4.800	2.900	3.287	11.420	4.407	1.074	2.069	10.202	5.161	1.828	1.215	9.343
8	76.667	3.333	4.600	2.779	3.150	11.083	4.113	0.780	2.266	10.199	4.946	1.613	1.321	9.254
9	73.333	3.333	4.400	2.658	3.012	10.745	3.839	0.506	2.439	10.172	4.731	1.398	1.428	9.161
10	70.000	3.333	4.200	2.538	2.876	10.409	3.583	0.250	2.593	10.126	4.516	1.183	1.536	9.069
11	66.667	3.333	4.000	2.417	2.739	10.072	3.344	0.011	2.727	10.060	4.301	.968	1.642	8.975
12	63.333	3.333	3.800	2.296	2.602	9.735	3.121	(0.212)	2.842	9.975	4.086	.753	1.749	8.882
13	60.000	3.333	3.600	2.175	2.465	9.398	2.913	(0.420)	2.941	9.874	3.871	.538	1.855	8.783
14	56.667	3.333	3.400	2.054	2.328	9.061	2.719	(0.614)	3.024	9.757	3.656	.323	1.962	8.695
15	53.333	3.333	3.200	1.933	2.191	8.724	2.538	(0.795)	3.092	9.625	3.441	.108	2.068	8.401
16	50.000	3.333	3.000	1.813	2.055	8.388	2.368	(0.965)	3.148	9.481	3.226	(.107)	2.176	8.509
17	46.667	3.333	2.800	1.692	1.918	8.051	2.368	(0.965)	3.011	9.144	3.011	(.322)	2.282	8.415
18	43.333	3.333	2.600	1.571	1.780	7.713	2.368	(0.965)	2.874	8.807	2.796	(.537)	2.389	8.322
19	40.000	3.333	2.400	1.450	1.643	7.376	2.368	(0.965)	2.737	8.470	2.581	(.752)	2.496	8.229
20	36.667	3.333	2.200	1.329	1.506	7.039	2.368	(0.965)	2.600	8.133	2.366	(.967)	2.602	8.135
21	33.333	3.333	2.000	1.208	1.369	6.702	2.368	(0.965)	2.463	7.796	2.151	(1.182)	2.709	8.042
22	30.000	3.333	1.800	1.088	1.233	6.366	2.368	(0.965)	2.327	7.460	1.935	(1.398)	2.817	7.950
23	26.667	3.333	1.600	0.967	1.096	6.029	2.368	(0.965)	2.190	7.123	1.720	(1.613)	2.924	7.857
24	23.333	3.333	1.400	0.846	0.959	5.692	2.368	(0.965)	2.052	6.785	1.505	(1.828)	3.030	7.763
25	20.000	3.333	1.200	0.725	0.822	5.355	2.368	(0.965)	1.915	6.448	1.290	(2.043)	3.137	7.670
26	16.667	3.333	1.000	0.604	0.685	5.018	2.368	(0.965)	1.778	6.111	1.075	(2.258)	3.244	7.577
27	13.333	3.333	0.800	0.483	0.547	4.680	2.368	(0.965)	1.641	5.774	.860	(2.473)	3.350	7.483
28	10.000	3.333	0.600	0.363	0.411	4.344	2.368	(0.965)	1.505	5.438	.645	(2.688)	3.458	7.391
29	6.667	3.333	0.400	0.242	0.274	4.007	2.368	(0.965)	1.368	5.101	.430	(2.903)	3.564	7.297
30	3.333	3.333	0.200	0.121	0.137	3.670	2.368	(0.965)	1.231	4.764	.215	(3.118)	3.671	7.204

Averages

	Net Plant	Book Dep'n	Return	Equity Return	SL Inc. Tax	SL Fixed Chg.	DB Dep'n	DB Excess	DB Inc. Tax	DB Fixed Chg.	SYD Dep'n	SYD Excess	SYD Inc. Tax	SYD Fixed Chg.
Arith.	51.667	3.333	3.100	1.873	2.123	8.556	3.333	0	2.123	8.556	3.333	0	2.123	8.556
P.W.6%	69.458	3.333	3.932	2.375	2.692	9.957	3.954	0.621	1.999	9.254	4.225	.892	1.681	8.946

2/2/59

EXHIBIT II(a)

FIXED CHARGES WITH CONTINUOUS GROWTH
$100 ORIGINAL PLANT, $10 PER YEAR GROWTH

Based on: Debt 50% @ 4.75% Interest
Equity 50%
Total Return 6.00%

30-Year Life - Retirement End Year 30
Income Tax Rate 53.125% (Composite Fed. & St.)

Year	Begin. Gross Plant	Dep'n $	Res. For Dep'n	Begin. Net Plant	Return	Equity Return	Straight Line			SYD Method				
							Inc. Tax	Fixed Chg.	Gross Plant %	Dep'n	Excess	Inc. Tax	Fixed Chg.	Gross Plant %
1	100	3.333	3.333	100	6.000	3.625	4.108	13.441	13.441	6.852	3.119	0.573	9.906	9.906
2	110	3.667	7.000	106.667	6.400	3.867	4.383	14.450	13.136	6.882	3.215	0.739	10.806	9.824
3	120	4.000	11.000	113.000	6.780	4.096	4.540	15.320	12.766	7.291	3.291	0.912	11.692	9.743
4	130	4.333	15.333	119.000	7.140	4.314	4.889	16.362	12.586	7.677	3.344	1.099	12.572	9.671
5	140	4.667	20.000	124.667	7.480	4.519	5.122	17.269	12.335	8.043	3.376	1.295	13.442	9.601
6	150	5.000	25.000	130.000	7.800	4.713	5.341	18.141	12.094	8.387	3.387	1.503	14.303	9.535
7	160	5.333	30.333	135.000	8.100	4.894	5.547	18.990	11.863	8.710	3.377	1.719	15.152	9.470
8	170	5.667	36.000	139.667	8.380	5.063	5.738	19.785	11.638	9.011	3.344	1.948	15.995	9.409
9	180	6.000	42.000	144.000	8.640	5.220	5.916	20.556	11.420	9.291	3.291	2.186	16.826	9.348
10	190	6.333	48.333	148.000	8.880	5.365	6.080	21.293	11.207	9.549	3.216	2.436	17.649	9.289
11	200	6.667	55.000	151.667	9.100	5.498	6.231	21.998	10.999	9.786	3.119	2.696	18.463	9.232
12	210	7.000	62.000	155.000	9.300	5.619	6.368	22.668	10.794	10.001	3.001	2.967	19.267	9.175
13	220	7.333	69.333	158.000	9.480	5.728	6.492	23.305	10.593	10.195	2.862	3.248	20.061	9.119
14	230	7.667	77.000	160.667	9.640	5.824	6.601	23.908	10.395	10.367	2.700	3.541	20.848	9.064
15	240	8.000	85.000	163.000	9.780	5.909	6.697	24.477	10.199	10.518	2.518	3.843	21.623	9.010
16	250	8.333	93.333	165.000	9.900	5.981	6.778	25.011	10.004	10.647	2.314	4.156	22.389	8.956
17	260	8.667	102.000	166.667	10.000	6.042	6.848	25.515	9.813	10.755	2.088	4.481	23.148	8.903
18	270	9.000	111.000	168.000	10.080	6.090	6.902	25.982	9.623	10.841	1.841	4.816	23.896	8.850
19	280	9.333	120.333	169.000	10.140	6.126	6.943	26.416	9.434	10.906	1.573	5.160	24.633	8.798
20	290	9.667	130.000	169.667	10.180	6.150	6.970	26.817	9.247	10.949	1.282	5.517	25.364	8.746
21	300	10.000	140.000	170.000	10.200	6.163	6.985	27.185	9.062	10.971	0.971	5.884	26.084	8.695
22	310	10.333	150.333	170.000	10.200	6.163	6.985	27.518	8.877	10.970	0.637	6.263	26.796	8.644
23	320	10.667	161.000	169.667	10.180	6.150	6.970	27.817	8.693	10.949	0.282	6.650	27.497	8.593
24	330	11.000	172.000	169.000	10.140	6.126	6.943	28.083	8.510	10.906	(0.094)	7.049	28.189	8.542
25	340	11.333	183.333	168.000	10.080	6.090	6.902	28.315	8.328	10.842	(0.491)	7.458	28.871	8.491
26	350	11.667	195.000	166.667	10.000	6.042	6.848	28.515	8.147	10.756	(0.911)	7.880	29.547	8.442
27	360	12.000	207.000	165.000	9.900	5.981	6.778	28.678	7.966	10.649	(1.351)	8.310	30.210	8.392
28	370	12.333	219.333	163.000	9.780	5.909	6.697	28.810	7.786	10.520	(1.813)	8.752	30.865	8.342
29	380	12.667	232.000	160.667	9.640	5.824	6.601	28.908	7.607	10.370	(2.297)	9.204	31.511	8.292
30	390	13.000	245.000	158.000	9.480	5.728	6.492	28.972	7.429	10.198	(2.802)	9.667	32.147	8.243
31	300	10.000	145.000	155.000	9.300	5.619	6.368	25.668	8.556	10.000	0.000	6.368	25.668	8.556
32	300	10.000	145.000	155.000	9.300	5.619	6.368	25.668	8.556	10.000	0.000	6.368	25.668	8.556
33	300	10.000	145.000	155.000	9.300	5.619	6.368	25.668	8.556	10.000	0.000	6.368	25.668	8.556

30-year total income taxes   186.695   131.952
Permanent saving   54.743

*

EXHIBIT II(b)

FIXED CHARGES WITH CONTINUOUS GROWTH
$100 ORIGINAL PLANT, 5% PER YEAR COMPOUND GROWTH

Based on: Debt 50% @ 4.75% interest
Equity 50%
Total Return 6.00%

30-Year Life - Retirement End Year 30
Income Tax Rate 53.125% (Composite Fed. & St.)

Year	Begin. Gross Plant	Dep'n $	Res. For Dep'n	Begin. Net Plant	Total Return	Equity Return	Straight Line			STD Method				
							Inc. Tax	Fixed Chg.	Gross Plant	Dep'n	Excess	Inc. Tax	Fixed Chg.	Gross Plant
1	100.00	3.333	3.333	100.000	6.000	3.625	4.108	13.441	13.441	6.452	3.119	0.573	9.906	9.206
2	105.00	3.500	6.833	101.667	6.100	3.685	4.176	13.776	13.120	6.559	3.059	0.709	10.309	9.618
3	110.25	3.675	10.508	103.417	6.205	3.749	4.249	14.129	12.815	6.672	2.997	0.852	10.732	9.734
4	115.76	3.858	14.366	105.252	6.315	3.815	4.324	14.497	12.523	6.791	2.933	1.000	11.173	9.652
5	121.55	4.051	18.417	107.184	6.431	3.885	4.403	14.885	12.246	6.915	2.864	1.157	11.639	9.575
6	127.63	4.254	22.671	109.213	6.553	3.959	4.487	15.294	11.983	7.046	2.792	1.323	12.130	9.504
7	134.01	4.467	27.138	111.339	6.680	4.036	4.574	15.721	11.731	7.183	2.716	1.496	12.643	9.434
8	140.71	4.690	31.828	113.572	6.814	4.117	4.666	16.170	11.492	7.327	2.637	1.677	13.181	9.367
9	147.75	4.925	36.753	115.922	6.955	4.202	4.762	16.642	11.264	7.479	2.554	1.868	13.748	9.305
10	155.14	5.171	41.924	118.387	7.103	4.292	4.864	17.138	11.047	7.638	2.467	2.068	14.342	9.245
11	162.90	5.429	47.353	120.976	7.259	4.385	4.970	17.658	10.840	7.804	2.375	2.278	14.966	9.187
12	171.05	5.701	53.054	123.697	7.422	4.484	5.082	18.205	10.643	7.979	2.278	2.500	15.623	9.134
13	179.60	5.986	59.040	126.546	7.593	4.587	5.199	18.778	10.455	8.163	2.177	2.731	16.310	9.081
14	188.58	6.285	65.325	129.540	7.772	4.696	5.322	19.379	10.276	8.356	2.071	2.975	17.032	9.032
15	198.01	6.600	71.925	132.685	7.961	4.810	5.451	20.012	10.107	8.559	1.959	3.231	17.792	8.985
16	207.91	6.930	78.855	135.985	8.159	4.929	5.586	20.675	9.944	8.778	1.848	3.492	18.581	8.937
17	218.31	7.276	86.131	139.455	8.367	5.055	5.729	21.372	9.790	9.001	1.725	3.774	19.417	8.894
18	229.23	7.640	93.771	143.099	8.586	5.187	5.879	22.105	9.643	9.236	1.596	4.070	20.296	8.854
19	240.69	8.022	101.793	146.919	8.815	5.326	6.036	22.873	9.503	9.483	1.461	4.380	21.217	8.815
20	252.72	8.423	110.216	150.927	9.056	5.471	6.200	23.679	9.370	9.743	1.320	4.704	22.183	8.778
21	265.36	8.844	119.060	155.144	9.309	5.623	6.373	24.526	9.243	10.015	1.177	5.046	23.199	8.742
22	278.63	9.287	128.347	159.570	9.574	5.784	6.555	25.416	9.122	10.301	1.014	5.406	24.267	8.709
23	292.56	9.751	138.098	164.213	9.853	5.953	6.747	26.351	9.007	10.631	0.880	5.749	25.353	8.666
24	307.19	10.239	148.337	169.092	10.146	6.130	6.947	27.332	8.897	10.916	0.677	6.180	26.565	8.648
25	322.55	10.751	159.088	174.213	10.453	6.315	7.157	28.361	8.793	11.246	0.495	6.596	27.800	8.619
26	338.68	11.288	170.376	179.592	10.776	6.510	7.378	29.442	8.693	11.594	0.306	7.031	29.095	8.591
27	355.61	11.852	182.228	185.234	11.114	6.715	7.610	30.576	8.598	11.952	0.100	7.497	30.463	8.566
28	373.39	12.445	194.673	191.162	11.470	6.930	7.854	31.769	8.508	12.332	(0.113)	7.982	31.897	8.543
29	392.06	13.057	207.740	197.367	11.843	7.155	8.109	33.019	8.422	12.734	(0.333)	8.486	33.396	8.518
* 30	411.66	13.721	221.461	203.920	12.235	7.392	8.378	34.334	8.340	13.157	(0.564)	9.017	34.973	8.496
31	332.24	11.074	127.535	210.779	12.647	7.641	8.660	32.361	9.746	13.597	2.523	5.800	29.521	8.885
32	343.85	11.461	133.746	216.315	12.979	7.841	8.886	33.326	9.692	14.268	2.807	5.705	30.145	8.767
33	355.79	11.858	140.094	222.044	13.323	8.049	9.122	34.303	9.641	14.981	3.123	5.583	30.764	8.647

* 30-year total income taxes 173.175 115.848
Permanent saving 57.327

| 221.461 | 252.919 | | 173.175 | 647.555 | | | 115.848 | 590.228 |

EXHIBIT I

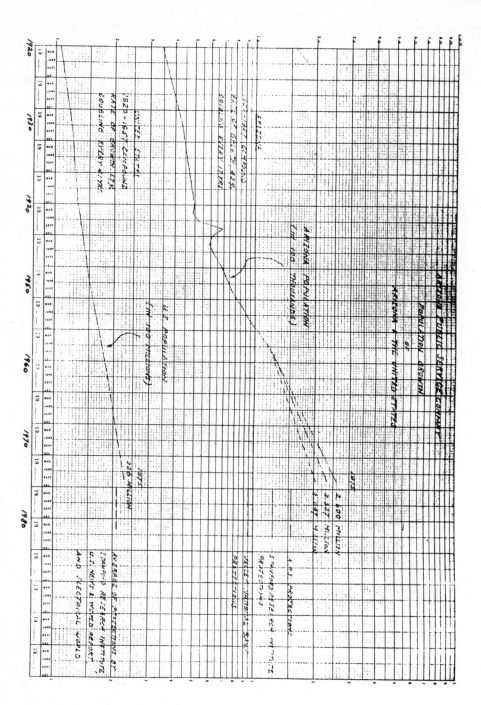

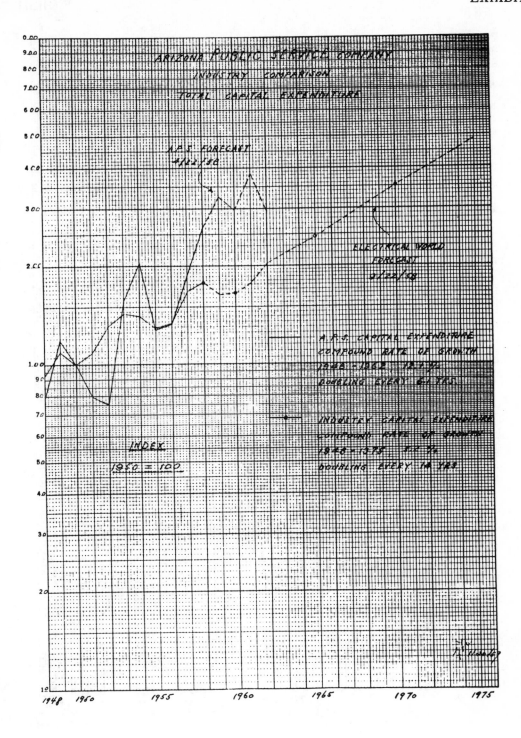

EXHIBIT IV(

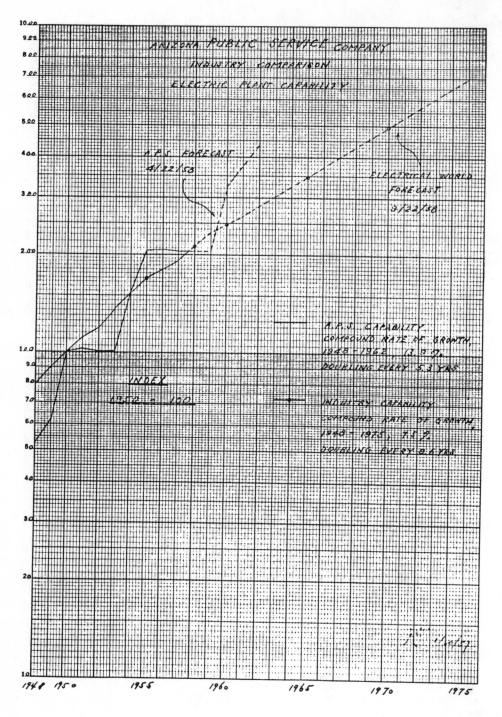

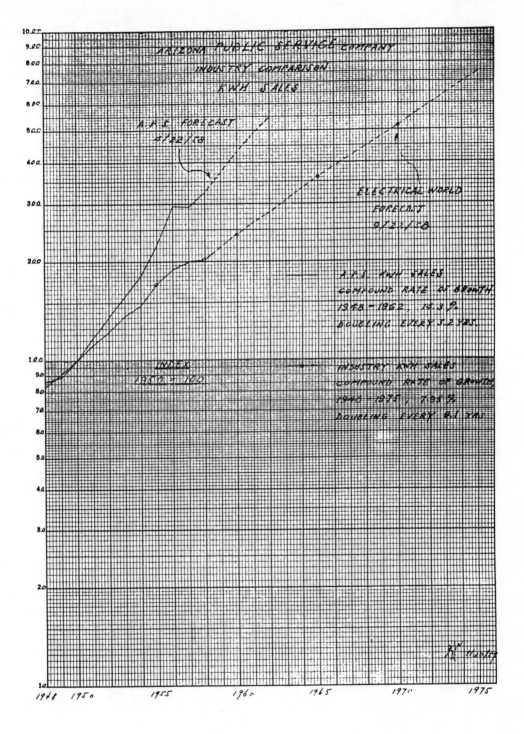

EXHIBIT V

MILLIONS OF DOLLARS

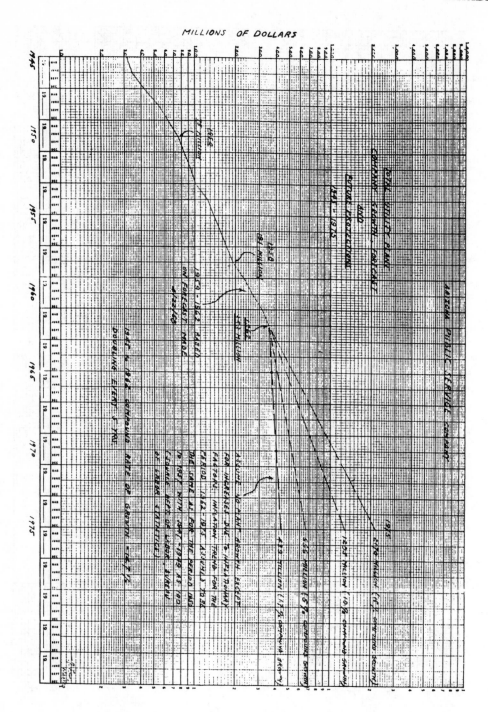

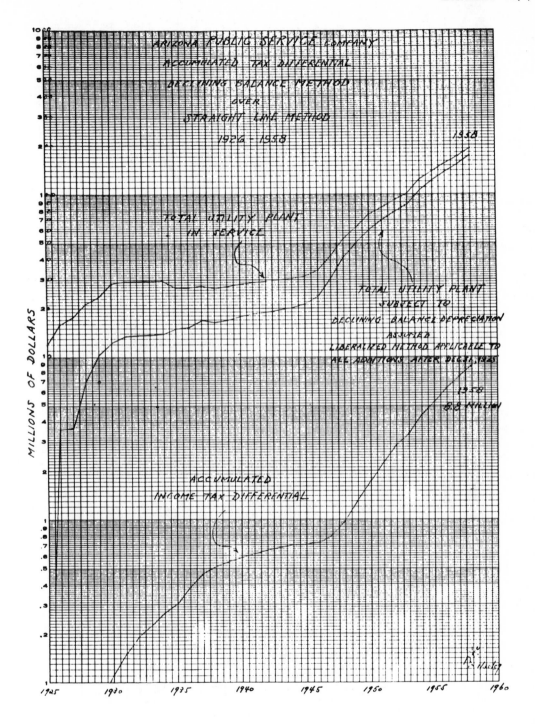

ARIZONA PUBLIC SERVICE COMPANY
ACCUMULATED TAX DIFFERENTIAL
DECLINING BALANCE METHOD
OVER
STRAIGHT LINE METHOD
1926 - 1958

EXHIBIT VI(b)

ARIZONA PUBLIC SERVICE COMPANY
DECLINING BALANCE DEPRECIATION 1926 - 1958
COMPUTATION OF TAX DIFFERENTIAL DECLINING BALANCE OVER STRAIGHT LINE
(Thousands of Dollars)

Year	Asset Balance Jan 1	Current Additions	Current Retirements	Asset Balance Dec. 31	Average Balance	Average Reserve Before Depr.	Net Depreciable Balance	Declining Bal. 7.18%	Depreciation Straight Line 3.55%	D.B. Over Straight Line	Rates %*	Income Tax Differential	Accumulated Differential
1926	$ 3,591	$ 3,591		$ 3,591	$ 1,795		$ 1,795	$ 129	$ 64	$ 65	13.500	$ 9	$ 9
1927	3,644	53		3,644	3,617	$ 129	3,488	250	130	120	"	16	25
1928	7,025	3,381		7,025	5,334	379	4,955	356	191	165	12.000	20	45
1929	10,034	3,052	$ 43	10,034	8,030	713	7,317	525	288	237	"	28	73
1930	12,553	2,562	43	12,553	11,293	1,195	10,098	725	405	320	"	38	111
1931	13,341	871	83	13,341	12,947	1,858	11,089	796	465	331	"	40	151
1932	13,560	338	119	13,560	13,450	2,552	10,898	782	483	299	13.750	41	192
1933	13,694	282	148	13,694	13,627	3,201	10,426	749	489	260	"	36	228
1934	13,932	397	159	13,932	13,813	3,796	10,017	719	496	223	"	39	267
1935	14,996	1,223	159	14,996	14,464	4,357	10,107	726	519	207	17.316	36	303
1936	15,189	353	160	15,189	15,093	4,923	10,170	730	542	188	"	82	385
1937	16,845	1,819	163	16,845	16,017	5,491	10,526	756	575	181	43.635	79	464
1938	16,259	(410)	176	16,259	16,502	6,078	10,424	748	592	156	34.236	53	517
1939	16,863	782	178	16,863	16,561	6,649	9,912	712	595	117	"	40	557
1940	17,846	1,181	198	17,846	17,354	7,173	10,181	731	623	108	26.782	29	586
1941	18,436	730	190	18,436	18,141	7,710	10,431	749	651	98	33.297	33	619
1942	18,972	733	197	18,972	18,704	8,266	10,438	749	671	78	41.968	33	652
1943	19,457	694	209	19,457	19,215	8,811	10,404	747	690	57	"	24	676
1944	20,043	802	216	20,043	19,750	9,346	10,404	747	709	38	"	16	692
1945	21,044	1,223	222	21,044	20,543	9,874	10,669	766	737	29	"	12	704
1946	23,793	2,977	228	23,793	22,419	10,415	12,004	862	805	57	39.864	23	727
1947	30,722	7,164	235	30,722	27,257	11,045	16,212	1,164	979	185	"	74	801
1948	41,103	10,623	247	41,103	35,913	11,969	23,944	1,719	1,289	430	"	171	972
1949	50,279	9,455	279	50,279	45,691	13,424	32,267	2,317	1,456	861	43.635	343	1,315
1950	61,276	11,359	362	61,276	55,778	15,421	40,357	2,898	2,002	896	"	391	1,706
1951	69,515	8,724	485	69,515	65,395	17,896	47,499	3,410	2,348	1,062	51.934	567	2,272
1952	78,212	9,290	593	78,212	73,864	20,767	53,097	3,812	2,652	1,160	53.125	616	2,888
1953	87,302	9,812	722	87,302	82,757	23,921	58,836	4,224	2,971	1,253	"	666	3,554
1954	106,133	19,649	818	106,133	96,718	27,375	69,343	4,979	3,472	1,507	"	801	4,355
1955	122,475	17,261	919	122,475	114,304	31,485	82,819	5,946	4,104	1,840	"	979	5,334
1956	137,207	15,758	1,026	137,207	129,841	36,459	93,382	6,705	4,661	2,044	"	1,086	6,420
1957	151,927	15,969	1,249	151,927	144,567	42,026	102,541	7,362	5,190	2,172	"	1,154	7,574
1958	172,144	21,658	1,441	172,144	162,036	48,044	113,992	8,185	5,817	2,368	"	1,258	8,832

* Composite rate for Federal and Arizona income taxes, excluding excess profit taxes.

1/21/59
P.Z.C.

EXHIBIT VI(b)

ARIZONA PUBLIC SERVICE COMPANY
DECLINING BALANCE DEPRECIATION, 1926 - 1958
DEPRECIATION RESERVE
(Thousands of Dollars)

Year	Reserve Jan. 1	Current Retirement	Reserve Dec. 31 Before Depr.	Average Reserve	Allowable Depreciation	Reserve Dec. 31 After Depr.
1926					$ 129	$ 129
1927	$ 129		$ 129	$ 129	250	379
1928	379		379	379	356	735
1929	735	$ 43	692	713	525	1,217
1930	1,217	43	1,174	1,195	725	1,899
1931	1,899	83	1,816	1,858	796	2,612
1932	2,612	119	2,493	2,552	782	3,275
1933	3,275	148	3,127	3,201	749	3,876
1934	3,876	159	3,717	3,796	719	4,436
1935	4,436	159	4,277	4,357	726	5,003
1936	5,003	160	4,843	4,923	730	5,573
1937	5,573	163	5,410	5,491	756	6,166
1938	6,166	176	5,990	6,078	748	6,738
1939	6,738	178	6,560	6,649	712	7,272
1940	7,272	198	7,074	7,173	731	7,805
1941	7,805	190	7,615	7,710	749	8,364
1942	8,364	197	8,167	8,266	749	8,916
1943	8,916	209	8,707	8,811	747	9,454
1944	9,454	216	9,238	9,346	747	9,985
1945	9,985	222	9,763	9,874	766	10,529
1946	10,529	228	10,301	10,415	862	11,163
1947	11,163	235	10,928	11,045	1,164	12,092
1948	12,092	247	11,845	11,969	1,719	13,564
1949	13,564	279	13,285	13,424	2,317	15,602
1950	15,602	362	15,240	15,421	2,898	18,138
1951	18,138	485	17,653	17,896	3,410	21,063
1952	21,063	593	20,470	20,767	3,812	24,282
1953	24,282	722	23,560	23,921	4,224	27,784
1954	27,784	818	26,966	27,375	4,979	31,945
1955	31,945	919	31,026	31,485	5,946	36,972
1956	36,972	1,026	35,946	36,459	6,705	42,651
1957	42,651	1,249	41,402	42,026	7,362	48,764
1958	48,764	1,441	47,323	48,044	8,185	55,508

1/21/59

Exhibit VI (c)

ARIZONA PUBLIC SERVICE COMPANY
ASSUMPTIONS USED IN COMPUTING ESTIMATED TAX
DIFFERENTIAL DUE TO LIBERALIZED DEPRECIATION
FOR YEARS 1926 - 1958

Arizona Public Service Company came into existence on March 1, 1952, as a result of a merger between Arizona Edison Company, Inc., Central Arizona Light and Power Company, and the Northern Arizona Light & Power Company, a subsidiary of the Central Arizona Light and Power Company.

Arizona Edison Company, Inc., was organized June 24, 1935 following the transfer to receivership of the former Arizona Edison Company. This latter company acquired many of its gas and electrical facilities as far back as 1911, and some of the facilities, in turn, were acquired by the respective units as early as 1904. Many of the records pertaining to various plant additions and retirements in the earlier years of the company were not available. Due to this reason, a set of assumptions were made as to various changes in plant prior to 1950.

While assumptions are made for our illustration of the arithmetic of the declining balance method here, it is to be noted that had the records of the early years been meticulously kept, the resultant figures thus available would not result in any material differences from the figures we have arrived at in our assumptions herein.

1. Liberalized depreciation began in year 1926 for additions after year 1925, continuing through 1958.

2. The percentage of estimated depreciable plant, income tax basis, to total book utility plant (after deducting rapid amortization property, water, ice and other properties) for years 1925 through 1949 is the same as for the average for the years 1950 through 1958.

3. The retirements for years 1925 through 1949 are at the same percentage as for the average for the years 1950 through 1958.

4. The ratio of electric and gas properties for years 1926 through 1949 is the same as the average ratio for years 1950 through 1958.

5. The percentage for depreciation for years 1926 through 1949 is the same as the composite rate computed for both electric and gas combined for years 1950 through 1958.

6. Retirements on additions to plant began in the fourth year, continuing thereafter at the same percentage as computed for the years 1950 through 1958.

7. The income tax rates are the composite rates for Federal and State of Arizona income taxes.

8. For the years in which there were progressive Federal income tax rates, the highest rates applicable were used.

9. Excess profits tax rates were not included.

10. Removal cost and salvage were in the same amounts and thus offset each other.

1/21/59
P.Z.C.

EXHIBIT VII(a

MILLIONS OF DOLLARS

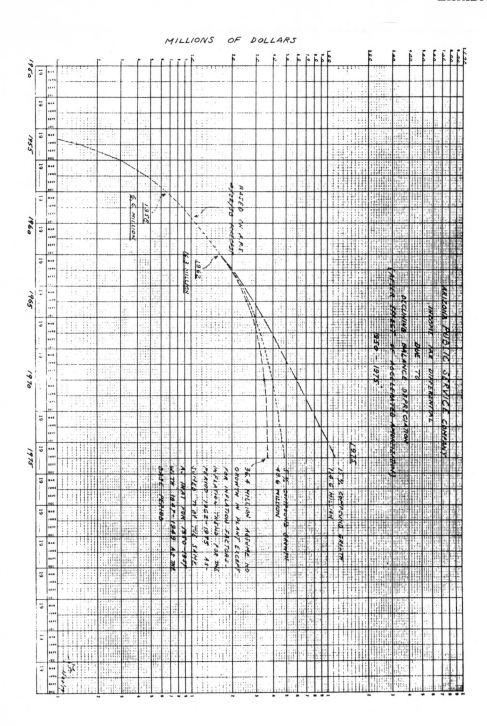

ARIZONA PUBLIC SERVICE COMPANY
INCOME TAX DIFFERENTIAL - ACTUAL AND ESTIMATED
1951 - 1975
(Millions of Dollars)

Year	Accelerated Amortization	Actual 1954-57	Estimated 1958-62	Liberalized Depreciation (1)			(2)			(3)		
				Projected 1963-75	Total	Accumulated Tax Diff'l	Projected 1963-75	Total	Accumulated Tax Diff'l	Projected 1963-75	Total	Accumulated Tax Diff'l
1951	0				0	0		0	0		0	0
52	0				0	0		0	0		0	0
53	0.1				0.1	0.1		0.1	0.1		0.1	0.1
54	0.2	0.1			0.3	0.4		0.3	0.4		0.3	0.4
55	0.7	0.4			1.1	1.5		1.1	1.5		1.1	1.5
56	0.9	0.6			1.5	3.0		1.5	3.0		1.5	3.0
57	0.9	0.8			1.7	4.7		1.7	4.7		1.7	4.7
58	0.8		1.1		1.9	6.6		1.9	6.6		1.9	6.6
59	0.6		1.5		2.1	8.7		2.1	8.7		2.1	8.7
1960	0		2.1		2.1	10.8		2.1	10.8		2.1	10.8
61	(0.2)		2.7		2.5	13.3		2.5	13.3		2.5	13.3
62	(0.2)		3.2		3.0	16.3		3.0	16.3		3.0	16.3
63	(0.2)			3.9	3.7	20.0	4.1	3.9	20.2	3.8	3.6	19.9
64	(0.2)			3.6	3.4	23.4	4.4	4.2	24.4	3.3	3.1	23.0
65	(0.2)			3.3	3.1	26.5	4.7	4.5	28.9	3.0	2.8	25.8
66	(0.2)			3.1	2.9	29.4	5.1	4.9	33.8	2.6	2.4	28.2
67	(0.2)			3.0	2.8	32.2	5.6	5.4	39.2	2.3	2.1	30.3
68	(0.2)			2.8	2.6	34.8	6.2	6.0	45.2	1.9	1.7	32.0
69	(0.2)			2.6	2.4	37.2	6.9	6.7	51.9	1.6	1.4	33.4
1970	(0.2)			2.4	2.2	39.4	7.7	7.5	59.4	1.3	1.1	34.5
71	(0.2)			2.3	2.1	41.5	8.7	8.5	67.9	1.0	0.8	35.3
72	(0.2)			2.2	2.0	43.5	9.7	9.5	77.4	0.8	0.6	35.9
73	(0.2)			2.0	1.8	45.3	11.1	10.9	88.3	0.6	0.4	36.4
74	(0.2)			1.9	1.7	47.0	12.5	12.3	100.6	0.3	0.1	36.4
75	(0.2)			1.8	1.6	48.6	14.2	14.0	114.6	0.2	0	36.4

(1) Assume a net compound growth of 5%.
(2) Assume a net compound growth of 15%.
(3) Assume no growth except for inflationary factor. Inflation trend for 1962-1975 assumed to be the same as that for 1950-1957 with 1947-1949 as base period.

Exhibit VIII

Exhibit VIII is a copy of Securities Act of 1933 Release No. 4010, a copy of which is included on pages 19-21.

LLOYD, HORN, MEGARGEE & STEEDLE
Counsellors at Law
Atlantic City, New Jersey

1421 Atlantic Avenue

January 29, 1959

Securities and Exchange Commission
Washington 25, D. C.

Re: Securities Act of 1933, Release No. 4010
Securities Exchange Act of 1934,
Release No. 5844
Public Utility Holding Company Act
of 1935, Release No. 13894

Gentlemen:

In connection with your Notice of Intention
to Announce Interpretation of Administrative
Policy, dated December 30, 1958, as to which you
stated that interested persons might file comments
on or before January 31, 1959 we understand that
a number of companies affected by the proposed
interpretation have requested that the time for
comments by interested parties be extended for at
least thirty days, and that, thereafter, a public
hearing be held at which those interested may present oral arguments and file briefs.

Atlantic City Electric Company believes that
this matter is of such importance as to warrant
the allowance of the additional time requested and
the holding of a public hearing and it, therefore,
joins in the request that the time be extended for
at least thirty days and that a public hearing be
held.

Very truly yours,

/s/ JOHN LLOYD, JR.

John Lloyd, Jr., Counsel for
Atlantic City Electric Company

LAW OFFICES OF

ROSS, MARSH & FOSTER

725 Fifteenth Street

Washington 5, D. C.

March 24, 1959

Re: Securities Act of 1933
Release No. 4010
Securities Exchange Act of 1934
Release No. 5844

Honorable Orval L. DuBois
Secretary
Securities and Exchange Commission
Washington 25, D. C.

Dear Sir:

Atlantic City Electric Company (Atlantic) herewith submits its views and comments pursuant to notice issued in the above matter on December 30, 1958.

Atlantic is principally a distributor of electric power in some 377 communities in southern New Jersey. Atlantic's rates and accounting are subject to the jurisdiction of the New Jersey Board of Public Utility Commissioners. A relatively small amount of electric energy is interchanged with the Philadelphia Electric Company, a non-associated company, which gives rise to the filing of reports with the Federal Power Commission. Its stock is listed on the New York Stock Exchange and the Philadelphia-Baltimore Exchange.

Under the notice of proposed interpretation this Commission would require Atlantic to alter and change the accounting for $4,007,357, recorded in Atlantic's 1958 report to stockholders as retained earnings-- restricted. This amount arises from the accrued taxes deferred under accelerated amortization and liberalized depreciation. Unless Atlantic so complies in its financial statements, including reports to stockholders, such statements will be presumed by the SEC to be "misleading or inaccurate", despite disclosure contained in the certificate of the accountant and footnotes to the statements.

Without minimizing the importance of the arguments against the proposed notice of policy interpretation made by others, Atlantic wishes to stress a matter of great significance to it. The New Jersey Board of Public Utility Commissioners, which agency has complete regulatory jurisdiction over Atlantic, has authorized it to account for the deferred taxes arising from accelerated amortization and liberalized depreciation in a restricted surplus account. As heretofore indicated, in its most recent annual report to stockholders for the year 1958, Atlantic has included such deferred taxes as part of retained earnings, but restricted, all as provided by the authorization of the New Jersey regulatory authority, with appropriate notes denoting this fact. The requirements of the Federal Power Commission are also indicated by appropriate notes. Thus, the requirements of both agencies having regulatory authority over Atlantic's rates and accounting are disclosed.

In commenting on the instant proposal by this Commission, Honorable Jerome J. Kuykendall, Chairman of the Federal Power Commission (FPC) has stated in his letter of February 12, 1959:

> "We ⌈FPC⌉ believe that the force of this Commission's ⌈FPC's⌉ accounting jurisdiction requires that prescribed classifications be observed in financial statements distributed to the public, including prospective investors". (Emphasis supplied)

Thus the FPC claims that with respect to companies subject to FPC accounting jurisdiction it is the agency with jurisdiction over financial statements distributed to the public, including prospective investors. If this be true the SEC could not lawfully require any accounting classifications in financial reports which conflict with FPC accounting requirements. It appears that the SEC may have provided for the adoption of the FPC requirements respecting deferred taxes in this proceeding on the mistaken assumption that FPC has superior authority with respect to financial reporting by companies subject to FPC jurisdiction.

This raises a threshold question of the authority or jurisdiction of the SEC over the financial statements of Atlantic, a company which is subject to the accounting jurisdiction of the New Jersey Board of Public Utility Commissioners as well as to that of the FPC.

If the FPC is correct in its view,[1] then the SEC is without juris-diction in the premises. Certainly the assertion of jurisdiction by the FPC over the very matters which Congress lodged specifically with the SEC--"financial statements distributed to the public, including prospec-tive investors"--requires a determination in limine in this proceeding. This issue is not avoided by prescribing that (notice footnote 4) those companies subject to the uniform system of accounts of the FPC shall use the balance sheet captions and classification of deferred taxes prescribed by that Commission in its Orders Nos. 203 and 204. The basic issue here is whether the SEC can make any order in the premises in view of the FPC's allegation of jurisdiction over the subject matter. If arguendo the FPC has jurisdiction over the financial statements distributed to the public,[2] then it follows that the SEC cannot act in the very same matter.

It is clear that Congress conferred upon the SEC jurisdiction over security issues by virtue of the provisions and purposes of the Securities Act of 1933 and the Securities Exchange Act of 1934 dealing with dis-closure and financial statements.[3] By applying the FPC requirements as to the accounting to be followed in financial statements by Atlantic the maxim "delegato potestas non potest delegari" is violated. Congress has delegated the authority to the SEC but this delegation of authority does not empower the SEC to sub-delegate the authority to another independent agency by application of its requirements which were adopted without

---

[1] Although the SEC has exercised its jurisdiction over financial reports for over 25 years the FPC has not until now ever contended that its authority was paramount to that of the SEC.

[2] Atlantic does not concede that the FPC classification requires Atlantic to refrain from reporting the deferred taxes in a restricted surplus account in reports other than those required to be filed with the FPC.

[3] 15 USCA sections 77g, 77h, 77j, 78(1); A. C. Frost & Co. v. Couer D'Alene Mines Corp., 312 U.S. 38.

consideration of the policies of the Securities Act of 1933, and the Securities Exchange Act of 1934.[4] This is more than a mere delegation of a ministerial function to a subordinate.

Under this proposal, without a hearing or record before the SEC, Atlantic is compelled to follow and comply with the requirements prescribed by another agency charged with other responsibilities. Nor is there any assurance that the FPC will not change or alter its accounting requirements in the future. Compare FPC Order No. 171, issued April 21, 1954, (19 F.R. 2450), setting up Account No. 259 (Reserve for Deferred Income Taxes) with FPC Order No. 203, issued May 29, 1958, substituting for Account No. 259 a new Account 266. Does the SEC intend to adopt ipso facto any and all changes that the FPC may prescribe and intend that Atlantic will be ipso facto bound thereby? Is Atlantic thus relegated to another agency with respect to the matters over which SEC has primary jurisdiction? This is the very thing proscribed by the first Morgan case, (Morgan v. U.S., 298 U.S. 468). As the Court there stated: (298 U.S. at 481)

> "That duty [to decide] cannot be performed by one who has not considered evidence or argument. It is not an impersonal obligation. It is a duty akin to that of a judge. The one who decides must hear."

Moreover, if it is assumed that the SEC has authority to delegate its authority, there is no reason why it should confine its delegation to the FPC. Conceivably, it could by the same expedient as proposed here apply the accounting requirements of other agencies, state or federal. If such a delegation were valid it would be more reasonable to apply the accounting requirements of the state regulatory agency which has the most complete regulatory responsibility over the activities of Atlantic.

---

[4] Congress by Sec. 204(h) of the Federal Power Act provided that where the FPC has jurisdiction over the security issues compliance with FPC requirements will also suffice in lieu of "reports, information, and documents required under Section 7 of the Securities Act of 1933 and Sections 12 and 13 of the Securities and Exchange Act of 1934." Congress significently (sic) left to the SEC the determination of requirements under these Acts in all other instances.

The New Jersey Board of Public Utility Commissioners has jurisdiction over the issuance of securities by Atlantic and under Section 204(f) of of the Federal Power Act the FPC is specifically excluded from such regulation under such circumstances. The New Jersey Board also has jurisdiction over all of Atlantic's rates, except that concerning a relatively small interstate exchange.

It is not open to doubt that a respectable body of state regulatory agencies have prescribed "restricted surplus" accounting for deferred taxes. This being so, such accounting is not and cannot be misleading. As the proposed notice recognizes, a deferral of taxes results from the operations of Sections 167 and 168 of the Internal Revenue Code. Atlantic agrees with this Commission that during the period when tax deductions under Sections 167 and 168 exceed those under normal depreciation the income account should be charged with an amount equal to the reduction in income taxes, with a reversal by crediting income when the tax depreciation is less on the same properties. This accords with the authorizations of the New Jersey authorities.

The purpose of the Commission's proposals in this proceeding is to prevent "misleading or inaccurate" financial statements to be issued to the public, including investors, under the authority of the Securities Act of 1933 and Securities Exchange Act of 1934. Yet, the Commission proposes that a complete disclosure of the accounting required by a state commission in a financial statement by Atlantic and others so situated will be "presumed to be misleading or inaccurate." It is hard to see how an administrative determination could be more arbitrary.[5] The method used by Atlantic in reports to stockholders has accurately disclosed the accounting requirements of each agency having regulatory jurisdiction. To do otherwise would be misleading in fact. Any policy adopted by SEC

---

[5] The notice gives no reason in law or basis in fact for the Commission determination that restricted surplus accounting will be presumed to be misleading or inaccurate.

that would prevent the present method of reporting which is in fact not misleading or inaccurate is arbitrary.[6]

This Commission is seeking to determine what account or accounts in the balance sheet may contain the tax credits in question without misleading the public in financial reports. With respect to public utility operating companies such as Atlantic this Commission should determine that reports disclosing the requirements of the state regulatory commission and footnoting the requirements of the federal regulatory commission are not misleading or inaccurate but are proper. To lodge the tax deferral in restricted surplus is not misleading, since the origin and derivation of the amount is known and certain and fully disclosed.

This Commission in exercising its jurisdiction should accommodate the requirements of the regulatory agencies, both state and federal, where possible. But the responsibility of this Commission in this proceeding is only the determination of what in fact is misleading or inaccurate in financial reports, not the determination as to which requirement is preferable as between state and federal regulatory commission accounting requirements. Each regulatory commission has its own rate and concomitant accounting jurisdiction. The requirements of each must be disclosed in financial reports in order to present investors with all the facts. The public interest would best be served by permitting Atlantic to follow its present form of disclosure in financial reports. Since the FPC does not have jurisdiction over Atlantic's security issues, it is more reasonable, for purposes of disclosure in relation to security issues, to adopt the state regulatory requirements and accommodate the interests of the state. Certainly the SEC cannot give the FPC jurisdiction over the accounting requirements in connection with Atlantic's security issues because this

---

[6] It should be observed that the Commission is not promulgating an accounting rule as such but only a policy statement that surplus accounting will be presumed to be "misleading". In FCC v. American Broadcasting Co., 347 U.S. 284, the Court held that the FCC by agency action could not construe the "give away" programs as illegal, if they were not in fact illegal.

would be granting by indirection authority which Congress has explicitly denied to the FPC in Section 204(f) of the Federal Power Act, in deference to state regulation.

The inclusion of the tax deferral in restricted surplus enables Atlantic to borrow on a more favorable basis, and it is to the advantage of the rate payers as well as stockholders that borrowing be accomplished on the most favorable terms.

By accounting for the tax deferral in restricted surplus, advantage is taken of the plain fact that the financial community takes the restricted surplus into account as part of equity in determining capitalization ratios for purposes of rating the bonds of utilities. The more favorable the capitalization ratio -- the greater the ratio of equity to bonds in the overall capitalization -- the more favorable is the bond rating, and accordingly, the more favorable is the interest rate on new indebtedness. Moreover, by increasing the equity ratio in relation to outstanding debt, an increase in debt financing can be accomplished without changing the pre-existing capitalization ratio. For every dollar of the tax deferral in restricted surplus, and assuming a one-to-one capitalization ratio, it is possible to borrow an additional dollar of debt without impairing the capitalization ratio and without adding to equity capital. Further, debt financing is less costly than equity financing, with the additional advantage that interest payment on debt is a tax deductible expense.

In the current tight money market with relatively high cost of money, it is to everybody's advantage that financing be accomplished in the most beneficial manner. The Florida Railroad and Public Utilities Commission expressed the view as succinctly as any: 4 P.U.R. 3d. 91, 92 (1954)

"Based upon the circumstances of applicant as stated in the application as amended, * * * [and because] the applicant would in all probability experience a more receptive market when selling its securities were the Restricted Surplus permitted to be included as capital equity in the determination of capitalization ratios, the commission hereby permits such inclusion by applicant of Restricted Surplus. However, such Restricted Surplus may not be used for the payment of dividends."

In 1958, Atlantic spent $16,103,000 for new plant and equipment. The proposed construction program for 1959 involves estimated expenditures approximating 13 million dollars. The additional capital required for the 1958 construction (including retirement of outstanding short term notes) was obtained through the sale of First Mortgage Bonds, Preferred and Common stock, as well as internally generated funds. In order to go forward with its utility service on the most advantageous basis from the standpoint of the public interest, Atlantic should not be prevented from financing on the best possible terms so long as its financial statements are accurate and fully understood. To require Atlantic to depart from the method authorized by the New Jersey authorities will be of direct and immediate consequence to the rate payers who will be required to support the increased cost of financing. Both Congress and the courts recognize the weight of local laws in the administration of a federal statute. Davies Warehouse Company v. Bowles, 321 U.S. 144, 154-155.

In conclusion, Atlantic respectfully submits that this Commission, and not the FPC has jurisdiction over disclosure in financial statements; that this Commission cannot delegate the accounting requirements to be followed in financial statements to the FPC; that this Commission should not adopt the FPC accounting requirements as its own to be followed in financial statements; that this Commission's proposal to interpret as a matter of policy restricted surplus accounting for tax deferrals as "misleading" or "inaccurate" is arbitrary and without basis in fact or law; that restricted surplus accounting is expressly authorized by the New Jersey Board of Public Utility Commissioners having jurisdiction over almost all of Atlantic's utility operations; that the accounting requirements of both the state and federal regulatory authorities are fully disclosed in Atlantic's financial statements; and finally that such disclosure is not misleading or inaccurate and Atlantic should therefore be permitted to continue its present method of reporting the tax deferrals in its financial statements.

Pursuant to notice issued January 28, 1959, as amended by notice issued February 25, 1959, Atlantic City Electric Company hereby indicates its intention to appear at the public hearing on this matter and requests thirty minutes to make its oral presentation.

Respectfully submitted,

ATLANTIC CITY ELECTRIC COMPANY

/s/ By _____ BRADFORD ROSS _____

Bradford Ross
Ross, Marsh & Foster, Its Attorneys

BANGOR AND AROOSTOOK RAILROAD COMPANY

Bangor, Maine

January 20, 1959

Securities & Exchange Commission
Washington 25, D. C.

Attn: Orval L. DuBois, Secretary

Gentlemen:

Under date of December 30, 1958 your
Commission released a proposed announcement
relative to policy regarding balance sheet treatment of credit arising from reduction of income
taxes.

We assume that, when and if an interpretation or regulation is propounded in the premises,
there will be a specific exemption for railroads
which are required to keep their accounts pursuant to rules and regulations of the Interstate
Commerce Commission.

As you undoubtedly know, the Interstate
Commerce Commission has views somewhat different
from those of the proposed interpretation. We
would dislike being in the position of having to
violate the rules and regulations of at least
one, and perhaps at times both, of the two
regulatory bodies.

We would appreciate it if your Commission
will consider this problem before releasing the
proposed interpretation.

Yours very truly,

/s/ JOHN E. HESS

John E. Hess
Vice President - Finance

jehw

SECURITIES AND EXCHANGE COMMISSION
Washington 25, D. C.

January 29, 1959

Mr. John E. Hess
Vice President--Finance
Bangor and Aroostock Railroad Company
Bangor, Maine

Dear Mr. Hess:

Thank you for your letter of January 20, 1959, commenting on our proposed statement regarding balance sheet treatment of credit arising from reduction of income taxes.

It appears that you may have overlooked General Instruction I of our Form 10-K which permits your company to file with us a copy of your report to the Interstate Commerce Commission. No change in this instruction is contemplated as this procedure is prescribed by Sec. 13(b) of the Securities Exchange Act of 1934.

Very truly yours,

Andrew Barr
Chief Accountant

Enclosure

BANGOR HYDRO-ELECTRIC CO.

ROBERT N. HASKELL
PRESIDENT

33 State Street
Executive Offices
Bangor, Maine

January 28, 1959

Securities & Exchange Commission
Washington 25, D. C.

Attention: Mr. Orval L. Dubois, Secretary

Gentlemen:

This letter offers our comments on the Notice
of Intention to Announce Interpretation of Administrative Policy released by the Commission on
December 30, 1958. Bangor Hydro-Electric Company
has issued securities pursuant to the Securities
Act of 1933 and files annual reports pursuant to
the Securities Exchange Act of 1934.

Your release effectively supports a general
principle of deferred tax accounting with which
we are in agreement. We are disturbed, however,
by the exception related to public utilities under
regulatory decrees ordering the so-called "flow
through" approach, or by indirection seeking the
same end result by denial actions related to tax
normalization. If this type of exception is to
have Commission recognition we believe that any
operating statement that includes Section 167 tax
deferrals as a part of net income, or any balance
sheet wherein any part of surplus came from tax
deferrals should be clearly disclosed and the disclosure should indicate the exact amounts so
included in both the operating statement and the
balance sheet.

The writer's concept of the basic philosophy
of your S.E.C. operation is to insure that security
owners and purchasers have as full and as accurate
financial information as may be and since operating statements of a company have the principle
function of facilitating estimates of future
earnings, S.E.C. requirement of full disclosure
of net income sources should be a mandatory
requirement.

If tax deferrals, undisclosed, are included
in operating statements, the investor must assume,
all unknown to him, the risks inherent in Congressional amendments to Section 167 and in the
future conclusions of future regulatory bodies.
We would view with misgivings any inference that
some future regulatory body would impose rates on
future customers sufficient to pay for the "windfalls" reflected in an earlier policy of expedi-
ency that gives to current rate payers the benefit of current tax deferrals.

In summary, we agree with your administrative policy but suggest that in your consideration of proper balance sheet treatment you go to
the source from which surplus does accrue; namely,
the operating statement, and do what can be done
to inform investors the exact dimension of any
"earnings" coming from the fiction that tax
deferrals are tax reductions. Only by that action
do we believe you will accomplish clarity and
equity out of this fog that so surely surrounds
investors, security analists and regulatory bodies
in the accounting treatment of the liberalized
depreciation provisions in the 1954 Code.

Very truly yours,

/s/ R. N. HASKELL

R. N. Haskell
President

CALIFORNIA ELECTRIC POWER COMPANY

JOHN A. TALLEY
VICE-PRESIDENT
AND COMPTROLLER

2885 Foothill Boulevard
San Bernardino, California

March 17, 1959

Securities and Exchange Commission
Washington 25, D. C.

Re: Securities Act of 1933
Releases No. 4010 and 4038

Gentlemen:

Release No. 4010, dated December 30, 1958, stated that you had under consideration the announcement of an interpretation of administrative policy on financial statements regarding balance sheet treatment of credits equivalent to the reduction in income taxes.

The proposed balance sheet treatment is set forth in the first paragraph of the proposed announcement as follows:

"Notice is hereby given that any financial statement which designates as earned surplus or its equivalent or includes as a part of equity capital (even though accompanied by words of limitation such as 'restricted' or 'appropriated') the accumulated credit arising from accounting for reductions in income taxes for various items including those under sections 167 and 168 of the Internal Revenue Code of 1954, filed with this Commission dated as of December 31, 1958, or thereafter, will pursuant to the administrative policy

on financial statements announced in
Accounting Series Release No. 4, be
presumed by this Commission 'to be misleading or inaccurate despite disclosure contained in the certificate of the accountant
or in footnotes to the statements provided
the matters involved are material.'"
(Emphasis added.)

Release No. 4010 also sets forth the proposed income statement treatment of such credits.
This is covered in the third paragraph of the
proposed announcement which reads as follows:

"In order that the net income from operations of a corporation which deducts
liberalized depreciation or accelerated
amortization for tax purposes but only
normal depreciation in its books of
account be not overstated in the earlier
years and understated in the later years,
it is necessary, except in rare cases,
to charge current income with an amount
equal to the tax reduction. The exception to this procedure is found in those
cases described in paragraph 8 of
Accounting Research Bulletin No. 44
(Revised), Declining-Balance Depreciation,
issued in July 1958 by the Committee on
Accounting Procedure of the American
Institute of Certified Public Accountants.
The contra credit should be accumulated
in an appropriately captioned balance
sheet account and returned to income
proportionately in later years when the
depreciation then allowed for tax purposes is less than the normal depreciation charged to income in the books of
account."

Release No. 4038 advised that interested
persons could submit written views and comments
on the proposed interpretation of administrative
policy on or before March 25, 1959. California
Electric Power Company's views are that the pro-

posed interpretation should not be adopted by
the Securities and Exchange Commission. Its
reasons are as follows:

Under Accounting Series Release No. 4,
financial statements may be presumed to be
misleading or inaccurate despite full disclosures
only where such statements are prepared in
accordance with accounting principles for which
there is no substantial support. The proposed
interpretation of that Release, which would
require the use of a "normalization" procedure
except in those rare cases described in paragraph 8 of Accounting Research Bulletin No. 44
(Revised), could be justified only on a finding
that there is no substantial support for the so-
called "flow-through" method except in such rare
cases. Such a finding cannot be supported by
the facts.

Under the Uniform System of Accounts
prescribed by the Federal Power Commission, and
particularly under Order No. 204, Docket No. R-159,
utility companies subject to that Commission's
jurisdiction can properly use flow-through
accounting in the treatment of liberalized depreciation or accelerated amortization, or both.
California Electric Power Company, for example,
is utilizing flow-through accounting in its
treatment of accelerated depreciation and normalization accounting in its treatment of accelerated
amortization. Can the Securities and Exchange
Commission properly find that accounting principles authorized and prescribed by the Federal
Power Commission are misleading and inaccurate
on the grounds that they have no substantial
support?

Similarly, many state regulatory commissions
authorize flow-through accounting irrespective
of whether utility companies under their jurisdiction may properly be classified as rare cases
under Accounting Research Bulletin No. 44. Here
again, the facts belie any finding that there
is no substantial support for such accounting
procedures.

We submit that so long as there is substantial support for flow-through accounting and
so long as adequate disclosures are made in
connection with financial statements, the public
interest is fully and properly protected. The
Securities and Exchange Commission should not
adopt the proposed interpretation of administrative policy.

Our final comment is that if, in spite of
the reasons advanced in opposition, the Commission
decides to adopt the proposed interpretation, it
should first either eliminate the words "for
various items including those" which we have under-
lined above in the quotation of the first paragraph of the proposed announcement, or it should
enumerate those items in order to obviate misunderstanding and confusion.

Very truly yours,

CALIFORNIA ELECTRIC POWER
    COMPANY

/s/ By JOHN A. TALLEY

Vice-President and Comptroller

THE CALIFORNIA OREGON POWER COMPANY

Medford, Oregon

January 27, 1959

VIA AIR MAIL - SPECIAL DELIVERY

Securities and Exchange Commission
Washington 25, D. C.

Attention: Orval L. Dubois
Secretary

Re: Securities Act of 1933
Release No. 4010
Securities Exchange Act of 1934
Release No. 5844

Gentlemen:

Your Notice of Intention to Announce Interpretation of Administrative Policy, dated December 30, 1958, was received by this Company on January 12, 1959. This notice states that the Commission has under consideration the announcement of an interpretation of administrative policy on financial statements regarding balance sheet treatment of credits equivalent to the reductions in income taxes, as set forth in the notice. It is also stated that, in view of the amounts involved, any interested person may file comments on or before January 31, 1959.

The California Oregon Power Company, an operating electric utility, from time to time issues securities under the Securities Act of 1933 and makes periodic reports to the Commission under requirements of the Securities Exchange Act of 1934. This Company has, with respect to certain of its property additions subsequent to January 1, 1954, availed itself of the provisions of Section 167 of the Internal Revenue Code of 1954 and it has reflected on its corporate books of account, as reported to the Commission, the actual taxes paid pursuant to liberalized depreciation claimed under said Section 167. This reporting has been in conformity with the uniform systems of accounts prescribed for use by the Company by the State Commissions of California and Oregon, within whose jurisdiction the Company operates.

By reason of the use of Section 167 liberalized depreciation in the manner stated, the proposed interpretation of administrative policy regarding balance sheet treatment of this item is of utmost importance to this Company and it desires to have additional time within which to understand the full import of the proposed interpretation and to file its views thereon. Because of the importance with which the Company regards the proposed interpretation and the various very serious effects which it could have upon the Company, and because of the short period of time allowed for the making of comments on this interpretation, the Company respectfully requests that the time within which interested parties may submit their comments be extended for at least 30 days beyond January 31, 1959.

In further support of this request, it is pointed out that the import of certain portions of the proposed interpretation is not entirely clear. For example, it is not clear whether the interpretation would require a transfer from Earned Surplus to a Reserve for Deferred Taxes of the tax savings that flowed through to Income since 1954 or only in the first year in which a financial statement is filed after the new interpretation becomes effective, if adopted. Further, it is not clear what would be required to establish to the satisfaction of the Commission that a Company falls within the exception referred to in the third paragraph of the proposed announcement.

Very truly yours,

/s/ F. C. BASH

F. C. Bash
Vice President and Treasurer

FCB:po

SECURITIES AND EXCHANGE COMMISSION
Washington 25, D. C.

February 2, 1959

Mr. F. C. Bash
Vice President and Treasurer
The California Oregon Power Company
Medford, Oregon

Dear Mr. Bash:

As you see from the enclosed release, the Commission has extended the time for comment for approximately the thirty days requested in your letter of January 27, 1959, and has also set a date for a public hearing on the matter.

The third paragraph of our release to which you refer in your last paragraph recognizes by quotation in footnote 3 a paragraph in Accounting Research Bulletin No. 44 (Revised) which your certifying accountants, Haskins & Sells, I presume will take into consideration this year. Evidence that regulatory authorities having jurisdiction in rate matters will not permit deferred tax accounting with respect to accelerated depreciation should be produced. I note from your report to stockholders for 1957 that the balance sheet treatment advocated in our release has been adopted by you with respect to emergency facilities.

Very truly yours,

Andrew Barr
Chief Accountant

Enclosure

THE CALIFORNIA OREGON POWER COMPANY

Medford, Oregon
February 13, 1959

Mr. Andrew Barr
Chief Accountant
Securities & Exchange Commission
Washington 25, D. C.

Re: SECURITIES ACT OF 1933
Release No. 4010
SECURITIES EXCHANGE ACT OF 1934
Release No. 5844

Dear Mr. Barr:

Your reply of February 2, 1959 to our letter
of January 27, 1959, regarding the above releases,
refers to a quotation in Footnote 3 of a paragraph
from Accounting Research Bulletin No. 44 (Revised),
and you state:

"Evidence that regulatory authorities
having jurisdiction in rate matters
will not permit deferred tax accounting with respect to accelerated depreciation should be produced."

The retail rates of this Company for electric
service in Oregon, which account for about 77% of
the Company's total retail revenues, are under the
jurisdiction of the Public Utility Commissioner of
Oregon. The remainder of the Company's operations
are in California.

We submit herewith a copy of a letter to this
Company from the Public Utility Commissioner of
Oregon relating to the accounting and rate making
treatment of liberalized depreciation under
Section 167 of the 1954 Internal Revenue Code.
We shall appreciate your advice as to whether the
enclosed letter is sufficient to bring the company
within the exception contemplated in Footnote 3
and the related text of your release, and, if not,
what additional would be required.

Very truly yours,

/s/ F. C. BASH

F. C. Bash
Vice President and Treasurer

FCB:pq
Enclosure

STATE OF OREGON
Public Utility Commissioner
Salem

January 9, 1959

In reply please refer
to File No. 5501

The California Oregon Power Co.
Medford, Oregon

Attention: F. C. Bash, Vice President
& Treasurer

Gentlemen:

This will acknowledge your letter of
January 7, 1959 regarding accounting for income
taxes as reduced by the use of liberalized depreciation as permitted under Section 167 of the 1954
Internal Revenue Code.

Under the Uniform System of Accounts for
Electric Utilities adopted by the Commissioner by
Order No. 3917 dated December 21, 1936 and as
supplemented by Order No. 5002 dated December 1,
1937 and effective January 1, 1937 (which Order's
are still in effect for Electric Utilities under
the jurisdiction of the Commissioner) it is
proper procedure for an Electric Utility to
account for reduced income taxes due to liberalized depreciation as permitted by Section 167 of
the 1954 Internal Revenue Code, by recording
actual taxes that are paid as tax expense and
also to show in like manner its tax expense on
financial statements and annual reports to the
Commissioner.

This office is of the opinion, with respect
to a utility using such accounting for the tax
effect of liberalized depreciation, that this
method should also be followed for rate making
purposes and consistently applied to property
additions on which liberalized depreciation is
taken.

In view of the foregoing, I see no reason
to take exception to this method of accounting
for income taxes with the understanding that such
method will be followed consistently in the future.

Very truly yours,

/s/ HOWARD MORGAN

Howard Morgan
Commissioner

HM:DMF

SECURITIES AND EXCHANGE COMMISSION
Washington 25, D. C.

February 25, 1959

Mr. F. C. Bash
Vice President and Treasurer
The California Oregon Power Company
Medford, Oregon

Dear Mr. Bash:

Receipt is acknowledged of your letter of
February 13, 1959, enclosing a letter from the
Public Utility Commissioner of the State of Oregon
and inquiring as to whether this letter is sufficient "evidence that regulatory authorities having
jurisdiction in rate matters will not permit
deferred tax accounting with respect to accelerated
depreciation."

Item 8 of Accounting Research Bulletin No. 44
(Revised), to which I referred in my letter of
February 2, 1959, states that "accounting recognition need not be given to the deferment of taxes
if it may reasonably be expected that increased
future income taxes, resulting from earlier deduction of declining balance depreciation for income
tax purposes only, will be allowed in future rate
determination." It was our thought that Accounting
Research Bulletin No. 44 fully covered the accounting propriety of making deferred tax charges to
income with the exception noted in item 8, and
that the application of the exception would be
verified by the independent accountants. However,
it is becoming evident from the comments received
that further discussion of this point may be
necessary after consideration of all written and
oral comments.

A copy of Securities Act Release No. 4038
announcing the postponement of the public hearing
in this matter to April 8, 1959, is enclosed.

Very truly yours,

Andrew Barr·
Chief Accountant

Enclosure

BROBECK, PHLEGER & HARRISON
ATTORNEYS AT LAW

One Eleven Sutter Street
San Francisco 4

<u>AIR MAIL</u>   March 23, 1959

Mr. Orval L. Du Bois,
Secretary,
Securities and Exchange Commission,
Washington 25, D. C.

> Re: Securities Act of 1933 -
> Release No. 4010
> Securities Exchange Act of 1934 -
> Release No. 5844

Dear Sir:

On December 30, 1958, under the above release numbers, the Securities and Exchange Commission invited all interested persons to file written comments on the proposed interpretation of administrative policy on financial statements regarding balance sheet treatment of the accumulated credit arising from the recognition in such statements of the deferral to future periods of current reductions in income taxes. By subsequent releases, the time for submitting such comments has been extended to March 25, 1959. The following comments are submitted on behalf of The California Oregon Power Company (Copco) in response to the opportunity afforded by the Commission.

Pursuant to special orders of the state commissions in California and Oregon, Copco practices tax deferral accounting in respect of tax deferments under Section 168 of the Internal Revenue Code and places the deferred taxes in a reserve account in the manner contemplated by the proposed policy. Therefore, it is not concerned with the proposed administrative interpretation insofar as deferrals under Section 168 are concerned. However, Copco also avails itself of the liberalized depreciation provided for in Section 167 of the Internal Revenue Code in respect of which it has neither sought nor obtained special accounting orders of the state commissions which would be necessary in order for it to practice deferred tax accounting with respect to taxes deferred under Section 167.

By letter to Mr. Andrew Barr, chief accountant for the Commission, dated February 13, 1959, Copco requested advice as to whether or not the letter to it from the Oregon Public Utility Commissioner, dated January 9, 1959, a copy of which was sent to Mr. Barr, is sufficient to bring the Company within the exception contemplated in footnote 3 of the proposed administrative interpretation and, if not, what additional would be required. Mr. Barr's reply of February 25, 1959, does not definitely state whether or not the Oregon Commissioner's letter would be sufficient in this regard. Without assurance that it would be sufficient, Copco must oppose the proposed administrative interpretation as it relates to Section 167, and respectfully request the Commission not to adopt it.

The proposed exception is unsatisfactory because of its indefinite nature. While it is possible that the letter which Copco submitted to Mr. Barr would be construed by the Commission as qualifying Copco for exemption from the requirements of the policy, it is also possible to interpret it as being insufficient for that purpose and to hold that only a formal determination by a state commission that it will not permit deferral accounting in respect of Section 167 would exempt a company from compliance with the policy. This would force a company neither practicing nor desiring to practice such accounting to request a state commission for authority to practice such accounting in order to receive the requested denial, an obviously anomalous situation. Further, unless the Commission is willing to accept a predominantly subjective evaluation of the likelihood of the same state commission permitting the recovery of the increased taxes in later years, it would seem to be virtually impossible to satisfy that portion of the exception which provides:

> " * * * accounting recognition need not be given to the deferment of taxes if it may reasonably be expected that increased future income taxes, resulting from earlier deduction of declining balance depreciation for income tax purposes only, will be allowed in future rate determinations."

On matters such as this, there would appear to be no guarantee that the existing commission could speak for what any future commission in the same state might rule in respect of taxes allowed for rate-making purposes.

With respect to the merits of the proposed policy, it appears to Copco that deferred tax accounting such as that contemplated by the policy is not necessary to prevent financial statements from being misleading, so long as adequate disclosure of the existence and amount of tax deferments is made in the financial statements. The notes to the financial statements published by Copco for the year 1958 include the following statement with respect to taxes deferred under Section 167:

"The Company has elected, for income tax purposes only, the declining balance method of accelerated depreciation for mass property included in certain transmission and distribution property additions. As a result, provisions for income taxes are less and net income is more than they otherwise would have been by approximately $350,000 in 1958, $290,000 in 1957, $210,000 in 1956, $130,000 in 1955 and $43,000 in 1954. This "flow-through" practice is followed by the Company pursuant to advice of the Public Utility Commissioner of Oregon which indicates that this practice is recognized by him as proper for accounting purposes, and where used for accounting purposes should also be used for rate-making purposes. (Approximately 83% of the Company's property is located in Oregon, and 77% of its revenues are from within that State). The Public Utilities Commission of California, in a 1958 rate case decision, recognized the "flow-through" method for purposes of determining rates, but stated that the action taken therein was not to be understood as deciding the question of normalization of reduced income taxes in connection with the taking of accelerated depreciation. Hearings are currently being held by the California Commission to determine its policy in this regard.

The approximate amounts of depreciation and amortization of utility plant claimed or to be claimed for Federal income tax purposes are as follows:

	1958	1957
Depreciation	$3,440,000	$3,189,000
Amortization	4,608,000	4,761,000"

It is respectfully submitted that statements such as these could fully disclose the existence and extent of any tax deferment under Section 167 and enable any investor to consider the effect of such tax deferments in appraising the company's securities. The accounting being followed by Copco at the present time with respect to taxes deferred under Section 167 is in accordance with the uniform system of accounts for electric companies as prescribed by the Public Utility Commissioner of Oregon and the California Public Utilities Commission. If the proposed policy were enforced with respect to it, it would be necessary for the Company to obtain special permission of these commissions to depart from the Commission's uniform system of accounts.

One further objection to the proposed interpretation is that it is not clear whether it would require a transfer from earned surplus to a reserve for deferred taxes of the tax savings which flowed through to income since 1954 or only in the first year in which a financial statement is filed after the new interpretation becomes effective if adopted.

Very truly yours,

BROBECK, PHLEGER & HARRISON

/s/ By GEO. D. RIVES

George D. Rives

Attorneys for The California
Oregon Power Company

GDR:ef
(2)

cc: The California Oregon Power Company

CAROLINA POWER & LIGHT COMPANY

Raleigh, North Carolina

LOUIS V. SUTTON
PRESIDENT

January 26, 1959

Securities and Exchange Commission
Washington 25, D.C.

Gentlemen:

I respectfully request that Carolina Power & Light Company, an operating electric utility which is engaged in business in both North Carolina and South Carolina, be granted an extension of time until at least March 31, 1959, for the filing of written views and comments as to the Commission's intention to announce an interpretation of administrative policy on financial statements regarding balance sheet treatment of credits equivalent to the reduction in income taxes (Securities Act of 1933 Release No. 4010.

Very truly yours,

/s/ L. V. SUTTON

L. V. Sutton

LVS:JF

CAROLINA POWER & LIGHT COMPANY

LOUIS V. SUTTON
PRESIDENT

Raleigh, North Carolina

March 19, 1959

Securities and Exchange Commission
Washington 25, D. C.

Re: Securities Act of 1933
Release No. 4010

Gentlemen:

Carolina Power & Light Company ("Company"),
an operating electric utility which is engaged in
business in both North Carolina and South
Carolina, submits herewith in triplicate its
written views and comments on the Commission's
proposed interpretation of administrative policy
on financial statements regarding balance sheet
treatment of the accumulated credit arising from
the recognition in such statements of the deferral
to future periods of current reductions in income
taxes.

1. The Company is subject to regulation
    by the North Carolina Utilities Commission
    and by the South Carolina Public Service
    Commission as to rates, services, account-
    ing, and security issues. In certain of
    its activities the Company is subject to
    the provisions of Parts II and III of
    the Federal Power Act, including the
    requirement that it comply with the
    uniform system of accounts of the
    Federal Power Commission.

2. The Company holds necessity certificates
    that permit amortization over 60-month
    periods, for Federal income tax purposes,
    of approximately $38,000,000 of the cost
    of certain defense plant facilities

completed during the period 1952 through
1958 (Section 168 of the Internal Revenue
Code of 1954). That amount represents
57.7% of the entire cost of such facilities
but only 24.7% of the Company's total
construction expenditures of $153,900,000
during the same period.

3. Pursuant to an order entered by the
North Carolina Utilities Commission in
its Docket No. E-2, Sub 29 on January 26,
1953, and an order entered by the South
Carolina Public Service Commission in
its Docket No. 8541 on January 27, 1953,
copies of which orders are attached
hereto, the Company has recorded the
net reduction in Federal income taxes
resulting from amortization of defense
facilities as a credit to an account
entitled "Earned Surplus Restricted
For Future Federal Taxes on Income," and
corresponding charges have been made to
income.

4. It is the Company's view, and it respectfully submits, that the method of
accounting prescribed by the North
Carolina Utilities Commission and the
South Carolina Public Service Commission
in the above mentioned orders, for
recording and reporting the financial
results of its use of accelerated
amortization of defense facilities for
Federal income tax purposes, is consistent
with generally accepted accounting
principles and best portrays the purpose
of Congress in its enactment of this
legislation, that is, to create a source
of capital to encourage the expansion
of plant facilities in the interest of
national defense. Furthermore, the
method prescribed by these Commission
orders avoids the creation of inequities
between present and future ratepayers.

5. For the purposes of the Federal Power
   Commission the Company is required to
   follow the accounting treatment prescribed
   by that Commission in an order issued
   May 29, 1958, in its Docket No. R-159;
   however, as the Federal Power Commission
   noted in the following language of its
   order, such accounting treatment applies
   only to reports filed with the Federal
   Power Commission and does not supersede
   or render ineffective the requirements
   of the respective state commissions:

   "---. We regret the inconsistency
   which has arisen among the several
   state commissions. Under the circumstances, however, we see no
   reasonable solution to the problem
   for those utilities which are required
   by a state commission to report
   deferred taxes in a reserve or surplus
   account but to classify the deferred
   taxes in accordance with state
   requirements for state purposes, and
   to use the treatment specified by
   this order for the purposes of this
   Commission."

6. On the other hand the generality of the
   interpretation of administrative policy
   proposed herein by the Securities and
   Exchange Commission, which conflicts
   with the accounting treatment prescribed
   by the respective state commissions,
   might well have the effect of nullifying
   the orders referred to in paragraph 3
   above. In this connection it appears
   that Congress contemplated that as to
   regulated public utilities the Securities
   and Exchange Commission should not
   prescribe methods of accounting inconsistent with the requirements imposed on
   such utilities by state regulation.
   See: Section 79t (b), Title 15, United
   States Code.

7. The Company does not agree that its
   inclusion in its financial statements
   of the accumulated credit arising from
   accelerated amortization as earned
   surplus, with notations clearly indicating
   that it is restricted for future Federal
   taxes on income, is misleading or
   inaccurate in any way; and it is seriously
   concerned that the proposed interpretation of administrative policy herein
   not only states a contrary conclusion
   but might be construed as a determination by this Commission that the Company
   and others similarly situated heretofore
   have issued inaccurate and misleading
   financial statements, even though such
   statements were issued in compliance
   with orders of state regulatory commissions
   and have been filed with this Commission,
   without objection on its part, in connection with issuance of securities.

8. The application to regulated public
   utilities of this Commission's proposed
   interpretation of administrative policy
   herein is unnecessary in the public
   interest, and they should be exempted
   from such interpretation if it is in
   fact adopted.

Edison Electric Institute plans to represent
at the scheduled public hearing the interests of
its member companies, which include Carolina Power
& Light Company. The Company will not make a
formal appearance at the hearing, since we are
satisfied that our position will be adequately
presented there by the Institute and by other
operating electric utilities.

Very truly yours,

/s/ L. V. SUTTON

L. V. Sutton

LVS:jf

BEFORE THE

NORTH CAROLINA UTILITIES COMMISSION

In the Matter of	
CAROLINA POWER & LIGHT COMPANY,	DOCKET NO. E-2, SUB. 29
Ex Parte	O R D E R

On the 23rd day of January, 1953, Carolina Power & Light Company (hereinafter sometimes referred to as the "Company") filed with the Commission its Application for approval of procedures with respect to accounting for emergency facilities and the Federal Income Tax results of amortization of emergency facilities pursuant to provisions of Section 124A of the Internal Revenue Code.

Upon motion of counsel for the Company, the Application was filed and docketed and an immediate hearing was held by the Commission on the Application and the statements and representations of the Company's officials.

This Commission having given full consideration to the matter of accounting procedures to be followed by the Company in amortizing for Federal Income Tax purposes over a period of sixty (60) months that portion of the cost attributable to defense purposes, in accordance with the provisions of said Section 124A of the Internal Revenue Code, finds:

1. That the Company is a public utility engaged in the generation, transmission, delivery, and sale of electricity to the public for compensation, and is subject to the jurisdiction of this Commission with respect to rates, services, and accounting procedures;

2. That the Company holds Necessity Certificates under Section 124A of the Internal Revenue Code and may hereafter apply for such certificates with respect to emergency facilities hereafter constructed in the interest of national defense and attributable to defense purposes; that the costs of that portion of the emergency facilities attributable to defense purposes

under Necessity Certificates, which are now held by Company, aggregate approximately $16,420,900;

3. That such Necessity Certificates constitute authority to amortize for Federal Income Tax purposes over a period of sixty (60) months that portion of the cost of such facilities attributable to defense purposes; and

4. That the purpose of the special rapid amortization of the cost of emergency defense facilities is not to create additional income for Company, but simply to defer Federal Taxes on Income.

The Commission being of the opinion that said Application should be granted:

IT IS HEREBY ORDERED, ADJUDGED AND DECREED:

That Carolina Power & Light Company be, and it is hereby permitted and authorized to:

1. Amortize for Federal Income Tax purposes over a period of sixty (60) months that portion of the cost of such facilities attributable to defense purposes;

2. Provide on its books of account for depreciation on properties covered by Necessity Certificates at rates consistent with those for like property not covered by Necessity Certificates and, during the period of amortization of such emergency facilities, charge to the current provision for Federal Taxes on Income in operating expenses and concurrently credit "Earned Surplus Restricted for Future Federal Taxes on Income", amounts equal to the reduction in Federal Taxes on Income resulting from the accelerated amortization of such facilities for Federal Income Tax purposes and after expiration of the effective amortization period, and until "Earned Surplus Restricted for Future Federal Taxes on Income" applicable to specific facilities is exhausted or such facilities are retired

from service, charge "Earned Surplus Restricted for Future Federal Taxes on Income" and credit the current provision for Federal Taxes on Income with amounts equal to the increase in Federal Taxes on Income resulting from depreciation on the emergency facilities no longer being available for Federal Income Tax purposes, said charges and credits to the current provision for Federal Taxes on Income in operating expenses shall be made to a subdivision of Account 507, Taxes;

3. Follow the same procedures as are authorized in this proceeding with respect to any facilities hereafter constructed in the interest of national defense and attributable to defense purposes for which Certificates of Necessity may be issued to Company under authority of Section 124A of the Internal Revenue Code; and

4. Elect under the provisions of said Section 124A of the Internal Revenue Code at any time prior to completion of full amortization, to discontinue such amortization, exclude for Federal Income Tax purposes the amounts allowable under the Necessity Certificates, and return to normal depreciation allowable for Federal Income Tax purposes.

ISSUED BY ORDER OF THE COMMISSION, this 26th day of January, 1953.

NORTH CAROLINA UTILITIES COMMISSION

By: /s/ MYRTHA FLEMING

Myrtha Fleming, Chief Clerk

(SEAL)

State of South Carolina

THE PUBLIC SERVICE COMMISSION

Address Reply to:
Electrical Utilities Division
329 Wade Hampton State Office Building

Columbia, 1, S. C.
January 27, 1953

STATE OF SOUTH CAROLINA	BEFORE THE PUBLIC
COUNTY OF RICHLAND	SERVICE COMMISSION
In the Matter of	ORDER NO. E-707
CAROLINA POWER & LIGHT COMPANY,	DOCKET NO. 8541
Ex Parte	

CERTIFICATE OF AUTHORITY

TO: CAROLINA POWER & LIGHT COMPANY,
    RALEIGH, NORTH CAROLINA

On the 27th day of January, 1953, Carolina Power & Light Company (hereinafter sometimes referred to as the "Company") filed with the Commission its Application for approval of procedures with respect to accounting for emergency facilities and the Federal Income Tax results of amortization of emergency facilities pursuant to provisions of Section 124A of the Internal Revenue Code.

Upon motion of counsel for the Company, the Application was filed and docketed and an immediate hearing was held by the Commission on the Application and the statements and representations of the Company's officials.

This Commission having given full consideration to the matter of accounting procedures to be followed by the Company in amortizing for Federal Income Tax purposes over a period of sixty (60) months that portion of the cost attributable to defense purposes, in accordance with the provisions of said Section 124A of the Internal Revenue Code, finds:

1. That the Company is a public utility engaged in the generation, transmission, delivery, and sale of electricity to the public for compensation, and is subject to the jurisdiction of this Commission with respect to rates, services, and accounting procedures;

2. That the Company holds Necessity Certificates under Section 124A of the Internal Revenue Code and may hereafter apply for such Certificates with respect to emergency facilities hereafter constructed in the interest of national defense and attributable to defense purposes; that the costs of that portion of the emergency facilities attributable to defense purposes under Necessity Certificates, which are now held by Company, aggregate approximately $16,420,900;

3. That such Necessity Certificates constitute authority to amortize for Federal Income Tax purposes over a period of sixty (60) months that portion of the cost of such facilities attributable to defense purposes; and

4. That the purpose of the special rapid amortization of the cost of emergency defense facilities is not to create additional income for Company, but simply to defer Federal Taxes on Income.

The Commission being of the opinion that said Application should be granted:

IT IS HEREBY ORDERED, ADJUDGED AND DECREED:

That Carolina Power & Light Company be, and it is hereby permitted and authorized to:

1. Amortize for Federal Income Tax purposes over a period of sixty (60) months that portion of the cost of such facilities attributable to defense purposes;

2. Provide on its books of account for depreciation on properties covered by Necessity Certificates at rates consistent with those for like property not covered by Necessity Certificates and, during the period of amortization of such emergency facilities, charge to the current provision for Federal Taxes on Income in operating expenses and concurrently credit "Earned Surplus Restricted for Future Federal Taxes

on Income", amounts equal to the reduction in Federal Taxes on Income resulting from the accelerated amortization of such facilities for Federal Income Tax purposes and after expiration of the effective amortization period, and until "Earned Surplus Restricted for Future Federal Taxes on Income" applicable to specific facilities is exhaused or such facilities are retired from service, charge "Earned Surplus Restricted for Future Federal Taxes on Income" and credit the current provision for Federal Taxes on Income with amounts equal to the increase in Federal Taxes on Income resulting from depreciation on the emergency facilities no longer being available for Federal Income Tax purposes, said charges and credits to the current provision for Federal Taxes on Income in operating expenses shall be made to a subdivision of Account 507, Taxes;

3. Follow the same procedures as are authorized in this proceeding with respect to any facilities hereafter constructed in the interest of national defense and attributable to defense purposes for which Certificates of Necessity may be issued to Company under authority of Section 124A of the Internal Revenue Code; and

4. Elect under the provisions of said Section 124A of the Internal Revenue Code at any time prior to completion of full amortization, to discontinue such amortization, exclude for Federal Income Tax purposes the amounts allowable under the Necessity Certificates, and return to normal depreciation allowable for Federal Income Tax purposes.

This 27th day of January, 1953.

BY ORDER OF THE COMMISSION.

/s/ EDWARD WIMBERLY

Vice-Chairman

(SEAL)

Attest:

/s/ J. N. LAND, JR.

Executive Secretary

CENTRAL ELECTRIC & GAS COMPANY

144 South 12th Street
Lincoln 1, Nebraska

January 27, 1959

Securities and Exchange Commission
Washington 25, D. C.

Gentlemen:

This letter is being written on behalf of the following registered companies of which I am Secretary-Treasurer:

Central Electric & Gas Company
Central Telephone Company
Southeastern Telephone Company

In response to comments requested with respect to SEC release dated December 30, 1958, it is our view that the accumulated credit arising from reductions in income taxes because of the use of accelerated depreciation provisions, as provided in the Internal Revenue Code of 1954, should be treated as a reserve in the balance sheet of the reporting company. We cannot see how the contra to the expense charge (Provision for Deferred Income Taxes) can be considered as a credit to common stock equity and included in restricted earned surplus or its equivalent in the related balance sheet.

Yours very truly,

/s/ L. T. NELSON

L. T. Nelson
Secretary-Treasurer

LTN:Z

CENTRAL VERMONT PUBLIC SERVICE CORPORATION

Seventy Seven Grove Street
Rutland, Vermont

January 30, 1959

Securities and Exchange Commission
Washington 25, D. C.

Attention: Honorable Orval L. DuBois,
Secretary

Re: Securities Act of 1933, Release No. 4010
Securities Exchange Act of 1934,
Release No. 5844
Public Utility Holding Company Act of
1935, Release No. 13894

Gentlemen:

We have your Notice of Intention to Announce
Interpretation of Administrative Policy released
by your Commission on December 30, 1958 in which
you advised interested parties that you have under
consideration announcing an interpretation of
administrative policy on financial statements
regarding balance sheet treatment of credits
equivalent to the reductions in income taxes.
You also suggested that written views and comments
by interested persons be submitted for your
consideration.

We have applied for and received from the
Defense Production Administration, Necessity
Certificate No. TA - NC - 4907 dated July 20,
1951 and Necessity Certificate No. TA - NC - 16184
dated April 9, 1952. Under these authorizations
and pursuant to Section 124A of the Internal
Revenue Code of 1939 or Section 168 of the Internal
Revenue Code of 1954, depreciation claimed in
Federal Income Tax and Vermont State Franchise
Tax returns in the subsequent years for the
covered property additions was accelerated. The

amount of the resulting tax reductions was calcu-
lated annually and an equivalent amount charged
to the income account and credited to Earned
Surplus - Restricted to Deferred Taxes on Income
and included in equity capital.

Also since 1954 we have been using the "sum-
of-the-years" method in calculating allowable
depreciation for income tax purposes as allowed
under Section 167 of the Internal Revenue Code of
1954 and in accounting for the resulting tax
reductions have been using the so-called "flow
through" method by order of the Vermont Public
Service Commission (copy attached). Since it is
reasonably expected that increased future income
taxes, resulting from the earlier deduction of
"sum-of-the-years" depreciation for tax purposes
only, will be allowed in future rate determinations,
we believe that we qualify for the exception as
provided for in paragraph 8 of Accounting Research
Bulletin No. 44 (Revised) referred to in your
Notice.

In the first paragraph of the proposed
announcement reference is made to accumulated
credit from accounting for reductions in income
taxes for "various items including those under
Section 167 and 168 of the Internal Revenue Code
of 1954." The reference to "various items" is very
broad and we would appreciate clarification as to
the nature and scope of this term.

In regard to the accounting for tax reductions resulting from the application of Sections
167 and 168 of the Internal Revenue Code of 1954
we feel that this accounting on all financial
statements for this Company should be in accordance with the orders of the Vermont Public Service
Commission who also have jurisdiction over our
accounting practices and procedures.

Our present accounting is in accordance with
these Commission Orders, and financial data of
this Company which has been released since the
provisions of Sections 167 and 168 have been
available to us has reflected this accounting.

We believe that the accumulation of tax deferrals resulting from the use of accelerated amortization for income tax purposes as allowed under Section 124A and 168 of the Internal Revenue Codes of 1939 and 1954 respectively is of an equity character rather than a liability because of their long-term nature and is therefore properly stated as a part of equity capital.

In order to maintain our financial reporting on a basis consistent with prior years, and to prevent conflict in financial reporting as between requirements of your commission which would result from your intended announcement, as we understand it, and the requirements of the Vermont Public Service Commission, we believe that financial statements of this Company prepared in accordance with the requirements of the Vermont Public Service Commission should be acceptable to your commission and not presumed "to be mis-leading or inaccurate despite disclosure contained in the certificate of the accountant or in foot-notes to the statements provided the matters involved are material."

Very truly yours,

CENTRAL VERMONT PUBLIC SERVICE CORPORATION

/s/ H. J. LYNE

H. J. Lyne, Comptroller

HJL/egz

STATE OF VERMONT

PUBLIC SERVICE COMMISSION

ORDERED that the following accounting procedures shall apply to emergency facilities for which Necessity Certificates have been issued and which domestic utilities operating in this State may elect or may have elected to amortize under the provisions of Section 168 of the Internal Revenue Code of 1954 of Section 124A of the Internal Revenue Code of 1939 in each case for the effective period of such amortization and to the reduction in taxes measured by income resulting from such amortization:

1. Each such utility shall provide on its books of account for depreciation of properties or facilities covered in whole, or in part, by Necessity Certificates at rates consistent with those for like property or facilities not covered in whole or in part by Necessity Certificates,

2. During any period of accelerated amortization of the costs of certified emergency facilities pursuant to said Section 168 of the Internal Revenue Code of 1954 of Section 124A of the Internal Revenue Code of 1939, to provide currently by charge to a subdivision of Account 507 entitled "Provision for Deferred Taxes on Income" and concurrently credit "Earned Surplus - Restricted to Deferred Taxes on Income" amounts equal to the reduction, resulting from the accelerated amortization, in taxes on or measured by income.

3. After the expiration of the effective amortization period and until "Earned Surplus - Restricted to Deferred Taxes on Income" applicable to specific facilities is exhausted, or such facilities are retired from service, it shall charge "Earned Surplus - Restricted to Deferred Taxes on Income" and credit a subdivision of Account 507, Taxes entitled "Portion of Current Taxes Deferred in Prior Years" with amounts equal to the increase in taxes, on or measured by income, resulting from earlier amortization of emergency facilities which are no longer depreciable for tax purposes.

4. It is ordered that the authority herein granted is subject to the express condition that the approval granted herein does not bind this Com-

mission as to any matter involved herein in any rate proceeding or other proceeding before this Commission in which a Vermont utility company may be a party, and the Commission reserves the right to change, modify, or cancel such authority at any time upon the application of any interested party or upon its own motion.

Dated at Montpelier, County of Washington and State of Vermont this 3rd day of December, A. D. 1958.

/s/   OSCAR L. SHEPARD

/s/   NORMAN LOWE

/s/   WILLIAM F. SINCLAIR

PUBLIC SERVICE
COMMISSION
OF VERMONT

STATE OF VERMONT

PUBLIC SERVICE COMMISSION

ORDER

1. That, unless otherwise specifically ordered, any electric and gas utilities doing business in Vermont which elect to avail itself of the liberalized depreciation permitted under Section 167 of the 1954 Internal Revenue Code shall record as tax expense on its books only the actual liability for Federal Income Tax and Vermont Franchise Tax.

2. Each such company which has elected to avail itself of liberalized depreciation under Section 167 of the Internal Revenue Code 1954 shall include in its Annual Report to this Commission a memorandum reporting the amount of the annual tax reductions due to use of liberalized depreciation and the total accumulation to date.

3. Tax reductions of electric and gas companies using liberalized depreciation under Section 167 of the Internal Revenue Code of 1954 to date which have been carried in a Reserve for Future Income Taxes are released of the restrictions imposed upon them and shall now revert to "Unrestricted Surplus in Account 271 -- Earned Surplus."

4. Depreciation on property subject to liberalized depreciation pursuant to the Company's election under Section 167 of the Internal Revenue Code of 1954, shall be recorded on the company's books of accounts in the same manner as its other properties, and the company shall accrue depreciation at rates consistent with its rates for like property not subject to liberalized depreciation.

5. The Temporary Order of February 29, 1956, as it relates to domestic electric and gas utilities, is hereby superseded by this Order.

6. It is ordered that the authority herein granted is subject to the express condition that the approval granted herein does not bind this Commission as to any matter involved herein in any rate proceeding or

other proceeding before this Commission in which a Vermont utility company may be a party, and the Commission reserves the right to change, modify, or cancel such authority at any time upon the application of any interested party or upon its own motion.

Dated at Montpelier, County of Washington and State of Vermont this 3rd day of December, A. D. 1958.

/s/ OSCAR L. SHEPARD

/s/ NORMAN LOWE

/s/ WILLIAM F. SINCLAIR

PUBLIC SERVICE
COMMISSION
OF VERMONT

THE CLEVELAND ELECTRIC ILLUMINATING COMPANY

F. WARREN BROOKS
VICE PRESIDENT
FINANCE

55 Public Square
Cleveland 1, Ohio

January 23, 1959

Securities and Exchange Commission
Washington 25, D. C.

Attention: Mr. Orval L. DuBois, Secretary

Gentlemen:

Under date of December 30, 1958, the
Securities and Exchange Commission issued a
release entitled:

Notice of Intention to Announce
Interpretation of Administrative
Policy.

This release relates to the accounting treatment to be accorded accumulated credits arising
from accounting for reductions in income taxes for
"various items" including those under Sections 167
and 168 of the Internal Revenue Code.

We are now studying the proposal covered by
the above release. In view of the importance of
the matter, and the possible impact on our Company
among others, we feel we should have time to
adequately prepare and file such written views and
comments as our further study may indicate to be
most helpful to your consideration of the adoption
of this policy statement. The time between the
date of receipt of your release and January 31 is
in our judgment too short a time to complete our
study and develop such comments as we feel would
best serve the purpose. Accordingly, we respect-

fully request that the Commission grant an extension of the January 31, 1959 filing date to
March 31, 1959.

It is also respectfully requested that the
Securities and Exchange Commission set a time and
place at which interested parties may appear
before the Commission to present arguments and to
file briefs relative to this matter. We would
appreciate being advised of such time and place if
the Commission grant this request.

An early reply with respect to these requests
will be appreciated.

Very truly yours,

/s/ F. WARREN BROOKS

F. Warren Brooks

THE CLEVELAND ELECTRIC ILLUMINATING COMPANY

F. WARREN BROOKS
VICE PRESIDENT
FINANCE

55 Public Square
Cleveland 1, Ohio

March 20, 1959

Securities and Exchange Commission
425 Second Street, N. W.
Washington 25, D. C.

Attention: Mr. Orval L. DuBois, Secretary

Gentlemen:

> Re: Notice of Intention to Announce
> Interpretation of Administrative Policy
> Securities Act of 1933 - Release No. 4010
> Securities Exchange Act of 1934 - Release
> No. 5844
> Public Utility Holding Co. Act of 1935 -
> Release No. 13894
> Investment Company Act of 1940 - Release
> No. 2814

Pursuant to the invitation for views and comments by interested persons contained in the above Notice, The Cleveland Electric Illuminating Company herewith respectfully submits in triplicate, its statement in opposition to the proposed interpretation of Administrative Policy.

Our Company is an electric utility company subject to regulation by the Public Utilities Commission of Ohio as to rates, issuance of securities, accounting practices and other matters. We are not subject to the Holding Company Act of 1935 or the jurisdiction of the Federal Power Commission.

The use of rapid amortization and accelerated depreciation by our Company for tax accounting purposes only has produced and will continue to produce substantial annual income tax reductions which generate funds available for capital uses for significant periods of time.

These tax reductions are in essence deferrals
of a tax otherwise incurred in the current year,
and for that reason, pursuant to orders of the
Public Utilities Commission of Ohio, our Company
"normalizes" income taxes by charging an amount
equal to these annual tax reductions as an
expense. Pursuant to orders of the Public
Utilities Commission of Ohio, we classify the
corresponding credits with respect to rapid
amortization tax reductions as "Earnings Retained
in the Business - Restricted for Future Federal
Income Taxes", and the corresponding credits with
respect to accelerated depreciation tax reductions are classified as "Reserve for Future
Federal Income Taxes".

We believe that income taxes should be
normalized, and that preferably the corresponding
credits with respect to both rapid amortization
and accelerated depreciation should be classified
as restricted equity accounts. We are therefore
opposed to the Commission's proposal to forbid
registrants to classify these credits as
restricted equity in their financial statements.

The reasons for our position are as follows:

1. In cases where there is substantial
   variation in accounting practice it
   is inappropriate for the Commission
   to invoke the conclusive presumption
   of A.S.R. No. 4 to impose uniformity.
   Of 30 state commissions prescribing
   normalization by utilities with
   respect to rapid amortization, 13
   provide for a credit to restricted
   equity, 11 provide for a reserve, and
   6 permit either. Of 21 state commissions prescribing normalizations with
   respect to accelerated depreciation,
   4 provide for a credit to restricted
   equity, 11 to a reserve, and 6 allow
   either.

2. Accounting Research Bulletins, state statutes and administrative orders and actual accounting practice provide substantial authoritative support for classifying accumulated tax reduction credits as restricted equity.

3. Such classification of these credits is accurate and consistent with the nature of these accumulated tax reductions and is not misleading. An appropriate title on the equity account plus an explanatory note can fully explain the source, purpose and future use of these credits.

4. Non-equity classification of these credits tends to mislead investors as to the real value of their investment and lenders as to the equity cushion supporting their claim, and analysts tend to be mislead into not giving proper weight to a significant source of capital.

5. The statutory authority of the Commission to prescribe accounting rules is limited to carrying out the policy of adequate disclosure. The proposed application of A.S.R. No. 4 will not materially serve that policy and therefore would be in violation of the Commission's authority. Furthermore, the proposed application would be in violation of Section 13 (b) of the Securities Exchange Act of 1934 and Section 20(b) of the Holding Company Act of 1935; and

6. The proposed announcement would have undesirable retroactive effects, if as indicated in the Notice it would apply to all financial statements dated on or after December 31, 1958, regardless of when filed.

Each of these reasons is more fully developed
in the Company's Statement in Opposition. The
Commission is hereby respectfully requested to
allot to Theodore J. Horvath, Esquire, counsel
for The Cleveland Electric Illuminating Company
not more than fifteen minutes at the public
hearing on this proposal to make a brief oral
statement on its behalf.

Respectfully yours,

/s/ F. WARREN BROOKS

F. Warren Brooks

UNITED STATES OF AMERICA

BEFORE THE

SECURITIES AND EXCHANGE COMMISSION

In the Matter

of

THE SECURITIES AND EXCHANGE COM-
MISSION'S NOTICE OF INTENTION TO
ANNOUNCE INTERPRETATION OF
ADMINISTRATIVE POLICY (Securities Act
of 1933, Release No. 4010; Securities
Exchange Act of 1934, Release No. 5433;
Public Utility Holding Company Act of 1935,
Release No. 13894; Investment Company Act
of 1940, Release No. 2814).

STATEMENT IN OPPOSITION TO THE PROPOSED
INTERPRETATION OF ADMINISTRATIVE POLICY

The Facts Involved

Section 167 of the Internal Revenue Code of 1954 (the "Code") allows a taxpayer to use "accelerated" depreciation methods for tax purposes, regardless of whether any such method is used for corporate accounting purposes. Section 168 of the Code allows a taxpayer, upon satisfying certain conditions, to amortize an asset over a period of five years for tax purposes regardless of the period of amortization or depreciation employed for corporate accounting purposes. (For convenience, the depreciation and amortization provisions of Sections 167 and 168 of the Code will sometimes be collectively referred to as "accelerated depreciation.")

Use of accelerated depreciation for tax purposes only provides larger depreciation deductions for a taxpayer in the early years of the useful life of the asset involved than would be allowable in those years were the income taxes computed on the basis of straight line depreciation methods. In later years of the useful life of the asset involved, depreciation deductions are smaller. As a consequence, in the early years of the life of the asset there is a reduction in income taxes over those which would otherwise be payable, and there is an increase in the later years. Various methods are used by companies to reflect such tax differences in their accounts.

We are advised by our certified public accountants that most industrial companies employing accelerated depreciation for tax purposes also use it for corporate accounting purposes. This presents no accounting problem. Relatively few industrial companies use accelerated depreciation for tax purposes only.

Use of accelerated depreciation for tax purposes only is prevalent mainly among regulated public utilities where the accounting problems are specialized due to the fact of regulation. The accounting treatment of these tax differences by public utilities varies in accordance with the requirements of the regulatory agencies having jurisdiction over their accounts. Some utilities allow the tax differences to "flow through" to surplus. The majority "normalize" annual income, i.e., an amount equivalent to the annual income tax reduction arising in the early years from use of accelerated depreciation for tax purposes only is charged against annual income and a corresponding credit is made to an equity or deferred or reserve account. In the later years the process is reversed to the relief of operating expenses. A few deduct the tax difference as an additional amount of depreciation. Invariably, the treatment employed is explained in a note to the financial statements.

The Issue

The Securities and Exchange Commission ("Commission") proposes to announce a new "Interpretation of Administrative Policy" with respect to the balance sheet classification of accumulated income tax credits ("Credits") resulting from use of normalization to account for income tax reductions arising from use of accelerated depreciation for tax purposes only.

The proposed announcement provides that:

" . . . any financial statement which designates as earned surplus or its equivalent or includes as a part of equity capital (even though accompanied by words of limitation such as 'restricted' or 'appropriated') the accumulated credit arising from accounting for reductions in income taxes for various items including those under sections 167 and 168 of the Internal Revenue Code of 1954, filed with this Commission dated as of December 31, 1958, or thereafter . . . "

will be presumed to be misleading because such classification is based upon accounting principles for which there is no substantial authoritative support. This proposed policy would be based upon application of the Commission's Accounting Series Release No. 4 ("ASR No. 4"), which provides for such a presumption where "substantial authoritative support" for the accounting principles employed in the financial statements of a registrant is considered to be lacking.

The proposed policy is not confined to the question of credits arising from normalization of tax reductions generated only through use of accelerated depreciation. The announcement refers to accounting for tax reductions in income taxes "for various items" including accelerated depreciation. However, the following discussion will be confined primarily to accelerated amortization and depreciation aspects of the proposal. The announcement also indicates that the Commission proposes to require use of normalization in financial statements of registrants where material reductions in income taxes are generated by use of accelerated depreciation for tax purposes only.

The Cleveland Electric Illuminating Company ("CEI") feels that annual income should be normalized to appropriately account for the deferral of income taxes arising out of use of accelerated depreciation for tax purposes only. Normalization is appropriate because the tax liability is not avoided; it is postponed. It does not necessarily follow, however, that the corresponding credits should be classified as a non-equity account. This statement is directed to the reasons why the Commission should continue to allow registrants to classify these accumulated credits as restricted equity accounts.

CEI takes the position that:

I. It is not appropriate to invoke the conclusive presumption of Accounting Series Release No. 4 in an area where accounting authorities subscribe to varying accounting treatments.

II. There is substantial authoritative support for the accounting principle which provides for classifying accumulated tax credits as equity.

III. Such classification of these credits is not inaccurate or misleading.

IV. The classification of these credits as a deferred tax account or a reserve may be misleading and inaccurate.

V. The proposed application of ASR No. 4 would be in violation of the statutory authority of the Commission.

VI. The proposed announcement would have undesirable retroactive effects.

I. It Is Not Appropriate To Invoke The Conclusive Presumption Of ASR No. 4 In An Area Where Accounting Authorities Subscribe to Varying Accounting Treatments

The presumption in the first sentence of ASR No. 4 is invoked even though there are ". . . disclosures contained in the certificate of the account or in footnotes to the statements provided the matters involved are material." The presumption, though apparently rebuttable, is quite strong. The second sentence of ASR No. 4 provides that if the Commission has previously expressed its position on an accounting principle by rules, regulations, or official releases, including opinions of its Chief Accountant, its use, though explained in a note, will be presumed to be misleading or inaccurate even if the registrant can show the existence of substantial authoritative support. Thus, once an announcement of policy, such as is proposed in this instance, is made, the presumption under ASR No. 4 becomes conclusive. The impact of the second sentence of ASR No. 4

is to impose uniformity of accounting methods upon all registrants once the Commission has announced its position, on the ground that adequate disclosure so requires.

Through formal orders or otherwise, approximately thirty-two state commissions have set forth accounting procedures for accelerated amortization. Thirteen states normalize with a credit to restricted surplus; eleven normalize with a credit to a reserve account; six permit a credit to either restricted surplus or a reserve account; and two have directed still other procedures. Relatively few states have spoken definitely on the rate treatment of accelerated amortization.

Approximately twenty-nine state commissions have adopted formal orders, or their equivalent, fixing the accounting or rate-making treatment, or both, for liberalized depreciation. On the accounting level, four states have either authorized or directed the use of a restricted or appropriated surplus account; six have permitted the use of either restricted surplus or a tax reserve; eleven have prescribed or authorized a tax reserve method; and one has provided for a totally different accounting procedure. In the rate-making area, ten states have denied "normalization"; ten states have permitted normalization; and in one state, normalization was allowed in one case and denied in another.

Thus, in a sizeable number of states, utility companies, pursuant to the regulations of their state commissions, have been accumulating credits arising from the normalization of income taxes in restricted surplus accounts. This is not a situation where a few authorities refuse to conform to a generally accepted practice. There is substantial variation among many legally responsible agencies.

It is understandable that the Commission might feel that uniformity of treatment of these accumulated tax credits is desirable. It is perhaps unfortunate that there is such a wide difference in treatment, especially among public utilities.

This being the present situation, however, it hardly seems appropriate for the Commission to attach the stigma and legal consequences of inadequate disclosure to use of a principle of accounting which, though controversial, is employed by a substantial number of registrants pursuant to the requirements of regulatory agencies having accounting authority.

II. There Is Substantial Authoritative Support For The Accounting Principle Which Provides For Classifying Accumulated Tax Credits As Equity

From the language of the proposed announcement it appears that the Commission places substantial reliance upon the Accounting Research Bulletins ("ARB") of the American Institute of Accountants. ARB's are the accounting profession's vehicles for pronouncing "generally accepted accounting principles," and, therefore, it is understandable that the Commission would resort primarily to these announcements as an authoritative source of accounting principles.

It should be remembered, however, that these pronouncements do not always evidence unanimity of opinion or practice among accountants. Furthermore, ARB's, while they in terms apply to all enterprises, are primarily attuned to the needs and problems of unregulated industrial and commercial companies. As a result, it is not uncommon for regulatory agencies to require public utilities to follow accounting principles other han those pronounced in ARB's.

It is a fact which must be given recognition and weight by the Commission that there are other sources of substantial accounting authority which the business community is not at liberty to ignore. Various judicial and administrative agencies of state and federal governments have the legal authority to prescribe accounting principles and methods, especially for public utilities. State statutes also prescribe accounting principles. In reality, so far as regulated industry is concerned, principles announced by the accounting profession are substantial authority only to the extent recognized and enforced by law. These other sources, together with actual accounting practice, should be taken into account when considering whether a particular practice lacks substantial authoritative support.

A. The Accounting Research Bulletins

The Commission refers principally to ARB No. 44 as the substantial authority regarding the proper classification of these accumulated tax credits. Examination of other formal pronouncements of the accounting profession reveals that its position regarding these credits is not as fixed as the announcement of the Commission indicates.

ARB No. 44, itself, does not expressly and clearly specify the classification which should be made of these accumulated credits arising from accelerated depreciation under Section 167 of the Code. Paragraph 4 of that Bulletin does clearly provide for normalizing income to account for "deferred" income taxes. But nowhere in that Bulletin is there an express recommendation as to the balance sheet classification to be made of the corresponding credits. There is only a passing reference in paragraph 5 to a "deferred tax account" couched in language which indicates an assumption that the corresponding credit will be so classified. Other treatment of these credits is not expressly ruled out. ARB No. 44 is conspicuously incomplete so far as analysis and discussion of the balance sheet credit are concerned. This is not surprising in view of the strong dissents to the adoption of ARB No. 44, Revised, made by Messrs. Halvorson, Jennings and Powell of the AIA Committee on Accounting Procedure.

In recognition of the authority of regulatory agencies over the accounts of public utilities, paragraph 8 of ARB No. 44 recognizes a practice other than normalization. "Flow through" of deferred income taxes to surplus is provided for where normalization is not allowed by a regulatory agency for rate purposes. Where "flow through" is used, all that is recommended from the standpoint of <u>disclosure</u> is an explanation of the reduced tax component of income in a note. See, ARB No. 44, paragraph 9.

ARB NO. 43, Chapter 9, Section C, paragraph 12, dealing with such credits arising from rapid amortization under Section 168 of the Code, is admittedly more precise in recommending classification of these credits as a deferred account outside of the capital section. Perhaps this is understandable because reduced tax accumulations from Section 168 amortization are generated for a relatively short period of time (but the use of the funds so generated is extended over the life of the asset, often a much longer time). But even so, the statement in paragraph 12 is that such classification is "desirable." Other treatment is not expressly ruled out in this portion of ARB No. 43.

Chapter 10, Section B of ARB No. 43, dealing with accounting treatment of income taxes specifically covers the balance sheet treatment of various deferred tax charges and estimated tax liability items. It is there stated in paragraph 11 that classification of accumulated tax reduction items charged against income as a deferred-charge account is preferable, but it is also stated in paragraph 14, entitled "Special Treatment," that

"Where the treatments recommended above are considered to be not practicable, the amount of taxes estimated to be actually payable for the year may be shown in the income statement, provided that the pertinent facts, including the amount of the increase or decrease attributable to other accounts, are clearly disclosed either in a footnote or in the body of the income statement." (Emphasis added).

Thus, this paragraph of ARB No. 43 recognizes in general terms what was specifically recognized in ARB No. 44, namely, that there may be some situations in which normalization may be "not practicable." The accounting profession obviously has recognized in ARB No. 44 that the requirements of a regulatory agency may make it "not practicable" to normalize. It is equally "not practicable" for an accountant to fail to respect and accept as substantial accounting authority the order of a regulatory agency requiring a modified form of normalization, i.e., a charge to income and a credit to restricted equity.

B. There Is Substantial Authoritative Support In Statutes And State Regulation

These credits do not represent a present legal obligation to pay a sum of money. Though these credits represent an accumulation of liabilities as that term is broadly defined in ARB No. 9, they are not in the same category as current or other liabilities classified outside the capital section of the balance sheet. The very nature of this tax benefit is such that the funds generated thereby are made available for a relatively long period of time for capital or equity use, especially in the case of public utilities. Such long term funds are more properly classified as capital than liability items. The accumulation of these funds in a credit account represents a liability only in the sense that such accounting recognizes that certain funds, properly generated by current income, will be needed, after a period of capital use, to pay a tax bill to be incurred subsequently because of events which occured in the current year. The fact remains, however, that these accumulations legally belong to the equity owners of the enterprise.

These accumulated credits are legally available for any corporate use, including the payment to shareholders on dissolution and, in many jurisdictions, as dividends, unless set aside for other use. For example, in the State of Ohio dividends are payable "out of surplus." Section 1701.33(A), Revised Code of Ohio (R.C.). "Surplus" is defined as the excess of a corporation's "assets over its liabilities plus stated capital." Section 1701.32(A), R.C. The word "liabilities" as used in the definition of surplus is limited to its legal meaning, i.e., a debt or obligation. Stated differently, "liability" includes only those items which upon dissolution would have to be paid or provided for before shareholders may receive distribution. See Thomas vs. Matthews, 94 Ohio St. 32, 113 N.E. 669 (1916).*

The only limitation in Ohio upon using these accumulated credits for dividends is the business judgment rule, which requires the board of directors, when declaring a dividend, to take into account the needs for funds to provide for possible losses in future years. Lamb v. Lehmann, 110 Ohio St. 59, 143 N.E. 276 (1924). This legal rule is merely a recognition that in the case of dividends (but not dissolution), material future needs for funds should be considered.

In point of fact, the decision of management to normalize is the exercise by it of its business judgment, under Ohio law, to the effect that the amount deducted from current income is considered not available for dividends, but such amount is unquestionably available for any other equity use.

Because these credits clearly represent equity funds in the legal sense, it is understandable that many state accounting authorities have adopted the accounting principle of normalization modified by classifying the resulting credits as restricted equity. Normalization, so modified, embodies the virtues of both normalization and flow through -- current income is charged with a cost properly attributable to it and capital is

---

*Section 1701.38(A), R.C., requires an Ohio corporation to present to its shareholders at or before each annual meeting an annual report including a balance sheet containing a " . . . summary of the assets, liabilities, stated capital, and surplus . . . " Ohio, therefore, requires an accurate showing of the portion of the assets available to shareholders either as dividends or on dissolution.

credited with funds which in fact are available over a long term for any equity use. The conceptual difficulty scholars of accounting might have in finding a charge to income credited to retained equity is dissipated when it is realized that these tax deferral provisions of Congress have created a new class of capital, namely, significantly long term, but not permanent, equity capital generated out of income.

C. Actual Accounting Practice

For several years, practicing accountants of national reputation have been certifying financial statements of utilities showing these accumulated credits as restricted equity with appropriate disclosure in notes. To make these certifications, these accountants obviously concluded that equity classification was consistent with generally accepted accounting principles. We are advised by our certified public accountants that the general practice of accountants is to rely upon the orders of state regulatory agencies in this matter as a basis for certification without a stated exception provided disclosure is made by a note.

Even after the revision of ARB No. 44 in August, 1958, reputable accountants have been certifying statements of public utilities following orders of regulatory agencies. One cannot help but feel that accountants must consider that ARB No. 44, when read together with No. 43, Chapter 10 B, contains sufficient flexibility for recognition of regulatory or legal accounting authority or that such authority takes precedence.

III. Classification Of These Credits As Equity Is Not Inaccurate or Misleading

As pointed out in Part II, above, it is true that the funds represented by these credits belong to the equity owners. The credits do not represent a present legal obligation to pay a sum. Legally events could intervene to prevent the tax bill from falling due as expected. The long term availability of the generated funds justifies their characterization as equity. Such characterization is consistent with the purposes of Congress embodied in Sections 167 and 168 of the Code. Congress intended that these depreciation provisions be employed as a means of generating funds available for capital purposes. Shareholders and the investing public, having familiarity with these fund generating tax provisions, expect such funds to be used for equity purposes. Therefore, it is not only technically accurate to classify these credits as equity, but it is consistent with the generally accepted understanding as to the nature of these funds.

If these credits represent a kind of liability which must be shown outside the equity section of the balance sheet to avoid misleading investors, then use of flow through is even more misleading because it causes the credits to be included in equity with no identification whatsoever (other than a note). None-the-less, the accounting profession recognizes in its ARB's the appropriateness of the use of flow through so long as disclosure is made in a note.

All that is reasonably necessary to avoid the possibility that classification of these credits as equity might be misleading is to adequately disclose the probability that the funds will be needed at a future time to offset portions of future tax bills. This is accomplished by labeling the account "restricted" and further stating its expected future use "for future federal income taxes." The precise nature of the future need (as well as the source) is easily explained by use of a note, the contents of which the Commission has authority to prescribe in the interest of adequate disclosure.

The only significant added effect of the Commission's proposed policy would be a requirement of uniformity of classification by all registrants. Uniformity is not a necessary element of adequate disclosure, especially where accounting practice is widely divergent. In such a case the public is accustomed to variation. Uniformity should be required, in the interest of adequate disclosure, only in those cases where an accounting principle is so well established and known by the public that deviation would very likely be overlooked even if disclosed in a note. That is not the situation with respect to classification of these credits. Uniformity in this case does not materially serve the purpose of adequate disclosure.

IV. The Classification Of These Credits As A Deferred Tax Account May Be Inaccurate and Misleading

A reserve or deferred account placed outside the capital and equity sections of the balance sheet implies to the investor that there is a claim against the enterprise which would have to be recognized in the event of immediate dissolution. Stated differently, there is an implication that a prior claim to the funds represented by such account is certain. Of course, such is not the fact with respect to these credits. To this extent the investor is misled as to the real value of his investment and lenders are misled into thinking that the equity supporting their claims is smaller.

We are informed that it is a general practice among many financial analysts, when computing capital ratios and setting bond ratings, to exclude from consideration as capital, items not classified as capital in the financial statements. Thus, use of a deferred account for these credits tends to foreclose the consideration of such amounts in determining bond leverage and related credit ratings. On the other hand, classification of these credits as an equity item, restricted and properly explained in a note, results in appropriate consideration by analysts. In this regard a non-equity classification is misleading because it causes analysts to disregard an item which materially enhances the financial strength of a company simply because these credits represent large amounts of money available for long periods of time for capital purposes.

The Federal Power Commission has sought to solve this problem by classifying these credits as neither a liability nor an equity account, but as a new item labeled "accumulated deferred taxes on income." Federal Power Commission Order No. 204, Docket No. R-159, May 29, 1958. While this label may accurately describe the source of these credits, it still solves no problem because of its improper location in the balance sheet. Of the three choices of classification — liability, hybrid or equity — the last is technically and practically the most accurate and appropriate. If recognition is to be given to the hybrid nature of these credits, it perhaps should be done by recognizing a fourth class of capital by placing "accumulated deferred taxes on income" in the capital portion of the balance sheet.

V. The Proposed Application of ASR No. 4 Would Be
   In Violation Of And Inconsistent With The Statutes
   And Rules Administered By The Commission

A. The Disclosure Acts

Section 19(a) of the Securities Act of 1933 ("1933 Act") authorizes the Commission to prescribe accounting rules to carry out "the purposes of the . . . (1933 Act) . . ." Similar accounting rule-making authority is granted the Commission in Section 13 of the Securities Exchange Act of 1934 ("1934 Act"), and Section 38 of the Investment Company Act of 1940 ("1940 Act"). The purpose of these Acts is to protect the investing public by requiring that certain communications containing adequate disclosure of all material facts including financial statements be used in certain security issue and trading transactions. Thus, the Commission's authority under these Acts to prescribe accounting standards is limited to fulfilling its duty to insure adequate disclosure. No power is granted to prescribe uniform accounts and classifications among registrants.

Congress was aware when these Acts were enacted that other agencies, state and federal, are charged with the duty to prescribe uniformity in accounts. In Section 13(b) of the 1934 Act, Congress provided:

". . . but in the case of the reports of any person whose methods of accounting are prescribed under the provisions of any law of the United States, or any rule or regulation thereunder, the rules and regulations of the Commission with respect to reports shall not be inconsistent with the requirements imposed by such law or rule or regulation in respect of the same subject matter, and in the case of carriers subject to the provisions of section 20 of the Interstate Commerce Act, as mended, or carriers required pursuant to any other Act of Congress to make reports of the same general character as those required under such section 20, shall permit such carriers to file with the Commission and the exchange duplicate copies of the reports and other documents filed with the Interstate Commerce Commission, or with the governmental authority administering such other Act of Congress, in lieu of the reports, information and documents required under this section and section 12 in respect of the same subject matter."

During debate on the adoption of the 1934 Act, Senator Barclay remarked:

"It does not seem to me it (Sec. 13) gives the commission any power to impose on a corporation any particular method of bookkeeping . . . "

"It does not require them to adopt a set of books to suit us or the commission. It authorizes the commission to require the company to advise it by what bookkeeping method of its own it has arrived at those conclusions." 78 Cong. Rec. 8282.

Section 20(b) of the 1935 Act, discussed in part B of this Part V, infra, expressly directs the Commission not to prescribe for companies subject to that Act accounting rules inconsistent with state and federal public utility regulatory agencies. It is true that, except for Section 13(b) of the 1934 Act, the disclosure acts do not in so many words contain the limitation found in Section 20(b) of the 1935 Act. But, if the Commission cannot issue an overriding federal accounting rule even under a statute like the 1935 Act which gives it the broad power to prescribe a Uniform System of Accounts, it certainly cannot issue such an overriding accounting rule under the much more limited accounting powers granted to it by the disclosure acts. Congress obviously did not intend that the Commission consider uniformity to be an essential ingredient of adequate disclosure.

The Commission has acknowledged its limited authority under the disclosure statutes. Regulation S-X does not specify a system of accounts with detailed classifications. Rule 3-07(a) of the Regulation contemplates changes in accounting principles or practice or changes in the application thereof, so long as there is disclosure in an appropriate note to the financial statements. And, ASR No. 4 itself is general in referring to "substantial authority" for the principles employed. Flexibility was obviously intended. The first sentence of ASR No. 4 contemplates that registrants shall determine the classification of items in their statements so long as the classifications are truthful and supported by substantial authority. (Of course, ASR No. 4 becomes inflexible when its second sentence is applied to foreclose resort to accounting authority other than that announced by the Commission as substantial.*) Rule X-13B-1(a) recognizes the limitation in Section 13(b) of the 1934 Act. Rule X-14A-3(b) provides that the annual report accompanying or preceding the proxy statement of

---

* The second sentence of ASR No. 4 may be invalid to the extent that it imposes uniformity where substantial authority exists for more than one accounting principle on the same subject.

management shall contain "such financial statements . . . as will, <u>in the opinion of the management</u>, adequately reflect the financial position and operations of the issuer . . . in any form deemed suitable by management." (Emphasis added.) The theme of all these rules is disclosure, not necessarily uniformity. Now the Commission proposes to consider conformity to one particular accounting standard by all registrants as essential to the policy of adequate disclosure.

As pointed out above, actual disclosure is accomplished without classifying these credits outside equity. Therefore, it is very questionable that the proposed announcement can be supported as being necessary to carry out the purposes of these Acts.

Moreover, the proposed policy will have the effect of overriding the legitimate exercise by various state and federal commissions of their unquestioned plenary power to prescribe the accounting of public utilities. Business decisions are made and rate and capital matters are decided upon the basis of the accounts so established. Publication of different accounts has the natural tendency of forcing management and regulatory bodies to conform in their practices in order to keep faith with representations to investors. This, in turn, necessarily affects business decisions and regulation based upon such accounts. In this way, the Commission, more than any other regulatory body, could greatly influence the course of utility regulation. Therefore, the Commission should be extremely cautious when considering whether to require uniformity where other agencies have chosen not to be uniform.

B. The Holding Company Act

The Holding Company Act of 1935 ("1935 Act") is a regulatory act and not merely a disclosure statute. The accounting authority of the Commission is correspondingly more broad and includes the power to prescribe a uniform system of accounts. However, even in this statute in which Congress went beyond the policy of disclosure and granted the Commission regulatory power over books of account, pre-emption of accounting regulation by other agencies was carefully avoided. Section 20(b) of the 1935 Act provides that:

"(b) In the case of the accounts of any company whose methods of accounting are prescribed under the provisions of any law of the United States or of any State, the rules and regulations or orders of the Commission in respect of accounts shall not be inconsistent with the requirements imposed by such law or any rule or regulation thereunder; nor shall anything in this title relieve any public-utility company from the duty to keep the accounts, books, records, or memoranda which may be required to be kept by the law of any State in which it operates or by the State Commission of any such State. But this provision shall not prevent the Commission from imposing such additional requirements regarding reports or accounts as it may deem necessary or appropriate in the public interest or for the protection of investors or consumers."

The Commission has adopted Rule U-28 under the 1935 Act which provides that:

"No registered holding company or subsidiary thereof shall distribute to its security holders, or publish, financial statements which are inconsistent with the book accounts of such company or financial statements filed with this Commission by, or on behalf of, such company . . . "

It can hardly be said that the classification of a balance sheet account as non-equity rather than equity as prescribed by a state agency would merely constitute an "additional requirement"; it would be "inconsistent" under Section 20(b). Therefore, the proposed interpretation and application of ASR No. 4 would violate Rule U-28 and Section 20(b) of the 1935 Act and to that extent could have impact only upon utilities not subject to that Act. In this respect, the only practical objective of the proposed change - uniformity - would be frustrated.

Moreover, Congress could not have intended that financial statements based upon a state ordered accounting principle could be considered misleading by the Commission if filed by a registrant not subject to the 1935 Act, while a financial statement based upon the same principle could not be considered misleading because filed by a registrant subject to that Act.

VI. The Proposed Announcement Would Have
Undesirable Retroactive Effects

According to its terms, the proposed announcement would affect all financial statements dated December 31, 1958, or thereafter, regardless of when filed. Registrations filed and even effective prior to the announcement date would be within the express terms of the new policy and therefore conclusively presumed to be misleading. Such retroactive rule-making is of doubtful validity and in any event is unfair and not necessary in view of the past practice of the Commission to accept equity classifications.

Furthermore, if there was no substantial authority for the equity classification on December 31, 1958, there was none as far back as July, 1958, when ARB No. 44 revised was issued and perhaps there was no authority as far back as the issuance of ARB No. 43, at least with respect to rapid amortization. Thus, the propriety of numerous certifications is brought into question. Furthermore, the possibility of suits for civil liabilities under Sections 11(a) and 12(1) of the 1933 Act becomes a reality. From this standpoint it is unwise for the Commission to employ the vehicle of adequate disclosure to require these credits to be classified as non-equity.

CONCLUSION

For these reasons, the Commission should not adopt the proposed change in administrative policy.

Respectfully submitted,

/s/ LEE C. HOWLEY
Lee C. Howley, Esq.
Vice President and General Counsel

/s/ THEODORE J. HORVATH,
Theodore J. Horvath, Esq.
Senior Counsel

THE COLUMBIA GAS SYSTEM, INC.

CHARLES H. MANN
TREASURER

Address reply to
120 East 41st Street
New York 17, N. Y.

March 24, 1959

Securities and Exchange Commission
Washington 25, D. C.

Attention: Mr. Orval L. DuBois, Secretary

Gentlemen:

This letter is in reference to Release
No. 4010, Securities Act of 1933, titled "Notice
of Intention to Announce Interpretation of
Administrative Policy". By the issuance of
Releases 4023 and 4038, the Commission extended
the time for submitting views and comments to
March 25, 1959, and announced a public hearing on
April 8, 1959.

For the reasons clearly set forth in your
announcement, the companies comprising the
Columbia Gas System are in complete agreement
with the theory of deferred tax accounting where
liberalized depreciation is claimed for income
tax purposes, but only normal depreciation is
recorded on the books of account.

We think that this accounting treatment is
particularly applicable to regulated public
utilities and have successfully advocated this
treatment before the Federal Power Commission and
several State regulatory commissions (see FPC
Opinion at Docket No. G-6358 re Amere Gas Utilities
Company, et al). Attached hereto and made a part
of our comments is the statement of the Columbia
Gas System Companies filed on September 6, 1957 at

FPC Docket No. R-158, which sets forth in greater detail our position with respect to this accounting treatment.

Our Companies also desire to have time allotted to them at the public hearing on this matter to be held April 8, 1959.

Very truly yours,

/s/ C. H. MANN

Enclosure

UNITED STATES OF AMERICA

BEFORE THE

Federal Power Commission

In the Matter of	
Amendment of Uniform System of Accounts for Natural Gas Companies Respecting Treatment of Deferred Taxes on Income.	Docket No. R-158

STATEMENT OF COLUMBIA GAS SYSTEM COMPANIES

RICHARD A. ROSAN
and
W. ARTHUR BATTEN
120 East 41st Street
New York 17, N. Y.

JOHN P. RANDOLPH
1625 I Street, N.W.
Washington 6, D. C.

September 6, 1957

INTRODUCTION

At Docket G-6358 in the so-called "Amere Case," the Commission held lengthy proceedings concerning the appropriate treatment of the liberalized depreciation elections permitted by Section 167 of the Internal Revenue Code of 1954 for accounting and rate purposes. That proceeding was instituted by nine subsidiaries of The Columbia Gas System, Inc. However, the Commission permitted interventions by many parties, many of whom were in no way served or affected by the Columbia Gas System companies involved, for example, the Wisconsin Public Service Commission and the City of Detroit. Hearings were held, exhaustive briefs filed and oral argument held before the full Commission, so that all interested parties had an opportunity to be heard and to impress their views upon the Commission.

The Commission's Decision at Docket G-6358, issued June 30, 1956, sets forth the broad principles which should control in the treatment of liberalized depreciation for regulated companies subject to its jurisdiction. That Decision is sound.

The issue presented at Docket R-158 (and also at R-159) is merely to prescribe the accounting regulations which will properly effectuate such Decision of the Commission. It is the purpose of this Statement to set forth briefly our overall position with respect to the subject of liberalized depreciation as permitted by Section 167 of the Internal Revenue Code of 1954 and with respect to that part of the proposed rule making entitled Account 259.3—Reserve for Deferred Taxes on Income—Other.

A. ACCOUNTING RULES WITH RESPECT TO LIBERALIZED DEPRECIATION PERMITTED BY SECTION 167 OF THE 1954 INTERNAL REVENUE CODE SHOULD BE ADOPTED.

1. Congressional Intent. In order to effectuate the clear and obvious Congressional intent, it is essential that liberalized depreciation for tax purposes be recognized for what it is, namely, a deferral

2

of taxes. The accounting rule should recognize and effectuate this intent. The proposed Account 259.2 does this.

2. Not a Tax Reduction. Liberalized depreciation does not reduce taxes. It is an arrangement whereby the taxing authority—the U. S. Government—has permitted in the interests of the national welfare, the deferral of taxes. Nothing in the Reports of the Senate or the House of Representatives, or in the legislation itself, can lead to any conclusion but the fact that Congress intended and, in fact, passed legislation which created a deferral of taxes, and not a reduction in taxes.

There is no merit in the contention that because of anticipated growth in utility plant the effect of Section 167 is not to defer taxes, but to reduce taxes. The Commission's Order at Docket G-6358 concisely analyzed and answered this argument by stating:

> "It is clear that the charging of greater depreciation during the early life of property and the charging of less during the later life operates to create a deferral of income taxes. The fact that there may be continuing additions to plant, year by year, with the result that there will be a balance in the reserve account at all times in the foreseeable future, does not prove that there is no tax deferral. On the contrary, it proves that there is a continuing tax deferral so long as additional facilites are being installed. This is precisely what Congress intended."

The proposed accounting rule properly recognizes this conclusion.

3. Consumer Not Prejudiced. Proper accounting for liberalized depreciation does not result in higher rates to the consumer. Deferred accounting is a proper method of having consumers, present and future, get the tax benefit which results from, and is synchronized with, the depreciation expense which such consumers are asked to bear. The proposed Account 259.2 accomplishes this.

4. No Windfall to Stockholders. Proper accounting treatment is necessary in order to prevent a current windfall to the utility. It is also necessary in order that the investor is not required, by reason

3

of the election of liberalized depreciation, to absorb future tax liabilities, because the Company might not be able to recoup adequate rates from the consumer. The proposed Account 259.2 accomplishes this.

5. Loss of Valuable Right. Proper accounting for deferred taxes gives recognition to the fact that by using liberalized depreciation for tax purposes (but not for book purposes), the company has used up a valuable right.

6. Current Money Situation. Recently, the cost of raising capital by utilities has sharply increased. Thus, making available to utilities cash, which Congress has permitted through the deferral of tax liability, can have but one result—namely, a tendency to reduce the cost of capital to finance needed expansion of all utility services, both electric and gas.

The increase in the interest rates paid on the various bonds and debentures of natural gas companies issued during the first six months of 1957 (about 1% to 1½% in a six-months period) has been as great or greater than that experienced by other types of utilities. This may very well indicate that the past ability of natural gas companies to attract capital and construct facilities is not as "extraordinary" as suggested by the Commission's Order of June 30, 1956.

7. Conclusion. We submit, therefore, that an accounting rule should be adopted which will accomplish: (i) the objectives of Congress, (ii) the protection of consumers, both present and future, (iii) the prevention of windfalls to present investors, and (iv) the recognition, accounting-wise, of the transaction for what it really is, namely, a deferral of taxes.

B. SPECIFIC COMMENTS WITH RESPECT TO PROPOSED ACCOUNT 259.2—"RESERVE FOR DEFERRED TAXES ON INCOME—LIBERALIZED DEPRECIATION."

1. We agree with and endorse subparagraphs A and B of Account 259.2.

4

Some questions have been raised as to the propriety of requiring the maintenance of a Reserve Account, as distinguished from a Restricted Surplus Account to reflect the deferred tax.

(a) The fact that this Commission might require the accounting for deferred taxes in a reserve, while a State Commission might require the same company to reflect it in a restricted surplus account, presents no difficulty. There are many situations where the accounts required by a State differ from the Federal Power Commission. It is easy to maintain ledger sheets with different headings. Consequently, the argument for uniformity is not persuasive.

(b) We see no great problem whether the reserve is nominated "Restricted Surplus," or "Reserve for Deferred Taxes." Because the reserve reflects a deferred tax, we prefer and endorse the reserve method in the proposed rule. In this connection, the Commission is referred to the persuasive concurring opinion of Commissioner Thompson in the Application of the Public Service Company of Colorado, No. 45017, dated January 5, 1956, excerpts from which are set forth in Appendix A hereto.

2. We have no objection to subparagraph C of Account 259.2 which provides for vintage accounting for each class, group or unit as to which different liberalized depreciation methods and service life expectancies have been used. Such accounting is not estimated to impose an undue burden on our companies; the method is good accounting; and it will give complete control of these accounts in future years.

On the other hand, we understand that there is some objection to said provision for vintage accounting. We point out that subparagraph C merely provides for mechanics, as distinguished from substance. Since it is mere mechanics, it is possible that this provision could be modified to meet the objections of other parties by providing that the records be kept by vintage on a "gross" or "overall basis" without breakdown into class, group or unit. This could be accomplished by having paragraph C of Account 259.2 revised to read substantially as paragraph C in proposed Account 259.3—Reserve for Deferred Taxes on Income—Other.

3. In our written comments to the Commission, we indicated disagreement with the first sentence of paragraph D which provides that the accounting treatment is not "mandatory." In fairness, as between the regulatory agency, the consumer and the stockholder, the use of liberalized depreciation for tax purposes by a regulated utility should be recognized for what it is, namely, a deferred tax liability. Thus, the accounting procedure being prescribed should be mandatory. The benefits from the use of liberalized depreciation for tax purposes should not be allowed to flow through to income, since it is not, in our opinion, an income item. Clearly, as the Commission found in G-6358, the use of liberalized depreciation merely operates to create a deferral of income taxes. It should be accounted for as such. Failure to make the proposed accounting rule mandatory may result in income statements which fail to reflect correctly the operating results of the company.

C. ACCOUNT 259.3—"RESERVE FOR DEFERRED TAXES ON INCOME—OTHER" SHOULD BE ADOPTED.

Certain Columbia Companies presently have pending before the Commission rate cases in which it is their position that in rate proceedings the tax effect of intangible well drilling costs should be normalized so that the tax benefit would by synchronized with the depreciation expense charged to the consumer. The position with respect to intangible well drilling costs is identical with the position concerning liberalized depreciation. In both cases, Congress offers an incentive through tax legislation to accomplish certain objectives considered in the national interest. Such tax benefit should not be passed on 100% to the present consumer, with the possibility that future consumers who will pay part of the depreciation expense

6

associated with today's intangible well drilling costs will receive no offsetting tax benefit. The failure to normalize the tax benefits of intangible well drilling through proper accounting procedures can result in wide swings in the earnings of a company. The accounting by the deferred method, which would be possible under the proposed Account 259.3, represents, in our opinion, a step forward. Accordingly, we urge its adoption and the subsequent implementation of its adoption in appropriate cases, including those involving intangible well drilling costs.

Respectfully submitted,

RICHARD A. ROSAN, *Counsel for*
United Fuel Gas Company,
The Ohio Fuel Gas Company,
Atlantic Seaboard Corporation,
Home Gas Company,
Kentucky Gas Transmission
Corporation, and
Amere Gas Utilities Company

Dated: New York, N. Y.,
September 6, 1957

7

APPENDIX A

Concurring Opinion of Commissioner Thompson of the Public Utilities Commission of the State of Colorado in its Application of Public Service Company of Colorado, Application No. 13856, Decision dated January 5, 1956:

"I concur with the majority, that the applicant should be authorized to make provision for expected future income tax liability in this matter by making charges against current revenues. I do not agree that the balance sheet account should be denominated as earned surplus. This is not a matter merely of semantics. Words express thoughts; these words do not characterize my thinking on the matter.

"The 1954 Internal Revenue Code permits all taxpayers to reduce their immediate taxes by increasing their depreciation expense charges as to certain properties. This increases the taxpayer's current net income after taxes by the amount of the immediate tax reduction. In the case of public utilities, whose rates are regulated, this would tend to result in reduced rates, although in the present case the reduction at most would not amount to more than a few cents per year per customer.

"Further, it is expected that the taxes saved now will have to be paid later, because the Code provisions only change the emphasis of the depreciation charge to the early years of the property's life. The applicant here merely seeks to level out this tax situation so that over the coming years its net income will be normalized. To do this, it wants to set aside money from its present revenues, as though the full tax expense were currently payable, so that it will have money to pay the higher future tax. This seems to me to be sound accounting procedure, and good business practice.

"The justification for this procedure is the expectation of a future tax expense. We are merely permitting a normalizing charge as a bookkeeping expense now, to provide money for the expense when it actually arises. The effect is to overcharge ratepayers now in some slight degree, so that they will bear a fair

8

share of the true burden of expense to be incurred. This expense is a true operating expense—it is not a deduction from surplus. It is not an expense the stockholder must pay, but is one the rate-payer must pay. The money set aside is a provision for a future expense—in truth, a reserve; it is not something temporarily withheld from stockholders, which otherwise they would ordinarily receive—that is, it is not a surplus item, restricted or otherwise."

COLUMBIA GAS SYSTEM SERVICE CORPORATION

RICHARD A. ROSAN
VICE PRESIDENT AND COUNSEL

Address reply to
120 East 41st Street
New York 17, N. Y.

April 3, 1959

Mr. Andrew Barr
Chief Accountant
Securities and Exchange Commission
Washington 25, D. C.

Dear Mr. Barr:

We have considered carefully the contribution which we could make at the oral argument to the Commission's knowledge with respect to Release No. 4010. Since our views will be amply represented by other participants, and since our accounting for liberalized depreciation is controlled by the Uniform System of Accounts promulgated by the Federal Power Commission (pursuant to which we account for liberalized depreciation in a Tax Reserve account), we have determined that it is unnecessary for us to make an appearance at the oral argument before the Commission. Accordingly, we relinquish the 15 minutes allotted to The Columbia Gas System, Inc.

Thank you for your courtesies in this matter.

Faithfully yours,

/s/ RICHARD A. ROSAN

COMMONWEALTH EDISON COMPANY

72 West Adams Street
Chicago 90, Illinois

January 23, 1959

Securities and Exchange Commission
Washington 25, D. C.

Attention: Mr. Orval L. DuBois
          Secretary

Gentlemen:

    Commonwealth Edison Company favors the
adoption of the announced interpretation of
administrative policy on financial statements
regarding balance sheet treatment of credits
equivalent to the reduction in income taxes as
outlined in your Notice of Intention dated
December 30, 1958.

    The proposed interpretation of administra-
tive policy is in accord with our view that a
company which deducts liberalized depreciation
or accelerated amortization for tax purposes but
records only normal depreciation on its books of
account should charge current income with an
amount equal to the resulting tax reduction and
concurrently credit a balance sheet account which
clearly indicates by its title and balance sheet
position that the accumulated credit is an accrued
liability of the company. Consequently, we believe
that this credit should not be shown as earned
surplus or equity capital.

                    Yours very truly,

                    /s/ GRANT H. WIER

                    Grant H. Wier
                    Comptroller

CONSOLIDATED EDISON COMPANY OF NEW YORK, INC.

CHARLES E. EBLE
PRESIDENT

4 Irving Place
New York 3, N. Y.

January 19, 1959

Securities and Exchange Commission
Washington 25, D. C.

Attention: Mr. Orval L. DuBois, Secretary

Gentlemen:

We refer to the notice of intention to
announce "an interpretation of administrative
policy on financial statements regarding balance
sheet treatment of credits equivalent to the
reductions in income taxes" released by the
Commission under date of December 30, 1958
(Securities Act of 1933 Release No. 4010; Securities Exchange Act of 1934 Release No. 5844; Public
Utility Holding Company Act of 1935 Release
No. 13894; Investment Company Act of 1940 Release
No. 2814).

We have discussed the subject matter of the
Release with representatives of Central Hudson
Gas & Electric Corporation, Long Island Lighting
Company, New York State Electric & Gas Corporation,
Niagara Mohawk Power Corporation, Orange and
Rockland Utilities, Inc. and Rochester Gas and
Electric Corporation, all of whom are in agreement that the interpretation of administrative
policy proposed by the Commission impinges on an
important area of State regulation in such a
manner as to give rise to the possibility of a
very substantial conflict with local regulatory
authority. Moreover, it is not clear whether the
interpretation of administrative policy proposed
by the Commission is intended to proscribe the use

of "flow-through" accounting (except in the
instances referred to in foot-note 3 of the
Release), as well as to proscribe the inclusion
in surplus or equity capital accounts of accumulations resulting from the use of normalizing or
deferred tax accounting procedures. In these
circumstances, it is submitted that your
Commission should supply a more detailed and
specific statement of the modifications proposed
and should provide for public hearings upon the
proposal.

It is also the view of the Companies above
named that more time is required for the preparation of statements of their positions and that
more informative responses to the Commission's
invitation for the submission of views and
comments would be obtained if the time for submission of such views and comments were extended.
Accordingly, these Companies have authorized us
to say that they join with us in a request that
the Commission supply a more detailed and specific
statement of the modifications proposed, extend
to at least February 28, 1959 the time limit for
submission of views and comments, and provide for
public hearings upon the proposal.

Respectfully submitted,

CONSOLIDATED EDISON COMPANY OF
NEW YORK, INC.

By__/s/__C. E. EBLE_____
President

SECURITIES AND EXCHANGE COMMISSION
Washington 25, D. C.

January 28, 1959

Consolidated Edison Company of New York, Inc.
4 Irving Place
New York 3, N. Y.

Attention: Mr. Charles E. Eble, President

Gentlemen:

As requested in your letter of January 19
and in similar letters from others, the
Commission has published the enclosed release
extending the time for comment and announcing
a hearing on our proposed statement relating to
balance sheet treatment of amounts arising in
deferred tax accounting.

In preparing the release of December 30,
1958, it was assumed that all utility companies
and their certifying accountants were familiar
with Accounting Research Bulletin No. 44
(Revised) issued by the Committee on Accounting
Procedure of the American Institute of Certified
Public Accountants. It is our understanding
that the paragraph of this bulletin quoted in
our footnote 3 recognizes "flow-through" accounting where authorized for rate making by regulatory authority having jurisdiction in a particular case.

Your comments on this point and any others
requiring clarification or further discussion
will be helpful.

Very truly yours,

Andrew Barr
Chief Accountant

Enclosure

LAW OFFICES OF
LeBOEUF, LAMB & LEIBY

15 Broad Street
New York 5, N. Y.

March 5, 1959

Hon. Orval L. DuBois, Secretary
Securities and Exchange Commission
425 Second Street, N. W.
Washington, D. C.

Re: Accounting Series Release 4010, etc.

Dear Sir:

Enclosed are the comments of Consolidated Edison Company of New York, Inc. with reference to the above-numbered Release. In addition to the three copies required by the Release, we enclose an additional ten copies, for the convenience of the Commission.

We hereby request thirty minutes of time to make an oral presentation on behalf of Consolidated Edison Company of New York, Inc. at the hearing in connection with this matter scheduled to be held by this Commission on April 8, 1959.

Very truly yours,

/s/ CAMERON F. MacRAE

Enclosure

UNITED STATES OF AMERICA

Securities and Exchange Commission

In the Matter	
of	
Proposed interpretation of administrative policy on financial statements regarding balance sheet treatment of credits equivalent to the reductions in income taxes	Securities Act of 1933—Release Nos. 4010, 4023 Securities Exchange Act of 1934—Release No. 5844 Public Utility Holding Company Act of 1935—Release No. 13894 Investment Company Act of 1940—Release No. 2814

STATEMENT ON BEHALF OF CONSOLIDATED EDISON COMPANY OF NEW YORK, INC.

LeBoeuf, Lamb & Leiby,
15 Broad Street,
New York 5, New York,
*Attorneys for Consolidated
Edison Company of New York, Inc.*

Cameron F. MacRae,
Alfred E. Froh,
Of Counsel.

UNITED STATES OF AMERICA

Securities and Exchange Commission

In the Matter of Proposed interpretation of administrative policy on financial statements regarding balance sheet treatment of credits equivalent to the reductions in income taxes	Securities Act of 1933— Release Nos. 4010, 4023 Securities Exchange Act of 1934—Release No. 5844 Public Utility Holding Company Act of 1935—Release No. 13894 Investment Company Act of 1940—Release No. 2814

STATEMENT ON BEHALF OF CONSOLIDATED EDISON COMPANY OF NEW YORK, INC.

This statement which is submitted on behalf of Consolidated Edison Company of New York, Inc. (Consolidated Edison) is directed to the subject matter of the Commission's notice of intention to announce interpretation of administrative policy "on financial statements regarding balance sheet treatment of credits equivalent to the reductions in income taxes" (Securities Act of 1933 Release No. 4010, etc.).

Consolidated Edison is a New York public utility company engaged in the generation, manufacture, purchase and sale of electricity, gas and steam. It supplies electric service in the Boroughs of Manhattan, The Bronx, Brooklyn, Richmond, and Queens excepting the Fifth Ward (Rockaway District), all in the City of New York, and in Westchester County excepting the northeastern portions thereof; gas service in the Boroughs of Manhattan and The Bronx, in the First and Third Wards of the Borough of Queens, and in the more populous parts of Westchester County; and steam service in a part of the Borough of Manhattan. It controls, through ownership of all the voting stock,

---

Emphasis and bracketed matter in quotations in this memorandum are supplied unless otherwise noted.

2

Consolidated Telegraph & Electrical Subway Company, a New York corporation, which owns a system of underground conduits used principally by Consolidated Edison.

Without waiving its contention that, as a matter of law, it is not subject to the Public Utility Holding Company Act, Consolidated Edison files annual exemption statements pursuant to Rule U-2.

Securities of Consolidated Edison are listed on the New York Stock Exchange.

Consolidated Edison is now and has been for many years subject to the jurisdiction of, and regulation by, the Public Service Commission of the State of New York, which relates principally to its rates and service, the issuance of securities, and the keeping of its accounts.

Consolidated Edison is not subject to the jurisdiction of the Federal Power Commission under either the Federal Power Act or the Natural Gas Act.

From the foregoing it will be seen that the accounting regulations of the Securities and Exchange Commission, to which the proposed interpretation of administrative policy is directed, have impact upon Consolidated Edison in connection with the Securities Act, the Securities Exchange Act and the Public Utility Holding Company Act.

The particular phase of accounting to which the proposed interpretation of administrative policy relates is a matter of substantial importance and interest to Consolidated Edison.

Consolidated Edison's Accounting Procedure in Connection with Accelerated Amortization under I.R.C. Section 168

Consolidated Edison has received certificates of necessity under Section 168 of the Internal Revenue Code permitting the accelerated amortization of portions of facilities having an aggregate cost subject to accelerated amortization of 55 million dollars, of which 50 million dollars has already been amortized. The Company has followed a procedure of normalization accounting in connection with the tax deferment resulting from amortization under these necessity certificates.* Under this procedure an amount equivalent to the resulting

---

* Although accelerated amortization is being used for tax purposes, normal depreciation in amounts prescribed by the New York Public Service Commission is being recorded for general accounting purposes.

3

tax deferment is charged to operating revenue deductions in each year of the five-year amortization period and concurrently credited to a segregated surplus account; and in each subsequent year during the remaining life of the facility a proportionate amount of the total equal to the increase in income taxes resulting from the prior use of accelerated amortization is credited to operating revenue deductions and concurrently debited to the segregated surplus account.

The segregated surplus resulting from this process of normalization amounted to $21,044,119 at December 31, 1958; commencing in 1960, the balance will be gradually reduced through credits to operating revenue deductions, as described above.

Consolidated Edison's Accounting Procedure in Connection with Rapid Depreciation under I.R.C. Section 167

As permitted under Section 167 of the Internal Revenue Code of 1954, Consolidated Edison has elected to use one of the rapid depreciation methods (sum of the years-digits) on property additions made after December 31, 1953, for calculating Federal income taxes; although it has continued to make normal depreciation provisions for general accounting purposes. This has resulted in increasing net income, through reductions of federal income tax accruals, by approximately $1,409,000 in 1955, $2,697,000 in 1956, $3,991,000 in 1957, and $5,117,000 in 1958. Projections made by Consolidated Edison show that the annual amount of such tax reductions will continue to increase for a number of years, approaching a maximum of 18 million dollars. These projections further demonstrate that the time (if ever) at which net income may be reduced by reason of an increase of federal income tax accruals, resulting from the amount of rapid depreciation deductible for federal income tax purposes declining below the normal statutory depreciation, would be so far in the future (one hundred years or more) that the tax reductions referred to represent reductions rather than deferrals of federal income taxes. Accordingly, the Company has not adopted any normalizing or deferred tax procedure with respect to tax reductions resulting from the use of rapid depreciation, but has recorded the actual tax liability so that the reductions "flow through" to net income.

4

The New York Public Service Commission has held hearings in 1952 and 1956 to consider the accounting treatment of tax reductions resulting from accelerated amortization under necessity certificates and from the use of rapid depreciation and its decision in the matter is still pending. In view of the fact that the accounting procedures being followed by Consolidated Edison in connection with accelerated amortization and rapid depreciation have been explained in detail at such hearings and have been reported to the New York Commission in periodic reports filed by Consolidated Edison beginning with the year 1952 as to accelerated amortization and the year 1955 as to rapid depreciation, all without objection being raised by that Commission, Consolidated Edison has assumed that its accounting procedures in this connection do not require express approval of the New York Public Service Commission.

Ambiguity of Commission's Notice

Under date of January 19, 1959, Consolidated Edison addressed a communication to this Commission in which it was pointed out that the Commission's Release No. 4010 does not make clear whether the interpretation of administrative policy proposed by the Commission is intended to proscribe the use of "flow-through" accounting (except in certain instances referred to in footnote 3 of the Release), as well as to proscribe the inclusion in surplus or equity capital accounts of accumulations resulting from the use of normalizing or deferred tax accounting procedures, and requesting that the Commission supply a more detailed and specific statement of the modifications proposed.

In replies addressed to Consolidated Edison and to a similar inquiry made by the American Gas Association on behalf of its member companies, of which Consolidated Edison is one, the Commission's Chief Accountant seemed at first to clarify the matter by stating that the Commission's proposal "is directed *primarily* to secure uniformity in balance sheet treatment when deferred tax accounting is adopted".* but then he revived the uncertainty by referring to Accounting Research Bulletin No. 44 (Revised) issued by the Committee on Accounting Procedure of the American Institute of Certified Public Accountants.

---

* Letter to Managing Director, American Gas Association, January 28, 1959.

5

Therefore, it is thought desirable to address this statement to both features referred to above.

Summary Statement of Position

In summary, the position of Consolidated Edison with respect to the proposed interpretation of administrative policy is that substantial authority exists for recording in surplus account the accumulation resulting from normalizing or deferred tax accounting for deferment of Federal income taxes resulting from amortization under necessity certificates, and substantial authority also exists for the use of flow-through accounting in connection with reductions of federal income tax resulting from the use of rapid depreciation; and in these circumstances the Commission should not change its policy reflected in Accounting Series Release No. 4 of accepting disclosure in lieu of revision of the financial statements themselves. Moreover, it is questionable whether the Securities and Exchange Commission, within the ambit of its jurisdiction, could obtain any substantial degree of uniformity of accounting treatment and statement presentation even if the proposed interpretation of administrative policy were adopted.

I.

An inflexible requirement for the exclusion of deferred tax accumulations from surplus or equity accounts should not be imposed in the face of substantial authority allowing such treatment.

It has been the policy of this Commission, as officially promulgated in Accounting Series Release No. 4, to proscribe accounting treatment "for which there is no substantial authoritative support"; but to accept disclosure "if the points involved are such that there is substantial authoritative support for the [accounting] practices followed by the registrant." It is the position of Consolidated Edison that the policy laid down by Accounting Series Release No. 4 is a sound one which this Commission should continue to follow; and that since there is "substantial authoritative support" in favor of several alternative

6

methods of treating tax reductions arising from Sections 167 and 168 of the Internal Revenue Code, each of such accounting methods should be considered as proper by this Commission, providing only that there is full disclosure of the method being used, and the consequences resulting therefrom.

With particular reference to that accounting matter which the proposed notice of intention would clearly proscribe, namely, the inclusion in surplus or equity accounts of credits arising from deferred tax accounting for reductions resulting from the use of accelerated amortization or rapid depreciation, there is a large body of substantial authoritative support in favor of such accounting treatment, including the utility regulatory commissions of several States.

Some form of surplus treatment, whether restricted or otherwise, has been prescribed or allowed by State commissions in Alabama, Colorado, Florida, Kentucky, Michigan, New Jersey, New Mexico, North Carolina, Ohio, Oklahoma, South Carolina, Utah, Virginia, West Virginia, Washington and Wyoming.* Other State commissions have differed from this treatment, and a few of the commissions listed above have prescribed differing treatment in different cases. It is submitted, however, that the decisions of sixteen State commissions charged with jurisdiction over the accounting and rate regulation of utilities represents "substantial authoritative support", within the meaning of Release No. 4, for the accounting practices which they have prescribed in given cases.

The Federal Power Commission, while prescribing a non-equity classification for deferred tax credits for its own regulatory purposes, has recognized the divergency of views among the State commissions and the propriety of utilities following that treatment which is prescribed by their State commission. In its Order No. 204 (issued May 29, 1958) in Docket R-159, that Commission stated:

---

* Ala.—*Alabama P. Co.*, Order No. 1679, Feb. 28, 1955; Colo.—*Colorado Cent. P. Co.*, 21 PUR 3d 491; Fla.—*Florida P. & L. Co.*, 4 PUR 3d 91; Mich.—*Indiana & Mich. E. Co.*, 11 PUR 3d 470; N. J.—*Public Serv. E. & G. Co.*, letter dated Dec. 8, 1955; N. M.—*PSC Gen. Order No. 18* (see 10 PUR 3d 281); N. C.—*Carolina P. & L. Co.*, 97 PURNS 111; Ohio—*Ohio P. Co.*, Order No. 23,321, Aug. 27, 1952 (see 1953 CCH Util. L. Rep. ¶16,938); Okla.—*Public Serv. Co. of Oklahoma*, 12 PUR 3d 246; S. C.—*Lockhart P. Co.*, 1957 CCH Util. L. Rep. ¶17,562; Utah—*Utah P. & L. Co.*, 11 PUR 3d 477; Va.—*General Tel. Co. of the Southeast*, 14 PUR 3d 239; W. Va.—*Wheeling Electric Co.*, Case 4305, June 30, 1955; Wash.—*Pacific P. & L. Co.*, 1953 CCH Util. L. Rep. ¶16,469; Wyo.—*Utah P. & L. Co.*, 12 PUR 3d 489.

7

"* * * We regret the inconsistency which has arisen among the several state commissions. Under the circumstances, however, we see no reasonable solution to the problem for those utilities which are required by a state commission to report deferred taxes in a reserve or surplus account but to classify the deferred taxes in accordance with state requirements for state purposes, and to use the treatment specified by this order for the purposes of this Commission."

It would seem that an accounting practice prescribed by the number of regulatory agencies above listed and recognized by the Federal Power Commission should not be presumed by this Commission to be misleading.

On the other hand, where the accounting and rates of a utility company are under the control of a local regulatory agency, financial statements which deviate substantially from those required by and submitted to the local agency may in a given case tend to be highly misleading. Where the local regulatory agency regards the accumulated tax deferments as equity and does not require deduction from the rate base, such accumulations do for all practical purposes represent equity.

It is Consolidated Edison's view, without going into an extended discussion of the various other possible forms of accounting treatment, that there is no one form of accounting which in every case can be regarded as completely accurate in the absence of footnote disclosure. It is therefore submitted that an accounting method which has been prescribed by the substantial body of authority referred to, and particularly where the authority at the same time has the power to prescribe rates and limit earnings, should not, when coupled with adequate disclosure, be deemed misleading or proscribed by this Commission for any purpose. To the contrary, this Commission should continue the sound policy promulgated in Accounting Series Release No. 4 more than 21 years ago.

8

II.

Flow-through accounting accompanied by proper disclosure should not be limited to those situations described in footnote 3 of the notice of intention.

The notice of intention appears to imply that flow-through accounting will not be permitted except in those exceptional situations enumerated in Accounting Research Bulletin No. 44 (Revised) issued by the Committee on Accounting Procedure of the American Institute of Certified Public Accountants (ARB 44 Revised), and particularly paragraph 8 thereof which is quoted in footnote 3 of the notice of intention.

It is Consolidated Edison's position, as indicated above, that where there is substantial authority for an accounting practice this Commission should continue its policy of allowing such practice, provided it is accompanied by full disclosure. There is a substantial body of authority in favor of flow-through accounting with respect to tax reductions resulting from rapid depreciation in situations other than those so restrictively described in paragraph 8 of ARB 44 Revised.

Paragraph 8 of ARB 44 Revised would limit flow-through accounting to those situations in which the State Commission has not only prescribed the flow-through method for rate-making purposes, but in which it also may

"* * * reasonably be expected that increased future income taxes, resulting from the earlier deduction of declining-balance depreciation for income-tax purposes only, will be allowed in future rate determinations."

Apart from begging the question as to whether there ever will be any "increased future income taxes", this test is impracticable for two reasons:

First, it puts the accountant in a position of trying to forecast *future* action of a regulatory agency of unknown personnel, acting under unknown conditions of law and fact. This is clearly contrary to the precept expressed in Accounting Series Release No. 53 that "financial accounting * * * does not attempt to forecast the future."

9

Second, it is equally difficult to discern and specifically define the *current* rate-making policies of many of the local regulatory agencies with respect to tax reductions resulting from rapid depreciation. As the matter now stands, it appears that Indiana, Maine and Pennsylvania are the only states in which the problem has been clearly resolved in terms of a definitive rate-making policy with judicial affirmation, with Indiana allowing deferred taxes and Maine and Pennsylvania requiring flow-through treatment.* In other jurisdictions a preference for one method or the other has been indicated in individual rate decisions by commissions or courts.** In a number of states, there have been no commission decisions reported as to the rate-making treatment of tax reductions resulting from rapid depreciation. In view of the fact that most local regulatory agencies make their rate decisions on a case-by-case basis, and do not promulgate or publish immutable rate-making rules having universal application, it is doubtful whether the matter will ever be resolved with such definiteness and finality as to permit the application of the test set forth in paragraph 8 of ARB 44 Revised.

A substantial body of authority favors flow-through accounting in connection with tax reductions under I.R.C. 167

A proscription against flow-through accounting in situations which do not qualify for the exemption provided in paragraph 8 of ARB 44 Revised would fly in the face of a most substantial body of authority, consisting of State and Federal regulatory agencies which either require flow-through accounting, expressly permit it as optional, or have not proscribed it.

---

* *Public Service Co. of Indiana* v. *Indiana P.S.C.*, 22 PUR 3d 13 (Indiana Circuit Court, 1957) ; *Central Maine P. Co.* v. *P.U.C.*, 153 Me. 228, 136 A 2d 726. 21 PUR 3d 321 (1957) ; *City of Pittsburgh* v. *Pennsylvania P.U.C.*, 182 Pa. Super. Ct. 551, 128 A 2d 372, 17 PUR 3d 249 (1956).
** *Flow-through:*—California—*Citizens' Utility Co.*, 1958 CCH Util. L. Rep. ¶17,889 ; Illinois—*City of Alton* v. *Ill. Commerce Comm'n*, 26 PUR 3d 187 (Ill. Circuit Ct.) ; Missouri—*Empire Dist. Elect. Co.*, 22 PUR 3d 399 ; New Hampshire—*Public Serv. of N. H.*, 18 PUR 3d 523 ; New Jersey—*Bernards Water Co.*, 18 PUR 3d 92 ; New Mexico—(Public Service Commission) *Lea County Gas Co.*, 10 PUR 3d 399 ; North Dakota—*Montana-Dakota Utilities*, 1958 CCH Util. L. Rep. ¶17,855 ; West Virginia—*Hope Nat. G. Co.*, 23 PUR 3d 394.
Normalization:—Kansas—*Empire Dist. Elect. Co.*, 1958 CCH Util. L. Rep. ¶17,964 ; Kentucky—*Kentucky Util. Co.*, 1958 CCH Util. L. Rep. ¶17,925 ; Michigan—*Michigan Consol. G. Co.*, 1958 CCH Util. L. Rep. ¶17,851 ; New Mexico—(Corporations Commission) *General Telephone Co. of the Southwest*, 14 PUR 3d 243 ; Ohio—*Ohio Fuel Gas Co.*, 25 PUR 3d 207 ; Oklahoma—*Oklahoma N. G. Co.*, 26 PUR 3d 149 ; Wisconsin—*Wisconsin Fuel & L. Co.*, 12 PUR 3d 254 ; Wyoming—*United Telephone Co. of the West*, 23 PUR 3d 68.

10

At the extreme (which position is not advocated by Consolidated Edison), a substantial body of authority has taken the position that flow-through accounting with respect to tax reductions resulting from rapid depreciation constitutes the *only* manner of proper accounting. This position is largely based upon the view that such tax reductions constitute permanent savings rather than deferrals of taxes, and that setting up credits for taxes which probably never will be paid is unrealistic. Thus, the Committee on Accounts and Statistics of the National Association of Railroad and Utilities Commissioners has reported*

> "The Committee is convinced that the use of the liberalized depreciation procedures permitted by the 1954 Revenue Act results in tax reduction, not tax deferral, and that it would be contrary to sound accounting principles and to the provisions of the Uniform Systems of Accounts to record such tax reduction in a deferred credit account."

It is noteworthy that this Committee did not condition its views as to accounting procedure upon any fixed method of rate-making; indeed it indicated that normalization might be accepted for rate-making purposes, as distinguished from accounting.

Similarly, the NARUC Committee on Depreciation has stated**

> "In general this Committee favors the computation of depreciation expense for public utility accounting and rate purposes according to the straight line method and the recording of income taxes each year at the actual tax liability for that year."

A study of the effect of liberalized depreciation on the tax liability for future years by the Committee on Accounts and Statistics annexed to the report of the NARUC 67th Annual Convention at pages 439 *et seq.* demonstrates that the tax reductions will be permanent savings and should not in any sense be considered tax deferrals.***

---

* Report of NARUC 67th Annual Convention (1955), page 441.
** *Ibid.* page 436.
*** See studies to the same effect by Professor Robert Eisner "Depreciation Under the New Tax Law", 33 Harvard Business Review 66 (January-February 1955); E. Cary Brown, "The New Depreciation Policy Under the Income Tax; an Economic Analysis", 8 Nat'l Tax Journal 81 (1955); and Professor Sidney Davidson, "Accelerated Depreciation and the Allocation of Income Taxes", 33 The Accounting Review 173 (April 1958).

11

Commissioner Connole of the Federal Power Commission, who refused to participate in that Commission's Order No. 204 which permitted, but did not require, deferred tax accounting in connection with rapid depreciation under certain conditions (discussed more fully below), on the ground that the order "proceeds from an unsound premise", noted that

> "First, only if dollars of plant replacements are less than the dollars of plant retirements during an extended period will Federal income tax liability ever exceed the amount currently charged the income tax account during the period and result in a net reduction of the balance sheet account. But the possibilities of dollars retirements *at cost* ever exceeding dollars of replacements and extensions of facilities are non-existent in the utility industry generally. Therefore, there never will be a time 'when tax liabilities increase' and the proposed account 'Accumulated Deferred Taxes on Income' will never be debited." (Emphasis in original.)

The possibility of retirements ever exceeding replacements and extensions is perhaps not completely "non-existent" as suggested by Commissioner Connole. However, this contingency is clearly not so inevitable as to make deferred tax accounting the only non-misleading method of accounting for Section 167 reductions. If, indeed, Commissioner Connole, the NARUC Committees, and the other authorities cited are correct, deferred tax accounting is not only misleading, but is a misnomer, even if the variables of taxable profits and tax rate continued unchanged for an indefinite period into the future. Moreover any period of decline in total plant would have to coincide with a period when the company made a taxable profit for there ever to be a debit to any "deferred tax" accounts. Profitable operation coinciding with a decline in plant would appear to be, as a business matter, not very likely.

No statistical or mathematical refutation of the conclusions above discussed has been found, and indeed starting from certain premises the conclusions are mathematically inescapable. The premises upon which these studies are based, *i.e.*, maintenance or expansion of the level of plant investment, are fully applicable to Consolidated Edison's particular situation, and hence the conclusions reached are, for Con-

12

solidated Edison, completely valid. As has been noted (p. 3, *supra*) projections made by Consolidated Edison indicate that annual depreciation computed on the sum of the years-digits basis will be in excess of straight-line depreciation for a hundred years or more. At no time during this 100 year period would there be any reduction in the "deferred tax account" through payment of "deferred taxes". It is difficult to see how a requirement for maintaining an account reflecting a liability for deferred taxes that will not have to be paid for a century (if, indeed, they ever have to be paid) would be particularly helpful or informative to present day investors.*

Actually, of course, even if the level of plant investment is not maintained, there is no warrant for assuming that there will be any *liability* for deferred taxes arising out of Section 167 reductions. There can be no liability at any time, even if the extreme case of plant shrinkage be assumed, unless one assumes that certain highly variable factual conditions, *i.e.*, present tax rates and profits, will persist until such time as annual rapid depreciation becomes less than straight-line depreciation. As an indication of the remoteness of such time, it may be noted that even on a unit basis, sum of the years-digits annual depreciation rates will exceed straight-line rates for 21 years in the case of property having a 40-year life.

Among those state authorities which have repudiated "deferred tax" treatment for rapid depreciation are the Commissions and Courts of Pennsylvania and Maine. In *Central Maine Power Co.,* 17 PUR 3d 452 (1957) the Maine Public Utilities Commission noted that there was uncontradicted evidence (p. 463)

---

* Until the time comes (if ever it does come) when the "deferred taxes" have to be paid, the accumulations are available for all purposes for which any other equity capital is available, including protection of senior securities, distribution to equity holders on liquidation, and payment of dividends (except to the extent restricted by certain regulatory agencies, which may be indicated by appropriate footnote). In the light of the Consolidated Edison projections, it would seem that an income statement which failed to show the Section 167 tax savings as a part of net income available for all equity capital purposes would be seriously misleading; as would a balance sheet which classified the accumulations in the same sort of grouping with a reserve for depreciation or which in any other manner failed to indicate the equity availability (for at least a considerable period) of such funds. This would be particularly true with regard to securities representing term debt maturing prior to the date on which the increased tax burden, if any, would start to occur. The advocates of deferred tax accounting seem to fear that any other method would mislead investors into *overvaluing* equity securities. There is more danger that a deferred tax financial statement, by depressing earning and equity ratios, would mislead an investor into *undervaluing* senior securities.

13

"*   *   * that in the case of a utility which is growing the new tax method [rapid depreciation] results in a permanent savings."

Even apart from the questions of additions the Commission noted (*Ibid,* p. 463):

"A great deal of the plant of the company has a longevity of 50 to 100 years, and it is highly speculative to fix rates today on the possibilities of what may happen in such a distant future. It is, indeed, unrealistic to assume that taxes will remain at the present tax rate of 52% for so many years in the future."

This decision, and the views expressed, were approved by the Maine Supreme Court (*Central Maine P. Co.* v. *P.U.C.*, 153 Me. 228, 136 A 2d 726, 21 PUR 3d 321 (1957)).*

The Superior Court of Pennsylvania, in *City of Pittsburgh* v. *Pennsylvania P.U.C.*, 182 Pa. Super. Ct. 551 128 A 2d 372, 17 PUR 3d 249 (1956) rejected the utility's argument that the tax reductions pursuant to Section 167 constituted a mere deferral of tax liability, saying:

"In considering this approach the commission noted that whether there is or is not an actual tax saving or deferral depends upon the amount of new plant construction in 1954 and future years; and that, assuming the utility will add no additional plant after the test year, its actual tax liability relating to property presently being depreciated under the accelerated method will not be higher than under the straight-line method for the next seventeen years. Even under this extreme theoretical assumption it is impossible to say at this time what the taxes for this utility will be seventeen years from now. Although the depreciation deduction for any particular piece of property may be predicted and projected into the future, the tax which will be imposed cannot be determined. Taxes in future years will depend not only upon the amount of depreciation allowed, but upon other factors such as the gross income, expenses of operation, and the

---

* In *Re Bangor Hydro-Electric Company*, 1958 CCH Util. L. Rep. ¶18,178 the Maine Commission determined income taxes allowable for rate-making purposes on the basis of rapid depreciation even though the company did not elect to use any of the rapid depreciation methods permitted under I.R.C. Section 167.

14

tax rate. This contention of the utility erroneously assumes that these factors will remain constant."

In *City of Alton* v. *Illinois Commerce Comm'n.*, 26 PUR 3d 187 (October 24, 1958), the Illinois Circuit Court reversed a rate determination of the Illinois commission which had allowed "deferred taxes" as an expense, saying that the commission in so doing

"speculated on the future of such taxes, and on the prospects of future prosperity."

Those federal agencies dealing with the problem have addressed themselves chiefly to the issue whether "deferred tax" accounting will be allowed at all, rather than whether "flow-through" accounting will be allowed.

The extreme position has been taken by the Interstate Commerce Commission, which has refused to recognize any form of "deferred tax" accounting and requires all accounts to reflect only actual taxes, *i.e.*, flow-through accounting. See I.C.C. Notice to all Carriers Subject to Prescribed Accounting Rules, February 9, 1959, referring to rapid depreciation under Section 167.

The Civil Aeronautics Board had similarly, until March 12, 1958, prohibited any form of deferred tax accounting for tax reductions arising out of Section 167 or 168. On that date, by Regulation No. ER-230, it suspended such prohibition "temporarily", pending a final decision of the Board on rate treatment of accruals. Such temporary suspension does not require deferred tax accounting, however, and expressly it is applicable only "in the event a carrier elects to follow deferred tax accounting".

The Federal Power Commission, by Orders Nos. 203 and 204, has authorized deferred tax accounting in certain cases. Under Order No. 204 deferred tax accounting is permitted with respect to Section 167 or Section 168 tax reductions but only if the public utility or licensee shall

"(a) have filed with the Commission, copy of an order or other authorization by a state public service commission having jurisdiction, authorizing accounting for deferred taxes on income, [or] (b) in the absence of necessity of authorization by a state public service commission having jurisdiction, have filed with the

15

Commission a statement of proposed plan of accounting for deferred taxes on income."

Under Order No. 204, deferred tax accounting is expressly "not mandatory for any utility, which in accordance with a consistent policy, elects not to follow deferred tax accounting even though liberalized depreciation [or accelerated amortization] is used in computing taxes on income". In cases where a state commission having accounting jurisdiction has failed to act, *i.e.*, has neither expressly authorized nor refused to authorize deferred tax accounting, the Federal Power Commission has refused to regard such failure to act as compliance with either condition (a) or (b). In such cases it would seem that utilities are required to report to the Federal Power Commission on a flow-through basis.

As indicated more fully below, the authority of this Commission to override the accounting requirements of State and Federal agencies is limited. Aside from the question of this Commission's jurisdiction, however, it would seem that this Commission's policy of respect for the views of sister regulatory agencies, as well as a continuation of the long established policy of Accounting Series Release No. 4, should persuade this Commission not to adopt any policy which would proscribe the use of flow-through accounting by utility companies.

III.

The jurisdiction of this Commission over accounting practices of various corporations is so limited as to preclude the possibility that uniformity might result from the proposed policy.

While this Commission has broad powers to define accounting terms, in the exercise of its functions under the Securities Act of 1933, the Securities and Exchange Act of 1934, and the Public Utility Holding Company Act of 1935, its powers are not unlimited.

A general limitation upon this Commission's powers is that it must be exercised in accordance with the purposes of the various Acts. In each case, the primary purpose of the Commission's account-

16

ing jurisdiction is to prevent the dissemination of financial statements which would tend to mislead investors.*

It is Consolidated Edison's position that full disclosure is fully consistent with either equity treatment of deferred tax credits or with flow-through accounting; and that a proscription of these accounting methods not only is not necessary to fulfill the purposes of the various Acts, but in a given case, and particularly where the proscribed methods have been authorized or required by the rate regulatory agency, may *prevent* full and adequate disclosure.

In addition to this general limitation on the Commission's authority, specific statutory restrictions would preclude uniformity of the proposed policy. Section 20(b) of the Public Utility Holding Company Act provides:

> "In the case of the accounts of any company whose methods of accounting are prescribed under the provisions of any law of the United States *or of any State,* the rules and regulations or orders of the Commission *in respect of accounts shall not be inconsistent with the requirements imposed by such law or any rule or regulation thereunder;* nor shall anything in this title relieve any public-utility company from the duty to keep the accounts, books, records, or memoranda which may be required to be kept by the law of any State in which it operates or by the State commission of any such State. But this provision shall not prevent the Commission from imposing such additional requirements regarding reports or accounts as it may deem necessary or appropriate in the public interest or for the protection of investors or consumers."

The Commission in promulgating Rule U-27 has recognized this limitation on its authority. That Rule, insofar as pertinent, provides:

> "(a) Every registered holding company, and subsidiary thereof, which is a public-utility company and which is *not required* by either the Federal Power Commission or *a State commission to conform to a classification of accounts,* shall keep its accounts insofar as it is an electric utility company in the manner currently prescribed for similar companies by the Fed-

---

* See, *e. g., American P. & L. Co.* v. *SEC,* 158 F. 2d 771, 778, where the Court said that the Commission was given the power to regulate accounting practices in order to "insure investors a proper appraisal basis for subsidiary securities * * *"

17

eral Power Commission* and insofar as it is a gas utility company in the manner recommended by the National Association
of Railroad and Utilities Commissioners,** except any company
whose public utility activities are so limited that the application
to it of such system of accounts is clearly inappropriate * * *."

The legislative policy of Section 20(b) appears from the Senate
Report on the Bill (Report No. 621, 74th Congress, 1st Session, p. 9).

"With regard to the accounts of public utility companies
the committee has added an express provision in Section 20 to
prevent any possible encroachment upon the practice and jurisdiction of State commissions."

Thus, this Commission cannot prescribe accounting treatment
for holding companies or their subsidiaries inconsistent with that
of the State or Federal Commissions. This limitation on this Commission's authority extends beyond the Holding Company Act with
respect to such companies, however. A company which by virtue
of Section 20(b) must file financial statements consistent with State
regulatory requirements could not, in view of the provisions of
Section 15(e) of the Holding Company Act, prohibiting inconsistent
accounting, keep any inconsistent accounts for any other purpose.
Thus, such companies would appear to be wholly exempt from this
Commission's proposed policy.

Under the Securities and Exchange Act this Commission's authority is limited by the provisions of Section 13(b), which provides:

"* * * in the case of the reports of any person whose
methods of accounting are prescribed under the provisions of
any law of the United States, or any rule or regulation thereunder, the rules and regulations of the Commission with respect
to reports shall not be inconsistent with the requirements imposed by such law or rule or regulation in respect of the same
subject matter * * *."

It has already been noted that, with respect to flow-through accounting, the proposed policy of this Commission would be inconsistent

---

* Which allows flow-through accounting.

** Which recommends flow-through accounting in connection with rapid depreciation.

18

with the accounting procedures of the Interstate Commerce Commission, Civil Aeronautics Board and Federal Power Commission, which either prohibit deferred tax accounting or allow it at the option of the company as an exception to the general policy which favors flow-through accounting. Thus, companies under the jurisdictions of these three commissions would appear to be exempt from the proposed policy with regard to the Securities and Exchange Act.

With respect to the Securities Act, Section 19(a) invests this Commission with certain accounting jurisdiction but provides that

> "* * * insofar as they relate to any common carrier subject to the provisions of section 20 of the Interstate Commerce Act, as amended, the rules and regulations of the Commission with respect to accounts shall not be inconsistent with the requirements imposed by the Interstate Commerce Commission under authority of such section 20 * * *."

The Interstate Commerce Commission's requirement of flow-through accounting has already been noted (p. 14, *supra*).

These specific limitations on this Commission's jurisdiction would preclude any uniformity in accounting with regard to Section 167 or 168 tax deferrals, and to the extent that such uniformity is a goal of the proposed policy, it could not be realized. These exceptions to uniformity would be in addition to those which would arise under Footnote 3 of the Release 4010, *i.e.*, under paragraph 8 of ARB 44 Revised.

It may also be noted at this point that considerable confusion could be created with respect to the accounting on a consolidated basis of affiliated companies, where some of such companies would be exempt from the proposed policy by virtue of pertinent State or Federal regulatory orders while others would not be so exempted. It is submitted that the confusion that would result in such a situation would be symptomatic of the general confusion and misunderstanding which would result from the promulgation of a purportedly uniform accounting procedure which could not be uniformly enforced.

19

IV.

This Commission should not be bound by Accounting Research Bulletin 44 Revised.

This Commission's notice of intention, both by direct reference and by implication, appears to place great weight on the authority of ARB 44 Revised. While the promulgation of the notice of intention and the subsequent notice of hearing indicate that this Commission intends to give a full and fair hearing to other views, it is respectfully suggested that this Commission should not give such weight to ARB 44 Revised as would effectively nullify the procedural safeguards prescribed by the Administrative Procedure Act, which have been followed by this Commission both prior to and since such Act, and are being observed in this case.

ARB 44 Revised, it may be noted, was promulgated by a committee of a non-governmental group, with no procedure for the effective presentation of the views of others,* and (without reflecting on the integrity of any members of the actual committee involved) without any protection against bias or self-interest of the group or committee. Governmental action based on such private group decisions would clearly be improper (*Carter* v. *Carter Coal Co.*, 298 U. S. 238).

Aside from the impropriety of founding governmental action on private decisions, the manner of formulation of ARB 44 Revised places severe limitations upon the degree of authoritativeness which can be attributed to it. It is, of course, entitled to substantial respect as the collective opinion of twenty-one learned and respected certified public accountants.** However, even as an expression of the views of the accounting profession, ARB 44 Revised is not to be regarded as

---

* In sharp contrast with the procedure followed in the instant proceeding by this Commission, the AICPA Committee did not hold public hearings, although hearings were requested by the Edison Electric Institute and the American Gas Association.

** It is worthy of note that two of the distinguished members of the Institute's Committee on Accounting Procedure dissented clearly and unequivocally from the majority, noting their belief that the inflexible requirement for deferred tax accounting (except for the "rare cases" covered by paragraph 8) "calls for more extensive allocation of income taxes among periods of time than is necessary or desirable, *especially where the situation is such that the so-called tax deferment is in effect a permanent tax reduction.*"

20

binding. The manner of formulation of Accounting Research Bulletins has been the subject of professional review, and substantial
revision of procedure has been recommended by a Special Committee of the American Institute of Certified Public Accountants
on Research Program.* The recommendations call for a vastly
different procedure for promulgation of accounting precepts than
was followed in the formulation of ARB 44 Revised, including wide
dissemination of proposals both inside and outside the accounting
profession and the solicitation of both professional and non-accounting views prior to adoption of such proposals.

It is unnecessary to consider here whether such recommendations
go far enough; they do, however, point out a basic reason why ARB
44 Revised should not be accepted by this Commission with more
than the modicum of respect due to the opinions of its authors. It
is not, in fact, a result of a study with reference to views outside
of the ranks of certified public accountants. Although ARB 44 Revised involves utility and carrier rate regulation, it does not appear
that any regulatory agencies were consulted in any effective manner.**
The problems dealt with in ARB 44 Revised include problems of law,
economics, financial analysis, and business management; no professional or business group representing these specialized disciplines was
consulted prior to ARB 44 Revised being promulgated. As has been
partially indicated elsewhere in this memorandum, there has been far
from unanimous acceptance of the principles espoused in ARB 44
Revised as correct accounting principles by those regulatory agencies
and others dealing with the practical aspects of rapid depreciation
tax reductions.

It is Consolidated Edison's position that for the reasons previously
developed no accounting techniques thus far devised can accurately
report, without benefit of footnotes, the complex legal and economic
facts created by Sections 167 and 168 of the Internal Revenue Code of
1954. Deferred tax accounting is in this respect no more accurate
generally than flow-through accounting; and in many cases involving

---

* See the Committee's Report, The Journal of Accountancy, December, 1958.
** By letter of April 23, 1958, addressed to the Director of Research of the American
Institute of Certified Public Accountants, the NARUC Committee on Accounts and Statistics
urged the Institute in any Revision of ARB 44 that might be issued "to provide that the rule
of the proposed bulletin need not be applied to the financial statements of public utilities which
have followed the required accounting procedures of the regulatory agencies having jurisdiction."

21

Section 167 tax reductions (including Consolidated Edison's), deferred tax accounting would be misleading as contrasted with flow-through.

For all of these reasons, it is submitted that the respectable accounting authority of the group which promulgated ARB 44 Revised should not be allowed to override the substantial authoritative support for flow-through accounting not only within the accounting profession but in state and federal regulatory agencies, among lawyers, economists, and others.

In Conclusion

The proposed interpretation of administrative policy would reverse this Commission's policy of accepting financial statements which provide full disclosure and which are prepared in accordance with accounting principles having substantial authoritative support. The proposed new policy is not necessary to, and in particular cases may be detrimental to, the policy of complete and adequate disclosure; could not achieve uniformity; and is contrary to policy adopted by other federal regulatory agencies. This proposed policy should, therefore, be abandoned by this Commission in favor of a requirement of complete disclosure.

Dated: New York, New York,
March 5, 1959.

Respectfully submitted,

LeBoeuf, Lamb & Leiby,
15 Broad Street,
New York 5, New York,
Attorneys for Consolidated
Edison Company of New York, Inc.

Cameron F. MacRae,
Alfred E. Froh,
Of Counsel.

FLORIDA TELEPHONE CORPORATION

General Office
Ocala, Florida

MAX E. WETTSTEIN
PRESIDENT AND GENERAL MANAGER   March 2, 1959

Securities and Exchange Commission
Washington, D. C.

SUBJECT: Release No. 4010, Dec. 30, 1958
         Accelerated Depreciation -
         Administrative Policy
         Interpretation

Gentlemen:

Florida Telephone Corporation is an operating
telephone company which is using accelerated
depreciation for income tax purposes as provided
under the 1954 Internal Revenue Act.

The accounting and rate treatment prescribed
by the Florida Railroad & Public Utilities
Commission is a charge to current Income under a
special account called "Provision for deferred
Federal income taxes" and a credit to a balance
sheet equity account called "Retained Earnings or
Earned Surplus restricted for future Federal
Income Tax".

We have been using accelerated depreciation
(sum of the years digits) for income tax purposes
since 1954, the first year prescribed under the
prevailing Act, and over the five year period,
1954 through 1958, the accumulations to the
restricted retained earnings account have been as
follows:

	Year	Amount of Restricted Retained Earnings End of Year
	1954	$ 8,193
	1955	50,411
	1956	156,484
	1957	316,111
	1958	574,159
Est.	1959	874,159

Since the regulatory treatment prescribed in Florida calls for a retained earnings equity account, the proposed interpretation as prescribed in Release No. 4010 would be contrary to the prescribed accounting treatment established in this State.

Numerous utility companies are following a restricted retained earnings accounting treatment as part of the equity structure and as prescribed by the proper regulatory authorities. Financial analysts and others in such cases have interpreted it as part of the equity structure in computing debt and equity ratios and margins for additional financing. Severe hardship, increased costs, and the raising of large sums of new equity capital to supplant the sums lost by classification as a deferred tax reserve would be the result in many instances under the proposed interpretation under Release No. 4010.

Utilities in such states using accelerated depreciation as a straight "flow through" to unrestricted retained earnings would continue to gain the benefits of additional equity in their structures while utilities in other states with the restricted retained earnings treatment would be penalized under the proposed interpretation. This hardly seems consistent and fair to those utilities using the restricted retained earnings treatment prescribed by local regulatory authorities.

We are sure our views will be substantiated by many in the utility industry and we can see little to be accomplished under the proposed interpretation.

Sincerely yours,

FLORIDA TELEPHONE CORPORATION

/s/ MAX E. WETTSTEIN

Max E. Wettstein
President and General Manager

MEW/dl

GENERAL PUBLIC UTILITIES CORPORATION
AND SUBSIDIARY ELECTRIC POWER COMPANIES

67 Broad Street
New York 4, N. Y.
Telephone: WHitehall 3-5600

February 27, 1959

Securities and Exchange Commission
Washington 25, D. C.

Re: Securities Act of 1933 Release No. 4010

Dear Sirs:

We refer to the above captioned Release,
which was also published under three other Acts
administered by the Commission. The Release sets
forth a contemplated announcement of an interpretation of administrative policy regarding the
balance sheet treatment in financial statements
filed with the Commission of "the accumulated
credit arising from accounting for reductions in
income taxes for various items including those
under sections 167 and 168 of the Internal
Revenue Code of 1954" and permits submission of
written views and comments with respect to such
proposed announcement.

It is our view that, as applied to a registered public utility holding company and its subsidiaries, the proposed announcement is inappropriate, has no statutory foundation and should not
be adopted. Our reasons for these views are set
forth below.

The proposed announcement provides that, in
the case of public utility companies required to
comply with the uniform system of accounts of the
Federal Power Commission ("FPC"), the accumulated
credits in question shall be reflected (in balance
sheets filed with your Commission) by using the

balance sheet captions and classifications prescribed by the FPC in its Order No. 204, namely,
"Accumulated Deferred Taxes on Income." As the
FPC has stated, this classification is designed
to be a separate balance sheet category which is
neither a part of earned surplus nor a part of
reserves. It may well be that, in view of the
FPC's rate-regulatory and statistics-compilation
responsibilities, the establishment of such a
separate classification serves some useful purpose in the accounts maintained in accordance
with the requirements of the FPC and in reports
filed with it. However, as a means of disclosure
to investors, this separate balance sheet classification is less than helpful in the discharge of
your Commission's responsibilities. For example,
it is our understanding that the Wisconsin Public
Service Commission views the accumulated credits
in question as akin to depreciation and requires
that they be credited to a sub-account in the
depreciation reserve. Yet, your proposed
Release would apparently require a Wisconsin
public utility which was employing accelerated
depreciation for tax purposes but not for financial accounting purposes and which was required
to comply with the FPC's uniform system of
accounts to remove these accumulated credits
from its depreciation reserve and show them in
a separate balance sheet caption in any financial
statements filed with your Commission.

This example illustrates the basic defect
in your Commission's proposed announcement.
That proposed announcement would apparently use
the straight-jacket of a particular balance
sheet classification for these accumulated
credits and apply it to all public utility
companies without regard to the regulatory treatment of these credits in a particular
jurisdiction.

In the case of public utilities, the consequences of the employment of sections 167 and
168 of the Internal Revenue Code depend primarily upon the treatment accorded thereto by

regulatory commissions having jurisdiction for
rate-making purposes. Such consequences involve
not only the question of allowable operating
expenses (which is expressly dealt with in the
exception in paragraph 8 of Bulletin No. 44
(Revised) and in the third paragraph of, and
footnote 3 to, the proposed announcement) but
also the questions of capitalization ratios and
cost of capital. So long as such regulatory
agencies do not accord uniform treatment to this
item, a sound administrative policy cannot
require uniform reflection in either the income
statement or balance sheet.

Even more important than the lack of factual
foundation for the proposed administrative policy
is the lack of jurisdictional foundation.
Although the proposed announcement is captioned
under four Acts administered by the Commission,
it does not cite any specific provision of any
of those Acts which is relied upon as a legal
basis for the promulgation of the proposed
policy. In view of the importance of the subject, and the wide interest it has evoked over
the past several years, it would be helpful if
the Commission would specify, in advance of the
hearing upon this matter, the particular
statutory provisions relied upon as affording
a foundation for the proposed announcement. In
the absence of such a statement, we assume for
the balance of these comments, that, in so far
as the Securities Act of 1933 is concerned, the
Commission's primary reliance is on section 19
(a) thereof, and, in so far as the Public
Utility Holding Company Act of 1935 is concerned,
the Commission's primary reliance is on
sections 15 and 20 thereof.

Section 19(a) of the Securities Act confers
upon the Commission authority to make, amend or
rescind "such rules and regulations as may be
necessary to carry out the provisions" of that
Act, including rules and regulations governing
registration statements and defining accounting,
technical and trade terms used in the Act. It

also authorizes the Commission "for the purposes of" the Act to prescribe the form or forms in which required information shall be set forth, the items or details to be shown in the balance sheet and earnings statement, and the methods to be followed in the preparation of accounts, valuation of assets and liabilities, determination of depreciation and depletion, the differentiation of recurring and non-recurring income, etc. The question therefore presented by Securities Act Release No. 4010 is whether the policy therein set forth is necessary for the purposes of that Act. Since the purposes of the Act are to provide fair and full disclosure of the character of securities sold in interstate and foreign commerce and to prevent fraud in the sale thereof, the policy envisaged by the proposed Release can be justified under Section 19(a) only on the ground that failure to follow that accounting treatment would not provide the required disclosure and would be misleading or inaccurate.

In the case of a public utility, meaningful disclosure can be made of (a) the fact that sections 167 and 168 are being employed for income tax purposes but not for financial accounting purposes, (b) the fact that the employment of these deductions has reduced income taxes in specified amounts both in the current period and on a cumulative basis, and (c) the fact that the accounting being followed by the utility has been directed by a regulatory commission having significant rate-making jurisdiction over the utility's operations or, in the absence of such direction, the basis for the accounting treatment being accorded by the utility. However, characterization of these reductions in the balance sheet in the form proposed by the proposed announcement is not only not necessary to the purposes of the Act, but is indeed inconsistent with such purposes.

In so far as the Commission's Release is based upon its powers under the Holding Company Act, the proposed Release cannot be justified. Although Sections 15 and 20 of that Act give to the Commission broad powers with respect to

accounting of companies subject to that Act,
Section 20(b) of that Act specifically requires
that the rules, regulations and orders of the SEC
in respect of accounts shall not be inconsistent
with requirements imposed by the laws of any
State or of the United States or any rule or
regulation thereunder, upon a company whose
methods of accounting are prescribed under the
provisions of such law. In the case of a GPU
subsidiary, Pennsylvania Electric Company, that
company has, since 1953, been required by an order
of the Pennsylvania Public Utility Commission to
credit to restricted surplus the accumulated
credits resulting from charges equivalent to the
reduction in income taxes immediately payable as
a result of the accelerated amortization of two
specific facilities. So long as that order of
the Pennsylvania Commission is valid and outstanding, Section 20(b) of the Holding Company
Act expressly prohibits the SEC from requiring
Pennsylvania Electric Company to account for
these accumulated credits in some other fashion.
Moreover, Rule 28 of the Commission under the
Holding Company Act expressly requires Pennsylvania Electric Company to reflect in its
published financial statements the same treatment
of these accumulated credits which is accorded by
it to these credits in its books in accordance
with the Pennsylvania Commission Order.

As the Commission may be aware, the staff of
the Federal Power Commission has expressed the
view that the requirements of that Commission's
Order No. 204 extend to the balance sheet treatment accorded by Pennsylvania Electric Company in
registration statements filed with your Commission
(and apparently in all accounting and reporting
other than reports to the Pennsylvania Public
Utility Commission). It is the view of Pennsylvania Electric Company and this Company that the
staff of the FPC is in error, and there is
enclosed, as Appendix A, a copy of Pennsylvania
Electric Company's letter, dated February 4,
1959, to the Federal Power Commission. Of
course, if and to the extent that your

Commission's proposed action is based upon provisions of the Holding Company Act, Section 318
of the Federal Power Act would relieve Pennsylvania Electric Company from such obligation, if
any, as it might otherwise have by reason of
Order No. 204.

In at least two respects the proposed
announcement is significantly |ambiguous. The
first of these ambiguities centers about the
fact that the proposed announcement refers to
reductions in income taxes "for various items
including those under sections 167 and 168 of
the Internal Revenue Code of 1954." We have seen
a copy of Mr. Andrew Barr's letter dated
February 2, 1959 to Mr. Edwin Vennard in which he
states that he is sure that the members of the
Edison Electric Institute are familiar with the
Federal Power Commission Orders 203 and 204 which
provide accounts for items other than depreciation and that a similar provision was made by
the Civil Aeronautics Board in its regulation
No. ER-230. In this connection, it is significant to point out that, in its order No. 204, the
Federal Power Commission specifically pointed out
that, in adopting Account 266.3 entitled
"Accumulated Deferred Taxes on Income - Other,"
that Commission did so as a matter of convenience
only without specifying the purposes to which
that account may be put and that, before specifying such uses, that Commission would provide
for any further proceedings respecting such
account which may be necessary or appropriate.

The second respect in which the proposed
announcement is significantly ambiguous or inconsistent - and may be in conflict with order 204
of the Federal Power Commission - involves a
question of whether the proposed announcement
relates only to the balance sheet treatment or
also refers to the income statement. The first
paragraph of the notice states that the interpretation proposed is one "regarding balance
sheet treatment" of the credits in question.
However, the third paragraph of the proposed
announcement itself apparently refers to the

income statement and apparently would require,
except in cases described in paragraph 8 of
Bulletin No. 44 (Revised), that a reporting
company "charge current income with an amount
equal to the tax reduction." If we correctly
construe this paragraph, it is completely inconsistent with the requirements of the Federal
Power Commission's Uniform System of Accounts for
Electric Utilities, as amended by Order No. 204
of that Commission, cited by your Commission in
its Notice. Specifically, as the description of
Account 266 prescribed by that Order of the
Federal Power Commission makes clear, such account
may only be utilized by a public utility which
has filed with the Federal Power Commission a
copy of an order of a State Commission having
accounting jurisdiction which authorizes deferred
tax accounting or, in the absence of necessity
of such authorization, has filed with the Federal
Power Commission a statement of a proposed plan
of accounting for deferred taxes on income.
There are some utilities which, on the one hand,
are subject to State Commissions having accounting jurisdiction but have not received State
Commission authorization to utilize deferred tax
accounting and, on the other hand, are not within
the exception referred to in paragraph 8 of
Bulletin 44 (Revised). Thus, the Order of the
Federal Power Commission does not permit such
utilities to use deferred tax accounting but, by
the proposed announcement of your Commission,
they would be required to do so.

This letter is being filed in triplicate in
response to the Release referred to above. We
intend to appear at the hearing to be held on
March 25, 1959 and request that we be assigned
twelve (12) minutes for the oral presentation of
our views.

Very truly yours,

/s/ W. G. CHRISTIE

W. G. Christie
Comptroller

PENNSYLVANIA
ELECTRIC COMPANY

222 Levergood Street
Johnstown, Pennsylvania

February 4, 1959

Secretary
Federal Power Commission
Washington 25, D. C.

Dear Sir:

We acknowledge receipt, on Janurary 16, 1959, of your letter, dated January 15, 1959, relating to the consolidated balance sheet treatment accorded by this Company's parent, in a prospectus contained in a registration statement filed under the Securities Act of 1933, to the accumulated credits arising from the employment of accelerated amortization by this Company with respect to two certificated facilities. In your letter, you state that

"In the opinion of the staff, the accounting and reporting (exclusive of reports for State Commission purposes) of deferred taxes that your company is following, as revealed in the said prospectus, violates the accounting and reporting requirements of this Commission's uniform system of accounts, as amended by the Commission's order No. 204, dated May 29, 1958."

Although your letter of January 15th does not refer to the fact, it may assist your and the Commission's review of this matter if we call attention to the fact, under date of January 2, 1959, we transmitted to you a copy of the Order, dated December 22, 1954, of the Pennsylvania Public Utility Commission authorizing the subject accumulated credits to be credited to Account 271A - "Earned Surplus - Restricted."

Your letter does not deal with the merits of the accounting treatment prescribed by the Federal Power Commission's Order No. 204 and this letter also does not deal with that subject. Instead, your letter in essence poses two questions, namely, (1) whether the Staff of the Federal Power Commission is correct in its construction of the terms of Order No. 204 as requiring that the subject credits be classified in Account 266. "Accumulated Deferred Taxes on Income" in registration statements filed with the Securities and Exchange Commission under the Securities Act of 1933*, but not filed with your Commission and (2) if Order No. 204 is so construed, whether it would be valid.

In appraising these questions, it should be borne in mind that the Company has established, in conformity with Order No. 204, in its books of account an account denominated "Account 266. Accumulated Deferred Taxes on Income" and has noted thereon that said account is being maintained in accordance with said Order No. 204. Moreover, the Company has credited to said account the accumulated credits required to be credited to said account by said Order. Furthermore, although the Company has not filed any financial statements with your Commission since receipt of the Order of May 29, 1958, it contemplates that these accumulated credits will be shown in any such financial statements hereafter filed with your Commission (as, for example, in the Company's Annual Report on FPC Form 1) in Account 266. On the other hand, the Company is also reflecting these same credits on its books of accounts as credits to "Account 271A - Earned Surplus, Restricted," in accordance with the above mentioned Order, dated December 22, 1954, of the Pennsylvania Public Utility Commission, with a notation thereon that such credits are being made in accordance with that Order. Thus, the Company is keeping its accounts in precise compliance with applicable orders of both the Pennsylvania Public Utility Commission and the Federal Power Commission.

This dual account treatment on the books of the Company is explicitly recognized as appropriate - and, indeed, unavoidable - by the Commission's Order No. 204. In that Order, the Commission stated, in part:

"In view of the fact that some state regulatory commissions also having accounting jurisdiction have specified the restricted surplus treatment and others the reserve treatment, some parties urge that we adopt accounting provisions which would permit either a restricted surplus or a reserve treatment. In our opinion, this dual or alternative treatment would cause intolerable confusion and conflict in the Commission's prescribed accounting and would be contrary to the public interest. We regret the inconsistency which has arisen among the several state commissions. Under the circumstances, however, we see no reasonable solution to the problem for those utilities which are required by a state commission to report deferred taxes in a reserve or surplus account but to

---

*It may be noted that the Securities and Exchange Commission has asserted, by a Notice of Intention to Announce an Interpretation of Administrative Policy (Securities Act Release No. 4010), that it possesses jurisdiction to prescribe the balance sheet presentation of these items in financial statements filed with it.

classify the deferred taxes in accordance with state requirements for state purposes, and to use the treatment specified by this order for the purposes of this Commission.''

Apparently, the Staff construes the phrase ''for the purposes of this Commission'' as extending to and including financial statements contained in (i) applications relating to the issuance of securities by this Company (with respect to which, by virtue of Section 204(f), the Federal Power Commission has no jurisdiction) ·filed with other regulatory agencies, (ii) registration statements filed under the Securities Act of 1933 (again, over which the Commission has no jurisdiction), and (iii) reports to the Company's security holders. Likewise, the Staff construes the phrase ''in accordance with state requirements for state purposes'' as being limited to reports filed by the Company with Pennsylvania Public Utility Commission, even though that Commission has comprehensive regulatory jurisdiction with respect to the Company's business, including specifically jurisdiction with respect to the issuance of securities by the Company.

In appraising this contention by the Staff of the Federal Power Commission, it must be borne in mind that it was and is the intention of this Company to make clear by footnote to its financial statements contained in applications to other regulatory agencies having jurisdiction with respect to the issuance of securities by the Company, in registration statements under the Securities Act of 1933 and in reports distributed to the Company's security holders that, although the accumulated credits in question are shown in such financial statements in conformity with the order of the Pennsylvania Public Utility Commission as ''Earned Surplus - Restricted,'' nevertheless the Federal Power Commission's Order No. 204 requires that the credits be classified for the purposes of the Federal Power Commission as ''Accumulated Deferred Taxes on Income,'' a separate balance sheet category which is neither a part of earned surplus nor a part of reserves. Thus, all such financial statements will disclose the existence of these inconsistent orders.

We cannot believe that the phrase ''for the purposes of this Commission'' could have been intended by the Commission to extend to matters with respect to which the Commission has no jurisdiction or regulatory function and that the phrase ''in accordance with state requirements for state purposes'' could have been intended by the Commission to be limited simply to reports filed by the Company with the Pennsylvania Public Utility Commission and not to extend to financial statements relating to the issuance of securities, over which the Pennsylvania Commission does have comprehensive jurisdiction. Wholly apart from the question of jurisdictional power, the interpretation sought to be accorded by the Staff of the Federal Power Commission to Order No. 204 is inconsistent with the requirements of our dual sovereign system and with the spirit of accommodation to the requirements thereof elsewhere manifested by the Federal Power Commission in the same Order. For example, in the very next paragraph of the same Order, the Commission rejected the contention that it seek to make deferred tax accounting mandatory, and stated in that connection:

"This non-mandatory feature is desirable, among other reasons, to avoid to the extent possible conflict with requirements which may be prescribed by state regulatory authorities having major rate regulatory responsibilities, some of which may authorize and others deny deferred tax accounting."

Thus, the Federal Power Commission has stated that recognition of the "major responsibilities" of State Commissions in the field of the regulation of rates of electric utilities makes it appropriate that the State Commissions - and not the Federal Power Commission which regulates only a small part of the rates of electric utilities - shall possess the ultimate responsibility and authority to determine whether or not, and the extent to which, an electric utility is to be permitted to employ deferred tax accounting. This statement is implemented by the express provision of Account 266 prescribed by Order No. 204 which would preclude this Company from utilizing Account 266, even for the purposes of the Federal Power Commission, for the subject credits if the Pennsylvania Public Utility Commission had not issued its order, dated December 22, 1954.

It necessarily follows that the Federal Power Commission must have intended that, in areas where the State Commission possesses "major responsiblities" and the Federal Power Commission possesses no responsibilities the consequences which follow from the granting of authorization by the State Commission to employ deferred income tax accounting should be those prescribed by the State Commission, and not those prescribed by the Federal Power Commission.

That this must have been the intent of the Federal Power Commission is demonstrated by restating the matter in the following summary form:

1. The Federal Power Commission will not permit this Company to employ deferred tax accounting even for the purposes of the Federal Power Commission, unless authorized by the State Commission;

2. Compliance with the terms of the State Commission authorization requires that the balance sheet presentation of the accumulated credits resulting from such authorization be in accordance with the terms of such authorization, wherever the matter is one involving State Commission action;

3. The regulation of security issues by this Company does involve action by State Commission and not by the Federal Power Commission;

4. The balance sheet presentation of the accumulated credits in this Company's prospectuses and other items directly related to its security issues is, therefore, a necessary concern - and indeed a "major responsibility" - of the State Commission, whereas it is not a matter of responsibility, major or minor, of the Federal Power Commission;

5. Consequently, as between the Federal Power Commission and the State Commission, the balance sheet presentation of these accumulated credits in this Company's prospectuses and similar matters relating to security issues must be controlled by the State Commission.

Moreover, if it be assumed that the particular balance sheet presentation of this item employed in conection with prospectuses and financial reports distributed to security holders may have a direct bearing upon the Company's cost of capital and, therefore, ultimately upon its rates, it again appears clear that the Commission intended in its Order No. 204 that the State Commission's determination should be controlling in order to enable the latter to discharge its "major regulatory responsibilities" with respect to rates.

Of course, in a rate proceeding before the Federal Power Commission, these accumulated credits would be classified in Account 266, in determining the utility's rate base, capitalization structure, cost of capital and like matters. In this fashion, the recognition of the major rate responsibilities of the State Commission can be achieved without prejudice to the much more circumscribed rate regulatory responsibilities to the Federal Power Commission.

In summary, we believe that the opinion of the Staff expressed in your letter is inconsistent with the precise terms of the Commission's Order No. 204, is inconsistent with the rationale of that Order, and is inconsistent with the sound requirements of our Federal System with its dual sovereignty.

We now turn to a consideration of this jurisdictional question. We do not doubt, of course, that the Commission has authority under the Federal Power Act to require this Company as a licensee and public utility, to make, keep and preserve such accounts as the Commission may by rules and regulations prescribe "as necessary or appropriate for purposes of administration of this Act." Moreover, we do not contend that the fact that the State Commission has imposed upon this Company different accounting requirements relieves this Company from compliance with Order No. 204 in so far as compliance therewith is "necessary or appropriate for purposes of administration of" the Federal Power Act. As noted previously, the Company has established an account denominated "Account 266. Accumulated Deferred Taxes on Income" and has made and is making the credits to said account required by Order No. 204. The Company does not contend that this account is, in any respect, inferior to "Account 271A - Earned Surplus, Restricted" which, for more than four years, it has been maintaining and is presently maintaining in accordance with the Order of the Pennsylvania Commission and to which it has made and is making credits in accordance with that Commission's Order. So long as both Orders are outstanding and applicable to it, the Company proposes to continue to maintain both said accounts and to make credits thereto. However, since the accounts are duplicative, the Company cannot reflect both of them on any single balance sheet. The best that it can do in this respect is to reflect this item in the balance sheet in accordance with the Order of one Commission and, by footnote to such balance sheet, to indicate that the other Commission has directed that the item be reflected in a different manner. Consequently, in balance sheets filed with the Federal Power Commission, the item will be reflected in "Account 266, Accumulated Deferred Taxes on Income" and the footnote thereto will indicate that the Company has been directed by the Pennsylvania Public Utility Commission to reflect this same item in a different fashion, namely, in Earned Surplus, Restricted. On the other hand, in balance sheets filed with the Pennsylvania Public Utility Commission, the Company will reflect this item in "Account 271A - Earned Surplus, Restricted" and the footnote to that balance sheet will disclose that the Company has been directed by the Federal Power Commission to reflect this item in Accumulated Deferred Taxes on Income.

The jurisdictional question presented with respect to balance sheets filed elsewhere than with your Commission, for example, as a part of a registration statement or distributed to security holders, turns, then, on the issue of whether conformity to Order No. 204 in said balance sheets is "necessary or appropriate to the purposes of administration of" the Federal Power Act. Essentially, this issue is identical with that discussed above, namely, what is the meaning of the phrase "the purposes of this Commission" used in Order No. 204.

As previously indicated, Section 204(f) of the Federal Power Act expressly provides that the provisions of Section 204 of that Act (which generally require the Commission's approval with respect to the issuance of securities by a public utility)

"*** shall not extend to a public utility organized and operating in a State under the laws of which its security issues are regulated by a State Commission."

Since the Federal Power Commission is thus wholly deprived of jurisdiction with respect to the issue of securities by this Company, what basis can there be for the assertion that financial statements used in connection with such security issue involve matters which are necessary or appropriate in the administration of the Federal Power Act? Certainly, the Commission could hardly urge that because such balance sheet presentation might affect capitalization ratios and the attitudes of other regulatory agencies or purchasers of securities, or even compliance with the terms of outstanding securities, control of such balance sheet presentation in such a prospectus is necessary or appropriate to the administration of the Federal Power Act, since these are matters which directly affect the issue of securities and the Commission has no jurisdiction with respect thereto.

As heretofore stated, the balance sheet presentation of this item in registration statements or in financial reports distributed to security holders could affect the cost of capital of a public utility and thereby have some impact upon its rates. However, in Order No. 204 itself the Commission has expressly recognized that major rate regulation with respect to a public utility such as this Company lies with the State Commission and not with the Federal Power Commission. Consequently, the Commission could hardly urge that its own rate regulatory functions make it necessary or appropriate that the balance sheet presentation of this item utilized by this Company in connection with security issues conform to Order No. 204 and not conform to the Order of the Pennsylvania Public Utility Commission, which does possess major regulatory responsibilities.

If neither the regulation of security issues nor the regulation of rates makes it necessary or appropriate to the purposes of administration of the Federal Power Act that the Federal Power Commission control the prospectus balance sheet presentation of this item, what purpose of administration of the Act makes it necessary or appropriate that the Commission control such presentation? We can conceive of none.

The question of the Federal Power Commission's jurisdiction over accounts is not a new one. On numerous occasions, since the 1935 amendments to the Federal Power Act, the question of the authority of the Federal Power Commission to issue particular accounting directives has been presented. In each case, the Commission's authority has been sustained. However, in every case where the possibility of conflict with State requirements has been discussed, the Court has pointed out that the Federal Power Commission's Order does not affect action by the State Regulatory Agencies for State purposes. In no case has the Court held that the State Commission action, in discharging its regulatory responsibilities, is to be controlled by the action of the Federal Power Commission in areas where the Federal Power Commission has no regulatory responsibility.

Indeed, a careful reading of the decisions collectively referred to as the Arkansas Power & Light case, 156 F.2d 821, (C.A., D.C., 1946), 330 U.S. 802 (1947), 8 F.P.C. 106 (80 P.U.R.(N.S.) 193 (1949), 185 F.2d 751 (C.A., D.C. 1950), cert. den. 341 U.S. 909 (1951), and particularly the decisions relied upon by the Court of Appeals in the above-cited 1950 decision, make it clear that that case held no more than that the order of the Federal Power Commission directing the Arkansas Power & Light Company to record certain adjustments in its corporate accounts, was not invalid because that company was subject to the inconsistent accounting requirements of the Arkansas Public Service Commission. Although the matter of reflecting the orders of the State Commission and of your Commission in reports to security holders and others is discussed in the above-cited decision of your Commission, neither your Commission's order nor the decision of the Court of Appeals expressly dealt with that subject.

In obtaining judicial confirmations of its own Orders, the Federal Power Commission has been a vigorous proponent of the argument that its own accounting Orders do not control the rights of State regulatory agencies in the exercise of their own jurisdiction, nor relieve a public utility from compliance with the Orders of such State Commissions within their own realms. The position of the Staff set forth in your letter of January 15th would, in effect, reduce the accounting jurisdiction of the State Commissions simply to obtaining reports from utilities located in such States. If that position were sound, it would follow that a State Commission order approving a security issue could not impose any accounting condition, if such accounting condition conflicted with the requirements of the Federal Power Commission. The Staff's concept of the extent of the Commission's jurisdiction and of the limits upon State Commission jurisdiction would thus result in vesting the Federal Power Commission with the substance of authority in an area, namely, the issue of securities by this Company, where Congress expressly denied any jurisdiction to the Federal Power Commission and would leave the State Commission with only the shadow of authority in that area where Congress intended to leave the State Commission with unrestricted authority.

Under these circumstances, it is the view of this Company that its accounting is in agreement with that contemplated by the Commission's Order No. 204 and that its published reports are also in agreement with the Commission's Order No. 204 to the extent that such published reports are required to be in such agreement.

The issues which are posed by your letter stem, of course, from the fact that there is a conflict between the December 22, 1954 Order of the Pennsylvania Public Utility Commission and your Commission's Order No. 204, with respect to the account in which the accumulated credits arising from the use of accelerated amortization are to be recorded. The Order of the Pennsylvania Public Utility Commission was entered more than four years ago. Our Application to the Pennsylvania Commission at that time and its December 22, 1954 Order were in accord with similar prior applications to, and orders by, that Commission and simply followed the precedents which had been established by that Commission. It may be that, as a result of developments since the Pennsylvania Commission's Order was entered, that Commission takes a different view at the present time from that which was embodied in its December 22, 1954 Order. We are, therefore, sending a copy of this letter to the Pennsylvania Public Utility Commission and are requesting that they advise us of their views concerning the subject matter of this letter.

Very truly yours,

PENNSYLVANIA ELECTRIC COMPANY

By   Original Signed By:
      LOUIS H. RODDIS, JR.
      President

GULF POWER COMPANY

Pensacola, Florida

January 26, 1959

Mr. Orval L. DuBois, Secretary
Securities and Exchange Commission
Washington 25, D. C.

Dear Mr. DuBois:

Referring to the Commission's "Notice of
Intention to Announce Interpretation of Administrative Policy" relating to deferred income taxes
as set forth in release dated December 30, 1958,
we submit below for the consideration of the
Commission the reasons which make it appear
undesirable, in our opinion, for the Commission to
make an interpretation of administrative policy as
set forth in such release.

The undersigned company, Gulf Power Company,
is subject to regulation, including accounting
regulation, by the Florida Railroad and Public
Utilities Commission. This Commission has
prescribed that provisions shall be made, by
credits to "Earned Surplus Restricted for Future
Federal Income Taxes", of amounts equivalent to
the reduction in Federal income taxes resulting
from accelerated amortization and depreciation for
income tax purposes under Sections 167 and 168 of
the Internal Revenue Code of 1954. The company
has been so accounting and reporting, in accordance
with the treatment prescribed by such Commission,
since 1952 without objection by the Securities
and Exchange Commission or any other body having
jurisdiction or, for that matter, by any other
persons whatsoever.

Since 1954, in balance sheets contained in
reports to stockholders and in filings with the
Securities and Exchange Commission, "Earned Surplus
Restricted for Future Federal Income Taxes" has

been carried, not as a part of "Capitalization",[1] but as a wholly separate and correlative item. The basis and nature of the accounting has in instances also been described in an appropriate footnote.

In other words, as authorized by and in accordance with the prescription of the duly constituted public utility regulatory authority of the State of Florida having jurisdiction over such matters, and without objection or adverse comment by any others, this company for many years has been uniformly accounting for and reporting for all purposes the accumulated credit for deferred federal income taxes in a separate account entitled "Earned Surplus Restricted for Future Federal Income Taxes". Substantially all of the revenues of this company are derived under rates subject to regulation by the State commission and this company is primarily subject to such State commission's regulation in most other respects. There is, therefore, clearly substantial authoritative support for such accounting treatment.

The Federal Power Commission, in its Order No. 204, referred to in the Commission's Notice, states that where there is inconsistency between the requirements of such order and the accounting requirements of a State commission having juris-diction, a reasonable solution of the problem is "to classify the deferred taxes in accordance with state requirements for state purposes, and to use the treatment specified by this order for the pur-poses of this Commission". Pursuant to this suggestion, the company has, since the adoption by such order of appropriate amendments to the Federal Power Commission's Uniform System of Accounts pro-viding for the accounting treatment of amounts so accumulated for deferred Federal income taxes, entitled the account in which such amounts have

---

[1] Except in Annual Reports on FPC Form No. 1 which were filed as a part of Form 10K/U-5S.

been recorded as "Account 266, Accumulated
Deferred Taxes on Income" for the purposes of the
Federal Power Commission and "Account 271, Earned
Surplus Restricted for Future Federal Income
Taxes", for the purposes of the State commission,
and propose to report to each of the commissions
in accordance with its own requirements.

The company desires, and in the absence of
an announcement such as set forth in the
Commission's Notice, proposes to continue its
established practice in reports to stockholders
and in filings with the Commission, of reporting
the accumulated credit for deferred taxes in
accordance with the accounting prescribed by the
State commission, as a separate item on the balance
sheet, not a part of "Capitalization" and with an
appropriate footnote describing the requirements
of the Federal Power Commission's order.

It is submitted with all respect that there
can be nothing in such procedure which can fairly
be described as "misleading or inaccurate". Moreover, in the Public Utility Holding Company Act of
1935, one of the laws cited in the Commission's
Notice, it is specifically required of the
Commission that the rules, regulations and orders
of the Commission in respect of accounts "shall
not be inconsistent with the requirements imposed
by the law of any State or any rule or regulation
thereunder". It can hardly be considered consistent with this statutory injunction to make the
proposed announcement and thereby characterize as
"misleading or inaccurate" the method of accounting
prescribed by the duly constituted regulatory
authority of a soverign (sic) State.

Since the method of accounting and reporting
in published statements followed by this company
has been so followed for many years, in accordance
with requirements prescribed by the regulatory
commission having jurisdiction, without objection
by anyone and without any evidence that the procedure has been misleading to any security holder
(as it could hardly be since the origin and nature

of the items are fully described in the published
financial statements), the proposed interpretative
announcement, particularly in its apparent prohibition against captioning, in accordance with
the requirements of a State utility commission,
the accumulated credit "Earned Surplus Restricted
for Future Federal Income Taxes", even when
accompanied by a fully explanatory footnote, goes
far beyond anything required for the protection
of investors or consumers and appears to be contrary to the policy prescribed for the Commission
in the Public Utility Holding Company Act of 1935.

Very truly yours,

GULF POWER COMPANY

/s/ By L. T. SMITH JR.

Président

cc: Florida Railroad and Public
    Utilities Commission
    Tallahassee, Florida